Drinking and Crime

The Guilford Alcohol Studies Series

HOWARD BLANE AND DONALD GOODWIN, EDITORS

Drinking and Crime: Perspectives on the Relationships between Alcohol Consumption and Criminal Behavior
  James J. Collins, Jr., Editor

In preparation

Alcohol Problems in Women
  Sharon C. Wilsnack and Linda J. Beckman, Editors

Drinking and Crime:
Perspectives on the Relationships between Alcohol Consumption and Criminal Behavior

Edited by
JAMES J. COLLINS, JR.
Research Triangle Institute
Research Triangle Park, North Carolina

Foreword by
MARVIN E. WOLFGANG

THE GUILFORD PRESS
New York, London

©1981 The Guilford Press, New York
A Division of Guilford Publications, Inc.
200 Park Avenue South, New York, N.Y. 10003

Printed in the United States of America

Second printing, February 1984

Library of Congress Cataloging in Publication Data

Main entry under title:

Drinking and crime.

  (The Guilford alcohol studies series)

  Includes bibliographical references and indexes.

    1. Alcoholism and crime—Addresses, essays, lectures. I. Collins, James J., 1936– . II. Title. III. Series: Guilford alcohol studies series.

HV5053.D74   364.2′4   80-28046

ISBN 0-89862-163-1

To Mildred Reddy Collins and James J. Collins, Sr.

Contributors

Richard H. Blum, PhD
American Lives Endowment, Portola Valley, California

James J. Collins, Jr., PhD
Research Triangle Institute, Research Triangle Park, North Carolina

Stephanie W. Greenberg, PhD
Research Triangle Institute, Research Triangle Park, North Carolina

Claire Jo Hamilton, MA
Research Triangle Institute, Research Triangle Park, North Carolina

Kai Pernanen, MA
Alcohol and Aggression Study, funded by Health and Welfare Canada and Addiction Research Foundation of Ontario

Judy Roizen, PhD
Brunel University, London, England

Paul M. Roman, PhD
Department of Sociology, Tulane University, New Orleans, Louisiana

Acknowledgments

The editor of this book appreciates the careful work done by each chapter author. The state of current social psychological knowledge on the relationship between drinking and crime is well summarized by the contributions included in this volume.

Dr. Helen Erskine and Dr. Richard Barnes of the Center for the Study of Crime Correlates and Criminal Behavior of the National Institute of Justice each helped make this volume possible. Helen Erskine's wide-ranging intellectual interest in the subject matter helped broaden the scope of this book. She directed our attention to relevant materials that may otherwise have been omitted. Dick Barnes's active and open-minded cooperation is partly responsible for this book's publication.

The Research Triangle Institute has actively encouraged and supported publication of this book. Samuel C. Ashton and Drs. William C. Eckerman and Alvin M. Cruze were especially helpful.

Judy Whatley of the Center for the Study of Social Behavior at the Research Triangle Institute has spent many hours editing, organizing, and corresponding on behalf of the book. She has made important contributions to the style and readability of all the chapters in the volume.

Donna Albrecht and Brenda Young, also of the Center for the Study of Social Behavior at the Research Triangle Institute, have typed hundreds of pages of drafts and revisions with care and patience. Their important contribution is appreciated.

Finally, Rebecca A. McDiarmid has contributed to this book in unobtrusive but important ways. It is a pleasure to acknowledge that help here.

This book was, in part, prepared under Grant No. 78-NI-AX-0112 from the National Institute of Law Enforcement and Criminal Justice, National Institute of Justice, U.S. Department of Justice. Points of view or opinions stated in this volume are those of the authors and do not necessarily represent the official position or policies of the U.S. Department of Justice.

Foreword

There is a lot of drinking and a lot of crime in America. Most people who drink do not commit crime; whether most people who commit crime also drink is unclear. No one claims that committing crime causes drinking, but the suspicion that drinking causes crime has long been with us. The proposition seems fairly straightforward. However, this volume shows how difficult is the task of examining, testing, or proving the claim.

Alcohol comes in many forms and strengths. Persons who ingest it come in many styles too: by sex, age, race, height and weight, ethnicity, culture, and subculture. It cannot be gainsaid that these and other factors have varying influences on physical and emotional reactions to drinking alcohol. Even time is a condition to be considered: time of day when drinking, and the timing of a given quantity of alcohol. A myriad of situations surrounding the person who drinks can interlace in such a way that the concatenation can evoke behavior that is alien to, or enhancing of, a personality normally without alcohol. Crimes of cunning, stealth, or numerical complexity, like many white-collar crimes, are most unlikely to be performed efficiently under a heavy influence of alcohol. But *crimes passionel*, it has been asserted, are often the culmination of excessive drinking.

Notice the cautious language in these chapters, relative to the issue of alcohol and crime. *Cause* in the behavioral sciences is not commonly claimed, and, if it is, it is inferentially suggested from powerful and consistent correlations, often today through multivariate analyses. Relative to crime, the presence of alcohol may be a *contributing* factor, may be *positively correlated*, may be a *determinant*, but our scholars are generally unwilling to assert *cause*. And rightly so, for the best available evidence is sometimes contradictory and never fully compelling and convincing. Alcohol may arouse aggression or may augment aggressive behavior which may, in turn, result in criminal assault. But many other things also promote aggression, and even aggression aroused need not lead to criminal behavior.

The complexities are greater than these few examples, and the contributors to this volume have displayed and analyzed them with comprehensive and quality scholarship. They review and carefully criticize the literature, sifting through the old and the new, making methodological comments and cautious conclusions. There is probably no finer nor more thorough collection of writings on the topic. We are indebted to all of these scholars, especially to the capable, diligent editor/author, James Collins, for assembling such an extraordinary group, for consistent editing, and for writing his own contribution. A published product like this volume not only enlightens our disciplines; it also enhances the posture of the National Institute of Justice which encouraged and funded this undertaking.

Marvin E. Wolfgang

Preface

This volume examines a number of aspects of the relationship between alcohol consumption and criminal behavior. In recent decades alcohol consumption has been viewed as an important factor in the occurrence of crime. Research has repeatedly shown that alcohol is present in significant percentages of violent events. Serious criminal offenders have also been found to have drinking problems at rates higher than nonoffenders.

Findings showing that drinking often precedes criminal events and that disproportionate numbers of criminal offenders have drinking problems have occurred often enough that it seems reasonable to infer that drinking and crime are related to each other. Unfortunately, the complexity of the drinking–crime relationship and the absence of scientific rigor in much research on the issue make it difficult to spell out particular ways in which drinking contributes to the occurrence of crime.

Each of the chapters in this volume was written to summarize the state of the art of research and theory for selected aspects of the alcohol–crime relationship. The chapter foci were chosen because it is believed that future knowledge of how alcohol consumption "causes" criminal behavior will be served by summary statements of past work in these selected areas.

In the first chapter, Pernanen reviews theoretical aspects of the alcohol–crime relationship. Past work in this area has not been theoretically or conceptually sophisticated. Pernanen discusses the behavioral science theoretical enterprise in general, he applies an organizing scheme to the inferential problems of alcohol–crime research, and he also discusses a number of specific research findings in the violence area in terms of the inferential scheme.

In the chapter by Greenberg, the methodological aspects of alcohol–crime research are reviewed. Conceptual and definitional problems are discussed; and sampling and level-of-analysis issues, and hypothesis-formation aspects of past research are reviewed. These aspects of alcohol–crime research are discussed separately for research on the criminal event, research on the alcoholism of criminals, and research on the criminal careers of alcoholics.

In the third chapter, Blum focuses on the interrelationships between drinking, situational environment, and violence. He reviews much of the experimental literature on aggression and drinking, and also examines the relevance of cultural and group norms for the relationship of drinking and violence.

In the fourth chapter, Roman suggests an interpretive framework to incorporate cultural and situational factors into the study of drinking and crime. He then proposes a methodological approach to this study called "situational ecology."

The Collins chapter on alcohol careers and criminal careers examines the age variations that characterize drinking behavior and criminal behavior. Drinking problems and serious crime problems are found to cluster in the young adult male segment of the population. Findings suggest that this segment of the life cycle is important to the alcohol–crime relationship and should be a focus of future research.

The Roizen chapter focuses on the relationship between drinking and crime among Blacks. She finds some support for concentrating future research on this subpopulation. Although, in some aspects, the alcohol–crime connection appears to be more important in White than Black groups, there is some promise for analysis of the alcohol–crime relationship among Blacks that would focus on drinking–crime settings. In this regard, the Black tavern may be a fruitful focus.

In the chapter by Hamilton and Collins, the literature on the role of alcohol in family violence is reviewed. Much research in this area is poor in quality, but alcohol appears to be a factor with some capacity to explain family violence. The findings of this review indicate that alcohol is more relevant to wife beating than to child abuse.

The final chapter of the book contains a summary overview of the empirical, theoretical, and methodological aspects of the alcohol use–criminal behavior relationship. In this chapter, Collins summarizes the major issues covered in the previous chapters. Sociodemographic, sociocultural, social psychological, and psychological explanations are discussed. The fundamental and important problems of measuring the alcohol use and criminal behavior variables are also discussed.

The eight chapters in this volume have not appeared elsewhere in print. Earlier versions of the chapters were presented at a conference sponsored by the Center for the Study of Crime Correlates and Criminal Behavior of the National Institute of Justice in Arlington, Virginia, in October 1979. The purpose of the conference was the development of a future research agenda to address aspects of the relationship between drinking and serious crime. The original papers were written in support of that goal. They have been revised for publication here on the basis of discussion and criticism generated at the conference.

It is important to place research which has been or may be done on the alcohol–crime relationship into an historical and cultural context. Drinking practices as well as beliefs about the effects of alcohol on behavior have changed over the history of the United States. Rorabaugh (1979) and others have pointed out that per capita consumption of alcohol in this country was much higher in the 18th and 19th centuries. Our forebears drank much more alcohol than we do. Yet this consumption only began to be considered a serious social problem in the latter 19th and 20th centuries. Gusfield (1963) ascribes much of the change in public attitude toward drinking to ideological and political factors. In his view, the redefinition of drinking, especially as characterized in the Temperance Movement, was the result of changes in the distribution of social and political power in American society. The attack on drinking was in reality an attempt to bring official condemnation to bear against the lifestyle of a population segment that was gaining influence at the expense of other population segments.

It is clear that research which attempts to specify the effects of alcohol on behavior must take into account social perceptions about alcohol's effect on behavior. These social evaluations have been shaped by beliefs about the morality of drinking and by perceptions about the influence of drinking on behavior. There cannot be a purely scientific statement on the alcohol–crime connection. One need only consider the Prohibition Amendment to the U.S. Constitution and its aftermath for confirmation that logic and reason do not characterize public debate and control efforts about alcohol consumption.

When alcohol first began to be viewed as a problem in the United States, it was seen as a threat to public order and political stability, rather than as a criminogenic force related to violent and acquisitive crime directed against individuals (Rorabaugh, 1979, pp. 26–31). The concern about public order still characterizes some public debate about alcohol and crime, but recent years have seen attention turn from concern about public drunkenness as an offense against public order to concern with alcohol's effects on violent and property crime.

Modern concern about alcohol as a cause of such crime goes back about 100 years. Lombroso, the Italian criminologist considered by many to be the first modern criminologist, was convinced that alcohol was an important factor in criminality. Writing in the late 19th and 20th centuries, Lombroso based his conclusions on such diverse empirical evidence as the concomitant increases of crime and the level of alcohol consumption in modern society, and the correlation between the peaks in alcohol consumption and the peaks in criminal activity. Lombroso quoted Ferri's finding that, in France, serious assaults increased at the same time the new wine came in during November. He summarized as follows:

Alcohol, then, is a cause of crime, first, because many commit crime in order to obtain drinks, further, because men sometimes seek in drink the courage necessary to commit crime, or an excuse for their misdeeds; again, because it is by the aid of drink that young men are drawn into crime; and because the drink shop is the place for meeting of accomplices, where they not only plan their crimes but also squander their gains . . . it appears that alcoholism occurred oftenest in the case of those charged with assaults, sexual offenses and insurrections. Next came assassinations and homicide; and in the last rank those imprisoned for arson and theft, that is to say, crime against property. (Lombroso, 1968, pp. 95–96)

Since Lombroso wrote these words about three-quarters of a century ago, the dominant opinion about the role of alcohol in criminal behavior has not changed much. It is true that knowledgeable persons writing today are more conditional in their attribution of causality. It is also true that much more empirical research has addressed the question, but the vast majority of this research is hardly more sophisticated than some done in the last century. The use of incarcerated populations as the source of subjects for research on alcohol–crime questions is still the most common way to pursue evidence on individuals. This is true in spite of awareness that generalization from results of research on these populations is impossible or seriously problematic.

As the reader will see in the chapters that follow, the issues and methodological problems raised by consideration of the relationship between alcohol consumption and criminal behavior are complex ones. The scientific complexities of the research issues interact with another set of factors that have referents in the cultural and political spheres. Both the alcohol and crime issues elicit attitudes and reactions that have symbolic and value components; these nonrational components are difficult to integrate with the scientific enterprise. The chapters that follow necessarily grapple with scientific and nonscientific problems. The struggle has clarified issues and suggested future research directions.

James J. Collins, Jr.

Contents

Drinking and Crime

1 Theoretical Aspects of the Relationship between Alcohol Use and Crime

KAI PERNANEN

In this chapter, theories, models, hypotheses, other types of explanatory schemes, and some scattered variables or sets of variables, which have been brought forth in explanations of the association between alcohol use and crime, are discussed. In addition, a certain amount of extrapolation to new explanatory possibilities is attempted. In addition to investigating explanatory entities directly related to an association between alcohol use and crime, there is every reason to try to bridge the theoretical and empirical gap that exists between both general and crime-specific theories of crime or deviance, and theories on the concomitants and effects of acute alcohol use and alcoholism. Some empirical, theoretical, and prototheoretical findings regarding the effects of alcohol ingestion on perception, cognition, attitudes, and behavior are also extrapolated to provide explanatory models relevant for the association.

The discussion falls into six major sections. We present these in the order of appearance, which also should partly reflect an inherent logical progression. The major types of studies on the epidemiological level which form the basis of the statistical association are briefly reviewed. Some necessary formal distinctions are then presented as a preliminary to a discussion of individual level theoretical entities. These consist largely of models postulating physiological variables and processes which explain the occurrence of deviant behavior (predominantly aggressive behavior). Some further formal considerations of explanatory schemes are necessary for linking social theories of deviance and crime as well as other social theories with the individual-level theories. The discussion of social theories which comes next is tentative in nature, and the selection of theories for a brief discussion is largely determined by convenience. The tentativeness reflects the fact that social theories, perhaps by their very nature, are indeterminate as to the constellation of factors relevant for the use of in-

KAI PERNANEN. Alcohol and Aggression Study, funded by Health and Welfare Canada and Addiction Research Foundation of Ontario.

ference rules (models, theories) which predict individual behavior. In the final section of the chapter a summary of the discussion and some personal predilections of the author as to promises of theory are briefly presented.

Because of the lack of empirically tested substantive theories in the field, the following discussion includes many tentative models and empirical generalizations. For the same reason, the exposition is more formal and methodological in nature than would be the case in a well-researched area. The formal approach is also necessitated by the varied nature of the potentially relevant explanatory schemes which are available from both the individual and aggregate levels of theory and analysis, and from several different scientific disciplines. It is also required by the fact that very many of the attempts at explaining the association utilize not theories but what could be called "prototheories," using concepts such as "setting," "physiological characteristics," "personality," etc. It should be emphasized that the aim of the logicoformal scaffolding presented here is not to provide a rigid explanatory framework and to show how little we know, thus inducing despair, perhaps, but to provide a background against which to fit in explanatory entities and empirical findings and research projects. There is more reason for despair with blind adherence to one discipline and one-factor theorizing, since ultimately (although personal satisfaction may come easier) the overall goal of explanation cannot be reached. Some of the reminders implicit in the framework may be useful in any integrative attempt of explanations of human behavior.

The Association to Be Explained

The phenomenon which needs explaining is the apparent statistical association between alcohol use events and alcoholism or specific drinking patterns, on the one hand, and crime or deviant behavior, on the other hand. We start with a brief look at the evidence available on the existence of a statistical association. This consists basically of four different kinds. We start with the one that is most indeterminate as to the causal structure leading to the statistical association, and then proceed toward the most determinate with regard to the causal relationship between alcohol use and the occurrence of crime.

Trend Studies

The most indeterminate evidence is available from aggregate-level analyses of trends in per capita alcohol consumption and crime rates in a population. The evidence here is very scant, and recent attempts have been limited to Scandinavian studies. Lenke (1975, 1976) has shown a very high statistical correlation between rates of violent crime and alcohol consumption in several Scandinavian countries during the period 1960–1973. The fact that both alcohol consumption and crime rates showed a steady increase over the period could be explained by common developmental or evolutionary factors, as often is the case with covariation in trend figures. More convincing evidence of causal influences in Lenke's data are the irregularities in both curves, which tend to follow each other closely. Apparently, no studies exist which examine the relationship between per capita consumption of alcohol and other serious crime, although the data are readily available for a great number of countries and jurisdictions. This type of study is, of course, possible not only longitudinally but also across jurisdictions and nations for which aggregate consumption data and rates of violent crimes are available. However, a superficial examination of available data shows that—possibly due to differing drinking patterns, cultural concomitants of drinking, and/or differences in data collection methods and reliability of statistics or a host of other factors—this relationship would probably not be very strong even for violent crimes where the connection traditionally has been considered to be at its strongest. Thus, out of all the countries for which both statistics are available, France has the highest per capita consumption of alcohol, but it does not have a very high rank in homicide rates. Conversely, the highest homicide rates available are found in Central and South America, in countries which do not place very highly in per capita consumption of alcohol.

The statistical null hypotheses against which to test the significance of the relationship between per capita alcohol consumption and crime are also relatively easily available, and it is surprising that more studies have not been carried out at this level.

"Natural Experiments"

The second type of purely aggregate analyses which have been used to some extent are based on data provided by so-called natural experiments. The availability of alcohol is typically manipulated through increases in the price of alcohol, strikes by liquor store employees, introduction of new sales points (e.g., introduction of sale of beer through grocery stores), or by some other occurrence limiting or increasing availability of alcohol. The rates of crime during the period of limited or increased availability are compared to the rates before and after this period. This type of study, again limited to an examination of violent crime rates, has been carried out by Lenke (1975) in Sweden and by Takala (1973) in Finland. Both studies show clear decreases in rates of violent crime with decreased availability of alcohol.

The most important difference between conjunctive inspection of trends and natural experiments is that the presumed independent variable is manipulated directly in the latter, and thus alternative hypotheses invoking common-cause variables of a developmental or evolutionary nature are ruled out. However, positive findings in this type of analyses should not be taken to mean that a causal relationship on the individual level between alcohol use and an increasing aggregate tendency toward criminal acts has been established. There may still be common-cause factors on the individual level which explain the statistical associations, so that alcohol's physiological, psychological, or other effects do not have to play a part in the explanation of the connection on the aggregate level. It is, for example, possible that when the supply of alcohol is cut down, the frequency of social interaction (through partying, etc.) is also reduced, with a resulting decrease in the probability of interaction and, consequently, interpersonal crime. Thus, the frequency of interaction could be the main explanation of violence in a society. It may be possible to manipulate the level of social interaction in a population and thus perhaps change the rate of some crimes by manipulating the availability of alcohol, even though there is no causal link between alcohol consumption and probability of aggression or other forms of deviance. There are some indications that a model of this type may play a part in explaining the association between the rates of alcohol use and the rates of violence. Aho (1976) has shown that in Finland during the period 1956–1974, when both alcohol consumption and violent crime rates increased, the share of alcohol-related violent crimes did not increase. Expressed differently, when the rate of alcohol-related crimes of violence increased, so did the rate of violent crime in which neither the offender nor the victim had consumed alcohol. We return to Aho's interpretation of this finding in a later section.

Individual Coincidence Estimates

The most common level of empirical analysis contains individual-level data on alcohol use and crime. In studies using crime events as units of study, alcohol use by the offender or victim or both, preceding the crime event, is ascertained; and in studies of prison populations the long-term patterns of drinking, with particular emphasis on typical alcoholic drinking patterns and resultant problems, are typically investigated. Two recent reviews of the literature have looked at the evidence for the statistical association between alcohol use and crime based on this type of data, its basic methodological flaws, and the many different forms and loci of bias (Pernanen, 1976; J. Roizen & Schneberk, 1977a) so there is no need to duplicate the effort here.

Three different characterizations of these studies will serve to point out the shortcomings of this type of data and the type of analyses they have been subjected to. These characterizations are applicable both to the estimates of alcohol use in the event by offender and/or victim, and the estimates of the proportions of problem drinkers or alcoholics in prison populations or similar data bases. First of all, they have been labeled as "one-number estimates" (J. Roizen & Schneberk, 1977a). This can partly be taken as a criticism of the lack of elaboration of the figures of association over the values of third (or more) variables, which would lead us closer to a specification of the causal processes involved in producing the empirical relationship (H. Hyman, 1955; Rosenberg, 1968). Second, these estimates could be called "impact figures" since the results typically are presented without reference to expected values, either in the form of a control group, relating them to population base figures, or other methods of estimating the value of a null hypothesis which would define and quantify the hypothesis of no statistical association. (This could also be implied in the notion of "one-figure estimates.") Third, they are characterized later in this chapter as "coincidence" figures since they are based on samples which are selected by sampling along the dependent variable in the presumed causal relationship. All the issues referred to by these characterizations are brought up later in discussing current and potential explanations of the association.

Despite the shortcomings of these estimates, they are an unavoidable starting point for any attempts at explaining the statistical association, since they effectively make up the statistical association to be explained. Other types of estimates of a statistical association would change at least the aggregate structure of the models and theories which would make up such an explanation. The fact that the empirical evidence is rather unsystematic will not deter this discussion, since we are not trying to explain an association of a specific strength. Such an attempt will have to be put off into the indefinite future. Consequently, we do not systematically attempt to estimate the explanatory weight of (the empirical relevance of) the different explanatory schemes discussed here; this would be a rather hopeless task with the current state of knowledge.

The association expressed as alcohol involvement in the event (drinking by either offender or victim or both) in the most representative North American studies sets the figure at around 50% for violent crime, almost exclusively homicide. These impact figures of alcohol involvement seem to be used at times to suggest that 50–60% of homicides are directly caused by alcohol use and thus would not have occurred if there was zero alcohol consumption in the population. They dominate the discussion and popular views of the relationship to the extent that they seem to be taken to be almost synonymous with epidemiological findings in the area.

In addition to North America, even minimally systematic data seem to be available only for Finland, where the alcohol involvement figures for homicide and assault are somewhat higher: typically between 60 and 70%. It has been calculated that the rate of alcohol-involved homicides per 100,000 liters of absolute alcohol consumed in Finland in one year (1974) was almost twice as high compared to that of Canada (Pernanen, 1979b). It is quite possible that a large part of this difference can be ascribed to a more intensive recordkeeping of alcohol involvement in crime (particularly violent crime) in Finland. This fact in turn may partly rest upon different belief systems surrounding alcohol use and its effects in the two countries. On the other hand, it may also reflect different prevalence rates of high-risk drinking patterns and other factors directly related to alcohol use events.

With regard to the estimates of the proportion of alcoholics or problem drinkers among offenders committing various types of crime, the definitions of alcoholism and problem drinking differ so much that summary values are rather meaningless.

Crimes of violence are used here by way of illustration since they provide the most extensive data on the association. For a thorough review of the coincidence estimates between alcohol use and nonviolent crime, both as it pertains to alcohol use events and to long-term drinking patterns, the reader is referred to J. Roizen and Schneberk (1977a).

Experimental and Clinical Studies

Evidence for a net statistical association could, under ideal circumstances, be gleaned from experimental or clinical studies. At the present time, however, the gaps in the measures of the presumed independent variables of alcohol use between experimental studies and the epidemiological reality are large, and the size and significance of these gaps cannot be assessed with the empirical evidence and conceptual tools available. The same holds true, by ethical necessity, for many relevant dependent variables. Moreover, the presence of third (or more) variables in natural crime events (and in criminals) causally relevant in bringing about the statistical association has not been taken into account systematically in experimental studies, which further restricts their usefulness for this purpose.

Judged solely by their special methods of sample selection or self-selection, clinical studies seem to have more direct relevance to the assessment of the validity of the statistical association than typical experimental studies, particularly since the selection criteria are based on aspects of the independent variable, such as alcoholism, and on aspects of the dependent variable, such as violent tendencies. The potentially greater relevance stems from the likelihood that predisposing variables are conditionally relevant in explaining the association between alcohol use and crime. However, here also the links of causal determination and the empirical relevance of research and explanatory models are too complex and scantily researched to provide grounds for an assessment of the impact on the statistical association. Moreover, the generalizability, prevalence, and incidence of the variable values of experimental and clinical studies, and their settings are difficult to assess. For these reasons, discussions based on theories or models derived from or otherwise associated with experimental or clinical research are not used in this chapter to assess the validity of the aggregated statistical association, although any valid theories implicitly are relevant for this purpose.

Instead, the statistical associations between alcohol use and different crimes are accepted at face value, and theoretical evidence from clinical and experimental research is used in its most fruitful aspect in explanatory schemes which play a potential role in accounting for these associations.

The Major Assumption

The unavoidable major premise in any attempt to analyze theories or theorizing about the relationship between alcohol use and crime is that a net positive statistical association does hold true, at least on the aggregate level and in some fairly common and socially relevant circumstances. This assumption must be based on two further assumptions. The first assumption is that the estimates of the involvement of alcohol in crime occurrences and other relevant statistical data are relatively unbiased estimates of the true size of the statistical associations. The second implicit assumption is that, if a statistical test were possible, the null hypothesis of no association between alcohol use and criminal acts would be rejected. Alternative hypotheses attempting to "explain away" the association have been suggested, however, and they are discussed later.

The Explanatory Material and Tools

The different research traditions and methodologies which have brought forth the empirical research, theories, and other explanatory entities relevant for the explanation of the statistical relationship differ greatly in their emphases. The scope of the material is striking and brings with it inherent tensions which have to be resolved at least in principle, if not on the substantive level of theory.

Due to the polarities of different disciplines, methodologies, and theoretical emphases, a comparatively lengthy discussion of the formal properties of theories and models, and the requirements for their integration in explaining the statistical association between alcohol use and crime is necessary in this chapter.

We do not propose one global theory which would purport to explain the statistical association but instead suggest an organizing formal explanatory framework which will enable us to "fit in" what is known about the relationship. This way we can stay much closer to the facts and at the same time point out the location and nature of the gaps in theory and empirical knowledge. It might also assist us later in achieving an integration of theories into more general structures of wider applicability. In this section we look at the formal properties of the individual models and theories available, and in a later section we put forth the necessary formal properties that a causal accounting of the statistical association which integrates individual-level and aggregate-level theories will by necessity have. The concepts and interrelations between these, which are discussed later, are part and parcel of the very nature of scientific explanation.

The Material

Empirically, it is relatively convenient to delimit the study of the relationship between alcohol use and crime to detected and labeled crimes. Because of the relatively ready availability of data on crime events and individuals who have committed crimes, the choice is often not even a conscious one. On the theoretical level, this limitation should not occur. The scope of a theory should be determined by its explanatory power, not by the scattered empirical evidence available. This evidence is often truncated by limitations due to data sources, administrative interests, and specific research foci. "Crime," understood as deviant acts known to and recorded by the authorities, as an exclusive variable in an explanatory scheme is theoretically useful only under very specific assumptions. In the following we do not delimit the theoretical interests to crime but look inclusively at theories and empirical studies dealing with general deviance.

Both the label of "crime" and the label of "alcohol use" in effect represent many different types of events and variables. Even in the scientific literature, the term "alcohol use" typically, and very loosely, denotes a great number of different entities (Pernanen, 1976). These references are not specified to the extent that they could be, especially on the epidemiological level of inquiry. In this discussion "alcohol use" implicitly stands for a disjunction of at least the following: blood alcohol level, intoxication, amount of alcohol consumed, type of beverage consumed, congener content of beverage consumed, rising versus falling blood alcohol content (BAC), length of drinking occasion, long-term patterns of drinking, alcoholism, and sometimes even different variables present in the alcohol use event. Any combinations of these, summatively or in interaction (such as amount consumed plus rising or falling BAC), can determine manifest behavior and are thus included in the implicit disjunction. For any serious advance in theory, however, these different references of the term have to be explicated and kept apart. (See Pernanen, 1976, and Aarens, Cameron, Roizen, Roizen, Room, Schneberk, & Wingard, 1977, for discussions of the indeterminateness of the concept.)

It should thus be kept in mind that "alcohol use" in this chapter refers to a whole set of potential variables and combinations of these and could be read in a notation familiar from set theory as {alcohol use}. Sometimes the term is used more restrictively; this should be clear from the context. If special elements of this set (e.g., BAC) are intended, these are explicitly mentioned. The major distinction between situational aspects of alcohol use and long-term effects of alcoholic drinking patterns is signaled by referring to the former subset interchangeably by the expressions "alcohol use events," "alcohol use situations," "acute alcohol use," and easily detectable synonyms; and by referring to the latter by labels such as "chronic alcohol use," "long-term excessive alcohol use," and "alcoholism." The stigma of excessive drinking, its economic, social, interactional, and medical consequences, are best referred to as "problem drinking" or, in a more disjunctive fashion, as "drinking problems."

Needless to say, the specification of the relevant variables contained under the epidemiological labels has crucial implications for theoretical developments in the area. Regarding the other central variable, most often assumed to be the dependent variable in explanations of the association, the discussion concentrates on serious crime, but the theoretical perspective necessitates discussion of theories of other (more general or restricted) variables, ranging over a wide variety of behaviors. These include deviance, crime, violent crime, rape, robbery, homicide, child abuse, violence, family violence, aggression, property crime, arson, vandalism, and other potential references. In the following discussion "crime" and "deviance" should also generally be read in an implicit disjunctive set theoretical notation. Formally, all possible relationships between the elements of the sets would be represented by the Cartesian product of those sets: {alcohol use} × {crime}. In addition, as already mentioned, some interactive combinations of elements in the set of alcohol use variables are possible. Contemplating this way of representation may make us more sensitive to the indeterminateness of much of the discussion in this area. The notation is not used in this chapter, except to underscore the multiple references of the terms in certain contexts.

It seems clear that all the different relationships denoted by {alcohol use} × {crime} cannot exclusively be explained by the same theories or models. Some explanatory schemes would, in all probability, be applicable to alcohol involvement in deviant behavior in general, others to interpersonal, purely assaultive crime, other "submodels" to robbery and to rape, and a largely different set of models to property crimes. No satisfactory explanatory entity (theory or model) is available in sufficient detail to explain the alcohol involvement in all different types of crime.

There hardly is any more clear-cut case for the importance of interdisciplinary theorizing and research than that which can be made for explanations of the effects of mood-modifying drugs on human behavior. In addition to definite, although conceptually not easily delimited, and categorized effects on behavior, mood-modifying drugs (including alcohol) have been surrounded with informal and formal social arrangements, and societal reactive systems, which have partly determined social definitions and beliefs about the nature of the drugs and their users as well as the effects of the drugs. These social and cultural factors cannot be neglected in any attempts at explaining the psychological, behavioral, societal, and cultural phenomena associated with alcohol use.

In order to make the task more manageable, two substantive relationships which would fall within the formal framework of alcohol use and crime are not discussed here at any length, although they are worthy of serious empirical and theoretical attention. The relationship between alcohol use and crime, if broadly interpreted, could also cover the observed association between parental alcohol use and criminal acts of offspring. The empirical evidence implicates parental alcoholism and resultant emotional, social, and material deprivation as explanatory variables; and parental alcohol use patterns through modeling, availability of alcohol in the home, parental behavior under the influence, etc., could provide other types of mediating processes. This relationship is not included for consideration, since the relationship does not have a direct impact on the statistical association as reflected in coincidence figures, which is based on alcohol use and crime by the same individual. Trend studies and perhaps, to some extent, natural experiments deal only with aggregate figures and are indeterminate in this respect. Thus, it is conceivable that changes in per capita consumption will reflect changes in parental alcohol use, and that changes in crime rates will be made up partly by crimes committed by children and determined by these changes in alcohol use by parents. In accounting for the findings of purely aggregate-level studies, this possibility would have to be considered, its relevancy depending on the length of the time units of study.

Another aspect of the relationship between alcohol use events and violent crime which does not receive the attention it perhaps deserves is the role of alcohol use as an *issue* in violent events. This would seem to have a noteworthy prevalence in instances of family violence, judging from some preliminary data from a community study on alcohol use and aggressive behavior. (See Pernanen, 1979b, for an introductory presentation of this study.)

Empirical data on or theories of any connection between group violence or riots and alcohol use are unfortunately not available to any extent which would allow theoretical discussion. A more fanciful connection could be included if the designation "alcohol use and crime" is understood historically (and very inclusively), namely the one between the rise of organized crime in the United States and alcohol use during the Prohibition years.

The Tools: Formal Distinctions

Some formal distinctions of theories and empirical research methodology will aid in extracting the central features of theories and research of alcohol use and crime/deviance, in drawing the broad outlines of integrative attempts, and as aids in suggesting future developments. Formal properties of theories, models, and single variables are especially useful in any attempts at integrating theoretical entities which are ascribed to several different academic disciplines and in a field with major gaps in theoretical and empirical knowledge.

"Theories" and "models" are sometimes used here interchangeably but with models seen as more specific with regard to specification of conditions of applicability. Theories involve more generality by virtue of specifying relationships between fewer variables of wider applicability. Thus, models often "borrow" from several theories to attain predictability and explain occurrences. A good case can be made for a different and more precise distinction for the use of the two concepts. Thus Brodbeck (1959) assigns the term "model" to explanations which contain references to entities or variables which are not directly observable or measurable.

"Cause" and "causal" are used probabilistically to indicate the direction in chronological determination, in the same type of rather loose but not uncommon fashion. "Cause" is thus used here in a very general, formal way to indicate that if A did not occur before B in time, B would not occur or would not occur to the same extent or with the same probability. Its looseness in everyday usage does not prevent it from being used with serious consequences. It is, for example, embedded in the concepts and practices connected with "responsibility" and law.

With regard to theories or models, some standard distinctions with fairly standard labels are used. These types of models or theories include those postulating a direct-cause relationship between alcohol use and crime, models positing a common-cause variable, conditional or interactive relationships, and associations based on a conjunctive clustering of alcohol use and other factors due, for example, to cultural contexts of alcohol use.[1] In the case involving cultural context, the other factors, and not alcohol use, are causally active.

Schematically, the structure of these models can probably be best represented by arrow diagrams, and these are used in the following text to summarize and illustrate these formal properties of explanations of the association between alcohol use and crime. A direct-cause ("unconditional") relationship is simply represented by Diagram 1, the common-cause relationship by Diagram 2, and the conditional/interactive and conjunctive relationships by Diagrams 3 and 4, respectively:

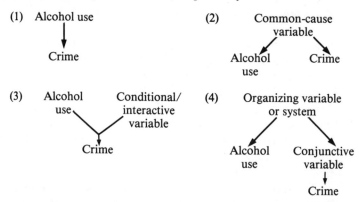

In the probabilistic scheme of explanation under which we, by necessity, are laboring, the arrows of the diagrams should be read as: "increases the probability of."

Empirically, the end result of all these formal designations of causal relationships—the direct-cause, conjunctive, conditional, interactive, and common-cause relationships—is a higher-than-chance association be-

[1]In this discussion the designated "interactive" is used to include conditional relationships as a special case.

tween alcohol use and crime. They may be combined in any number of ways in causal models and in more complex explanations linking alcohol use events or alcohol use patterns (e.g., alcoholism) to crime.

In the additional variables adduced in the explanations, a further distinction between situational and predisposing variables is made. Situational variables are those variables whose values show intraindividual variations over time, with a comparatively low degree of stable interindividual variations. Predisposing variables, on the other hand, show interindividual variation in a stable manner over time, with only relatively small intraindividual variation. Values for most variables show both types of variation, and the distinction, although heuristically valuable, becomes arbitrary at the borderlines. It is thus difficult to assign a definite label to variables which are based on cognition—on learning processes. Examples of predispositional factors are most convincingly taken from the biological and psychological variables which have been posited in explanations of the association between alcohol use and crime, while situational factors are taken from the immediate environment surrounding the act.

Situational and predisposing variables are extremely important since we have to discard "direct-cause" theorizing and accept that there is no one-to-one relationship between the effects of alcohol use and human behavior. We must thus acknowledge the existence of conditional/interactive factors, which, together with alcohol use, explain some crime occurrences. This has been shown by everyday, unsystematic observations and by both failures and successes of experimental studies.

Individual-Level Models

The formal explanatory distinctions outlined in the preceding section are partly applied in the following discussion of individual-level theories and models of alcohol's effects on behavior that are of potential relevance to the association between alcohol use and crime. The alternative strategy of ordering theories by discipline is intermixed with this formal categorizing when the nature of the variables in the theory or model clearly points to a certain discipline. This is most clearly the case with physiological, pharmacological, or general biological theories of alcohol effects. However, even with regard to these, conditional or interactive factors whose etiology is traceable to other disciplines are relevant. Empirical conditions of a predispositional or situational nature which interact with alcohol use in determining behavior, and the distribution of these conditions in the population are determined by theories which must include sociological and psychological variables. We return to this in the section on "explanatory accounting."

It is much easier to categorize variables into different disciplines than it is to classify models on the same basis, since the latter, sometimes explicitly, include variables from more than one discipline. In our thinking, models are primary, not variables. Paraphrasing Ludwig Wittgenstein on concepts and propositions (1961, p. 63), one could say: Only in the context of a theory does a variable have meaning. Theories and models explain, variables do not. In some multivariate techniques, single variables and groups of variables are said to "explain" a certain share of the variance in a "dependent" variable. It is unfortunate if such technical uses of the word "explanation" can lead to misconceptions regarding the nature of scientific explanation.

The relevant literature on the acute effects of alcohol on behavior has mainly focused on the measurement of aggressive behavior and is, by extrapolation, relevant most directly for alcohol's association with violent crime. The relevance of aggression theories for the explanation of general deviance or crime is difficult to assess, although psychoanalytical theories can be found which would provide the necessary connection.

Physiological Effects of Alcohol as Intervening Variables in the Explanation of Crime

In the models discussed in this section, direct causal effects of alcohol can be invoked to account for the epidemiological association between alcohol and aggression and violence. Other variables in addition to aggression which may enter explanations as intervening variables in the causal process are also discussed.

Experimental studies show equivocal results regarding the effects of alcohol on violence, whether "alcohol use" is explicated as BAC (within the range of BACs used), congener content, or as a total alcohol use event. This lack of clear tendencies is evident whether the subjects are humans, rats, or Siamese fighting fish (e.g., Bennett *et al.*, 1969; MacDonnell & Ehmer, 1969; Raynes & Ryback, 1970; Shuntich & Taylor, 1972). Thus, if we accept the statistical association between alcohol use and violent crime, and persist in regarding alcohol use as a potential independent variable, we must look for conditional values of third (or more) variables which interact with alcohol use to increase the probability of violent behavior and crime. We must also assume that these factors have not, neither explicitly nor implicitly, been taken into account in most experimental studies.

From what is known of the physiological processes associated with alcohol use, it is clear that physiological effects of alcohol covary with some other variables. This may lead to the emergence of a relatively strong relationship between alcohol use and deviant/violent behavior in one collection of individuals, with a certain patterning of activities connected with their alcohol use situations; and a weaker relationship, or none, between the two variables in another collectivity, with another patterning of concomitant variables. To take a very simple example, consumption of food at drinking occasions will slow down the absorption of alcohol into the bloodstream and attenuate the peak of BAC. If the probability of aggressive behavior, deviant behavior, risk taking, crime, etc., increases with increasing BACs (up to a point), the one collectivity which does not consume food at drinking occasions will show a stronger relationship between alcohol use and the criterion behavior. This, of course, assumes that we choose the mere presence of alcohol consumption, or amounts consumed, etc., out of {alcohol use} as our potential independent variables, and that we do not choose blood alcohol concentration, since BAC enters as a potential independent variable in which absorption rate is already controlled for.

As pointed out earlier, the models and theories discussed in the literature deal largely with alcohol's effects on aggressive behavior and are thus potentially applicable primarily to a theoretical discussion of violent crime. Perhaps (because of the lesser specificity and greater complexity of actual behavior involved in other forms of crime) it is difficult to imagine models explaining specific physiologically determined physical acts which would have face validity in explaining crimes other than violent crime and even less validity in explaining crime or deviance in general. In the latter case it would be easier to imagine a further intervening variable, such as risk taking, as a dependent variable in the models, with a great deal of indeterminateness regarding the outcome in the form of specific acts.

Disinhibition Models

The main properties of the disinhibition concept have been discussed elsewhere and are not reviewed here (Pernanen, 1976). It has been used predominantly as a concept describing behavior and also in referring to some formal explanatory features. Used as a formal concept, "disinhibition" potentially refers to an unlimited number of theories or models which have certain formal properties in common. As a concept describing the resultant behavior (the dependent variable values), it also refers to an unlimited number of theoretical schemes, that is, any that explain "disinhibited" behavior.

The idea of "disinhibition" as a formal concept is partly built into the most general features of the logic of explanation of an occurrence on the basis of a prevailing tendency. Its generality explains partly why the disinhibition concept is so popular and elusive. Substantive delimitations to this formal openness have historically been generated from psychoanalytical theory and, related to this, from (social) control theory of deviant behavior. However, the current use of the concept of "disinhibition" and the formulation of substantive research hypotheses allegedly linked to the concept do not show many vestiges of this historical and conceptual link. Instead, the use of the concept has shifted to a descriptive reference of behavior connected with alcohol use and a label of the formal properties of explanatory schemes of the type described.

Descriptively, the concept can be used to refer to a "disinhibition hypothesis" of alcohol use, that is, that alcohol use will lead to behavior which can be described as "disinhibited." This is, however, nothing more than an empirical generalization, and its confirmation should not be interpreted as confirmation of a disinhibition theory or model.

In addition, however, "disinhibition" has been used as a label of some specific and legitimate causal theories. The labeling of the theories as disinhibition theories would, in these cases, be based on an implicit reference to specific inhibition variables (initial conditions) and/or specific mediating processes.

Among the direct physiological models suggested, belongs the one according to which a neurophysiological mechanism mediated by blood alcohol disconnects the inhibitory functions of the cerebral cortex on the lower brain centers and thus disinhibits aggressive impulses (e.g., Sobell & Sobell, 1975). No empirical findings seem to be available to help either directly support or refute such a specific model, although Kalant (1961) has presented support for a modified version of the theory. By locating the processes resulting in aggressive behavior in psychological or in purely physiological processes below the level of consciousness, this model is impossible to test on the behavioral level. As far as is known to the author there is no clear-cut evidence available from neurological studies to support the existence of such a mechanism. However, this possibility would seem to deserve careful attention and empirical study. Extrapolations of findings from research on brain lesions and CNS excitation would seem relevant in this context. Even if such a mechanism is detected, however, nothing has been proven about the nature of the resulting behavior (and its other determinants). Just because a physiological inhibitory process has been eliminated does not mean that the resulting behavior will be what we describe as "free from inhibitions." The criteria are entirely different.

A finding which would seem to lend support to a theory based on the blocking of neural signals between the cortex and other brain centers is the finding that alcohol impedes the transmission of electrical currents in nerves generally (e.g., Chafetz, 1979). This fact can, however, also be used to corroborate other types of models than disinhibition models, which do not postulate a selective blocking which would "release" aggressive and presumably other antisocial impulses. (This disinhibition model has the properties of a social control model superimposed on neural processes. It may have more to do with remnants of psychoanalytical theorizing than with brain physiology.) Other consequences of this impediment to neural communication are quite likely in that they will inter alia affect perception and cognition. Although the author professes inadequate knowledge of brain physiology, it seems that this effect of alcohol is sufficiently iso-morphic with the basic assumption of a randomization effect on behavior cues to warrant integrative attempts in research and theory. (See later sec-tion on randomization of behavior cues as a mediating process in alcohol effects for more detail.)

The disinhibition concept as a direct-cause model of alcohol's effects on aggressive behavior has been refuted without question, not a very de-manding task since one negative instance is enough to accomplish this. The extravagant uses of the concept should not be allowed to hide the fact that it can have and has had legitimate explanatory uses. If one decides to label an explanatory model on the basis of the nature of the initial condi-tions postulated by the model, it seems that the concept could, in connec-tion with explanations of violent crime, be used to refer to models employ-ing variables and processes based on an "old grudge," displaced aggression, experimentally induced blocking of aggressive behavior, social inhibitions (Hetherington & Wrey, 1964), etc.

Control theories have had widespread support also in the explanation of crime and deviance, at least among psychoanalytically oriented research-ers, and within the context of these theories the most natural explanatory role of alcohol probably has been that of a "disinhibitor." "Disinhibi-tion" within the framework of a social control theory perhaps becomes coextensive with deviant behavior generally.

Epinephrine/Norepinephrine Secretion

As summarized by Roizen and Schneberk (1977a), theorizing on effects of alcohol on altered epinephrine/norepinephrine levels has posited two predominant models of action:

(1) Alcohol ⟶ Altered epinephrine/ ⟶ Stress ⟶ Aggressive
norepinephrine   behavior
activity

(2) Alcohol ⟶ Activation of specific ⟶ Aggressive behavior
chemical codes of ag-
gressive behavior,
epinephrine/nor-
epinephrine

The first of these models posits two levels of intervening variables, with presumably two levels of possible indeterminateness added as compared to a direct cause inhibition model. Even the second model—which, with only one level of potential indeterminateness, is closer to a direct cause model—cannot hold strictly true since alcohol use does not unfailingly lead to aggressive behavior. (As is well known from anybody's unsystematic observations or autoexperiments, this is rather the exception than the rule.) Thus, we have to assume a certain amount of openness in the posited causal links, and if we want to stick by scientific canons of causal accountability, we have to posit the existence of conditional or interactive variables, whose nature for the time being would be left open. There are undoubtedly individual differences in physiological processes and pharmacological reactions, and these should be specified as they pertain to any predominantly biological model. The additional gap of indeterminateness between these processes and the behavioral level would, of course, also need further study.

Temporal Lobe Dysfunction

This biophysiological model, in contradistinction to the two previously discussed, tries to explain an association between alcohol use and violence by the explicit use of a conditional/interactive model. It seems possible that biological disinhibition models can be made less deterministic and more conditional in nature by expending them to include individual variations in: (1) neural blockage, (2) strength of cerebral control, and (3) strength of the aggressive/antisocial impulses located in lower brain centers. In the same way, constitutional individual differences affecting the probability that alcohol will lead to changes in the epinephrine/norepinephrine levels could explain individual differences in behavior after alcohol use even with the same BACs (or other relevant values of other alcohol use variables).

Temporal lobe dysfunction has often been quoted as a determinant of "pathological intoxication"—a paradoxical state of consciousness caused by even relatively small amounts of alcohol (e.g., Cuthbert, 1970; Marinacci, 1963; Skelton, 1970). This diagram schematizes the outline of the model:

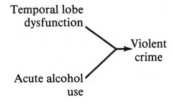

Temporal lobe
dysfunction

Violent
crime

Acute alcohol
use

Chronic excessive alcohol use or alcoholism seems to lead to epileptiform dysrhythmias in brain waves in some cases (e.g., Giove, 1964). If the independent effects of temporal lobe dysfunction are sufficient to increase the probability of violent crime, this would be a valid (nonconditional/noninteractive) causal model:

Chronic excessive   Temporal lobe   Violent
alcohol use ——▶ dysfunction ——▶ crime

Combining these two models, the cerebral dysfunction caused by long-term alcohol abuse would be an intervening variable in a causal model linking alcoholic drinking with alcohol use events in the same scheme (with alcohol use in the event as a conditional or interactive variable):

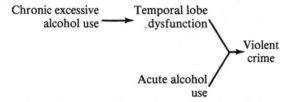

The prevalence and distribution of temporal lobe dysfunction independently of or caused by chronic excessive alcohol use in the general population or among alcoholics are not known. Thus, the extent to which this predisposing condition accounts for the association between alcohol use and (violent) crime cannot be assessed. We return to the importance of prevalence and incidence data for explanation of the statistical association and related matters in the section on integration of various models and theories.

The significance of other types of brain damage possibly caused by alcohol use has not received attention in discussions of crime or violence.

Hypoglycemia

Hypoglycemia has been mentioned as a factor responsible for violent behavior (e.g., Herman, Sesko, Trinajstic, Vidovic, & Cabrijan, 1970). Alcohol is known to cause hypoglycemia in individuals who are undernourished (e.g., Moynihan, 1965). Since much excessive alcohol use, especially among alcoholics, is associated with poor nutritional habits, this condition could be a factor in explaining part of the association between prolonged alcohol use events (and alcoholism) and violent crime. Vartia, Forsander, and Krusius (1960) suggest that hypoglycemia may become a chronic condition with alcoholics. The prevalence of hypoglycemia among alcoholics seems to be rather low (Herman et al., 1970), and this of course means that the value of this factor in explaining the observed relationship between alcoholism or alcohol use events and violent crime is limited. Hypoglycemia as a possible interactive predisposing factor in causing violent behavior in connection with acute alcohol use has not been discussed in the literature to the knowledge of the author.

Sleep Deprivation

Another intervening variable of potential theoretical relevance is sleep deprivation, in particular deprivation of rapid-eye-movement (REM) sleep. It has been shown in numerous experiments that acute alcohol use leads to deprivation of REM sleep (Greenberg & Pearlman, 1967; Gresham, Webb, & Williams, 1963; Gross & Goodenough, 1968; Johnson, Burdick, & Smith, 1970; Knowles, Laverty, & Keuchler, 1968; Yules, Freedman, & Chandler, 1966). The increased probability of aggressive behavior caused by sleep deprivation has been documented in several studies (see Gove, 1969–1970). Due to their drinking patterns, especially binge drinking, alcoholics are at high risk of exhibiting deprivation of REM sleep and consequent behavior disturbances. The possible interactive effects of sleep deprivation and (other) acute effects of alcohol on the probability of violence in alcohol use events have not received scientific attention but would seem to deserve systematic empirical study. To try to untangle the effects of sleep deprivation from the effects of stress induced by sleep deprivation may be difficult empirically. Effects of sleep deprivation may also be partly accounted for by a frustration–aggression theory, since stressful stimuli are perhaps less easily coped with in a sleep-deprived state, especially considering other, more direct effects of alcohol intoxication.

The prevalence of alcohol use events which cause sleep deprivation and the threshold values of sleep deprivation needed for aggressive behavior to occur are not known. Thus, any assessment of this model for an explanation of the statistical association between alcohol use and violent crime is not possible.

Paresthesia

The causal relevance of alcohol-induced paresthesia (Hartocollis, 1962) as an intervening variable in the escalation of violent crime has been hypothesized by Pernanen (1976). The effects of this factor on the probability of inception or escalation of violence have not been subjected to any tests in experimental research on alcohol effects. It would seem that experiments using electric shocks as obnoxious stimuli in eliciting aggressive responses could be modified to include this factor in the experimental set-up. Due to the effects of alcohol, it is possible that it has been implicitly included in many experiments. Independent and systematic variations of this variable in alcohol use experiments would enable an assessment of its causal significance.

Alcoholism as an Independent and Interactive Predisposing Factor

The preceding sections speculate on the predisposing conditional/interactive roles of temporal lobe dysfunction, hypoglycemia, and sleep deprivation in connection with alcohol use. Another potentially predispositional factor which has received at least implicit attention in the literature, in this context should be mentioned. This variable is alcoholism, or possibly some factors which are definitionally or causally related to alcoholism.

It is possible that the alcoholism syndrome—due to epileptiform cerebral changes, hypoglycemia, or deprivation of REM sleep as outcomes of alcoholic drinking, and acting as predispositional interactive/conditional factors—explains part of any excess violence committed by alcoholics in alcohol use events. This can be schematized as follows:

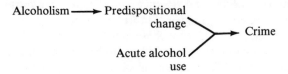

Alcoholism as a condition which directly increases the probability of violent behavior has been mentioned not infrequently in the literature (e.g., Antons, 1970; Hassall & Foulds, 1968). Alcoholism, as a cluster of definitional characteristics and effects of long-term alcohol abuse, may, via irreversible physiological/biological changes, also have main effects which increase the likelihood of crime (Pernanen, 1976). This, again, can be rendered in schematic form in the following manner:

$$\text{Alcoholism} \longrightarrow \underset{\text{changes}}{\text{Predispositional}} \longrightarrow \text{Crime}$$

In addition, the somehow circumscribed condition of alcoholism may by itself interact with acute alcohol effects to bring about an increased probability of these types of behavior:

The evidence available for this type of model has been reviewed in two fairly recent publications (Freed, 1978; Pernanen, 1976) and is not discussed here in any detail. The bulk of the experimental and clinical evidence rests on the differential effects of acute alcohol use on the mood of alcoholics compared to nonalcoholics.

Typical alcoholic drinking patterns, most obviously through the increased frequency of alcohol use events, probably increase the likelihood of aggressive reactions via the type of models discussed for alcohol use events, but these drinking patterns would have to be considered a conjunctive independent factor and not a predispositional attribute of alcoholics which would interact with alcohol use. Certain variables of a developmental or genetic nature have also been adduced in explanations of a higher probability of both alcoholism and crime. These are discussed briefly in connection with other common-cause models in the following section.

Other Interactive Predisposing Factors

A great many predisposing factors or processes of varying degrees of testability and theoretical value have been suggested in the explanation of deviant behavior, crime, and violence (socialization of a certain type, ability to delay gratification, degree of moral judgment, impulsivity, superego development, etc.). In order for these to help explain the statistical association with alcohol use, there would have to be a conditional or interactive relationship of these variables with alcohol use. This means that the probability of the criterion behaviors should be higher when individuals with these predispositions use alcohol (in a certain way) than could be expected from the simple additive effects of the predisposition and the alcohol use. This type of relationship has not been shown to hold true for very many of the predisposing variables put forth in explanations of deviance, violence, or crime.

Typically, when a predisposing variable is presented in the literature as having explanatory value with regard to increased aggressiveness or deviance after alcohol use, this explanatory role is not distinguished from its independent main effects. Thus, it is not satisfactorily explained how the effects of a certain type of socialization, or lack of integration into society (Boyatzis, 1975) or male sex roles (Lenke, 1976) or too rigid a socialization (Roebuck & Johnson, 1962), are exacerbated or otherwise affected by alcohol use. Sometimes an implicit, rather vague, disinhibition model seems to be invoked to account for this fact (e.g., Boyatzis, 1975; Roebuck & Johnson, 1962); however, it is often not accounted for at all (e.g., Lenke, 1976).

Situational Theories and Variables

Direct-cause models, as they are presently formulated at least, cannot explain the existence of an association between alcohol use and violence, deviance, or crime. This is because of both the interindividual and intraindividual variations in reactions to alcohol observed both systematically and unsystematically in experimental and natural settings. Due to the intraindividual variations, theories invoking only predisposing factors as conditionally relevant do not suffice. On the other hand, any models which only invoke situational variables as conditionally relevant do not suffice as explanations of the association either. The following discussion on situational models should be read in this light.

Conjunctive or Conditional Theories, Prototheories, and Variables

Although the importance of situational variables in determining behavior in alcohol use events has been acknowledged by many authors, no serious attempt at specifying the nature of these variables has been made. Thus, much of what goes under the label of theorizing are general prototheories pointing to one or more types of variables, which may have explanatory value. Other prevalent theorizing in the field is actually the discussion of one or more specific variables whose role in any theory is left largely open. References to situational factors remain at the general level of "setting," and very few studies have been carried out which would aid in this specification. Presence of other individuals in the setting has been shown by Hartocollis (1962) to increase boisterous and aggressive behavior of subjects who were given alcohol intravenously. Subjects tested individually, on the other hand, were "unusually friendly to those around them." Some methodological shortcomings of the study make generalizations difficult. Carpenter and Armenti (1972), in reviewing the experimental literature, have mentioned male drinking company as one conditional situational factor, but further specification would be needed as to characteristics of the males, their interaction, and characteristics of the situation, etc., since only a very small proportion of male drinking groups exhibit violence. No data exist from experimental studies to support any guesses about the characteristics of such company. Epidemiological studies have not compiled data on crime events relevant to an assessment of important characteristics of the drinking group. Systematic observational studies of value in this context are hard to come by.

With the present state of knowledge it is impossible to make any assessment of the explanatory relevance and role of any situational variables. A basic weakness is that no studies have been made in natural settings systematically comparing a nonalcohol condition to an alcohol condition. Thus, it is not possible to distinguish between the role of situational factors as conditional and as merely conjunctive variables in alcohol use events. Carpenter and Armenti (1972), in reviewing relevant experimental studies, seem to suggest that the main effect of variables in the setting independently (conjunctively) explain most of the behavior in alcohol use events: "It appears that the circumstances of drinking produce greater changes in behavior than the alcohol does" (p. 540).

As with many of the predisposing variables suggested in explanation of the relationship under study, authors often neglect to specify in what way their "favorite" variables conditionally increase the likelihood of deviance or violence in connection with alcohol use, compared to the independent effects of the variable and alcohol use itself. Thus, for example, competitive activities such as card games have independent effects on the probability of aggression which are sometimes not kept apart from the possible interactive effects of alcohol use. It should also be noted that any one of the possible valid theories (such as an extended frustration–aggression theory or a randomization theory; see later discussion) may explain this type of observed empirical regularities. The favorite choice seems to be, however, an explanation based on the physiologically disinhibiting properties of alcohol.

Taylor, Gammon, and Capasso (1976), in experiments designed to examine the conditional nature of reactions to frustrating stimuli in alcohol conditions, have shown convincingly an interactive relationship between alcohol consumption and threatening stimuli. Also, by using attribution of characteristics of the presumed opponent they show a promising theoretical openness in their work. Through the explicitly conditional methodology and measurements of attribution they move away from direct-cause thinking and from the rather narrow confines of "disinhibition" paradigms toward an inclusion also of the perceptual and cognitive effects of alcohol. This direction will probably lead to theoretical progress at this time.

Other situational features which are probably relevant to the explanation of the association, although their "accounting power" is not known, are the heightened probability of interaction (see the later discussion of spuriousness models) and the largely randomized cues available in some tavern settings (cf. the discussion on ritualization in Pernanen, 1976).

The significance of situational determination of crime in connection with acute alcohol use and alcoholism is underscored by the considerable field dependency and impulsivity of alcoholics (Gomberg, 1978), the fact that a large proportion of crimes can be characterized as crimes of opportunity (e.g., J. H. Goldstein, 1975), and the probably increased importance of immediate behavior cues in determining behavior in alcohol use events.

Increased situational determination of behavior would also mean that the availability of weapons and their cue value would be a more important factor in alcohol use events than in alcohol-free situations regarding the probability of interpersonal violence.

Intervening Variables

A number of empirical studies and connected theorizing have focused on variables which as such cannot be subsumed under violence, aggression, deviance, or crime but still seem to have semantical or empirical causal links with these presumed dependent variables. Here we mention some that apply to at least the "normal" range of acute alcohol use. (Intervening factors related to excessive use of alcohol in the event, such as sleep deprivation, are discussed in an earlier section.) These intervening variables may function in mediating processes between acute alcohol use and deviant behavior, and may thus have a role in the explanation of the statistical association. McClelland and Kalin and co-workers (Kalin, 1972; Kalin, McClelland, & Kahn, 1972; McClelland & Davis, 1972) conducted a series of studies designed to measure emotions and fantasy themes in social drinking situations. They found that alcohol use increased power concerns and power feelings among the subjects. Another potential intervening variable in an explanatory model of the relationship between alcohol use and general deviance or crime is risk taking (Cohen et al., 1958; Katkin, Hayes, Teger, & Pruitt, 1970; Sjoberg, 1969). The empirical evidence for the status of these two variables as intervening variables in linking acute alcohol use and aggressive behavior, violence, and crime is nonexistent but would seem to warrant closer analysis. The seeming relevance may stem largely from semantical connections between the concept of "power," with the concept of (potential) force, and "risk," with disregard for (potential) adversity such as physical punishment or sanctions in general. The latter concept is thus rather closely coextensive with the concept of deviance, and relevant alcohol effects are perhaps implicit in the notion of "drinking for courage."

The Frustration–Aggression Theory

The most common type of relevant controlled studies use the frustration–aggression paradigm in provoking experimental aggression. However, no attempts seem to have been made to take this paradigm into account in explaining the findings (Pernanen, 1976). Neither has the full potential of the frustration–aggression theory in explaning a greater probability of violent behavior in alcohol use events or by alcoholics been used.

Alcohol experiments using frustrating stimuli in eliciting aggressive reactions have, in effect, tested an interaction effect of alcohol use and frustrating or stressful stimuli (in alcohol conditions) versus the main effect of frustrating stimuli (in nonalcohol conditions).[2] Stressful stimuli could interact with alcohol use to produce a higher probability of aggression in alcohol use events as compared to nonalcohol situations. Consequently, the applicability of the theory and empirical findings is limited to alcohol use events in which frustrating stimuli are present. This type of stimuli constitutes only one set among possible conditional/interactive variables which could be used in experiments studying the effect of alcohol on aggressive behavior.

Pernanen (1976) has listed three ways in which the frustration–aggression theory could explain an increased probability of violence in alcohol use events. First, it could be used in explanations of the statistical association by assuming that there is a greater incidence of frustrating stimuli in natural alcohol use situations. The frustrating stimuli would then be a conjunctive variable explaining part of an association between alcohol use and violence. Second, if the aggression threshold is lowered in alcohol use situations (e.g., due to general or specific pharmacological actions of alcohol), quantitatively less frustration is needed to elicit aggression. Third, interactional cues which would not be perceived as frustrating in a sober state may be so interpreted in an intoxicated state due to a change in the conceptual model applied to the environment, perhaps based on the pharmacological effects of alcohol and/or social definitions of alcohol use, alcohol use effects, and alcohol use events.

Any combination of these three submodels could, of course, be relevant in explanations of subsets of violent behavior and violent crime.

Despite its situational focus, the frustration–aggression theory is probably applicable to more extended time frames, to contextual variables, and perhaps even to predispositional differences between individuals. For example, Dollard, Doob, Miller, Mowrer, and Sears's (1939) concept of "displaced aggression" points to a contextual extension potentially useful also for theorizing and experimentation on effects of alcohol use. It can, for example, be asked to what extent and in what type of situations alcohol facilitates the expression of displaced aggression.

Like other theories using aggression as the dependent variable, the ex-

---

[2]Strictly speaking, what has often been studied is probably an interactive relationship between alcohol use and perceived aggression of an alleged adversary in the experimental condition, with attendant attribution of responsibility and blame by the subjects.

tension of experimental findings relevant to the frustration–aggression theory to crimes of violence must assume the existence of an escalation process from mild forms of aggression to assault and homicide at the other extreme. This will serve partly as a link between the (by necessity) milder forms of aggression studied in experiments and the more severe reality tapped by typical epidemiological studies.

In order to keep these explanatory attempts in perspective it should again be stressed that the frustration–aggression theory as such is not sufficient for explanation of all violence, whether in connection with alcohol use or not, since it is a predominantly situational explanation. There are numerous indications that nonsituational predisposing factors are causally relevant.

Randomization of Behavior Cues as a Mediating Process in Alcohol Effects

A central assumption in direct-cause thinking and a prevalent one in disinhibition theorizing is that alcohol ingestion has unvarying qualitative effects on psychological states and consequent behavior. Aggression and other relevant behavior in connection with alcohol use would thus result largely independently of situational or individual predisposing factors. A more realistic assumption in the light of systematic research findings, everyday observations, and both successes and failures of controlled and associational studies is that any relevant direct effects of alcohol are qualitatively indeterminate in their emergent psychological and behavioral consequences. Instead, these are determined by the effects of alcohol in conjunction with other factors which vary largely independently of the values of the alcohol use variables.

Assuming that conditional variables of a situational nature are needed to explain and predict behavior in alcohol use events, there are still two alternative levels open for the resolution of the indeterminateness. One possibility is that given a detailed enough specification of "external" predisposing and situational determinants, a satisfactory explanation can be given by a listing of these and a specification of their internal relationships. However, a further level of indeterminacy is possible, which is based on the perceiving/cognizing individual and his/her structuring of the situation.

The effects of alcohol may, in fact, only determine certain formal boundary conditions for behavior. Within these limits, sociocultural, situational, and other types of factors would then determine the nature of actual behavior. In this way a wide variety of behavior in alcohol use events can potentially be explained, although (perhaps artificial) hopes of comparatively straightforward and strong explanatory and predictive power may have to be toned down. A model of alcohol effects in this vein which takes some experimental findings of alcohol on perceptual/cognitive functions as its starting point has been suggested by Pernanen (1976). Here this model is elaborated somewhat. The essentially stochastic model would attribute to alcohol disorganizing effects on cognitive functions which leave the determination of behavior more open to the effects of immediate situational cues. Moreover, based on some experimental findings on the influence of alcohol consumption on perceptual functions, the model posits a decrease in the perceived number of behavior cues, a narrowing of the perceptual field. The reduction of cues leads to a more random determination of behavior by the situational (environmental and internal) cues present. Intraindividually, this leads to a greater likelihood of affective fluctuations in behavior (and disoriented behavior on the instrumental level). In the interaction between individuals under the influence of alcohol, the smaller number of cues determining behavior on its part (in addition to perhaps more direct effects on cognitive structuring) leads to a greater likelihood of discrepant structurings of the situation and a consequent cognition of the other person's behavior as arbitrary. Perceived arbitrariness of behavior in turn has been shown to lead to aggressive reactions (S. Epstein & Taylor, 1967). The model partly covers the notion that people are more likely to misunderstand each other's intentions after having consumed alcohol. We have suggested elsewhere (Pernanen, 1976) that ritualization of drinking behavior in some societies may be a functional safeguard against misunderstandings and other undesirable consequences of the situational determination and the perceptual/cognitive impoverishment of behavior cues.

In this model it is assumed that alcohol has largely structural–quantitative effects on perception and cognition, and that these "work on" the raw material provided by the situation, the social definitions and personal predispositions. Alcohol causes a perceptual and cognitive impoverishment, and a randomization process, giving rise to unstable sets of behavior cues.

The disproportionate weight of immediate cues in the determination of behavior in alcohol use events is parallel to behavioral characteristics of alcoholics and some individuals who repeatedly commit certain types of crime. The determination of their behavior by the immediate situation has been suggested in the literature. It is related to the characteristic of extreme field dependency which seems typical of alcoholic behavior as ascertained in experimental studies (e.g., Gomberg, 1978). Difficulties in deferring gratification seem to be related to the same characteristic.

The cue selection which is normally (or in normal individuals) determined by an organizing and structuring of the situational elements is based on the orientation of the individual in the situation. The randomization model posits that this organizing "faculty" breaks down with certain types of alcohol use, and consequently the cue selection and resultant definition of the situation become more randomly influenced by situational cues. The process would have obvious parallels with the characteristics of impulsive behavior as described by J. H. Goldstein (1975): "Impulsive behavior implies that conscious, cognitive mechanisms which normally influence behavior are absent. What psychologists refer to as cognitive control over behavior, and what we generally call self-control, is minimized when a person acts impulsively" (p. 46). Perhaps a cognitive/conceptual impoverishment as a result of alcohol use leads to some effects found in aphasic patients: "Having lost their grip on universals, they stick to the immediate facts, to concrete situations" (Cassirer, 1944, p. 41). In general, there would perhaps be some theoretical gains in comparisons of alcohol effects with other forms of disturbances of the functioning of the central nervous system.[3]

Pliner and Cappell (1974) have suggested the concept of "plasticity" in referring to behavior affected by alcohol use. Descriptively this is probably a useful concept; for explanatory purposes an exposition of processes or hypothetical models thus labeled is needed. The end result of a randomization of determinants would probably be what descriptively could be labeled as "plasticity" in manifest behavior. Plasticity as a descriptive concept is useful also in extending the range of behaviors which can perhaps ultimately be explained by the same model(s).

On a more instrumental level, the randomization model would, with few additional assumptions, predict more risk-taking behavior as well as more extreme caution and greater fluctuations between these two extremes in alcohol conditions. The same type of effects will apply to frustrating cues in the situation; these will be perceived more randomly, and prediction of behavior thus becomes more difficult even in some fairly controlled settings. Concordance in both frustrating and nonfrustrating sets of cues will be more easily achieved, but these structurings will be more volatile and open to changes with new stimuli. Over a group of subjects, the model would predict more intraindividual and interindividual fluctuations. It is possible that a greater likelihood of an escalatory process can be deduced statistically from such a stochastic model. Likelihood functions based on the number, nature, and salience (strength) of behavior cues could predict either a fluctuation between alternative and behavioral extremes (based on discordant sequential cues) or a "snowballing" into escalation (based on concordant sequential cues). At this stage, this must

---

[3]"Drinking to forget" may in effect be based on the dissolution of cognitive control and the salient structurings of the individual's life situation with the help of alcohol.

be considered merely an interesting possibility. The deductions from the pure randomization aspect of the model supplemented by additional substantive assumptions will have to be worked out in detail.

To take the reasoning onto somewhat shakier ground, there is probably a greater degree of "mastery"—less ambiguity in the situational cues (especially when these are experienced as concordant)—due to the fewer number of cues perceived, cognized, and mentally processed. This may lead to a greater "feeling of power" among males in certain types of social situations (McClelland *et al.*, 1972) and perhaps to a greater prevalence of "feelings of womanliness" in female subjects in certain types of social situations (Wilsnack, 1974) in that one feels surer of oneself and of one's salient interpretation of the situation. However, we would have to make additional assumptions about salient structurings for men and women in order to incorporate these findings into the theory.

It should, perhaps, be emphasized that the cues in this type of model would have to be both internal (mental) and external (environmental) in nature. Kalant (1961) has summarized what many of us have probably noted in unsystematic observations: "The thought content, the emotional tone and the form of expression show progressive loss of relevance to the surrounding situation" (p. 11). (This does not mean that they have more relevance to internal cues, such as the thought content of the individual. Were we able to compare, the internal gap may prove as large as the environmental one.) If the perceptual impoverishment affects environmental cues to a larger extent than mental ones (e.g., at a certain stage of intoxication), there would be a greater determination of behavior by internal cues. Both randomizing of external cues and a proportionately greater determination by internal cues would predict the "unreasonableness" and unpredictability of an intoxicated person. The importance of even single cues to a person in such a state may perhaps be illustrated by the danger in uttering "just one wrong word" and the need to treat the person "like a child." To continue the speculations, a predominance of internal cues could explain a more stereotyped structuring of the environment and categorization of other persons, in it simplicity probably increasing the probability of a feeling of mastery or power, and also more readily coinciding with such sex stereotypes as "power" for (most) males and "womanliness" for (most) females.

In general the causes of alcohol-related violence and deviance may not be so different from the event-based etiology of sober deviance and violence. The excessive situational determination, impulsivity, inability to delay gratification, etc., which have been put forth in explanations of general deviance and crime, can be created artificially (as an analogue of sorts) by the use of alcohol.

The randomization theory and its specific assumptions have not been tested directly, but such tests are possible. Experimentation along the lines pointed out by the model may, due partly to its generality, be a small beginning toward the establishment of principles of "alcohol epistemology" and "alcohol phenomenology," which will help explain both why people drink and their behavior while drinking. That this type of "epistemology" and "phenomenology" will have a bearing on behavior models in sober individuals also is evident from the preceding remarks. (This should not be equated with the methodological phenomenology which has its adherents in sociology and whose tenets are much more far-reaching.)

It should be emphasized that other effects of alcohol are probably also relevant in explaining behavior in alcohol use events, more so in certain subcontexts than in others. Some of these may be structural or formal in nature, as postulated in the randomization model; others may well be qualitatively specific as to their effects on behavior. Empirically, such a combination of both qualitative and structural effects is, of course, quite possible and may in the end best explain behavior under the influence of alcohol. It seems that experiments can be designed to test theories combining both types of effects. Predisposing factors, determined, for example, by personality, socialization, social class, etc., probably also interact with these kinds of alcohol effects.

It may also be possible to have as a theoretical starting point the rather obvious isomorphism between a stochastic impediment of neural signals relevant for perception/cognition and the postulated randomization of cues, as mentioned in the earlier discussion on disinhibition explanations.

Common-Cause Explanation

A number of theoretical schemes try to explain the statistical association by postulating the existence of a third variable which varies independently of both alcohol use and crime, and which explains the increased probability of the occurrence of both. Some explanations discussed in this section have not been put forth explicitly but find some scattered empirical evidence in their favor in the literature. The common-cause models are of three basic types, which can be exhibited by means of arrow diagrams:

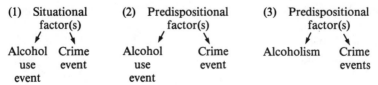

We treat these in this order in the following discussion.

Situational Common-Cause Factors and Alcohol Use Events

Some factors which vary intraindividually over time can partly explain both the occurrence of alcohol use events and an increased probability of violence in these. To the extent that these models explain a subset of (violent) crime in connection with alcohol use, the aggregate relationship would be spurious. Findings by McClelland and Kalin and their co-workers (McClelland *et al.*, 1972), Wilsnack (1974), and Boyatzis (1974) can be incorporated in a common-cause model. These studies found that individuals who drank more heavily in a social drinking situation were more likely to show power concerns or aggressive tendencies before drinking than were individuals who drank less. It is possible that individuals who are aggressively aroused before a drinking situation (or have a predispositionally aggressive personality) tend to drink more and exhibit more aggressive or violent behavior, with or without any main effects of greater alcohol consumption.

In another situational common-cause model, Macdonald (1961) suggested that alcohol use and homicidal behavior may both be caused by psychological conflicts. Stress situations in general may give rise to both (excessive) drinking and aggressive behavior. It would seem likely for instance, that a drinking spree and a domestic violent crime can both be determined by marital discord or other conflict. Interaction effects between stress or aggressive arousal and alcohol use would complicate any explanatory model but will have to be accepted as very possible. The former possibility has been suggested by Nicol, Gunn, Gristwood, Foggitt, and Watson (1973).

Predispositional Common-Cause Factors and
Alcohol Use Events

Common-cause explanations that have been suggested in the literature tend to utilize predispositional rather than situational models. Moreover, they mostly refer to the association between alcoholism and crime. However, individual characteristics such as personality disorders (Edwards, Hensman, & Peto, 1971) have also been adduced in explanations of both acute alcohol use and crime. One model suggested by Nicol *et al.* (1973) combines predisposing and situational variables in a common-cause framework. In this model, drinking is seen as a frequent response to stress in individuals exhibiting violent behavior tendencies. The violent tendencies are further enhanced by the pharmacological effects of "alcohol taken under these conditions," the authors suggest. Stress is also more likely to occur in these individuals, due to difficulties in establishing satisfactory relationships with other people. The model may be schematically illustrated with the following arrow diagram, borrowed from Pernanen (1976, p. 428):

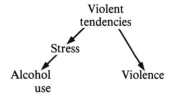

Generally the common-cause variables adduced for acute alcohol use and crime are the same as those found in the literature on crime and alcoholism. The increased probability of acute use among alcoholics is often not distinguished from alcoholism as an independent variable. Thus the discussion in the next section on common-cause models of alcoholism and crime is also potentially applicable to acute alcohol use.

Predispositional Common-Cause Factors and Alcoholism

Predispositional factors which have been suggested in common-cause explanations of the association between alcoholism and crime are developmental or constitutional in nature: childhood experiences such as parental neglect and lack of parental role models, affective disorders, organic brain disorders, psychopathic personality, emotional instability, "aggressive types," etc. The most cited studies in this research tradition are those by Robins, Bates, and O'Neal (1962), McCord and McCord (1962), and Glatt (1965). Antisocial behavior patterns in childhood could be seen as a symptom of a genetically determined propensity toward deviant behavior and crime that continues into adulthood or as an initial behavior pattern—a pattern that, through societal and interindividual reactions, is stabilized over the lifetime of the individual.

Wexberg (1951) has presented evidence that alcoholics have low frustration tolerance even before the onset of addiction. Possibly, low frustration tolerance has the dual role of causing both drinking and violent behavior in the same individuals, and acting as a predispositional factor situationally interacting with the effects of alcohol to further increase the probability of violent behavior:

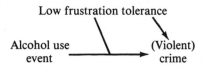

Along the same theoretical dimension, Hagnell *et al.* (1973) in Sweden also found an aggressive ("dangerous") subgroup of alcoholics. They suggested that the premorbid personality determines the type of alcoholic personality that emerges. Similarly, DeVito, Flaherty, and Mozdzierz (1970) found an "acting-out-prone" alcoholic group who drank alcohol to facilitate acting-out behavior.

As we stated earlier, the discussion of predispositional common-cause models which would explain at least part of the statistical association is inconclusive as to the direct causal contribution of the alcoholism syndrome and the contribution of acute alcohol use events which will occur with an increased probability among alcoholics. This can again be expressed by means of an arrow diagram. The literature does not distinguish clearly between Model (3) (shown at the beginning of this section) and the following model:

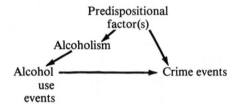

In future research and explanatory analyses it would be important to keep these two elements apart and try to assess the relative contributions to the statistical association of alcohol events and the alcoholism syndrome among alcoholics. Interactions are to be expected, as should be evident from the earlier discussion of alcoholism as an interactive predisposing variable.

Spuriousness Models

Data Bias

Strict adherence to methodological principles would require that we, even before having established a null hypothesis for our test of the statistical association between alcohol use and crime, already had established that the association was not due to any selective biases in the reporting of crime events. Such biases would cause us to either overestimate or underestimate the extent of acute alcohol use or alcoholism in the crime events or the criminals that form the analytical units.

A great number of different circumstances have been invoked to point out the probability of selective biases which tend to result in an overestimate of the involvement of alcohol in crime. These have been reviewed in some detail elsewhere (Pernanen, 1976, J. Roizen & Schneberk, 1977a), and thus only the ones of at least incipient theoretical interest are briefly discussed here. The screening process affects different types of crime in variable ways and may thus influence estimates of alcohol involvement in different degrees (e.g., Cohen, 1966; Macdonald, 1961), also depending on the type of crime.

Due to some effects of alcohol it can be assumed that, all else being equal, the offender who has been drinking has a greater risk of being apprehended than nondrinking offenders. Alcohol's effects in impairing motor coordination and slowing reaction time have been established without any doubt. These would leave the drinking offender at a disadvantage compared to nondrinking "colleagues." Acute intoxication and perhaps a pattern of long-term excessive drinking independently of acute alcohol effects will affect the cognitive functions of the offender and might cause him/her to leave clues which will lead to apprehension proportionately more often if the offender has been drinking than if he/she has not. Theories and empirical generalizations of the psychological effects of alcohol consumption reviewed in previous sections would also tend to predict the occurrence of factors increasing the probability of apprehension. For example, the increase in a tendency toward risk taking observed in experimental settings would explain at least part of an increased probability of being apprehended. The higher-than-average likelihood that alcoholics have of being known to the police and the use of alcohol for false courage are perhaps of less direct theoretical interest, although they are on a par with any other factors in an accounting of the influences of biasing factors on the estimate of the aggregate association.

On the other hand, if alcohol use were regarded as an extenuating circumstance by the arresting officer or in a court of law, the alcohol involvement in at least some forms of crime would be underestimated in police records and prison samples on the basis of this factor alone. Social belief systems regarding alcohol, its effects, and its relevance for ascriptions of personal responsibility are relevant in this context.

Coincidence estimates of alcoholism among perpetrators of various crimes based on prisoner samples will overestimate the true coincidence if alcoholics have a higher probability of arrest and conviction, and a longer average sentence. The latter could be true if alcoholics (due to a higher rate of commission, arrest, and conviction) are more likely to be recidivists and thus in all probability have longer terms of incarceration. On the other hand, alcoholics will in some jurisdictions be more likely to be sent to compulsory or semivoluntary treatment as part of their sentence, which will lead to too low an estimate of their share in some crimes and in some institutional settings.

The relevance of social definitions in biasing available estimates was mentioned in the preceding section. "Blaming alcohol" and other "neutralizing techniques" (Sykes & Matza, 1962) reflect popular norms and beliefs, individual rationalizations, and, in some jurisdictions, legal definitions.

Common-Cause Spuriousness

Even assuming that corrections of the estimates of alcohol involvement necessitated by data bias had been made, so that they reflect reality in an unbiased way, and assuming that the null hypotheses had been rejected on the basis of these corrected estimates, there still remain a few plausible alternative hypotheses which would deny alcohol use any causal role in the determination of crime occurrences. The models discussed earlier in the section on common-cause explanations are all cases of spuriousness models in that an independent variation of alcohol use in these models will not affect the probability of crime occurrences, and conversely, independent variation in crime occurrences will not affect the probability of acute alcohol use or alcoholism. In practical terms it means that however much we try to prevent or restrict the occurrence of alcohol use in any of its many aspects we will not be able to curtail crime or deviance, and vice versa.

In the common-cause models already discussed, the notion of spuriousness is easy to apply since the models are greatly simplified. In the complexities of the empirical world, however, attributions of spuriousness become more difficult. Thus, the explanation of the role of alcohol in developmental and career models is not limited to a role as an element in a simple common-cause model. In the following discussion of the possibilities of integrating explanatory schemes of careers in crime with theories of effects of alcohol use, it is noted that alcohol can enter the explanation of the aggregate association between alcohol use and crime in an indefinite number of ways. "Spuriousness" becomes a rather vacuous concept in such an explanatory scheme, with long links of probabilistic determination and varying explanatory roles of alcohol use. This is true of other types of social theories as well.

The many negative or equivocal findings in experimental studies of potential relevance to violent crime should not be given too much weight as an indication of the spuriousness of the relationship between alcohol use and crime, since, as we pointed out earlier, they generally do not take any potentially relevant conditional (both situational and predispositional) variables into account. (It could perhaps also be said that the association is spurious if it is seen to imply that alcohol use does not have any crime-reducing effects. This aspect is discussed later.)

Conjunctive Spuriousness Models

Some models would explain the association by invoking a third variable or cluster of variables which, through cultural clustering or structural force, are associated with alcohol use. These "third variables" and not alcohol are seen as the real causally effective variables varying independently of alcohol use. The association between alcohol and crime would thus come about through the fact that these factors occur in alcohol use situations or are clustered with alcoholic individuals (situationally or predispositionally) with a greater probability than in nonalcohol situations or with nonalcoholics. The most important difference between these models and common-cause models is that conjunctive factors do not determine the probability of alcohol use events or alcoholism occurrences.

Some conjunctive factors have been mentioned in the literature. These deal exclusively with factors causally relevant for the involvement of acute alcohol use in the crime event. Here only some are listed very briefly:

1. "Time-out" features of drinking occasions (MacAndrew & Edgerton, 1969). Social definitions of drinking events as periods of license are seen as explaining drunken comportment.
2. The "setting" of alcohol use. Bennett *et al.* (1969) seem to imply this, and Carpenter and Armenti (1972) use the presence of males in a drinking situation as one example.
3. The higher probability of interaction in alcohol use situations. The probability of interpersonal crime would thus not be greater than in situations in which the same number of individuals interact while not consuming alcohol. The effects or social and cultural connotations of alcohol use can also increase interaction through effects quite unrelated to violence or crime, and thus increase the risk of interpersonal crime.
4. Criminal contacts are made and/or crimes are planned in public drinking places, and drinking is thus associated with, but causally incidental to, the occurrences of crime after the alcohol use event.

Further conjunctive models which have not been directly used as such in the literature to the knowledge of the author, but which can be used in that way, are not hard to speculate on. These seem to be among the most plausible:

1. Accepting the frustration–aggression model, one could hypothesize that frustrating stimuli are present or occur in alcohol use events to a greater extent than in comparative events when alcohol is not used. This would be one instance of the influence of the setting of an alcohol use event. Increased interaction can also lead to an increased probability of encountering frustrating stimuli.

2. A selection procedure into subcultures determined by societal reactions which conjunctively select excessive drinkers or alcoholics and criminals into a subcontext or subculture of society could create an association between alcohol use and crime.

3. As noted earlier, belief systems regarding the effects of alcohol—or, more distributively, psychological "sets," cue values, or symbolic meanings of the presence or ingestion of alcohol—have been shown to affect behavior independently of any psychopharmacological effects.

With some of these conjunctive independent variables, a somewhat arbitrary line has to be drawn to delimit what is subsumed under the label of "alcohol use" and what falls outside this concept. The delimitation will determine whether the independently varied variable should be regarded as a conjunctive variable or included in {alcohol use}, in which case the relationship between the two variables would not, of course, be spurious. A good case in point is the symbolic effects of alcohol on behavior. Generally, the problems of delimitation are greater with the alcoholism label than with acute use. The former tends to be somewhat amorphous due in part to the varying nature of definitions and operationalizations in the literature, and the complex pattern of medical problems and behavior patterns in the etiology and effects of the syndrome.

Other conjunctive models are possible. In the light of the almost complete lack of empirical data to aid in accepting or rejecting such models, however, further speculation is unwarranted. Perhaps the ease of such speculations can serve as a warning against "theorizing" in the face of an empirical vacuum. Although explanations utilizing independent conjunctive variables are of less interest to nomothetic alcohol–crime theories, they are naturally on par with any other explanations in their impact for policy and other practical implications.

Integration of Individual-Level Models and Social Theories

Theories dealing with criminal behavior have evolved largely along different routes and in different academic fields from theories explaining alcohol use and its effects and the causative symbolic aspects of alcohol use. No serious attempt has been made to bridge this gap. A prerequisite for theoretical advance in explaining the association of alcohol with criminal behavior would be through conceptual and historical analysis of the development of these two sets of theories. An outcome of this analysis should be an attempted integration of these. Here only the bare logical scaffolding for such an integration is presented, together with scattered substantive elucidations of the integrative process.

One requirement for such integration is a closer specification of what could be called the "initial conditions" of a theory or model. Initial conditions are the conditions which have to be fulfilled for a theory or model to be applicable. The initial conditions pertain to the independent variable set: They specify what values or ranges of values these variables must have for the occurrence of the phenomenon to be explained. If the theory or model is expressed in hypothetical form as an "if–then" statement, some initial (antecedent) conditions are typically included in the if-clause. Disregarding for the moment the probabilistic nature of the inference rules that we deal with, we can illustrate this by the following deliberately simplistic predictive theoretical statement: If the blood alcohol level of male subjects reaches .15, then physiological disinhibitive processes will take place in the central nervous system, and aggressive behavior will result. Similarly another simplistic theoretical statement will predict criminal behavior: If the subject has been socialized not to ascribe a negative value to criminal behavior and has an opportunity with low risk of detection he/she will commit a property crime. More often than not the antecedent conditions are not all expressed in the hypothetical statement representing the theory or model. In fact, as Toulmin (1953) has shown, for example, in the natural sciences some theoretical statements (regularities) are elevated to a paradigmatic, almost tautological status. What remains for research is to find out and specify the region of applicability of these regularities. For reasons which we need not go into here, there are distinct advantages to making analytical propositions out of certain theoretical statements. With the theory as a new type of investigative tool its validity is no longer asked for, only its range of applicability. In this way, this type of theoretical statement is applied in a paradigmatic way to order the field of inquiry by providing definitions of the concepts used.

Some of the antecedent conditions are so implicit in the very training of a researcher or scientist that they are thought to be entirely redundant if expressed. The paradigms of social science also rest on this type of unexpressed conditions (Kuhn, 1970; Toulmin, 1953). Many of the implicit assumptions of relevant conditions are discrete and fairly trivial. Others are so general as to be metatheoretical in nature and so much taken for granted that only an intensive conceptual analysis will bring them out. For an integration of theories relevant to the association between alcohol use and criminal behavior, we can expect the latter type of assumptions to be of high importance, because of the different research traditions that current alcohol theories and crime theories have evolved from and are still part of. The former are part of what could be called a general "causal orientation," whereas the latter typically are part of a "symbolic orientation." Any general integrative attempt will not be able to disregard issues related to philosophy of science, philosophy of language, epistemology, and sociology of knowledge.

Theories, prototheories, and models of the effects of alcohol use on behavior typically do not specify the initial conditions under which they hold true to the extent that would be desirable and possible even under the present circumstances. Biological alcohol theories potentially relevant for explanations of criminal behavior have typically implied a direct-cause relationship, with alcohol use as the sole independent variable. Even these, however, often do not specify the relevant causal values of the alcohol use variable. None of the biological or psychological theories specify what blood alcohol level will lead to aggressive behavior. If blood alcohol level is the effective variable, or one of the effective independent variables, at least the lower and upper thresholds of causal effect should be defined. (The same explanatory role would of course be even better served by the specification of a dose–response function.) In fact, as we have seen, there is often not enough research data to distinguish between the different variables in {alcohol use}. The dichotomous general variable of alcohol use versus no alcohol use is what we have to be content with at this stage.

The conditionality of the relationship between alcohol use and different types of criminal behavior is another locus of initial conditions. Since the conditionality of the relationship with regard to other independent variables is often not explicitly acknowledged, we typically have no specification of required initial values, and even less a stimulus–response function of these.

No theories of criminal behavior have alcohol use in any of its aspects directly as one of its initial conditions. However, some of the effects or concomitants of alcohol use seem to overlap with some of the initial conditions postulated by theories of criminal behavior. As we have seen, this is true for the impulsivity, low stress tolerance, etc., which have been adduced as initial conditions, consequences, or concomitants of alcohol use, and as initial conditions in the explanation of criminal behavior. This type of overlap could form the basis for advances in theoretical integration.

In theorizing from a social conceptual framework, a neglect of the specification of initial conditions, even as a distant goal, leads to a neglect of the importance of differential distributions of initial conditions of individual-level models and event-based models which can explain the occurrence of criminal behavior (or alcohol use). Thus, global concepts such as societal values or subcultures are often introduced to explain an aggregate-level phenomenon or relationship without also considering or testing the possibility of differential individual predisposing or situational conditions in different subsegments of the population which could at least supplement the explanation of observed variations. In the following discussion we illustrate this with the concept of subcontext as opposed to the concept of subculture in the explanation of variations in the strength of the statistical association between alcohol use and crime in different subsegments of the population.

In ex post facto research, such as the theoretical analysis of the observed association between alcohol use and criminal behavior, the important distinction between (1) the validity of a theory and (2) the prevalence and incidence of the empirical conditions under which it is applicable and under which it can explain empirical phenomena is easily obscured. If a theory or model is valid, it will explain (and correctly predict) the occurrence of criminal behavior, assuming that the sufficient initial conditions postulated by it (such as certain types of alcohol use, stress, economic conditions, availability of means, and opportunity) do exist. The validity of a theory does not depend on whether it can explain any empirical phenomena; the empirical conditions for it may not exist. If they do exist the theory is applicable. In ex post facto explanation, where we already are faced with the occurrence of the phenomenon to be explained, both the validity and the applicability of the theory or model are presupposed. If a theory does not explain, for example, the occurrence of criminal behavior or variations in crime rates in a society, this can consequently mean that the theory is invalid, or valid but inapplicable. However, a negative finding is often taken to mean that a theory has been shown to be invalid under any set of circumstances. What in fact may be needed is a further specification of initial conditions, perhaps an explicit statement of a newly found conditionality of the relationship postulated in the theory. A focus on the range of applicability of a theory is often more fruitful than an attempted general corroboration or refutation of it.

A theory of criminal behavior can be perfectly valid and still not explain a single instance of crime in the empirical world. If empirical conditions change, the theory may become applicable and thus explain its share of crime occurrences. Similarly, a theory which would explain a great deal of the statistical association between alcohol use and crime in one population would not explain as much in another population or in the same population during another time period. Circumstances change and the explanatory value of a theory may be greater in some time periods and in some geographical, cultural, and jurisdictional areas than in others due to changes in the incidence or prevalence of initial conditions.

The lack of specification of initial conditions can thus obscure the central distinction between the validity and applicability of a theory or model. This leads to two unfortunate types of confusion. In individual-level theorizing, the lack of specification of initial conditions leads to exaggerated claims of the share of the association between alcohol use and crime which can be explained by one model. In social-level theories (since they are almost without exception based on ex post facto analyses), where initial conditions are not as easily observable as in controlled settings in which they are manipulated systematically, it reinforces the tendency to view different social-level theories as mutually exclusive. In fact there is room for a great number of both valid and applicable theories in the explanation of a unitary social phenomenon. The simple explanatory principle that theories do not contradict each other unless contradictory states of affairs can be deduced from the same initial conditions seems to be too easily forgotten in ex post facto analysis. Of equal general importance is the fact that the same empirical state of affairs can result from different initial conditions and mediating processes. Thus, criminal behavior can—without contradiction, and even within the same society—be caused by the processes related to membership in a subculture, structural strain leading to anomie, inversion of the normative rules of the parent culture, and many other social processes and component social and individual processes. Unfortunately, without a specification of necessary and/or sufficient initial conditions the theories are held as valid either under very general conditions or under an amorphously indeterminate disjunction of antecedent conditions. Consequently, the different theories of criminal behavior are often seen as mutually exclusive.

We have already stated that the quest for one all-encompassing general theory which would "explain" all or most of the association between alcohol use and crime seems very unrealistic. When the quest is formulated without heeding the distinction between the validity and applicability of a theory, one is led to believe that a general theory in this case would need to explain the distribution in the population of initial conditions relevant for all valid individual-level models, for example, why certain situational features are clustered to the extent observed with predisposing features of drinkers. This takes us far afield from any theories directly connecting alcohol use and crime. If, in addition, "alcohol use" is interpreted in its common, very general, sense, part of the association is explainable via, for instance, the effects of alcoholism on the probability of crime occurrence; and such a theory would also have to explain the frequency and distribution of alcoholics (over certain situations) in the population. The multiplicity of empirical and theoretical relationships between {alcohol use} and {crime} makes it more realistic to keep the theories apart as theories and to use them conjointly, in combinations adaptable to the requirements of the empirical world, in the explanation of the empirical association. Flexibility will be retained, and explanations will better adjust to the empirical distributions of relevant initial conditions in different populations.

Explanatory Accounting

The considerations in this and other sections of this chapter concerning the multiplicity of relationships between alcohol use and crime, the validity of theories and the extent of their applicability, the existence of potentially valid models from several academic disciplines, and connected with this, the existence of theories on both the individual level and the aggregate level of analysis, bring us to the concept of "explanatory accounting."

This is perhaps not the ideal label for this type of activity. Other potential candidates include "theoretical accounting" and "weighted explanation." However, the label chosen includes the two basic ingredients of the activity as well as or better than other candidates in the mind of this author. "Explanatory" stresses the importance of theories or models and does not exclude the potential role of empirical generalizations in the accounting activity, as the label "theoretical" would do. "Accounting" on its part hopefully brings out the quantitative aspect of the activity, its dependence on the prevalence and incidence of initial conditions, the quantifiable probabilistic nature of the inference rules, and the quantified end result— the estimates of statistical association—which we account for with the help of explanatory schemes.

The discussions in this chapter also partly utilize other forms of accounting of the statistical association which could perhaps be called "pre-explanatory" accounting. The two main forms of this are the assessments of the effect of (1) sampling biases and (2) the variables related to the establishment of a null hypothesis (this can also be conceptualized as explanatory accounting by means of conjunctive independent variables). When these are controlled for, the material for explanatory accounting remains.

In addition to providing a schematic outline for the integration of theories of alcohol use and the effects of alcohol use with theories of crime or deviance, the use of the framework of explanatory accounting will aid us in resolving the tension between individual-level theories and social- or aggregate-level theories. Furthermore, the formal explanatory scheme presented here will more easily than a global social theory take into consideration the undeniable multidisciplinary nature of the required explanations.

All this is accomplished at the cost of a certain amount of apparent determinateness which one single organizing theory might ideally provide. The formal scheme presented here is much more open than a global theory. It allows for the validity of an indeterminate number of both social-level and individual-level theories and models, and allocates explanatory weight to these not by how well these fit conceptually into a theoretical matrix, as a general organizing theory would, but by the extent to which the antecedent conditions postulated by the separate theories or models exist in the empirical world. Social-level theories would in this scheme mainly be used to predict the occurrence and distribution of (some of) the antecedent conditions of individual-level models and their configurations in a population.

It should again be stressed that the scheme is not meant as a strict guideline for explanation or research, and with such pretensions it would surely be generally rejected. In large measure its usefulness will consist in providing a formal background against which to place and assess past and future research and theorizing which deal with the validity, specification, and explanation of the statistical association between alcohol use and crime. The need for such a framework is especially great in an area where both the empirical and theoretical knowledge are scattered and contain large gaps. In addition, the approach set out here will hopefully provide a background which will remind us of the need for data on which to base null hypotheses in determining the strength of the association, especially in different subgroups of the population. It may also aid in underscoring the need to know the frequency and distribution of initial conditions, the possibilities of multidisciplinary determination and two-way causation between alcohol use and crime, the probable multivariate determination of crime and alcohol use, and the multiple relationships that can and probably do exist between {alcohol use} and {crime}.

In explanatory accounting of the observed statistical association we assume that the many different theories of criminal and deviant behavior are valid under different empirical conditions. Most directly relevant for the explanation of the association are those theories and models which connect alcohol use and criminal behavior. The association between alcohol use and criminal behavior consists of a combination of the contributions of different models which are valid within the limitations of the sufficient initial conditions. Depending on the prevalence or incidence of the combinations of initial conditions postulated by the theories, the different theories and models will have different "weights." That is, the more prevalent these initial conditions relative to the initial conditions of other valid theories, the larger the share which the theory can explain.

In a probabilistic explanatory scheme, the conditional probability of occurrence of the event to be explained, given the occurrence of the initial conditions, will also determine the "explanatory weight" of the theory in the given empirical circumstances. Some explanatory models can be very deterministic and almost infallibly explain and predict the occurrence of the criterion event under the initial conditions, but these still have little explanatory weight on the aggregate-level association because the prevalences or incidences of the initial conditions required are relatively low. Thus, the potential explanatory weight of XYY chromosome anomaly is very low in explaining crime, since the condition is relatively rare even if it were very deterministic, for which there is ample evidence to the contrary. Explanations can be valid and applicable, but they need not carry much explanatory weight, either due to low prevalence or incidence of initial conditions, or to low probabilistic power.

Explanatory accounting would look at the contribution that each theory makes to the explanation of the aggregate-level relationship: what share it can explain. Of central interest is the extent to which theories of alcohol use can directly explain crime occurrences or explain the occurrence of some initial conditions which form a subset of the initial conditions explaining the occurrence of crime, such as economic deprivation or membership in high-risk groups or subcultures. Of equal interest is the extent to which theories of deviance or crime can predict initial conditions for certain forms of alcohol use, perhaps alcoholism foremost among these. Examples of such possible integration between alcohol theories and deviance theories are provided later.

Consequently, we end up with not a unitary theory but with a scheme employing many different theories from different disciplines. One category of theories will explain or predict the occurrence of crime events or crime rates from a knowledge of the empirical occurrences and distributions of alcohol events, and other relevant predisposing or situational factors; others will do the same from the knowledge of patterns of long-term excessive alcohol use and concomitant relevant factors. Other theories again will predict and explain occurrences of alcoholism and alcohol use events in the population from the knowledge of the patterns of deviance and crime together with knowledge of other factors.

Some of the models relevant to an explanation of the association would in fact by themselves predict a negative association between some aspects of alcohol use and some forms of crime. These would also have to be taken into consideration in a true accounting of the statistical association.

Two limitations of the exposition of this chapter, if compared to the ideal state of affairs, are worth noting in this context. This will hopefully also aid in placing the theories discussed here on the "map" of a full explanation of the statistical association between alcohol use and criminal behavior. First of all, with only a few exceptions, it will not be possible to give a weight to the share of a theory in the composite explanation (its applicability), nor much assessment of the empirical evidence for or against the validity of a theory. This springs from the fact that the theories or theory fragments are mostly tentative in nature, with little material available for an assessment of either their validity or the prevalence and distribution of initial conditions.

A second limitation of this discussion is that, despite the exclusive emphasis to this point on explanatory schemes or variables which purport to explain the higher probability of crime in connection with alcohol use, its use also has effects which are likely to decrease the probability of at least some forms of criminal behavior, as was pointed out earlier. It is to be expected that some of the relevant empirical associations in {alcohol use} × {crime} are negative (or zero), while others are positive. The partial negative associations can be located either on the individual level or the aggregate level. On the individual level, hardly any feature of alcohol effects is as well known on the basis of everyday, unsystematic observations as alcohol's incapacitating effects on motor skills, especially with large amounts consumed. This has also been verified in numerous experiments on motor skills, reaction time, the coordination of motor functions, etc., much of it from traffic safety research. Alcohol's incapacitating effects have been mentioned as a discrepant feature in connection with surprisingly high acute alcohol involvements of apprehended offenders in property crimes and robberies (J. Roizen & Schneberk, 1977a).

A higher risk of apprehension may, of course, be a biasing factor in the available data. Two additional aspects should also be included for discussion in accounting for coincidence estimates. These are even more utopian at this stage of knowledge and are mentioned only to complete the background picture. First, theories which explain the occurrence of crime or deviance without alcohol use as one of the initial conditions should be included for discussion. Also, in an explanatory accounting scheme, other theories probably unrelated to both alcohol use theories and theories on crime or deviance will have to be invoked to explain the distribution of alcohol use events and the distribution of causally relevant predispositional and situational factors in these (and thus the prevalence and incidence of crime). On the other hand, if the theory posits a spurious relationship between alcohol use and crime, the distribution of conjunctive variables needs to be explained and/or predicted.

Factors which reduce the probability of criminal behavior can also be found in connection with long-term excessive use of alcohol. This is especially true for types of crime which require motor skills, access to and use of more or less sophisticated equipment, and a certain position in the social structure required for the opportunity to commit the crime. The possibility of a negative relationship between alcohol use and crime with reference to {alcoholism} can be deduced from Merton's theory of deviance, which views alcoholism as a "retreatist reaction" to deviance-producing structural strain or anomie as opposed to more active forms of reactions, of which some are criminal in nature (Merton, 1957).

Some forms of alcohol use may thus act as "suppressors" on the occurrence of some types of crime. Our estimates of the association are in all likelihood partly the net results of the crime-increasing and crime-reducing effects of alcohol use. The relevance of crime-reducing models for an explanatory accounting will depend on the type of estimate of the association that we are trying to account for.

Basically, there is nothing excitingly new about this outline. In a sense it has (fortunately) been implicit in much of research and theorizing carried out to date. Needless to say, we are far from having the means available for a complete explanatory accounting of any societal phenomenon. However, its special importance for a research strategy needs to be stressed. A systematic research strategy, especially if it is multidisciplinary in nature, has to keep in view, if not the end result, then at least the implicit logic of explanation. The remarks in this section would not be necessary if it were not for the widespread acceptance of physiological and other types of one-factor theories or prototheories to the apparent exclusion of other explanatory attempts, the equally widespread assumption that causal influence only goes in one direction, the assumption that explanations of the association are largely exclusive of each other, and the other narrow, implicit or explicit, viewpoints which have been discussed earlier.

Other structurings of the theoretical field which take into account both individual-level and aggregate or global explanatory schemes are perhaps possible. It is this author's belief, however, that none will take into account the theories and models from different levels and disciplines as well and stay as closely to testable empirical explanatory schemes as the one presented here. Whatever the explanatory structurings, if they are in the form of regression methods or path analysis, they do implicitly assume a structure which is isomorphic with the causal structure of empirical occurrences.

The Need for Integration of Theoretical Approaches

In scanning the social theoretical literature potentially relevant to an explanation of the association between alcohol use and criminal behavior, the most immediate complexity is introduced by the very fact that we are faced with explaining a relationship between two phenomena and not "just" the occurrence of one type of phenomenon. Thus, theories which explain the occurrence of criminal behavior and theories which explain alcohol use patterns or alcoholism are not strictly applicable as such. In most cases, a great deal of extrapolation has to take place.

Another point needs to be emphasized. By necessity, the explanation of the statistical association has to be carried out from an extensionalist point of view. Regardless of how much one subscribes to essentially intentional (or "phenomenological") theories of deviance or crime and behavior in general (in terms of meanings, beliefs, symbolism, attitudes, etc.), there is no denying that they have extensional and, in principle, quantifiable consequences. If they did not, they would hardly deserve attention in explaining the intrinsically quantitative measures of association.

An important point regarding the relationship between different theories of criminal or any other behavior has already been mentioned: Theories do not contradict each other unless they predict different behaviors from the same initial conditions. There is no need for a choice, once and for all, between different theories of criminal behavior, crime, or deviance. Neither is there a forced choice between different theories of the causal and symbolic effects of alcohol use in integrating these theories with theories of crime and deviance, as long as the theories are valid under specific initial conditions. The problem lies in the specification of empirical prevalence of antecedent conditions. Theories and models are more like "inference rules" which can have many uses in explanations, and not like static scaffoldings of one unchangeable explanatory scheme.

Individual-level theories of the type discussed earlier in this chapter serve as the actual inference rules or as descriptions of the mediating processes in the individual in relating alcohol use with crime, deviance, or aggression. Theories of deviance or crime and related empirical generalizations, on the other hand, potentially have a much more varied role in the explanation of the association. If we believe exclusively in the individual-level theories of pharmacological or symbolic effects, we largely leave to the social-level theories the role of determination of the occurrence and distribution of the relevant values of {alcohol use} and of any conditional/interactive situational or predisposing variables.

Very often there is, of course, disagreement about what the initial conditions are, and the identity criteria for "same behavior" are by no means agreed upon. In fact, there are a number of different legitimate types of criteria for what can be called the "same behavior," and theorists differ in their choice. The identity criteria seem to be largely determined by the theory chosen, and this does pose a serious epistemological dilemma.

Many theories of criminal behavior predict changes in stable characteristics of the individual which can potentially act as predisposing or
common-cause factors in alcohol use events or in the association between
long-term excessive alcohol use and crime. We should, however, not underestimate the potential of these theories to predict distributions in the
population of relevant situational factors or, as we might call them, subcontexts.

The discussion on the following pages deals with the potential integration of theories of alcohol effects and theories of deviance and crime. Not
much in the form of substantive advance in theory comes out. The discussion is limited to the general outlines of such an integration and provides
but a few illustrations of actual substantive integration. A more thorough
attempt at integration would bring about considerable benefit to both the
explanation of criminal behavior and the explanation of alcohol use patterns, in addition to the more immediate benefits to the accounting of the
relationship between the two phenomena.

The General Concepts of Deviant or Criminal Behavior and Their Formal Connections with Alcohol Theories

Some implicit assumptions about the concepts of criminal behavior and
deviance as used in general theories of these phenomena should be brought
out and examined for their possible impact on the crime-alcohol connection.

The most important of these is the nature of the identity criteria of the
concept of "deviance" or "crime." How do we decide that a given type of
behavior is criminal? There is nothing in the act which would, by itself,
enable us to classify it as a criminal or deviant act. We have to turn to the
definitions existing in the society under study to guide us in finding the
identity criteria for these concepts. These criteria are socially determined,
and as such they vary from culture to culture and from one time period to
another within the same society or jurisdiction. Criminal and deviant acts,
in other words, are defined by societal reactions.

In order to subsume all crime or deviance under a general theory, we
have to assume that something that is either conceptually or empirically
connected with the general definition of criminal or deviant behavior (independent of its differential extension over time and in different societies)
determines its occurrence.

Conceptually determined criteria are those based on the mere existence
of any norms or laws in a society and/or on the unspecified sanctions that
are by definition connected with these. One conceptual candidate is "inversion of societal norms," that is, negation of all legal norms. This type

of theory has been suggested as an explanation of juvenile delinquency (Cohen, 1955). When phrased as a highly generalized theory, it is perhaps a partially tautological theory of "defiance" as much as an empirical theory of "deviance." At least a tautological feature probably adds to its appeal. The other, more empirical and contingent, way in which the desired generality can be achieved is by using the existence or actions of social agencies and institutions (police, courts, and authority figures in general) whose existence is contingent on the existence of these norms and sanctions.

Alcohol theories which invoke the concept of "disinhibition" could most easily be integrated with the "inversion of norms" or "defiance" approach to the explanation of criminal behavior generally in connection with alcohol use events. This is true if inhibition is due to external social control or the internalized social controls of the superego, unless we specifically assume that the inhibition only applies to certain types of deviance, such as violence. ("Defiance" may imply too much of a conscious choice to be suitable in this context.) This limitation in the range of "inhibitions" seems to be implicit in much theorizing and empirical research on alcohol use effects, since the full range of what can be descriptively referred to as "disinhibited" behavior has not been studied.

In the section on individual-level models, a possible way in which acute alcohol effects can enter the explanation of general deviance or crime was discussed: Alcohol could, via perceptual/cognitive changes, affect the deterrent effects of sanctions. Experiments measuring risk-taking behavior after ingestion of alcohol have shown that alcohol possibly has effects which may affect some component variables of deterrence, such as perceived probability and severity of sanctions that seem to be conceptually related to the notion of risk.

Another way in which a general effect of the mere existence of laws and legal sanctions can be used to provide a basis for general theories of criminal behavior is through stochastic processes in the population at risk. It can be hypothesized that some individuals, due to biopsychological endowment or socialization, are prone to exhibiting excessive behavior, and wherever it conflicts, or happens to conflict, with legal norms it becomes by definition a criminal act. In fact, however, many criminals are selective as to the type of crimes they commit, but this process may be applicable to some extent to a segment of the population of crime committers. Whatever its prevalence, it affords a parallel to some alcohol effects on behavior, which can rightly be labeled excessive, or acting-out behavior. Such a theory of deviance and crime has close theoretical ties with the randomization theory of alcohol effects discussed earlier. It also seems to tie in with the excessive situational determination of the behavior of alcoholics

(Gliedman, 1956), violent individuals (Melges & Harris, 1970), and youths who exhibit deviant behavior (Jessor & Jessor, 1977).

Social Theories in an Illustration of Integrative Attempts

Most theories of criminal and deviant behavior, at least the predominantly sociological ones, actually consist of several component theories. These components address themselves to different variables and sometimes to different analytical units, and they naturally postulate different kinds of processes or relationships between the variables. Thus, for example, the differential association theory of criminal behavior assumes the existence of reference group theory, role theory, and learning theory—theories which are not specific to explanations of deviance or crime.

After early attempts at "biologizing" the explanations of crime in connection with the rapid development and consequent strong influence of the biological sciences in the 19th century, the direction in the last decades (despite scattered resurgences of biological/physiological theories, such as the "XYY syndrome") has been toward an emphasis on social–structural, (sub)cultural, and psychological (learning) theories. This fact leads to difficulties for attempts at integration or coordination of these theories with theories or theory fragments related to alcohol and its effects, which are largely physiological and psychological in nature, and for which biologizing explanations would have provided greater opportunities of painless integration. Sociological theories in general are, if not by their very nature at least by tradition and due to gaps in existing knowledge, indeterminate as to the "lower-level" theories and models which they often implicitly assume or make explicit general references to. They are also often indeterminate as to the direction and nature of causal determination, often just postulating patterned associations between phenomena. This leads to difficulties in attempts at integration with individual-level theories.

The following brief discussion does not do justice to the richness of etiological and associational detail in the presentation of theories. This is largely redundant for our purposes. Instead, we concentrate on the central themes of the theories, which are not based on the discussion of any one single author but on characteristics of the whole theoretical approach. Concentrating on the central theme of a theory probably leaves out some potential points of integration with theories of alcohol use and its effects, but otherwise we would make the exercise too unwieldy. The exclusion of other general theories of crime and all crime-specific theories should, of course, not be interpreted as a suggestion that these are any less important than these crime theories in integrative attempts. On the contrary, with regard to the latter type of theories, if cautious deductions from available coincidence estimates are allowed for the moment, there seem to be considerable differences in the alcohol involvement between different types of crime, and this could indicate the applicability of additional crime-specific theories of criminal behavior.

Considering that alcohol seems to have a strong association with serious forms of crime, both property crimes and crimes of violence, it is surprising that alcohol has only a peripheral role, if any, in theories of crime. Some general evolutional connections seem to exist between "disinhibition" theories of alcohol effects and psychoanalytical control theories of deviance, in that they seem to have evolved from the same matrix of psychoanalytical thought. A common ancestry can also be found for some developmental theories of alcoholism and developmental theories of criminal behavior, especially those which posit biological or psychiatric anomalies as the basic cause for both types of deviance.

In general, linkages between theories of crime and deviance, and their auxiliary theories (such as learning theory and role theory) and theories of alcohol use seem plausible for both chronic alcohol use and alcohol use events.

The neglect of any explanatory impact of alcohol use events, their effects, their symbolic significance, and their distribution in the population in the explanation of criminal behavior is, of course, not a mere oversight. It is part of a fairly systematic neglect of situational factors in general in a theoretical tradition which has largely chosen the individual and his/her characteristics as its theoretical loci. Thus, the role of situational determinants and their frequency and distribution are generally areas of indeterminacy in theories of criminal and deviant behavior.

There is undoubtedly explanatory value in all the main theories of deviance and crime. Some crucial questions for the problem at hand would be: To what extent are they selective or indeterminate as to the relationship between alcohol use and crime, what form would lower-level theories have to take in order to "fit" into these theories, and what variables covary with the variables in {alcohol use}? These are very central questions, but they will have to await further specifications of deviance theory, alcohol use theory, and theories of the effects and consequences of alcohol use. This is a process which could be started by a thorough analysis of the theories available. With the present state of knowledge there does not seem to be much sense in speculating on all the possible combinations of models and theories, and subvariables of {alcohol use} and {criminal behavior} relevant to explanatory accounting of the association.

In the integration of theories of alcohol effects and theories of criminal behavior, the dependent variables of a theory from one set should somehow be made to fit in with the independent variables of the other set. This may well be the case "internally" within the two sets of theories too, so that, for instance, in theory of deviance, social strain (anomie) theory of crime can explain some of the initial conditions which subculture theory of crime presupposes. This linkage of theories of deviance can probably best be illustrated with the help of an ideal-type concretization of a developmental theory.

The following example may also serve as an illustration of the sequential applicability of different theories of crime and alcohol use in an explanation of a criminal career. We can start by assuming that biopsychological factors in individuals, together with situational factors whose occurrence is determined by theories or empirical generalization at least partly extraneous to alcohol use or crime theories, determine their probability of engaging in certain types of (perhaps prealcoholic) drinking patterns. Societal reactions and sanctions increase the likelihood that these individuals with excessive drinking patterns will form affiliative drinking groups (reference group theory). Processes within these groups (e.g., Homans, 1950) form (or have formed) a common set of norms and values which now partly determine the actions of the individual (subcultural influences, learning theory). Values of the larger cultural matrix determine societal reactions toward this subculture. These reactions determine the structural position in society of the members of this subculture. The structural position, together with the influence of the larger cultural matrix which stresses acquisitory values (Merton's structural strain theory, 1957) determines, together with other factors (some of which may have to do with effects of acute or chronic alcohol use), the response of the individual to the structural strain (theories of individual stress tolerance). The individual's definitions relevant to crime may be predominantly positive due to subcultural influence, the requirements to keep up an addictive drinking pattern, and the aforementioned biopsychological factors. Thus, probability of criminal behavior is relatively great (differential association theory).

This simplified explanatory scheme shows how alcohol use can enter an explanatory scheme in several junctures, as a dependent variable in one juncture and as an independent variable for the next. It also shows that theories of acute alcohol effects are linkable with all forms of theories of criminal behavior and theories of chronic alcohol effects in a developmental explanatory scheme. In addition, this type of reasoning can be used to show how reverse causality (from crime to alcohol), common-cause causality, alcohol causality, and negative association theories can all determine the strength of a statistical association between crime and alcohol use. A similar scheme of reasoning could be set up in a tentative integration of different aspects of alcohol use and subcultural theories or structural strain theories. There is a great deal of potential linkage between different explanatory models (theories) and no valid reason why most should in any sense be considered as exclusive of each other. This is recognized in descriptions or explanations of concrete deviant careers and subcultures, although in theoretical treatises, "pure-essence" thinking often takes over in an idealized logical universe where diversity is seen as contradiction.

Most important of all, such reasoning should make us aware that theories are tools and not rigid, immutable scaffoldings.

Subcultures and Subcontexts. Criminological studies show that crime is unevenly distributed over different subgroups of populations under study, chosen by factors such as age, sex, and different indicators of social class and related concepts. There is less information on the differential alcohol involvement of crime among these subgroups, although this information would be necessary for our purposes.

Marginal subgroups within the larger societal matrix are often relevant disproportionately to their actual size, if crime is greatly concentrated in these subgroups. If these subgroups are also geographically clustered and, consequently, long-term interaction and "division of labor" result, subeconomies will emerge. If, in addition, shared behavior norms, shared objectives, and shared symbolic representations of the identity of the group which are separately identifiable from those of the larger inclusive culture are created, what can legitimately be called a subculture is formed. It is still far from adequately known to what extent clustering of crime and alcohol use results from the specific cultural aspects of some social groups or social categories through the learning of specific values and conduct norms, which determine the probability of crime or alcohol use patterns or both.

The processes by which alcohol would become clustered with crime in these subgroups should be explicated, analyzed on the theoretical level, and studied on the empirical level. There are a number of potential candidates for such processes. Among these are the social definitions and societal reactions, both formal and informal, which would tend to select individuals who exhibit excessive drinking patterns and other forms of deviance into areas of poor and cheap housing, and less surveillance of deviant behavior by the police and by nondeviant residents. Moreover, subcultural norms would probably grow out of necessities of survival in such a group of disadvantaged urban dwellers. (In this interpretation we select social processes in the group or subculture and in society as the theoretical loci.) In addition to the "push" of the larger social structure there will be a "pull" to attract individuals with certain proclivities as to crime and/or alcohol use, whatever the mediating processes which explain the occurrence of this "pull." In this way, the basis of recruitment to the subgroup or subculture may explain part of any clustering of certain alcohol use patterns and criminal behavior. (In this case the locus for theoretical interpretation is the individual.)

There is also a third possibility for theoretical locus. Assuming that there is more alcohol-involved crime in lower social strata (controlling for any higher values of the null hypothesis due to possibly a higher number of causally relevant alcohol use events per capita), we should also consider differences in the distributions of initial situational conditions which distinguish males from females, members of one social class from another, and members of different subcultures from each other. A high association between alcohol use and crime in ecological subunits and other types of subgroups of the population can thus have its origin in different frequencies and distributions of alcohol use events and causally relevant factors in these (such as behavior cues and contexts, e.g., frustrating stimuli), which increase the probability of crime occurrences. Theories of subcultures (as well as theories of mere subgroups and subcontexts) can also be used distributively to predict and explain situational/contextual aggregations of causally relevant factors.

It is of relevance for purposes of explanatory accounting that changes in the size of marginal subgroups, although small in relation to society as a whole, may have profound effects on the incidence of crime (Aho, 1976; Fattah, 1972). This is true especially of crimes for which the total population rates are low, such as homicide. The role of alcohol in the emergence and sustenance or purely conjunctive existence of such a subcontext or subculture will thus, to a considerable extent, determine the overall relationship between alcohol and crime as evidenced in the total statistics of the total society. (This is probably where selective police action also can have its largest impact on aggregated association figures.)

There have not been any analyses, either theoretical or empirical, on the explanatory weight that this type of clustering to marginal subgroups would have on the aggregated association between alcohol use and crime. An attempt at assessing the contribution of, for example, skid row to the alcohol–crime association would deserve scientific attention. On the side of the presumed dependent variable, the clearest instances of a subculture in the literature are probably juvenile delinquent gangs. Among these, the existence of subcultural norms and values, structural strains, and subcontexts which would explain a clustering of alcohol use and criminal behavior need further analyses in the context of the association.

Subgroups of the population and subcultures may also be different in their proclivities toward immediate or deferred gratification, which has been adduced as a factor in explaining acute alcohol use, alcoholism, and criminal behavior. Consequently, since this is one of the initial conditions in explanations of both alcohol use and crime in individuals, it can explain an alcohol–crime association both on the aggregate and the individual level as a common-cause factor. The possibility that subcultural beliefs, attitudes, and norms act as common-cause factors in explaining both criminal behavior and certain patterns of alcohol use is discussed in the next section.

There are naturally other possibilities open for explaining a high association between alcohol use and crime in subsegments of the population. Thus, among alcoholics, there could be a narrowing of technical means available for survival, partly brought about by societal reactions (e.g., by losing one's job due to drinking) which may leave crime as one of the few means available. A theoretically intriguing possibility is that the interactional behavior norms of alcoholic subcultures (especially skid row) may be determined to some extent by the acute effects of alcohol, so that they are, for example, largely situationally determined even among sober alcoholics.

In summary, in addition to direct conduct norms, subcultural values, and societal reactions, a high association between alcohol use and crime in subgroups of society (after the rejection of chance association) can be explained by a higher incidence of situational factors in alcohol use situations which are conducive to at least some types of crime. It can also be explained on the basis of the recruitment processes of individuals with certain predisposing characteristics which would increase the probability of an aggregate association between alcohol use and crime. These possibilities are, of course, not mutually exclusive.

An analysis of subcultures from our perspective would try to establish to what extent there is ecological, individual, and cultural overlap between subcultures of crime, subcultures of violence, and subcultures of certain (presumably excessive) patterns of alcohol use.

The Importance of Social Definitions and Belief Systems. The causal role of social definitions and belief systems concerning events, social objects, and states of affairs in general, and alcohol use events, the causal role of alcohol, and effects of alcohol in particular is potentially the most widely relevant and theoretically most fascinating of all. It touches on all aspects of determination of human behavior, including perception/cognition and epistemological problems. Social definitions largely overlap with "definitions of the situation" as these determine behavior on the individual level. As such they of course enter into all theories of human behavior which take cognitive elements into account. This covers all major sociological theories of deviance and crime, and many auxiliary theories used in specifying mediating processes of these theories. On the individual level, the individual's whole symbolic sphere of determination is influenced by socially determined conceptual structurings and belief systems, in that cue values, expectations, and individual "sets" are at least partially defined by these. The concept of subculture, needless to say, is defined by belief and value systems, and symbolic determination pervades any explanation of the crime–alcohol association in subcultural explanatory schemes. The accepted explanatory, causal, technical, esthetic, and moral paradigms of a society partially determine accepted and expected behavior under the influence of alcohol, provide the justifications for such behavior, and determine "the social definitions of alcohol as a cause of events" (J. Roizen & Schneberk, 1977a).

Social variables associated with cultural patterns, social definitions, and beliefs enter into practically all the different types of models and theories discussed in this chapter, and the ways in which the variables enter into them can differ from one theory or model to another. They determine the recording of events as deviance or crime; they are used as rationalizations or neutralization techniques of deviant, criminal, and any other type of behavior; they provide "reasons" for drinking; they determine selections of individuals to events and larger contexts; and they provide interpretations of behavior in interpersonal encounters. Among the biasing factors which have been mentioned as influencing the observed alcohol involvement in crime events are the possible uses of alcohol effects as morally and legally extenuating circumstances. These uses affect the observed association insofar as the criterion for the use of alcohol in the event is a report by the offender him/herself. The extent to which alcohol use is seen as an extenuating circumstance in legal definitions and moral beliefs differs from culture to culture, and it may thus explain part of any observed differences in alcohol involvement.

Distributively, social definitions can thus probably enter into many valid models explaining the occurrence of the presumed cluster of independent variables designated as "alcohol use" and the presumed dependent variable of crime or deviance and the joint occurrence of the two, in addition to relevant conditional/interactive factors, both situational and predisposing in nature. As a simple example of their distributive theoretical relevance with regard to the variables of alcohol use, social definitions determine the distribution and frequency of binge-drinking events in the population over a certain time period and thus (assuming that, e.g., BAC and/or sleep deprivation increase the probability of [violent] crime in alcohol use events) also partly determine the aggregate-level association between alcohol use and crime.

Cultural and subcultural factors pervade the initial conditions determining behavior in alcohol use events and by alcoholics. Thus, they enter relevant causal models in many ways beside their distributive significance in providing typical patterns and settings of drinking, in which alcohol use variables and different situational variables partly determine the outcome.

The role of cultural factors in determining the inception of aggressive encounters (and their potentially criminal outcomes) can be illustrated by some preliminary data from a recent community study of alcohol use and violence (Pernanen, 1979b, 1980). Questions on drinking occasions in an interview study of community residents provided information on whether the respondents "got angry" in their last drinking event and the perceived reason or cause for the anger. The open-ended question format provided a great variety in responses. These are indicative of the wide array of possible causal roles that alcohol can play in interpersonal encounters for which boundary conditions have been specified by societal norms and definitions (which in turn are partly determined by larger cultural systems and/or conglomerations). The findings are at this stage largely impressionistic, and a brief sketch of four forms of alcohol relatedness which were brought out will have to suffice:

1. Some incidents of anger were brought about by the cultural "time-out" features of the drinking occasion, probably combined with alcohol's effects in deviating from everyday norms, as when a husband dances for too long or too many dances with the same woman, or the wife is given a ride home in a stranger's car or disappears from the party for an hour.
2. In other incidents alcohol increased the probability of types of behavior which led to interpersonal friction, as when a person in the drinking group was "loud and embarrassing," inconsiderate, obnoxious, or abusive, or when the drinking guests did not leave when deemed proper by the host.
3. Certain behavior by other participants in a drinking occasion toward the drinker, such as protective behavior like taking away car keys, was felt by the object of such acts as an infringement on his/her rights or an embarrassment, and so were reactions of other people to the drinker's clumsiness, etc.
4. Several violent events in which the respondents of the survey had been victimized also revolved around the use of alcohol as an issue of contention, either acute alcohol use or excessive long-term patterns by a participant.

Thus, alcohol effects on behaviors in social situations, other than any direct effects on aggressive behavior and reactions to aggressive behavior, seem also to be important in explaining alcohol-related criminal behavior. Institutional requirements and public attitudes toward a person who has been drinking (or is "drunk") also increase the probability of violent confrontations. Persons who have been drinking are not allowed in many places and, after a point, not even in public drinking establishments. Such individuals are often forcibly removed (sometimes by specially designated role individuals). To the extent that the estimates of association between alcohol use and criminal violence are seen to imply a causal relationship between alcohol use and violent behavior unmediated by social processes, these findings corroborate the importance of spuriousness models as at least partial explanations of the association.

Judging from this evidence it is quite possible that the lower the acceptance of alcohol use, the tolerance of certain patterns of alcohol use or typical behavior in alcohol use situations, the greater the likelihood of alcohol-related violence. Thus, strict attitudes and negative reactions toward alcohol use and alcohol-related behavior may, especially if also reflected in alcohol policy, lead to relatively low consumption levels and consequent low prevalence of alcohol-related health problems and other problems; but on the other hand, they may lead to more interpersonally problematic situations (and more violence) in connection with alcohol use.

Lenke's (1975, 1976) findings showing that increased per capita consumption is associated with higher rates of violent crime do not contradict this type of hypothesis, since they were obtained in analyses based on the same society. Within one society, this type of result is to be expected if attitudes toward alcohol use and connected behavior have not changed during the study period, and increased per capita consumption only means a higher prevalence of relevant alcohol use events. This type of model would, in fact, partly explain a discrepancy between temporal and geographical correlations of per capita alcohol consumption and violent crime. It can be tested through specifically designed cross-cultural comparisons in which event-based data of alcohol-related violence and data on attitudes toward alcohol use and related behavior are collected.

It is possible to connect explanations involving the attitudes and reactions of others with the models discussed earlier using perceived arbitrariness and unpredictability of behavior after alcohol use as explanatory variables. The interactional role of other behavioral effects of alcohol on the reactions of other drinking participants in an alcohol use event may, of course, further increase the probability of a violent event. Thus, individual-level models of increased aggression by the drinker are also potentially relevant in explicating the interpersonal processes and escalation in violent events.

As mentioned earlier, social reactions (based on social definitions and moral, esthetic, explanatory, and technical paradigms regarding the proper use of alcohol, and on the real and perceived effects of alcohol) are causally relevant in the creation of subgroups, subcontexts, and subcultures which become the loci for individual- and aggregate-level association between alcohol use and crime. Potentially, societal reactions provide explanations of an association between alcohol use patterns and criminal behavior, generally if these reactions are directed against crime or deviance in general and certain patterns of alcohol use. These factors then will lead to a clustering of alcohol use and crime on the individual, ecological, and subcultural levels. The fact that both are socially defined as deviant behaviors can thus provide a common-cause (or conjunctive) link between alcohol use patterns and criminal behavior. Due to differences in these definitions we may thus have different statistical associations between alcohol use and crime in different cultures, although valid individual-level models may be equally applicable in these cultures.

Social definitions probably also have direct main effects on behavior in alcohol use events by determining the allowable limits of conduct under such circumstances, again making the alcohol–crime relationship partly spurious. J. H. Goldstein (1975), without discussing alcohol effects, mentioned the definitional determinants of aggression and violence by referring to socially defined "aggressible situations," which would include barrooms, public streets, and vacant lots but not, for example, churches.

Moreover, social definitions probably enter explanatory models directly and interact with the psychophysiological effects of alcohol in determining resulting behavior, for example, the occurrence of criminal acts. In the randomization model described earlier, the socially and culturally determined definitions and structurings of the situation provide the universe from which behavior cues are molded through the randomization process of alcohol. A conditional/interactive relationship between alcohol use and sociocultural definitions and beliefs, including those surrounding alcohol use, is by necessity implied in theories which take into account cognitive effects of alcohol use. Any individual-level theories which purport to explain behavior under the influence of alcohol have to provide some openness for symbolic determination, be they idiosyncratically individual or social in nature. This has been shown in numerous experiments in both alcohol and nonalcohol conditions.

In summary, socioculturally determined symbolic structurings of material, mental, and social reality are causally relevant: (1) distributively by determining the frequency and distribution of initial conditions of individual-level processes, (2) in interactional processes between individuals, (3) in providing the raw material for cognitive processes partially determined by the effects of alcohol, and (4) by providing beliefs, expectations, excuses, rationalizations, and neutralization techniques connected with alcohol use patterns, effects of alcohol, and behavior in alcohol use events. Considering all this, it is not surprising that the anthropological literature on the behavior of individuals from different societies is replete with accounts of very different types of behavior in alcohol use situations (e.g., MacAndrew & Edgerton, 1969; Washburne, 1961).

Integrative theoretical and empirical analyses regarding the two associated phenomena of alcohol use and crime can be extended to include any theories of criminal behavior. The indeterminacy which exists between the typically individual-level theories of alcohol effects and the typically social-level theories of criminal behavior can probably best be overcome by extending the framework of individual-level theories to include variations in socially determined variables. The potentiality exists for making all social-level theories and theoretical orientations of criminal behavior (structural strain or anomie theories, social control theories, differential association theories, subcultural theories, and social control theories), and their middle-range components relevant for the explanation of the alcohol–crime association. To the extent that the theories are both valid and applicable, they will explain their share of the statistical association between alcohol use and criminal behavior.

Summary and Concluding Remarks

The preceding discussion has moved freely between theory, empirical findings, and methodology. This is, of course, due to the fact that the matter at hand (i.e., theory) to a significant extent should be concordant with empirical findings. These in turn are largely determined by choice of methodology. Narrowness of methodology and analyses seriously limits theory, and vice versa. On the other hand, advances in methodology and analyses of empirical findings, and growth in substantive theory are inseparable.

Shortcomings of the present estimates of the association between alcohol use and crime hamper the development of theory in the explanation of the area: (1) The prevalent use of coincidence figures tells us nothing about the degree to which the estimates differ from what can be expected by chance. (2) The potential of even coincidence figures to shed light on theoretical questions has not been used; for example, elaborations over different subgroups, situations, or contexts of the studied populations have not been attempted. (3) The coincidence figures do not tell us anything about the risk that alcohol use events or alcoholism will lead to criminal behavior.

Attempts at explaining the statistical association should ideally be preceded by corrections for possible data bias and establishment of a null hypothesis. In addition, the strength of the associations should be estimated, not just the fact that they differ from zero. In this way the possible contributions of different explanatory schemes can be assessed. This has not been possible with the approaches used to date.

Part of a pervasive indeterminacy of the available explanations has to do with their status as "prototheories"; that is, they only specify the type of the determinant variable or variables. This is done through the use of labels of variable sets such as "setting," "personality," "childhood experiences," and "psychopathology." Second, often combined with this type of indeterminacy, attempts at explaining the association only specify variables which are believed to be of causal significance, without specifying mediating processes that are connected with alcohol use or specific alcohol use patterns; that is, the theory or model is incomplete. Sometimes the model itself is clearly implicit in the specification of the presumably causative variable; often it is a presumably bivariate linear direct-cause model since no further specification is provided. Plausible explanatory variables such as competitive activities or sex roles are put forth at times without specifying why they would increase the probability of crime specifically in connection with alcohol use.

There are two main sources of gaps in the theoretical knowledge of the relationship between alcohol use and crime. The first is the discrepancy that exists between theories of deviance or criminal behavior and the theories of alcohol effects, both symbolic and more directly causal, in both the acute and the more chronic aspects. The second gap is the related empirical and methodological one between the individual-level methods and models of experimental and clinical studies of the effects and meanings of alcohol use, and the standard methods and models of epidemiological analyses of the relationship between alcohol use and criminal behavior.

One central problem is how the findings and theories of different disciplines and problem areas of the same discipline and the findings from different types of samples in the same problem area fit into a general explanatory scheme. It is a major assumption in this chapter that such an integration is possible.

This discussion has presented some tentative ideas about an integration of theories on alcohol use and its effects and theories of crime and deviance. In the light of the indeterminateness of the theories with regard to each other, a more thorough integrative attempt would need a systematic injection of empirical findings wherever available. All major theories of deviant and criminal behavior should be subjected to a thorough conceptual analysis with special emphasis on the supplementary middle-range theories which are, at least implicitly, utilized by these theories. Theories attempting to explain specific types of crime also need such analysis as a preparatory step in integrative attempts. All this necessarily falls outside the scope of this chapter.

In order to try to bridge the existing gaps, a framework of "explanatory accounting" of the relationship has been used. Explanatory accounting is based on: (1) the validity, or probabilistic explanatory power of theories, and (2) the extent to which the initial conditions postulated by the theories hold true in the empirical world, that is, the extent to which the theory is applicable.

In all probability, many of the theories discussed in this chapter are valid, under certain specific circumstances. The greatest need at this stage would be to specify the different initial conditions (values of variables) which will have to be fulfilled for the models to have explanatory power. In other words, we would need to explicate the conditionality of the theories and models, and to specify the specific nature and values of the presumed independent variables in the explanations.

The suggested formal aspects of the integrative framework are a necessary feature of any attempt to account for any aggregate association which is multidisciplinary in its base. The large share of formal considerations in the exposition is a direct consequence of the lack of sufficiently determinate substantive theories, especially those on the aggregate level of theoretical analysis; the lack of specification of initial necessary and sufficient conditions of even the individual-level theories or models, which still labor largely under a direct-cause assumption; and a related lack of empirical generalizations regarding the incidence and distribution of causally relevant determinants (initial conditions).

An explicit assumption of this discussion is that no one theory or model will be able to provide the explanation for the totality of the observed statistical association(s) between alcohol use and crime, no matter how grand its scale. Partly, this is due to the fact that the referents of the concepts of both "alcohol use" and "crime," "criminal behavior," or "deviance" are so manifold. Furthermore, the existence and distribution of initial conditions for the applicability of any model or theory explaining (part of) the statistical association will have to be predicted or explained by other theories. Full theoretical closure is unattainable except in artificially manipulated conditions. Openness to the multiple possibilities of integration between discrete theoretical schemes and the idiosyncratic determination of important explanatory variables has to be accepted at this stage of knowledge.

Alcohol enters the explanatory accounting of the association between alcohol use and crime in a number of different models and sequences of models which determine the underlying causal processes. In addition to the pharmacological effects of alcohol, causal processes of a different kind are operating on another level. The "sets," "cues," expectations, meanings, and general symbolic connotations of alcohol use determine behavior independently of actual pharmacological effects and probably interact with these. Alcohol's effects on perception and cognition have been established in several experimental studies. It would indeed be surprising if these did not have an influence on the individual's definition of his/her situation and thus more directly on the tendency to deviate from accepted norms or established laws.

A third level of determination is the interpersonal one. On this level, alcohol use may not increase the probability of deviance and aggression through intraindividual processes, but other outcomes of alcohol use may be causally relevant through social interactional processes. Thus, the carelessness, inconsiderate behavior, clumsiness, and loudness which often accompany alcohol use no doubt lead to friction with other individuals and to the escalation of aggressive encounters to physical violence. Cultural values and social beliefs partly determine reactions toward a drinking individual and his/her behavior, and there probably exist differences in the "role" of the drunk in different cultures, depending on prevalent social beliefs and value systems.

A fourth level of determination is the sociocultural one, in which societal reactions, cultural conglomeration of activities and attitudes through social belief systems, etc., cause a clustering of alcohol use with criminal or generally deviant behavior. Empirical data supporting the relevance of all these levels of actions of alcohol have accumulated steadily, although a connection with criminal behavior has not often formed the basis of data collection and analyses.

Combinations of these different levels of determination will probably explain a major share of the statistical association. Thus, the randomization model explains deviance and general variability of behavior from a psychophysiological basis, not only by an extensional determination using situational, predispositional, and other types of variables but by postulating a randomization effect of alcohol on the selection of socioculturally determined cues for behavior and a resultant fluctuation, "inner-directedness," and seeming interpersonal arbitrariness of behavior. This intentional type of model can potentially explain a great variety of different types of behavior in connection with alcohol use.

The available estimates of the association between alcohol use and crime are composite outcomes of these different types of processes. Some valid theories or models would, in fact, predict and explain a decreased likelihood of criminal behavior connected with alcohol use under given circumstances. Many of the theories and models discussed in this chapter are not exclusive of each other but describe processes which take place in one and the same societal unit, during any specific period of study.

In "disaggregating" the causal processes resulting in statistical associations it should be remembered that causal processes between alcohol use and criminal behavior can proceed in both directions. Processes by which alcohol use, in any of its manifestations, leads to criminal behavior are supplemented by processes through which criminal behavior increases the probability of alcohol use events and alcoholism. This means that alcohol use events and patterns of alcohol use probably have consequences which constitute causally relevant factors for (i.e., initial conditions of) one or more theories of deviance or criminal behavior, and it means that theories on the consequences and concomitants of criminal behavior and deviance can determine some of the initial conditions of certain types of drinking events or long-term drinking patterns and thus predict behavior on the basis of theories of the narrowly causal or broadly symbolic role of alcohol. There is no contradiction between the two directions of relationship. The only question is how much of the aggregated statistical association is explained by each type of determination. We should beware not only of single-variable and single-theory explanations but also of one-directional explanations of the statistical association.

In future theoretical developments, integration can be attained through joint analyses of, on the one hand, theories on alcohol use and its concomitants and effects, and, on the other hand, theories of crime and deviance. These analyses would of necessity be both of a general nature and specific to different types of criminal behavior and deviance, and would be designed to cut down the considerable indeterminacy existing between theories of alcohol use and theories of criminal behavior. The need for conceptual analyses and substantive extensions is also evident regarding the individual-level theories internally. In the end, the explanation of "drunken comportment" may rest on the combination of some variation of a frustration or stress model, a well-defined disinhibition model, and a model built upon the cognitive, perceptual, and motivational effects of alcohol. Any such models will, however, have to take into account the characteristics of the individual and his or her social environment. The conditionality of all individual-level theories has to be made explicit and should form the basis for an empirical research approach which tries to specify the antecedent conditions for the validity of the theories and the prevalence and incidence of these conditions (i.e., the applicability of the theories) in different societal units.

Conceptual analyses of the current theories, theory fragments, and new empirical findings in the problem area should receive separate attention as an independent substrategy in a research program, and not be exclusively relegated to the role of preliminary considerations in individual research projects. Current theories on alcohol use, alcohol effects, and the scientific and popular notions of the relationship between alcohol use and crime should be analyzed from a historical–developmental and conceptual point of view.

In the empirical sphere, experimental and clinical research should be linked with epidemiological approaches in an integrated research program, where interpretations and theories based on associative relationships, are tested (to the extent possible) by means of controlled studies. In the same research program, the generalizability and explanatory import of clinical and experimental findings should be ascertained through the use of epidemiological methods. The impetus for such research will move both from epidemiological-level generalizations to the individual level of clinical and experimental studies, and vice versa. With this process will come finer specifications of both theory and empirical generalizations.

It is clear that the current emphasis on available police or court records has to be replaced, or at least supplemented, by specifically designed research projects if we are to make any significant advances in estimating the validity and strength of the association, and in assessing the validity and applicability of specific theories or models. Specifically designed research on the epidemiological level will aid in assessing the validity and applicability of practically all explanations on both the individual and social levels which are discussed in this chapter.

In addition to the minimal distinction between acute alcohol use events and patterns of long-term excessive alcohol use, and the rough dichotomy of use versus no use of alchol in the crime event, finer specifications of the alcohol use variable are needed. Amount of drinking is probably relevant in determining, for example, the degree of paresthesia and the extent and nature of sleep deprivation. Duration of drinking in the event is also a factor which perhaps, via the effects of sleep deprivation or stress, can provide important clues for advances in explanation of the association. The causal significance of rising versus falling blood alcohol levels, congener content of the beverage, etc., cannot be ruled out, and these variables deserve further scientific attention in the context of the relationship between alcohol use and crime.

The conditional nature of alcohol effects, with regard to both predisposing and situational characteristics, should be taken into account in planning both survey-type studies and clinical and experimental research. Partly because of this conditional nature of determination, key subgroups of the population (such as youth in general, young offenders, recidivist alcoholics, and members of certain subcultures) should be given special attention in epidemiological analyses and should be purposively selected for experimental or other controlled studies. Situational factors of a conditional nature should receive systematic attention in both survey-type and controlled studies. For survey-type studies this means a greater concentration on crime events and events of drinking as units of analysis, and for more controlled studies it implies more systematic manipulation of situational variables.

In view of the pervasive significance of cultural factors for all different levels of theory, cross-cultural replications of both epidemiological and controlled studies are of the highest priority.

Theoretical advances in an experimental substrategy should be achieved through the application of a wider range of variation in all relevant loci of controlled studies. The dependent variables in alcohol use experiments need to be extended to include deviant or quasi-criminal behavior generally. Typical experiments on aggression should include measurements also of other types of affective behavior including positive affect. The response-invoking stimuli need variation in that the exclusive reliance on the frustration–aggression paradigm, implicit in the "aggression machine" technique, should be complemented by other types of stimuli. It seems especially worthwhile to utilize stimuli which allow spontaneous selection of different types of cognitive cues of different affective content as bases for action. As mentioned earlier, the independent variable of alcohol use needs extension into higher amounts and blood alcohol levels, and longer durations of alcohol use events to correspond to alcohol use levels in relevant natural conditions (as ascertained by epidemiological means). The conditional nature of the relationship between alcohol use and criminal behavior should be acknowledged in the selection of relevant subject samples and in the manipulated variables of setting, human interaction, and expectations within the setting. The possibility of determination of alcohol use patterns by involvement in deviant and criminal behavior should also receive specific attention in an experimental substrategy. The same is true for situational common-cause and conjunctive models of the type discussed in this chapter.

Auxiliary research is needed to establish the levels of null hypotheses in the subpopulations of special interest; that is, those showing high alcohol involvement in crime. There is a great need for estimates of the true excess of alcohol involvement of different types of crimes in geographically, jurisdictionally, and culturally delimited populations and demographic subgroups of these populations. Auxiliary research attempting to assess the biases of different research methodologies, especially the use of police or court records or self-reports of crime, is long overdue. Of special interest in this context are truly event-based data on drinking occasions in the general population and subgroups of the population, asking for specific details about samples of actual (not just typical) drinking events.

A comparison of such auxiliary data of criminal events and drinking events in the general population (of interest also in their own right) with data from police and court records, and from interviews with offenders and victims will make possible an assessment of biases of event-based data in these widely used official records.

Much of future research in the area will probably be guided by preventive goals. It is clear that some prevention of alcohol-related crime can be accomplished without the knowledge of theories explaining, or processes mediating in, the genesis of the aggregated statistical association. For example, decreasing general availability of alcohol would, in many circumstances, decrease the incidence of alcohol-related crime. Other, less drastic measures, such as increased police surveillance in areas of high concentration of taverns, would probably also decrease this incidence. Studies measuring the effects of preventive policies and intervention, if these are not related to theoretical consideration, are not of immediate theoretical concern but would deserve systematic attention.

The emphasis in much of this chapter has been on the association between alcohol use and violent crime, and the explanation of this association. This is due to the fact that despite apparently strong statistical associations between alcohol use and crimes such as property crimes and arson, the empirical bases for these are even more scattered, and explanatory attempts have consequently been very limited.

The role of alcohol in the victimization aspect of crime has not been dealt with to the extent that it deserves in this discussion. That alcohol plays a major victimogenic role in crimes such as rape and robbery (e.g., Amir, 1971; Leppa, 1974; Normandeau, 1968) seems clear; in these types of crime the incapacitating effects of alcohol are more relevant than the ones principally reviewed here. (On the other hand, the theories and models discussed have a large role to play in the crime events in which victim precipitation is a contributing factor.) It would seem that cultural factors—especially cognitive, normative, and attitudinal structures, such as the "role of the drunk" in the society, in addition to more idiosyncratic factors related to ecology and surveillance in areas of high-risk drinking and possibly a higher probability of alcohol use by the offender if the victim has been drinking—will explain a large part of the victimogenic connection between alcohol use and these crimes.

Finally, the causative role of alcohol use in the processes leading to criminal behavior should always be seen in the context of other causal factors. In assessing the role of alcohol in the explanation of criminal behavior, it should be borne in mind that alcohol use by itself explains nothing, whereas alcohol use in combination with an assortment of other variables in several kinds of valid theories and models probably explains a not insignificant proportion of crime occurrences. Considering the conditional nature of the relationship between alcohol use and crime, it may not make sense to ask what share of crime occurrences or criminal behavior are explained by alcohol use. Instead, we should perhaps ask in what share of crime events alcohol is one of the causative factors. In this case we may find that stress, poverty, developmental factors, or other social and psychological factors would be causally involved in a larger share of such events even if the share of alcohol use were as high as 50% or more.

Acknowledgments

Several helpful comments by Dr. Richard Jessor on a draft of this chapter have probably influenced its substance and changed some of its emphases. The author would also like to express his gratitude to Kerstin Carsjo for her valuable assistance during the preparation of this work.

2 Alcohol and Crime: A Methodological Critique of the Literature

STEPHANIE W. GREENBERG

Introduction

The negative consequences of alcohol use for the individual and society have been claimed since biblical times. Deviance in general and criminal activity in particular are traditionally believed to be among the principal evils of drinking. The relationship between alcohol use and crime is thought to be particularly strong in the case of violent crime. Images of barroom brawls and family disputes escalating into homicides under the influence of alcohol are firmly fixed in Western cultures. Empirical evidence supports this view sufficiently enough that it has remained a major component in the conventional wisdom about alcohol use. As a result, public policy at the local, state, and federal levels has been aimed at controlling the consumption of alcohol and alleviating the effects of its excessive use. However, despite the cultural embeddedness of the link between alcohol and crime, the existing research leaves wide gaps in our understanding of this relationship. The purpose of this chapter is to examine the methodologies employed in the literature, critically evaluate them, and show how they affect study results.

Three principal questions are addressed in the literature:

1. What is the role of alcohol in the criminal situation?
2. What is the prevalence of alcoholism among criminals?
3. What is the criminal history of alcoholics?

The bulk of the literature concludes that there is a positive relationship between crimes, especially violent crimes, and the presence of alcohol in or

STEPHANIE W. GREENBERG. Research Triangle Institute, Research Triangle Park, North Carolina.

directly preceding the situation; that heavy use of alcohol is more prevalent among criminals than the general population; and that alcoholics have higher rates of criminality than the population as a whole. Thus, despite some variation in the findings among studies, the available evidence seems to support the notion that alcohol use and criminal behavior occur in the same place among the same group of people. However, the relationships that are established in the majority of studies are merely associational. These findings tell little about process and variation in a very complex phenomenon. A finer-grained view is required if simplistic understanding is to be avoided.

Several excellent critiques discuss the methodological weaknesses of the alcohol–crime literature (Bartholomew, 1968; Blane, 1965; R. H. Blum, 1969b; Cook, 1962; Goodwin, 1973; Lahelma, 1977; Pernanen, 1976; J. Roizen & Schneberk, 1977a; Tinklenberg, 1973). In general, the problems with the research fall into these categories:

1. Multiple and loosely defined concepts of alcohol use
2. Lack of uniformity in definitions of crime
3. Biased samples
4. Failure to control for relevant variables
5. Lack of information on the context in which drinking and crime co-occur
6. Inability to distinguish subgroups of alcohol users and offenders

This chapter attempts to illustrate how these and other problems in study design have affected results.

The discussion uses as its organizational framework the steps of the research process. It begins by discussing problems in hypothesis formation and continues through sample selection, definitions and data sources for alcohol and crime variables, and data analysis.

Most studies have failed to specify the nature of the relationships to be tested and the population or events to which the findings can be generalized. The research has therefore been conducted without a guide to study design. The inadequate conception of research questions is reflected in all succeeding phases of the studies: vague or inadequate definitions of crime and alcohol, samples selected for convenience rather than suitability to the research question, failure to take sample bias into account, and limitation of the analysis to bivariate correlation. Consequently, the research is unable to answer questions concerning the role alcohol use plays in the criminal event, the interaction between alcohol use and other characteristics of this event, the role of alcohol in the criminal career, and differences in these relationships among subpopulations of offenders and alcohol users.

This chapter does not deal with the following issues related to alcohol use and crime: drunkenness offenses, traffic offenses, suicide, and the prevalence of alcoholism in the families of criminals. First, drunkenness offenses are related to the excessive use of alcohol, either acute or chronic, by definition. Examining these offenses adds little to the understanding of the role of alcohol in the criminal event. Second, most traffic offenses, with the important exception of driving under the influence, are misdemeanors. The emphasis in most of the literature on alcohol and crime—and hence in this chapter—is on serious offenses. Third, the act of suicide usually lacks the element of human interaction, being internal to the individual (Pernanen, 1976). It is therefore not comparable to crimes in which the nature of direct interaction between victim and offender is critical in determining the outcome. Finally, alcoholism in the family of criminals has been considered to be a causal factor in the criminal career. This discussion, however, is concerned with the effect of more direct alcohol-related variables on crime.

Formation of Hypotheses

The formation of a hypothesis serves two major functions in research: It dictates the kind of data that must be collected to answer the research question, and it guides the organization of the analysis (Sellitz *et al.*, 1951). The absence of clearly defined hypotheses in the alcohol–crime literature has prevented it from addressing at least two critical issues: (1) the precise nature of the relationship between crime and alcohol and (2) the population or event to which findings are inferred. Each of these problems is discussed later as it relates to the role of alcohol in the criminal situation, the prevalence of alcohol use among criminals, and the criminal history of alcoholics.

Types of Relationships between Alcohol and Crime

The Criminal Event

J. Roizen and Schneberk (1977a) stated:

> The absence of a general theory or theories of alcohol-involved social problems has been a serious constraint on diversity in the collection of data about criminal events. . . . The contemporary empirical research on drinking and crime is associational research. There is active restraint on making causal claims although causal claims are often implicit in the structure of the research design. With few exceptions, the research is organized around neither an

alcohol theory or theories nor a crime theory. The question which then must be asked of this alcohol/crime data is whether crime, or some aspects of crime can reasonably be called a consequence of drinking or a drinking problem. (pp. 320–321)

This failure to incorporate a coherent conceptual framework into studies has resulted in descriptions of the role of alcohol in the criminal event in such vague terms as "associated with crime," "figured prominently," "played a role," and "involved." These terms tell nothing about the process by which a situation where alcohol is merely present escalates into a criminal event. Virtually no studies in the literature have formulated a research question that is more specific than, What is the relationship between alcohol use and crime? While the type of crime to be considered as the dependent variable is usually indicated, the independent variable, alcohol consumption, is rarely well specified. Conditional variables are almost never mentioned. Thus, the research is guided by the notion that a vaguely conceptualized independent variable is expected to have some form of association with a dependent variable, and that variation in this dependent variable can be completely explained by a single independent variable.

The vagueness of the research questions would be problematic in any study but is particularly so in alcohol–crime studies. One problem is that alcohol use often occurs among people who are at least casually acquainted. Crimes that have been found to covary with alcohol use, such as homicide and assault, also tend to occur among people who know one another. A study by the Vera Institute of Justice (1977) of felony arrests in New York City reported that in half of all murder arrests and 69% of felonious assault arrests, there was a prior relationship between the victim and the accused. The problem then is to distinguish criminal events where alcohol is merely present from those where it plays an active role (J. Roizen & Schneberk, 1977a). A second problem is that alcohol use is a commonplace activity in our society; crime occurs less frequently. An important task, therefore, is to distinguish the vast majority of drinking situations that do not result in crime from those that do.

Tinklenberg (1973) has stated that three factors must be taken into account in order to examine the role of alcohol in the criminal event—pharmacological, personality, and contextual effects. First, regarding physiological variables, specific types of alcohol (such as bourbon) are found to induce greater risk taking than equal amounts of other types (such as vodka) because of differing amounts of psychoactive agents other than alcohol. Second, individual response to alcohol varies and is dependent on such factors as weight, food ingestion, and drinking speed. Third, studies relating crime to the proportion of offenders or victims who drank prior to the crime never indicate how much time elapsed between the two events. The effect of alcohol on any situation is increasingly tenuous as time elapses from the last drink. Finally, there may be individual response variation as a function of prior experience with alcohol. Equal amounts of alcohol may produce a marked reaction in an individual with mild or moderate drinking habits but no reaction in an alcoholic because of the increased tolerance.

Personality factors are also expected to play a role in the alcohol–crime relationship. Individuals with various kinds of personality disturbances may experience a wide variety of problems in social functioning, including excessive use of alcohol and violent outbursts which may translate into assault, homicide, or rape. Some studies report an interaction effect between certain mental disorders and consumption of alcohol which results in sudden, uncharacteristic violence against others (Selling, 1940; Skelton, 1970). Therefore, the problem is to disentangle the effects of individual pathology, drinking, and criminal behavior.

Contextual effects have received little attention in the literature but are critical in the understanding of the development of drinking events into criminal events. Several studies show that homicides where alcohol is present are more likely to occur in the evening and on weekends than at other times (Herjanic & Meyer, 1977; LeRoux & Smith, 1964; Wolfgang & Strohm, 1956). There is also likely to be a prior relationship between offenders and victims of alcohol-related homicide (J. L. Baker, 1959; Herjanic & Meyer, 1977). Alcohol-related assaults and homicides tend to take place at home or in a bar (Gerson, 1978; Herjanic & Meyer, 1977; Mayfield, 1976; Wasikhongo, 1976). Studies measuring the presence of alcohol in both the offender and the victim of homicide, assault, or rape have found that in the vast majority of cases where alcohol was present in either the victim or the offender, it was present in both (Amir, 1967; Herjanic & Meyer, 1977; Hollis, 1974; Virkkunen, 1974; Wasikhongo, 1976; Wolfgang & Strohm, 1956). However, these characteristics describe leisure time interaction in general. These studies therefore yield little insight into the factors that escalate companionable drinking occasions into criminal events. They do not tell whether the presence of alcohol is simply associational or if it plays an active role.

It is not suggested that variables reflecting all three conceptual levels— physiological, psychological, and contextual—can or should be included in all studies of the alcohol–crime relationship. It is possible to confine hypotheses to a single conceptual level and assume that the effects of variables on the other levels are randomized. However, what is necessary is that recognition be given to the various ways in which alcohol might relate to the criminal event. This does not mean that causal statements, which would be extremely difficult to test stringently, should be made in hypotheses. Rather, hypotheses should be stated in terms of conditional probabilities.

Pernanen (1976) has suggested a number of hypothetical models that describe the role of alcohol. These are alternatives to the unidirectional, bivariate models that are implicit in most of the research. As an illustration of Pernanen's discussion, we use the results of two studies which found that an argument preceded homicide in a majority of cases where alcohol was present and in less than half the cases where it was absent (Herjanic & Meyer, 1977; Virkkunen, 1974). The effect of alcohol on violent crime could be conditional; that is, alcohol increases the probability of violence but only when an argument erupts. The relationship could be interactive; that is, when alcohol and an argument co-occur, the probability of violence is greater than the sum of the probabilities when either alcohol or an argument, but not both, is present. A common-cause explanation might mean that alcohol use increases the probability of both an argument and violence, but the latter two are not causally related. More probably, alcohol use might increase the likelihood of an argument, which increases the likelihood of violence. This is an intervening relationship.

This level of specificity in hypothesis formation has at least two advantages. One is that competitive theories of the effect of alcohol on human behavior can be tested. This is not possible when such vague terms as "associated with," "played a role," or "involved" are used. Second, a focus is provided for subsequent phases of the research process, such as the appropriate population from which to sample and the utilization of comparison groups and control variables.

Alcoholism among Criminals

A number of studies have examined the prevalence of the excessive use of alcohol or alcoholism, as these are variously defined, among identified criminals. (See Chapter 5, this volume, for a theoretical and empirical discussion of the role of alcohol in the criminal career.) While there is considerable variation in the findings among both studies and types of criminals, the modal finding is that between one-quarter and one-third of the samples had a history of chronic alcohol abuse. J. Roizen and Schneberk (1977a) compared the drinking history of prison samples with drinking prevalence in the general population. They found that the prevalence of drinking problems in prison samples was higher than comparable measures of drinking problems in the general population. However, they pointed out that prisoners appear to have higher rates of many different problems than does the general population, such as low education, high unemployment, and high divorce rates.

Apparently, there are two implicit hypotheses in this research. One is that the higher rate of alcoholism among identified criminals is evidence that alcohol played a causal role in the event that resulted in imprisonment. The second is that alcoholism in and of itself leads to a life of crime, ostensibly because of its destruction of moral fiber (J. Roizen & Schneberk, 1977a). However, studies of alcoholism among prisoners seldom actually test the hypotheses that seem to be implied.

With regard to the first implicit hypothesis, that alcoholism leads to crime because of the disinhibiting effects of alcohol use, few studies measure differences in alcohol consumption between alcoholics and nonalcoholics during the criminal event. Thus, it is impossible to evaluate whether alcoholism or alcohol use is the relevant independent variable. Studies that do compare differences in drinking in the criminal event between alcoholic and nonalcoholic offenders find that a higher percentage of alcoholics were drinking prior to the crime than were nonalcoholics (Mayfield, 1976; D. P. Miller, 1964; Rada, 1975). But since alcoholics are more likely to be drinking at any given time than are nonalcoholics, there is no way to know whether alcoholism has an effect on the criminal event above and beyond the effects of alcohol. In one of the most detailed studies in the literature on the relationship between drinking history and the use of alcohol during the crime, Mayfield (1976) found that over one-third of the problem drinkers who were intoxicated during the crime thought it was an irrelevant factor, compared to about half of the entire sample who were intoxicated during the crime. Thus, according to one study, it was perceived that alcohol played no direct role in the crime for a substantial proportion of alcoholics.

In order to assess whether alcoholism exerts an effect independent of the effect of drinking during the criminal event, it is necessary to treat the two as separate and distinct variables. There are several hypothetical relationships between alcoholism, drinking, and the occurrence of a crime. The effects of alcoholism on the criminal event could be conditional on the presence or absence of alcohol; when alcoholics are not drinking they may not be any more prone to criminal behavior than are nonalcoholics. Alcoholism would have a direct causal effect only if alcoholics were prone to criminality regardless of whether they were drinking at the time. Finally, there may be an interaction effect between alcoholism and alcohol on the criminal event; alcoholics could be more or less prone to criminality when drinking than would be expected from the direct effects of alcoholism or drinking. Most of the available research is incapable of testing such hypotheses because these studies emphasize individual-level characteristics. The implicit research question suggests a combination of individual- and event-level data.

The second underlying hypothesis is that a life of crime is one of many negative consequences of excessive drinking. However, few studies address such questions as: Does alcohol use facilitate the criminal career because of its disinhibiting effects? Does alcoholism impede the criminal career because of its disintegrating effects on the personality? Does the peak of criminal activity correspond to the peak of drinking activity? These questions cannot be addressed by most studies since samples usually reflect the prevalence of alcoholism at a point of failure in the criminal career, that is, imprisonment. Pittman and Gordon (1958) have suggested that public inebriates are examples of failed criminals. Arrests for serious offenses in their sample declined or stopped after age 35, and the individuals settled into a pattern of chronic drunkenness offenses. Pittman and Gordon view this as a response to career failure. Cook (1962) and Goodwin (1973) have suggested that drinking may be more relevant to the criminal career than alcoholism. Acute excessive drinking may bolster courage sufficiently to commit a crime, while alcoholism may damage the ability to execute the carefully made plans that are necessary for some crimes, particularly property crimes.

Hypotheses addressing the long-range effects of alcoholism on the criminal career should be stated in terms of the probable course of the career in the presence and absence of alcoholism. The effect of excessive drinking on the criminal career, at discrete points in time, should also be incorporated into the model.

The Criminal Career of Alcoholics

The problems in hypothesis formation concerning the prevalence of criminality among populations of identified alcoholics are similar to those for the prevalence of alcoholism among criminals. The research indicates that samples of identified alcoholics have far higher rates of criminality than would be expected in the general population. However, it is necessary for hypotheses to specify whether the criminal career is a consequence of alcoholism or the reverse.

Pittman and Gordon (1958) found that criminality preceded chronic alcoholism and that non-alcohol-related offenses decreased as arrests for drunkenness increased. They suggested that alcoholism may be interpreted as an adaptation to a failed criminal career. But alcoholism may be an adaptation to failure in "legitimate" careers as well. Lindelius and Salum (1975) found a relationship between crime and alcoholism among hospital admissions for acute, excessive drinking and admissions of homeless men but not among voluntary admissions to a psychiatric institute. While not career criminals, this last group may have experienced failures and problems in adjustment analogous to those in the first two groups. Given that alcoholics tend to be identified by various medical and mental health agencies fairly late in life (approximately 40% of the Lindelius & Salum, 1975, sample was over 50 years old), the most advanced stages of alcoholism represent a career endpoint in many cases. The question then becomes, Is alcoholism a consequence or a cause of career failure? Is this equally true for alcoholics with and without a criminal background? It may be that criminals who continue to succeed never turn to alcohol. On the other hand, alcoholism may convert a successful criminal into a public inebriate. The problem is to delineate at what point in the course of career development (both criminal and noncriminal) excessive use of alcohol begins and what effect this has on subsequent career patterns.

The Problem of the Null Hypothesis

A major problem in interpreting the results of the literature on the relationship between crime and alcohol is the lack of a null hypothesis, either stated or implied. The null hypothesis provides a link between the particular sample being examined in a given study and the population from which the sample was drawn. It states that there is no difference between groups or no relationship between variables in the population. The researcher then compares sample results to the null hypothesis and decides, according to specified criteria, how likely it is that differences between results and the null hypothesis could have been caused by chance sample fluctuations. If the null hypothesis is rejected, we are reasonably certain that the study sample was not drawn from a population where the null hypothesis was true. Few studies specify to what population they wish to generalize. Hence, there is no way to evaluate whether observed relationships or group differences are a result of pure chance or represent true relationships or group differences. (Problems in sample selection also make it difficult to generalize beyond the study sample. These are discussed in the next section.)

Several authors have pointed out the difficulties in establishing a null hypothesis concerning the effect of alcohol in the criminal event (Amir, 1967; LeRoux & Smith, 1964; Pernanen, 1976; Tinklenberg, 1973; Wolfgang & Strohm, 1956). Nevertheless, this is a necessary first step simply to support the assertion of an association, leaving aside the question of the nature of this association. Pernanen (1976) has discussed the concept of the population at risk. This is the total number of individuals in a given time and place who are exposed to the risk of an alcohol-related crime either as victim or offender. It is necessary to compare the number of alcohol-related crimes to the size of the population at risk of experiencing this event. For example, it was mentioned earlier that alcohol-related violent crimes are most likely to occur on evenings and weekends, often in bars. However, such times and places have the largest population at risk and would therefore be expected to have the greatest proportion of alcohol-related crimes. Other contexts with smaller at-risk populations may in fact have a larger per capita share of alcohol-related crime. Wolfgang and Strohm (1956) applied this reasoning to their finding that alcohol-related homicide is more likely to take place among Blacks and males than among Whites and females. However, they suggest that the social norms may be such that a greater proportion of Blacks and males drink during informal social interaction and, hence, constitute a larger at-risk population than Whites and females. If the number of alcohol-related homicides were compared to the at-risk population, the opposite findings concerning race and sex might pertain.

Similar problems exist in establishing the at-risk population when measuring the prevalence of alcoholism among criminals. A number of studies show considerably higher prevalence of various measures of problem drinking among prison populations than in the general population. However, the general population is not the appropriate population at risk. Young, Black, urban males tend to be overrepresented in prison populations. This same group also has a high prevalence of heavy drinking and social and medical problems resulting from excessive drinking (Robins & Guze, 1970). If prison samples were compared to that portion of the general population with similar social and demographic characteristics, the differential may be reduced or even eliminated.

In establishing the at-risk population for measuring the prevalence of criminality among alcoholics, it is necessary to take into account important subpopulations within this group. Alcoholics who are so identified because of physical or psychiatric symptoms may represent a very different population than those who are labeled as alcoholics by the law, that is, for drunk driving, public inebriety, vagrancy, and the like (Lindelius & Salum, 1973, 1975). The evidence suggests that only the latter group has higher rates of criminality than the general population in the same age–sex group. Therefore, inferences to the entire population of alcoholics based solely on the legally defined group will be misleading.

Sample Selection

The major source of sample bias in the literature on the relationship between alcohol and crime is the selection of criminals or alcoholics that have been identified as such by an agency of social control: the police, a prison, a psychiatric hospital, or the like. For example, the process by which an individual is arrested, brought to trial, convicted, and sentenced, is highly selective. Therefore, samples based on populations at any of these stages in the criminal justice system are not representative of the universe of offenders. But the presence of alcohol in the crime or an offender who is an alcoholic is likely to introduce yet another complicating factor in this selection process. Thus, estimates of the prevalence of alcohol in the criminal event, the prevalence of alcoholism among criminals, and the criminal history of alcoholics are almost certainly biased based on samples of those officially identified and processed by the criminal justice or treatment systems. As is discussed later, there is often more than one source of sample bias in each of these three types of studies. Each source of bias may have an opposite effect on the results. The difficulty lies in assessing both the effect of each type of bias and their combined effect on study results.

The Criminal Event

Table 2.1 summarizes the percentage of victims or offenders in whom alcohol was present during the crime, as reported in a set of 35 studies. Some studies dealt with the role of alcohol consumption in only one type of criminal event, such as homicide, while others included two or more types of crimes. These studies do not exhaust the total number of studies in this area. However, most of the frequently cited studies are included, and an attempt was made to cover a wide range of research methodologies.

This table clearly shows the difference in attention paid to personal crimes versus property crimes. There were 28 studies of alcohol involvement in homicide but only between three and six studies for the four types of property crimes. The small number of studies that include information on property crimes suggests a limited view of the role of alcohol in the universe of types of criminal events. Perhaps the culturally ingrained expectation that alcohol is relevant primarily to violent crime has created a self-fulfilling prophecy in the literature.

The results of these studies may not represent the true population of criminal events for at least two reasons: (1) the types of crimes most likely to involve alcohol may receive differential treatment in the criminal justice system, and (2) within types of crime, those where alcohol was present may receive differential treatment.

With regard to the first source of sampling error, alcohol-related crimes may be over- or underrepresented in offender samples because of differential handling by the police and courts of crimes where alcohol is most likely to be involved. The evidence suggests that alcohol-related crimes tend to

TABLE 2.1. Alcohol Involvement in the Criminal Event, by Type of Crime[a]

Percentage of crime victims or offenders where alcohol was present during criminal event	Frequency of studies							
	Homicide	Sexual offenses	Aggravated assault	Robbery	Burglary	Larceny	Auto theft	Forgery/ bad checks
0–10	2	—	—	—	—	1	—	—
11–20	4	—	1	1	1	—	—	—
21–30	—	2	2	—	—	—	—	—
31–40	2	1	—	—	2	—	—	—
41–50	2	3	1	—	—	1	1	1
51–60	4	1	—	1	1	1	1	2
61–70	4	1	3	2	1	1	1	—
71–80	2	—	—	1	—	1	—	—
81–90	7	—	—	—	1	—	—	—
91–100	1	1	1	—	—	—	—	—
TOTAL STUDIES[b]	28	9	8	5	6	5	3	3

[a]These percentages reflect the presence of alcohol, as defined in a variety of ways, immediately prior to or during the crime. The numbers upon which the percentages are based are therefore either total cases (victims) or total offenders. In studies where drinking on the part of both victims and offenders is reported, the percentage of victims only is reported in this table.

[b]This table is based on the findings of 35 studies. The grand total does not add to 35 because some studies include data on only one type of crime, while others include two or more types of crime and therefore appear in more than one column.

81

involve violence against other persons, particularly aggravated assault and homicide. For each of these crimes, in half or more of the studies examined, a majority of the victims, offenders, or both drank prior to the crime. (This is consistent with Pernanen's, 1976, estimate that 50 to 60% is the best estimate of alcohol involvement among homicide offenders. Most studies of nonviolent crimes also show that the majority of offenders, victims, or both drank prior to the crime. However, this statement is based on far fewer studies than is the case for violent crimes, particularly homicide.) In addition, studies show that offenders were more likely to be known to their victims in homicides involving alcohol than in non-alcohol-related homicides (J. L. Baker, 1959; Herjanic & Meyer, 1977). Herjanic and Meyer, in fact, found that 44% of homicide victims who were drinking were killed by a friend, compared to 25% of nondrinking victims. Finally, alcohol-related assaults and homicides tend to take place at home or in a bar, rather than on the street (Gerson, 1978; Herjanic & Meyer, 1977; Mayfield, 1976; Wasikhongo, 1976). Each of these characteristics has implications for the treatment of the case in the criminal justice system.

Treatment of domestic assault cases by the police often precludes their entry into the criminal justice system and into corresponding records. Two recent studies of police intervention in family disputes indicate that the police rarely make arrests in such cases (Bard & Zacker, 1974; Zacker & Bard, 1977). However, a study of family court cases found that drunkenness in one party is the best predictor of family violence (Byles, 1978). Family quarrels which sometimes involve both alcohol and assaultiveness may be considered too unimportant or private by the police to require arrest. Thus, such cases may be underrecorded in police statistics. Also, the distinction between reported crimes and recorded crimes should be kept in mind. An alleged crime may be reported to the police, but if the officer who responds to the call decides that no crime has been committed, the event will not be recorded in the official police statistics.

The disposition of assault cases, when they do result in an arrest, suggests that alcohol-related crimes may be underrepresented in prison samples. A recent study by the Vera Institute of Justice (1977), which traced the disposition of felony arrests in New York City, found that assault had a high arrest rate, but the rates of convictions and lengthy sentences for this offense were low. One reason for this may be the high proportion (69%) of victims with a prior relationship with the offender. Prior relationships were cited by prosecutors as the most frequent reason for case dismissal. Plaintiffs who are friends or relatives of the defendant often fail to give the prosecutor necessary information on the case or fail to appear at the trial. While a prior relationship may be conducive to arrest because of the ability of the victim to identify the offender, such cases are less likely to come to trial than are cases involving strangers. Cases that are tried which involve acquaintances are less likely to result in convictions and sentences than are cases involving strangers. This negative relationship between closeness of relationship and conviction was also found in a study of arrest dispositions in Washington, D.C. (Forst, Lucianovic, & Cox, 1977). If alcohol-related crimes take place disproportionately among friends and relatives, alcohol-related assault in particular and personal crimes in general may be underrepresented in prison populations. The following example illustrates what may be a common occurrence in alcohol-related crimes:

> An auxiliary police officer watched a woman approach a man as he emerged from a liquor store. It was dark. The officer thought he saw a knife flash in her hand, and the man seemed to hand her some money. She fled, and the officer went to the aid of the victim, taking him to the hospital for treatment.
>
> The officer saw the woman on the street a few days later and arrested her for first degree robbery on the victim's sworn complaint. It was presumably a "high quality" arrest—identification of the perpetrator by an eye-witness, not from mugshots or a line-up, but in a crowd. Yet, shortly thereafter, this apparently airtight case was dismissed on the prosecutor's motion.
>
> What the victim had not explained to the police was that this defendant, an alcoholic, had been his girlfriend for the past five years; that they had been drinking together the night of the incident; that she had taken some money from him and got angry when he took it back; that she had flown into a fury when he then gave her only a dollar outside the liquor store; and that she had slashed at him with a pen knife in anger and run off. He had been sufficiently annoyed to have her charged with robbery, but, as the judge who dismissed the case said, "He wasn't really injured. Before it got into court they had kissed and made up." In fact, the victim actually approached the defense attorney before the hearing and asked him to prevail upon the judge and the Assistant District Attorney (ADA) to dismiss the charges against his girlfriend. (Vera Institute, 1977, p. xii)

The tendency for alcohol-related violent crimes to take place in bars and at home may counteract the possibilities for underestimation discussed in the previous paragraph. Normandeau (1968) found that the likelihood of arrest decreased as the amount of time between the occurrence of the crime and the report to police increased. Forst et al. (1977), in their study of arrest dispositions in Washington, D.C., found that the greater the amount of elapsed time between the occurrence of the crime and the arrest, the lower the likelihood of conviction. It might be expected that crimes occurring in homes and public gathering places would have a shorter lag time between occurrence and arrest than street crimes because the offender can be identified more readily. This could result in an overestimate of alcohol-related crimes in both arrest and prison populations.

There appear then to be at least two competing sources of bias in crimes where alcohol is likely to be involved. On the one hand, prior association between the victim and assailant increases the likelihood of arrest but decreases the likelihood of conviction and sentencing. On the other hand, the locations in which alcohol-related crimes tend to occur would be likely to increase the probability that the crime will be reported and decrease the time between the occurrence of the crime and the arrest. This last situation would increase the probability of conviction. Taking all of these possible sources of bias into account, arrestee samples would be expected to show a higher proportion of alcohol involvement than prison samples.

Little information exists on the specific effect of alcohol involvement in the criminal event on subsequent criminal justice proceedings. J. Roizen and Schneberk (1977a) have argued that a victim who has been drinking prior to the crime is less likely to report the crime to the police for fear of not being believed. This would result in an underestimate of the alcohol factor in official crime statistics. On the other hand, an offender who has been drinking may be more likely to be arrested because of incompetence in avoiding the police. This is a source of upward bias in arrest data.

T. Epstein (1977) has discussed the role of alcohol in convictions and sentences. The two key concepts that determine the role of alcohol in criminal trials are voluntary action (actus reus) and criminal intent (mens rea). When intoxication is believed to cause the absence of either voluntary action or criminal intent, intoxication is viewed as the cause of the crime, and the individual is excused. However, the problem is in deciding when intoxication is sufficiently severe to obliterate criminal intent or voluntary action. The rule in most states is that intoxication is not a legitimate defense except in three cases: a long-term condition of insanity due to habitual drinking, an involuntarily contracted state of intoxication, and an inability to form a specific criminal intent in offenses where that form of intent is an essential element. Regarding this last point, the absence of specific intent does not necessarily mean the individual is regarded as innocent. He or she may be convicted of a lesser offense which does not require proof of specific intent. Wolfgang and Strohm (1956) have argued that judges may reduce a conviction from first to second degree murder on the basis of the belief that alcohol consumption reduces or eliminates the ability to form specific intent. Myers (1976) found that drinking prior to the crime was associated with case dismissal in a substantial proportion of moderately serious offenses. This would result in a reduction of alcohol-related offenses in prison samples. The reduction of charges from more to less serious offenses would also decrease the number of alcohol-related offenses in prison samples because of the reduction or elimination of prison sentences.

In order to explore the actual effects of these various sources of bias on study results, the data presented in Table 2.1 were disaggregated into sample types. The focus on serious crimes in this literature is emphasized in the population from which the samples were selected. Prisons were the single most common source of samples (with the exception of medical examiner reports in homicides). Out of a total of 35 studies, nine used prisoner samples (Abrahamsen, 1950; J. L. Baker, 1959; Banay, 1942; Bartholomew, 1968; Leven & Vandre, 1961; Matheson, 1939; Rada, 1975; Scott, 1968; Selling, 1940); nine used medical examiner reports (S. Baker, Robertson, & Spitz, 1971; Cleveland, 1955; Haberman & Baden, 1974; Harlan, 1950; Hollis, 1974; LeRoux & Smith, 1964; Spain, Bradess, & Eggston, 1951; Westermeyer & Brantner, 1972; Wilentz, 1953); seven used police reports (Amir, 1967; Bett, 1946; Connor, 1973; Malik & Sawi, 1976; Marek, Widacki, & Hanausek, 1974; Pittman & Handy, 1970; Wasikhongo, 1976); four used samples of accused offenders (Cassity, 1941; Christian Economic and Social Research Foundation, 1976; East, 1939; Gillies, 1965); two used arrest records (Shupe, 1954; Steward, 1964); and four used a combination of police and medical examiner records (Herjanic & Meyer, 1977; Mayfield, 1976; Virkkunen, 1974; Wolfgang & Strohm, 1956). Since seriousness of the offense is an important determinant of both receiving a prison sentence and the length of the sentence (Vera Institute of Justice, 1977), the reliance on prison populations eliminates less serious offenses from consideration. Bartholomew (1968) has suggested that the relationship between alcohol use and serious crime might weaken if samples included minor offenders punished by fines or probation.

The studies show considerable variation in the percent of alcohol involvement in the criminal event. However, several patterns emerge. First, there is a tendency for percentages to be higher in studies using police reports and arrests than in prison samples. In studies drawing samples from police reports and arrest records, the median percentages of alcohol involvement are 66.3% and 66%, respectively. In contrast, the median is 43.8% in prison samples. Thus, samples selected from populations in relatively early stages of the criminal justice process show a higher rate of alcohol involvement. These conclusions are based on a small number of studies, but the evidence does nonetheless suggest that alcohol-involved cases have a higher rate of attrition than do other cases. One possible explanation for this is an increased probability of reduction of charges in cases involving alcohol. This would result in either the elimination or reduction of prison sentences, thereby reducing the number of alcohol-related crimes in prison populations.

A second pattern is the generally more consistent rates of alcohol involvement in studies selecting samples of homicide victims from medical examiner or coroner reports. These percentages are based on the presence or level of alcohol in the blood or urine. In all studies but one (Hollis, 1974), the measurements are available for victims only. This is because the test must be made within 6 hours of alcohol consumption, making it possible only for rapidly apprehended offenders. The range of percentage points was 57.7 (from 30.8% to 88.5%) in studies sampling from medical examiner or coroner's reports, compared to 94.5 (from 5.5% to 100%) in prison samples and 79 (from 9.1% to 89%) in police record samples. The percentage spread was almost identical to that in arrest samples, which ranged from 43% to 100%. One reason for the greater uniformity of results in medical examiner samples is that techniques for measuring blood or urine concentration of alcohol are more standardized than those used in the criminal justice system to measure the presence of alcohol. (The biasing effects of measurement techniques are discussed under the heading Definitions and Data Sources.) The median percentage of alcohol involvement, 64%, is most comparable to those in samples of police reports and arrests. This may be because all three sample types reflect a similar stage in the criminal justice process, prior to conviction and sentencing.

Finally, there are no consistent differences in studies using the same type of sample in alcohol involvement in crimes against persons versus crimes against property. In fact, there is more variation in percent of alcohol involvement within types of crimes than within sample types. This suggests that the emphasis on alcohol involvement in personal crimes, both in the literature and in the public view, may be unwarranted.

The evidence indicates that the type of sample used has an important effect on study results. The attrition of cases in general and alcohol-involved cases in particular in the criminal justice process appears to be a factor which influences results. This attrition rate is likely to vary between jurisdictions. Jurisdictional differences in handling alcohol-related cases therefore should be taken into account when selecting samples in future studies. Other factors that should also be considered in attempting to select a representative sample are: (1) the effect of alcohol consumption on the probability of arrest and (2) the effects of conditions associated with alcohol-related crimes, such as prior relationships between victim and offender and the location of the crime, on the rate of reporting to the police and the likelihood of arrest and conviction. It is impossible to generalize to all criminal events from any one type of sample, but more recognition should be accorded to types and amounts of bias that result from each type.

Alcoholism among Criminals

Table 2.2 summarizes the findings of 17 studies on the prevalence of alcoholism, as this is variously defined, among criminals. The percentage of criminals with chronic alcohol problems is lower on average than the percentage of alcohol-involved crimes. This would be expected since chronic alcohol abuse is much rarer than alcohol consumption. In addition, alcoholism among criminals is more prevalent among auto theft and forgery offenders than among offenders in other serious crimes. This was not the case, it will be recalled, in studies of alcohol involvement in the criminal event.

J. Roizen and Schneberk (1977a) have demonstrated that criminals show higher rates of alcoholism than the general population when comparable measurements are used. The figures in Table 2.2 support this contention. However, when Roizen and Schneberk compared general population samples that were similar to prison populations (i.e., young and male), the differences were reduced. These differences might be further reduced if samples even more representative of the known criminal population were used.

Of the 17 studies of alcoholism among criminals, all but three utilized samples selected from prisons. (The following studies selected their samples from prisons: Apfelberg, Sugar, & Pfeffer, 1944; Banay, 1942; Bartholomew, 1968; Berg, 1944; Goodwin, Crane, & Guze, 1971; Leven & Vandre, 1961; Maule & Cooper, 1966; Mayfield, 1976; Nicol *et al.*, 1973; Rada, 1975; Scott, 1968; Tripkovic, 1967; Tupin, Mohry, & Smith, 1973; and Winkler, Weissman, & McDermaid, 1954. Two studies [California Department of Public Health, 1961; Selling, 1940] utilized samples of convicted felons. One study sampled arrestees [McGeorge, 1963].) This concentration on prison inmates is likely to result in overestimation of alcoholism in the universe of criminals. Several studies show that alcoholic prisoners are more likely to be recidivists than are nonalcoholic prisoners (Bartholomew, 1968; California Department of Public Health, 1961; Miller, 1964). Other research indicates that prior criminal history is one of the most important determinants of conviction and length of sentence (Forst *et al.*, 1977; Vera Institute of Justice, 1977). Therefore, the fact that alcoholics tend to have longer criminal careers than others (though they may not necessarily commit more serious crimes) means that they are more likely to be sentenced to prison and to receive longer sentences than nonalcoholics convicted of the same crime. This supposition is supported by the findings of a study of convicted male felons, which shows that only 25% of convicted alcoholic felons received probation, compared to 50% of nonalcoholics (California Department of Public Health, 1961). But because alcoholics have a greater probability of appearing in prison popula-

TABLE 2.2. Prevalence of Alcoholism among Criminals, by Type of Crime

Percentage of alcoholic offenders	Frequency of studies										
	Homicide	Sexual offenses	Robbery	Aggravated assault	Burglary	Larceny	Auto theft	Forgery/bad checks	Unspecified violent crime	Unspecified property crime	Unspecified crime
0–10	1	2	—	—	—	1	—	—	1	—	—
11–20	—	1	2	—	2	1	—	—	—	2	—
21–30	3	2	2	2	—	—	—	—	2	1	—
31–40	1[a]	2	—	2	1	—	1	1	—	1	—
41–50	—	—	—	—	1	—	1	1	1	—	3
51–60	—	—	1[b]	—	—	—	1	—	—	—	1
61–70	—	—	—	—	—	—	—	—	—	—	—
71–80	—	—	—	—	—	—	—	—	—	—	—
81–90	—	—	—	—	—	—	—	—	—	—	—
91–100	—	—	—	—	—	—	—	—	—	—	—
TOTAL STUDIES[c]	5	7	3	2	3	2	2	1	4	4	4

[a]This study combines 80% homicide offenders and 20% aggravated assault offenders (Mayfield, 1976).
[b]This study combines robbery and assault (McGeorge, 1963).
[c]This table is based on the findings of 17 studies. The grand total does not add to 17 because some studies include data on only one type of crime, while others include two or more types of crime and therefore appear in more than one column.

88

tions does not necessarily mean that criminals have higher rates of alcoholism than individuals in the general population with similar demographic and economic characteristics. It only means that one subset of criminals has a higher rate.

There are at least two hypotheses as to why alcoholics have a higher rate of recidivism and therefore a greater likelihood of appearing in prison populations. One is that certain subsets of alcoholics actually do commit more crimes than nonalcoholics (see the following section). Another is that alcoholics, who by definition are often intoxicated, are incompetent at avoiding arrest. They may also commit a number of minor offenses and thereby bring themselves to the notice of police. This contention receives support in a study of prisoners serving sentences for armed robbery (Petersilia, Greenwood, & Lavin, 1978). It was found that alcoholic prisoners had committed the fewest total serious offenses and the lowest number of violent crimes but had the highest percentage of offenses resulting in arrests and the highest ratio of convictions per offense. A study of convicted male felons showed that alcoholics were only half as likely to receive probation as nonalcoholics even when prior arrest history was held constant (California Department of Public Health, 1961). Thus, alcoholism appears to affect the probability of appearing in prison populations, independent of the effect of recidivism. By selecting samples almost exclusively from prisons, studies of the prevalence of alcoholism among criminals are unable to separate the effects of higher recidivism and greater probability of arrest and conviction among alcoholics from an actually higher rate of alcoholism. It is recognized that the true population of criminals is impossible to sample, but greater diversity in the types of samples used would increase the validity of alcoholism prevalence estimates.

The Criminal Career of Alcoholics

Table 2.3 summarizes the findings of several studies on the previous criminal career of identified alcoholics. The percentages indicate non-alcohol-related offenses only, since alcoholics, by definition, would be expected to have high rates of arrests for drunkenness. The results indicate higher levels of criminality than are likely to exist in the general population. However, what is of principal interest is the variability of the percentages. The proportion of alcoholics with prior criminality, as this is variously defined, ranges from 10.9% to 90.7%. This reflects differences in populations of alcoholics. The highest percentage is derived from a sample of convicted felons with a drinking problem (California Department of Public Health, 1961). The lowest percentage is based on a sample of voluntary admissions to an outpatient clinic for the treatment of alcoholism

TABLE 2.3. Prevalence of Prior Criminal Activity among Alcoholics

Percentage arrested or convicted of non-alcohol-related offense	Study
10.9	Bartholomew and Kelly (1965)
11.5	Lindelius and Salum (1975)
41.7	Lindelius and Salum (1975)
76.7	Lindelius and Salum (1975)
90.7	California Department of Public Health (1961)
69.0	Pittman and Gordon (1958)

(Bartholomew & Kelley, 1965). In general, the higher percentages are based on samples of institutionalized alcoholics, that is, registered homeless men (Lindelius & Salum, 1975), convicted felons (California Department of Public Health, 1961), or men serving sentences of one or more months for public intoxication (Pittman & Gordon, 1958). The lower percentages are based on voluntary admissions for treatment, as in an outpatient clinic (Bartholomew & Kelley, 1965), a psychiatric institute (Lindelius & Salum, 1975), or a hospital ward for the treatment of acute excessive drinking (Lindelius & Salum, 1975).

The evidence suggests that there are a number of distinctly different populations of alcoholics, each with a different level and pattern of prior criminality. At one extreme are alcoholics with no higher prevalence of prior criminality than persons in the general population with similar economic and demographic characteristics (Lindelius & Salum, 1975). Samples showing these results are likely to be selected from voluntary admissions to private psychiatric hospitals or mental health clinics.

At the opposite extreme are alcoholics who are also convicted felons. Members of this population have lengthy criminal histories relative to both other populations of alcoholics and nonalcoholic convicted felons. This group may represent those with failed criminal careers. Problem drinking may have prevented a successful criminal career or may be the result of continued failure for other reasons. If there is a decline or halt in drinking, the individual may cease criminal activity (Goodwin et al., 1971). If drinking continues, the end result may be a string of arrests for chronic public drunkenness—the "revolving-door" alcoholics. This pattern is likely to develop with increasing age. Pittman and Gordon (1958) found a biphasic pattern in their sample of chronic inebriates. Multiple arrests for serious offenses seemingly unrelated to heavy drinking took place prior to age 40. After age 40, virtually all arrests were for drinking or drinking-related crimes. Thus, samples of "revolving door" alcoholics seem to reflect the population of alcoholic convicted felons who continued to drink heavily after release from prison. The former group represents a "snapshot" of the latter group at a later period in life.

An intermediate group is perhaps represented by individuals hospitalized for symptoms of acute excessive drinking. This group is characterized by males in their 20s who drink heavily and experience a variety of social problems related to drinking, including arrests for fighting, job difficulties, and an unstable home life. These problems may be a direct result of heavy drinking, but both may be caused by an underlying personality disorder or an unstable family background (Cahalan & Room, 1974; Robins & Guze, 1970; Robins, Murphy, & Breckenridge, 1968). Both drinking and crime may decline with increasing age as individuals "mature out" of antisocial behavior. A small proportion, though, may become part of a criminal subculture and engage in increasingly serious crimes. Those who fail are likely to be captured in samples of convicted felons.

Definitions and Data Sources[1]

One of the major problems in interpreting the results of studies on the role of alcohol in the criminal event or the criminal career is the lack of clarity and uniformity in definitions of crime and alcohol use. This is explained in large part by the paucity of well-defined hypotheses. The researcher is therefore provided with no guide as to how the independent and dependent variables should be operationalized, that is, what dimension of each variable should be emphasized. Thus, it is sometimes unclear whether the offender or victim has had a single drink or is on the verge of unconsciousness at the time of the criminal event, or whether a convicted felon has been intoxicated just a few times in his or her life or has sustained organ damage from chronic alcohol use. The problem is compounded by the use of different data sources, each with its own bias. Definitions and data sources are discussed together since the two are often inseparable.

The Criminal Event

The three most frequently used measures of the presence of alcohol in the criminal event are police judgment, self-reports, and the concentration of alcohol in the blood or urine. Pretrial psychiatric examinations are also

[1]This section was prepared with the assistance of Charlene Potter.

occasionally used to obtain information on the presence of alcohol in the criminal event.

Blood or urine alcohol concentration is frequently used to measure the presence or level of alcohol in victims of homicides, because victims of "all sudden, medically unattended, traumatic or potentially unnatural deaths" are automatically sent to the medical examiner's or coroner's office in most jurisdictions (Haberman & Baden, 1974). If the victim has not been dead for more than 6 hours, a test of the presence and/or level of alcohol may be made. Some studies imply that this is automatically done in all cases and give no indication of the proportion of cases in which the test is not made. Others, however, indicate that blood alcohol is measured only in those cases where alcohol is implicated as a factor in the death (Haberman & Baden, 1974).

The major advantage of this measure is that it is relatively standardized. In the preceding discussion on sampling, it was found that studies utilizing medical examiner's or coroner's reports to measure alcohol involvement in the criminal event yielded fairly uniform results. While the blood or urine alcohol concentration does not reflect physiological, psychological, and contextual differences in the effects of alcohol on behavior, it seems to be the most precise and reliable measure currently available. One disadvantage of this measure is that there is no consensus on the amount of alcohol necessary to define an individual as acting "under the influence." This is probably a result of individual variation in the effects of alcohol on behavior. Some studies define acting under the influence as .10% or above of blood or urine alcohol concentration (Haberman & Baden, 1974; Herjanic & Meyer, 1977; Shupe, 1954); others define it as .15% (Cleveland, 1955; Wilentz, 1953); another uses 150 mg per 100 ml or more (LeRoux & Smith, 1964); while another does not specify the definition (Virkkunen, 1974). This lack of consensus affects the interpretation of results since the more stringently "acting under the influence" is defined, the smaller the percentage of cases that will satisfy the criterion.

It should be noted, however, that the lack of comparability in defining intoxication is far more problematic in other measures of alcohol use. A more serious disadvantage is that the test must be done within 6 hours of alcohol consumption. This constraint makes if difficult to measure consumption in offenders, in victims of crimes other than homicide, and in victims of homicide where the body is not discovered immediately or the victim dies in the hospital. While one study found that 71% of suspects are apprehended within 30 minutes of the offense (Forst et al., 1977), substantially more time may elapse before a blood or urine test can be made. Therefore, studies using this technique are confined almost exclusively to measuring alcohol in victims. This presents an incomplete picture of the role of alcohol in the criminal event. Furthermore, it is difficult to utilize this measure in crimes other than homicide because of the difficulty in locating victims and offenders within 6 hours. Victims of homicide, a crime with a high reporting rate, are automatically sent to the medical examiner or coroner, but there is no organized means of dealing with victims of other crimes. This is particularly true for crimes with low reporting rates. The only means of circumventing the 6-hour constraint would be to equip all police officers with blood- or urine-testing kits, the feasibility and legality of which is questionable. In general, though, this method provides the most precise and reliable estimates of alcohol involvement in the criminal event.

One of the most common measures of alcohol involvement is police judgment at the time of the crime. This method has at least three major disadvantages. One is the lack of well-specified standards for defining the role of alcohol in the criminal event. Terms such as "alcohol factor," "under the influence," "present," "drinking," and "excessive drinking" are found in police reports. These terms have neither clear meaning nor comparability across studies. Furthermore, police judgment is likely to vary between situations, individual officers, and jurisdictions. A police officer's evaluation of the role of alcohol is also likely to be affected by factors unrelated to the event itself. For example, the officer may overemphasize the role of alcohol if he or she knows that an offender is an alcoholic. By the same token, if the officer knows that the victim is an alcoholic, he or she may decide that the victim provoked the crime and not make an arrest (J. Roizen & Schneberk, 1977a).

Another problem is that the role of alcohol may not be the most important piece of information that the officer must obtain. He or she may be far more concerned with obtaining information directly relevant to making a charge. Therefore, details that might be critical in determining the effect of alcohol may be omitted (Christian Economic and Social Research Foundation, 1976). The problem is aggravated when there is a long delay between the offense and the apprehension because of the difficulty in reconstructing the events. While this is the case independent of the issue of alcohol involvement, alcohol-related details may be especially spotty because of their lack of immediate relevance to the case. Police judgment is probably most valid and reliable for crimes with a high reporting rate and a short lag time between occurrence and arrest.

Finally, there may be little agreement between police and participants' judgment about the role of alcohol. A study of police intervention in family disputes found that the police concurred in less than half of the cases where the complainant alleged drunkenness on the part of the offender (Bard & Zacker, 1974). The reasons for this discrepancy are unclear. However, the sole reliance on police judgment provides only one view of the situation, a view that is often after the fact.

Pretrial psychiatric examinations suffer from many of the same problems as police judgment. There are no uniform definitions of alcohol involvement or intoxication to apply to the criminal event. The assessment of the role of alcohol in the crime may therefore vary among situations and psychiatrists. In addition, the psychiatrist may be more concerned with establishing the mental state of the accused than in obtaining information on the amount, pattern, and context of drinking by the offender and victim (East, 1939). This may result in an underestimate of the role of alcohol in the criminal event.

Self-report by offenders or victims is one of the most frequently used sources of information on alcohol involvement in the criminal event. Self-reports typically take the form of interviews by police at the time of the arrest or interviews of prisoners by social workers, psychiatrists, or researchers. Self-reports have the obvious advantage of tapping information on an event about which the respondent has first-hand knowledge. However, there are at least four major problems with this data source. One is memory decay. The greater the period of time between the event and the interview, the more spotty the report. This is particularly problematic in studies using prison samples, where there may be a considerable time lag, especially for offenders serving long sentences. A second and related problem is that the victim or offender may experience memory distortion if he or she were drinking during the event. A third problem is that the quality of the information elicited is in part a product of the quality of the questions asked. Police investigators or psychiatric evaluators of prisoners may ask only general questions concerning alcohol involvement because this is not the main purpose of their interviews. Finally, victims and offenders may have specific motives for either under- or overemphasizing the role of alcohol. J. Roizen and Schneberk (1977a) reported that victims may choose not to mention that they were drinking at the time of the offense for fear of being perceived responsible for the crime. Offenders may overemphasize the role of alcohol as a means of deviance disavowal. Aarens *et al.* (1977) stated that "a crime attributed to drunkenness may provide an agreeable explanation for that crime because it does not so strongly imply a challenge to the legal norm implied in the crime (thou should not steal) or attest to the criminal's essential deviance—the alcohol presence in the event may suggest that the act was essentially unthinking and not a reflection of the actor's enduring self" (p. 8). However, the evidence suggests that deviance disavowal is not a major source of bias in self-reports of alcohol use by offenders during the criminal event (Bartholomew, 1968; McCaghy, 1968; J. Roizen, 1977). A number of studies have been done on the related issue of the validity of self-reports of drug abuse. These studies have generally found that addict responses concerning both drug use and criminal behavior are consistent with other sources of the same information (Ball, 1967; Cox & Longwell, 1974; Maddux & Desmond, 1975; Nurco & DuPont, 1977; Stephens, 1972).

Examining the 35 studies of the role of alcohol in the criminal event, the two most common data sources in the studies of all crimes except homicide are police records and self-reports. Blood alcohol concentration is the most common source in homicide studies. Of the 35 studies, nine used self-reports (Abrahamsen, 1950; Banay, 1942; Bartholomew, 1968; Leven & Vandre, 1961; Marek et al., 1974; Matheson, 1939; Rada, 1975; Scott, 1968; Selling, 1940); nine used police records (Amir, 1967; J. L. Baker, 1959; Bett, 1946; Christian Economic and Social Research Foundation, 1976; Connor, 1973; Malik & Sawi, 1976; Pittman & Handy, 1970; Steward, 1964; Wasikhongo, 1976); ten used blood or urine alcohol concentration (S. Baker et al., 1971; Cleveland, 1955; Haberman & Baden, 1974; Harlan, 1950; Hollis, 1974; LeRoux & Smith, 1964; Shupe, 1954; Spain et al., 1951; Westermeyer & Brantner, 1972; Wilentz, 1953); three used pretrial psychiatric examinations (Cassity, 1941; East, 1939; Gillies, 1965); and four used a combination of data sources, including blood alcohol concentration, police reports, or interviews with offenders (Herjanic & Meyer, 1977; Mayfield, 1976; Virkkunen, 1974; Wolfgang & Strohm, 1956). The last three data sources—blood or urine alcohol concentration, pretrial psychiatric examination, and combination of sources—were used only in studies of homicides. (The sole exception is a study which measured the urine alcohol concentration of offenders apprehended within 6 hours of the crime [Shupe, 1954]. This study includes offenders in eight major crimes.)

Homicide studies revealing both the presence and absence of alcohol in the blood of the victim and whether the victim was under the influence of alcohol show that half or more of those with any traces of alcohol had consumed a sufficient amount to be defined as under the influence (Cleveland, 1955; Herjanic & Meyer, 1977; LeRoux & Smith, 1964; Wilentz, 1953). The same holds true in the single study of offender self-reports that measured both drinking and intoxication (Leven & Vandre, 1961). The same finding pertains in studies using self-reports of offenders in other crimes, both violent and property (Bartholomew, 1968; Leven & Vandre, 1961; Rada, 1975). This suggests that when participants in the criminal event drink, they do so to the point of drunkenness. This critical distinction is missing in 28 of the 35 studies, which measure only presence or absence of alcohol. This finding also suggests that the roles of victim and offender are emergent in the situation, rather than a clear-cut predator attacking an innocent victim.

That the roles of the victim and offender are emergent is supported by studies showing drinking and/or intoxication by both parties (Amir, 1967; Herjanic & Meyer, 1977; Hollis, 1974; Mayfield, 1976; Pittman & Handy, 1970; Virkkunen, 1974; Wolfgang & Strohm, 1956). About an equal proportion of the victims and offenders drank at the event, when alcohol was present at all. Furthermore, alcohol was present in both parties in the vast majority of cases when it was present in either (Amir, 1967; Hollis, 1974; Wasikhongo, 1976; Wolfgang & Strohm, 1956). For example, Amir found that alcohol was present in less than one-quarter of rape victims and less than one-third of rape offenders. However, it was present in both in 21% of cases. It was rare for only the victim or the offender to be drinking. Studies showing the drinking behavior of both parties have variable results, ranging from 21% in Amir's rape study to 80% in Hollis's homicide study, with most studies falling in the one-half to two-thirds range. Clearly, there are other factors at work in violent crimes. However, these studies show that when alcohol is present at all, it tends to be present in both parties. Thus, alcohol appears to be only part of a complex interpersonal dynamic rather than the sole determinant of the criminal event. Unfortunately, most studies are unable to shed much light on this dynamic because they report use of alcohol or drunkenness for only one of the two parties.

It was mentioned earlier that blood or urine alcohol concentration is usually not used to measure alcohol in the offender because of the time lag between consumption and apprehension. However, two studies, Hollis (1974) and Shupe (1954), used this technique for offenders. The former shows the percentage of homicide offenders and victims where alcohol was present, and the latter shows the percentage of offenders under the influence for each type of serious crime. The Hollis study measured the presence of alcohol in the blood of all cases of criminal homicide in Memphis, Tennessee, over an 8-year period. It was possible to measure blood alcohol in only 50 offenders who were immediately apprehended, out of a total of 372 cases. Alcohol was present in a substantially higher percentage of both victims, 82%, and offenders, 86%, than in studies which utilized blood alcohol concentration for victims only and another data source for offenders, such as police reports or self-reports (Herjanic & Meyer, 1977; Mayfield, 1976; Virkkunen, 1974; Wolfgang & Strohm, 1956). In these studies, the percentages varied between one-half and two-thirds of victims and offenders. This suggests that the offender is more likely to be immediately apprehended in cases involving alcohol (J. Roizen & Schneberk, 1977a). In fact, in the Hollis study, alcohol was present in 82% of the homicide victims in cases where the offender was apprehended within the requisite 6 hours but in only 74.1% of all homicide victims. That alcohol use decreases the offender's ability to escape detection is further supported by the results of the Shupe study. This study showed the urine alcohol concentration of individuals immediately apprehended and arrested for felonies in Columbus, Ohio, between 1951 and 1953. When the proportion of offenders under the influence of alcohol (urine alcohol of .10% or more) is compared to studies utilizing offender self-reports of intoxication, the Shupe study shows consistently higher proportions of alcohol involvement for all serious offenses. Thus, while the measurement of alcohol involvement in crimes by blood or urine alcohol concentration has several advantages, its major disadvantage is that it is likely to overestimate alcohol use when it is used for offenders. One explanation for this is the inability of drunken offenders to avoid arrest.

The potential problems with using police judgment as the data source were discussed earlier. A related and more common data source in the studies examined was the full police report. Of the nine studies relying on police records, eight used the full report, and only one (Christian Economic and Social Research Foundation, 1976) used police judgment only. The two share many of the same problems as a source of information on the role of alcohol in the criminal event, but the police report has some unique difficulties. Police reports are a combination of statements from the arresting officer, the victim, the offender, and witnesses. Each source of information may use different terms to mean the same thing or the converse. The independent variable is therefore a conglomerate of many different terms and perceptions. There is often no clear definition even within a study, let alone comparability across studies. A related problem is that each source of information—the arresting officer, the victim, the offender, and witnesses—is likely to have a different perception of the course of events and the role of alcohol in these events. Obtaining information from all relevant parties is obviously necessary for the police to reconstruct the situation. However, studies do not indicate how often information is provided by each source and discrepancies between sources. It would be particularly interesting to separate out self-reports by offenders, since police records represent an early stage in the criminal justice process prior to the selection that takes place at trial and sentencing.

Studies using self-reports to measure alcohol consumption almost invariably draw their samples from pretrial or prison populations. As was mentioned earlier, offenders in crimes with an alcohol factor may be selectively eliminated in the criminal justice process. This is likely to be the reason that self-reports yield lower estimates of alcohol involvement than do police records. This argument is supported by the results of the only study that utilized self-reports from other than prisoners or defendants prior to trial. A study by Marek *et al.* (1974) measured the alcohol consumption of robbery victims in Cracow, Poland. The proportion that was intoxicated is substantially higher than the proportion of intoxicated robbery offenders as measured in studies using prisoner self-reports (Banay, 1942; Leven & Vandre, 1961). The results of the Marek study may even be an underestimate since victims are sometimes unwilling to report that they were intoxicated at the time of the crime. The evidence therefore suggests that the use of prisoner self-reports is likely to underestimate the prevalence of alcohol in the criminal event.

In summary, there are at least four major problems with definitions of the presence of alcohol in the criminal event. First, the majority of studies report alcohol use by only one party in the event, not by both. Limiting the data to the drinking behavior of the offender only or the victim only precludes analysis of the role of alcohol in the interpersonal dynamics from which the crime emerges. This results in an extremely narrow view of the alcohol–crime relationship. Second, there is often no distinction made between the mere presence of alcohol and intoxication. This is an important difference since the evidence suggests that when alcohol is present in the criminal situation, it is often present to the point of drunkenness. Knowledge of only the presence or absence of alcohol does not distinguish this event from commonplace drinking situations in which no crime occurs. Third, the criteria used to measure drunkenness are seldom reported. This is particularly problematic in studies defining alcohol use through police records or offender self-reports. Thus, there is no way to evaluate the comparability of findings between studies. Finally, different data sources reflect distinct points in the criminal justice process. This has an impact on study findings because of the apparent selective treatment of alcohol-related cases in this process. It appears that cases with an alcohol factor are selectively weeded out of the criminal justice system. For this reason, self-reports by prisoners often show less alcohol involvement than blood or urine alcohol.

This discussion has thus far focused on problems in the measurement of alcohol use. However, definitions of crime can also be problematic. Wolfgang and Strohm (1956) state that some studies combine criminal and noncriminal homicide. This is particularly true in medical examiner and coroner reports. However, a comparison of results between studies using blood alcohol concentration that specified criminal homicides with those that combined criminal and noncriminal homicides yielded no noticeable differences. Other types of studies also combine different crimes into a single category. Murder and manslaughter are sometimes combined (Leven & Vandre, 1961); various types of violent crimes may also be undifferentiated (Mayfield, 1976; Bartholomew, 1968). J. Roizen and Schneberk (1977a) pointed out that assault is often combined with attempted assault, especially in studies using police reports. This may result in a lower estimate of the role of alcohol than would be the case if assaults actually carried out were separately examined. Finally, prison studies define crime as the crime for which the offender was convicted rather than the crime that was actually committed. It was suggested earlier that alcohol involvement sometimes results in mitigation of charges. Therefore, studies categorizing the alcohol involvement by type of crime among prisoners may combine the crime actually committed with the crime for which the offender was convicted, often a less serious version of the actual crime.

Alcoholism among Criminals

A lengthy literature has developed since the early 19th century on the definitions of alcoholism. (See Glaser, Greenberg, & Barrett, 1978, for a discussion of the history of alcoholism definitions.) A multitude of terms have been used over the years, and this diversity is reflected in studies of alcoholism among criminals. Terms such as "chronic alcoholic," "alcohol addict," "problem drinker," and "alcohol-involved" appear in these studies. Criteria used for categorizing individuals as alcoholics are rarely the same from one study to another and are sometimes not even indicated. For this reason, it is difficult to compare results among studies.

Although many vague and unrelated terms have appeared in the alcoholism literature (Siegler, Osmond, & Newell, 1968), Cahalan, Cisin, and Crossley (1969) noted that most alcohol studies are guided by three broad conceptual models of alcoholism. The first conceptual framework has been termed the "vice model." The act of drinking is considered a crime to be dealt with by formal legal sanctions, or as a bad habit requiring that the individual be treated. Second is the disease model of alcoholism which was formulated by E. M. Jellinek (1952, 1960). According to Jellinek's model, there are five distinct forms of alcoholism, only two of which qualify as a disease. Five criteria must be met in order to qualify as one of the disease types: increased tolerance to alcohol, adaptive cell metabolism, withdrawal symptoms, craving, and either loss of control over the amount of alcohol consumed during drinking occasions or inability to abstain for more than a day or two (Glaser et al., 1978). Third is the social problems model, which emphasizes the effect of drinking on the individual's personal, work, and other social relationships.

Numerous classificatory schemes, conceptual definitions, and operational indicators have emerged from these three general models. Cahalan and Room (1974) have categorized these various definitions and indicators into three general sets of variables: (1) amount, pattern, and style of drinking behavior; (2) psychological involvement of the drinker; and (3) physiological and social consequences of drinking.

Of the 17 studies of alcoholism among criminals examined in this chapter, four studies defined alcoholism in general terms such as "addicted," "alcoholic," or "intemperate" (Apfelberg *et al.,* 1944; Banay, 1942; McGeorge, 1963; Winkler *et al.,* 1954). Four defined it in terms of quantity and/or frequency (California Department of Public Health, 1961; Maule & Cooper, 1966; Selling, 1940; Tupin *et al.,* 1973). Five defined alcoholism as some combination of drinking amount and pattern, psychological involvement, and physiological and social consequences of drinking (Bartholomew, 1968; Goodwin *et al.,* 1971; Leven & Vandre, 1961; Mayfield, 1976; Rada, 1975). Four studies did not fall into any of these three categories (Berg, 1944; Nichol *et al.,* 1973; Scott, 1968; Tripkovic, 1967). Thus, almost no two studies use the same indicator or combination of indicators of alcoholism. Widely differing stages and dimensions of alcoholism are included in the definitions. Therefore, it is difficult to compare results between studies. (It is noteworthy that the range of percentages and the median percentage are very similar among the three most frequently used definitions: quantity/frequency [median of 26% with a range of 8–56%], combination measures [median of 35% with a range of 17.6–43%], and general terms such as "addiction" [median of 29.5% with a range of 12.8–45%].)

There are a number of more specific problems in addition to the general problem of lack of comparability between studies. One is that some studdies do not indicate the criteria used to categorize an individual as alcoholic. They simply state that the individual is "addicted to alcohol" or is an "alcoholic." These studies are usually based on psychiatric evaluations. It is impossible to know whether the same term is used to indicate different patterns of deviant drinking. More importantly, in diagnosing alcoholism among identified criminals, psychiatrists may use other problems in personality and social adjustment as evidence of alcoholism (Banay, 1942; Winkler *et al.,* 1954). Such problems may co-occur with alcoholism, particularly in a criminal population, but are not necessarily directly related to drinking. Criteria used to support the diagnosis of alcoholism may be more specific to drinking behavior in a noncriminal population where general adjustment problems should be less frequent.

A second and related problem is that the combination measures which include problems with interpersonal relationships as a result of drinking are almost tautological when applied to a criminal population. This is particularly true for prison samples, which comprise all but three of the studies. Bartholomew (1968) stated:

> The vast majority of prisoners have, by definition, a disturbance or interference with their inter-personal relations and their smooth social and economic functioning. Further, it can prove almost impossible to distinguish between an effect due to alcohol(ism) and one due to a basic personality disturbance that also, as one aspect of the psychopathy, involves drinking to excess. (p. 74)

One item that is almost invariably included as a problem in interpersonal functioning is arrests for public drunkenness or drunk driving. This is likely to increase the proportion of prisoners categorized as alcoholics, since, as noted in the section on sample selection, alcoholism increases the likelihood of being known to the police, which increases the probability of receiving a prison sentence for a crime. An arrest for public drunkenness or drunk driving is a likely way for an alcoholic to become known to the police. In fact, the highest percentage of alcoholism, 64%, was found in a study which used prior arrests for drunkenness as its sole criterion for alcoholism in a prison sample (Berg, 1944). Alcohol-related arrests tend to be the most common symptom of alcoholism in prison populations (Leven & Vandre, 1961; Mayfield, 1976) and in general population samples of young males (Robins *et al.,* 1968; J. Roizen & Schneberk, 1977a). The explanation for this is that young males are the most likely to drink in public and consequently have the highest risk of exposure to police (Cahalan & Room, 1974). Thus, the inclusion of alcohol-related arrests in measures of alcoholism in prison populations is likely to increase the prevalence estimates.

The Criminal Career of Alcoholics

The results of studies of the criminal history of identified alcoholics are affected by two definitional problems: (1) whether alcoholism is defined in physical or sociolegal terms and (2) whether crime is separated into alcohol-related and non-alcohol-related offenses.

Lindelius and Salum (1973) examined a sample of patients admitted to a hospital in Stockholm, Sweden, for "acute psychiatric sequels of alcohol abuse." They found that the relationship between alcoholism and criminality varied according to the definition of the former. There was no relationship when alcoholism was defined in physiological terms. Patients with the most serious physical symptoms had a lower percent of prior criminality than those with less serious symptoms. In contrast, there was a strong relationship between alcoholism and criminality when the former was defined in legal terms, the number of convictions for drunkenness. The greater the number of convictions, the more likely the individual was to have a non-alcohol-related criminal record. Definitions of alcoholism that differ in the degree to which they emphasize physical versus social symptoms are likely to reflect two distinct populations of alcoholics. The Lindelius and Salum (1973) study shows that alcoholism can reach a very advanced state in terms of physical damage with little accompanying criminality. Samples of chronic public inebriates, on the other hand, may have less physical damage but have extensive criminal records, because for some members of this group, alcoholism represents the endpoint of a failed criminal career (Pittman & Gordon, 1958). (See the section on sample selection for a discussion of sampling problems.)

The level of specificity in definitions of prior criminality can also affect results. Several studies have found that offenses directly related to drinking account for a large proportion of prior crime (Bartholomew & Kelley, 1965; Lindelius & Salum, 1975; Pittman & Gordon, 1958). For example, in a sample of chronic public inebriates, Pittman and Gordon (1958) found that public intoxication accounted for over three-fourths of all arrests, and almost one-third of the sample had never been arrested on any other charge. Another one-third of the sample had only been arrested for offenses that appeared to be related to drinking, such as disorderly conduct and vagrancy. Only one-third had ever been arrested for non-drinking-related crimes. Therefore, it is essential for studies to distinguish types of offenses when examining prior criminality of identified alcoholics to avoid the tautology of arrests for intoxication.

Problems in Analysis

The lack of a conceptual framework in most studies on the relationship between alcohol and crime was discussed in the beginning of this chapter. The absence of clearly defined hypotheses is felt throughout the research process, but it creates perhaps the most serious problems in the analysis of the data. Data analysis in much of the literature is confined to a simplistic bivariate model. Control variables and comparison groups are seldom used. This type of analysis is capable of providing only a superficial understanding of the role of alcohol in the criminal event, the prevalence of alcohol use among criminals, and the criminal career of alcoholics.

The Criminal Event

R. H. Blum (1969b) has argued that, "Rare to the point of uniqueness will be the case of the nondrinker turned criminal by a single exposure to alcohol or the case of the normal, moderate or heavy (nonproblem) drinker who, with no history of personal or social troubles, commits a criminal act when drinking" (p. 1474). Blum further posited that alcohol (and psychoactive drugs in general) may modify existing traits but does not cause any specific behavior. Nevertheless, the assumption of a single-variable, direct-cause relationship underlies the bulk of the research. This single-variable model provides little enlightenment as to how an alcohol-using situation escalates into a criminal event. This chapter does not attempt to exhaust all possible variables that should be controlled, but several general classes of variables that seem critical are discussed.

At least four general factors should be considered as relevant control variables: drinking patterns, personality characteristics, contextual effects, and norms relating to frequency and acceptability of drinking among various race, sex, and economic groups. Of the 35 studies reviewed here that examined the role of alcohol in the criminal event, 14 of them failed to include more than one independent variable. The many factors that could modify the effect of alcohol were ignored.

Twelve studies included more detail on drinking patterns than simply "present" or "absent." Most of these studies differentiated between drinking and intoxication prior to the crime. However, they provided no other relevant information on drinking patterns, such as time lag between alcohol consumption and the crime or individual variation in response to alcohol as a result of prior drinking experience or other factors. Tinklenberg (1973) has suggested that such information on drinking patterns is critical in the evaluation of the role of alcohol in crime.

Only two studies examined personality factors in conjunction with alcohol effects. These studies suggest that individuals with certain types of mental disorders are likely to become violent only when they drink, and then the violence is extreme (Selling, 1940; Skelton, 1970). In such cases, alcohol is not the single direct cause of violence. Rather there is an interaction effect between alcohol and the personality disorder.

Ten of the studies examined contextual variables, such as whether the victim and offender were both drinking, the location of the event, and the day and time. Such information can provide important clues about what differentiates drinking events that culminate in a crime, a relatively rare phenomenon, from drinking events that do not, an extremely common phenomenon. The structure of the drinking situation may determine whether the disinhibiting effects of alcohol are maximized, minimized, or even reversed. (Situational influences on the behavioral effects of psychoactive substances have been studied most frequently for amphetamine use [S. W. Greenberg, 1976].)

Norms governing the frequency, patterns, and acceptability of drinking differ by race, sex, age, and economic status. That the relationship between alcohol use and crime is strongest for young, Black, low-income males is not surprising since drinking is highly prevalent in this group. This group has many other problems as well, including a high rate of criminality. The two challenges for analysis, then, are to measure the frequency of alcohol-related crimes relative to the frequency of drinking and the frequency of criminal behavior. Unfortunately, only five studies controlled for such variables as age, sex, and race. The great majority of studies therefore provide no benchmark by which to compare the co-occurrence of drinking and crime, let alone the causal relationship between the two.

It is an unrealistic goal for research in this area to strive to prove causality. The effects of psychoactive agents on human behavior are too variable to isolate a direct causal nexus. However, the research design should enable conditional, probabilistic statements to be made. Therefore, it is necessary for the design to flow from an explicit hypothetical model of the relationships between alcohol use, the criminal event, and other variables that are expected to modify this relationship.

Alcoholism among Criminals

There are at least three major analysis issues in the study of the prevalence of alcoholism among criminals: (1) delineation of the role of chronic alcoholism versus acute excessive alcohol use in the criminal event, (2) selection of an appropriate comparison group, and (3) analysis of the role of alcoholism from the perspective of the criminal career.

Of the 17 studies of alcoholism among criminals, only four examined drinking behavior during the criminal event (Banay, 1942; Mayfield, 1976; D. P. Miller, 1964; Rada, 1975). All four studies found that the great majority of alcoholics, between two-thirds and 100%, were drunk during the crime. The Mayfield, Miller, and Rada studies report far lower percentages among nonalcoholics. (Unfortunately, the Banay study measured drinking during the crime among "primary intemperates" but not among the rest of the sample.) However, this is not unexpected since alcoholics are more likely to be drunk at any given time than nonalcoholics. In addition, Mayfield found that over one-third of the alcoholics who were drunk at the crime thought their drunkenness was irrelevant to the crime. The problem for analysis, then, is to examine whether alcohol plays a different role in the criminal event for alcoholics and nonalcoholics. This necessitates the comparison of criminal behavior between the two groups both when intoxicated and when sober. In this way, the incremental effect of intoxication on crime can be measured and compared. Any difference between the two groups in this incremental effect may be attributed to the effect of alcoholism, assuming other differences between the two groups have been controlled. The existing research, however, either ignores the frequency of intoxication among alcoholics during the crime or measures it only for the crime for which the individual was arrested or imprisoned.

The second problem is the selection of an appropriate comparison group. The prevalence of alcoholism appears to be far higher among criminals than in the general population. However, when J. Roizen and Schneberk (1977a) compared similar measures of alcoholism between a sample of prisoners and a general population sample of males under age 40, the differences were substantially reduced. But even limiting the general population sample to young males may not provide a sufficiently comparable group. Race, economic status, and urban or rural residence are variables affecting both the probability of alcoholism and imprisonment. Comparison groups should take these factors into account. It is likely that differences in alcoholism between prisoners and the general population would be further reduced, would perhaps even disappear, if subgroups within general population surveys were better matched to prison samples.

The third analysis problem is that few studies view alcoholism within the context of the criminal career (Collins, Chapter 5, this volume). Goodwin *et al.* (1971) found that juvenile delinquency was more common among alcoholic than nonalcoholic felons. Robins and Guze (1970) found that Black males living in an urban ghetto were more likely to become alcoholics if they were first arrested as teenagers. This suggests that criminality precedes alcoholism. However, once an individual is imprisoned for a crime, continued excessive use of alcohol increases the probability of subsequent arrests (Goodwin *et al.,* 1971). While these studies offer insight into alcoholism as one outcome of early deviance and as a factor in continued criminality, more information is needed on its role in the criminal career. Differences in career patterns of alcoholic and nonalcoholic criminals should be compared. The bulk of the current research reflects only the presence or absence of drinking problems at some point in the past among imprisoned criminals. A career perspective necessitates the collection of longitudinal data that can capture the interplay between criminal and drinking behavior as they both progress through time. Also important to know is the nature of the relationship between alcoholism, family and job problems, and the course of the criminal career. Differential access to criminal opportunities should also be considered. For example, D. P. Miller (1964) found, in a sample of convicted felons, that forgery was the most common offense among White alcoholics, robbery was most common among Black alcoholics, and narcotics offenses were most common among Mexican-American alcoholics. This reflects the relative economic positions of Blacks and Whites and the greater access of Mexican-Americans to the major source of heroin in the United States. Other studies (Christian Economic and Social Research Foundation, 1976; Pittman & Gordon, 1958) indicate that drunkenness charges as a proportion of total offenses increase with age. More lucrative criminal opportunities may be closed to older alcoholics because of continued failure at crime, analogous to what might occur in the legitimate occupational world.

The end result of the analysis of criminal careers should be the delineation of a typology of roles that alcoholism plays in criminality, from the petty criminal whose illegal activities are an outgrowth of the skid row sub-culture to the individual whose alcoholism followed a long criminal history.

The Criminal Career of Alcoholics

The data analysis in this area tends to be the most comprehensive and care-fully controlled of the three types of studies. The work by Lindelius and Salum (1973, 1975) and Pittman and Gordon (1958) takes particular care to examine differences in number and types of crime by age group. These studies show that arrests, particularly for non-alcohol-related crimes, are highest among alcoholics below age 40. The rate of arrest for nonalcohol offenses is lower in older age groups at a given point in time and also de-creases as individual alcoholics grow older. Some alcoholics may become chronic public inebriates as an adaptation to a failed criminal career, as Pittman and Gordon suggest. Others may "mature out" of both crime and heavy drinking and hence no longer appear in samples of identified al-coholics. Age is thus an essential control variable in the study of the rela-tionship between alcoholism and the criminal career. (See Collins, Chap-ter 5, this volume, for more elaboration on this point.)

Another relevant control variable is the way the alcoholic is officially identified. Alcoholics labeled as such through the criminal justice system —as public inebriates (Pittman & Gordon, 1958), vagrants (Lindelius & Salum, 1975), or convicted felons (California Department of Public Health, 1961)—have longer and more serious criminal histories than those who are medically or psychiatrically identified (Bartholomew & Kelley, 1965; Lindelius & Salum, 1973, 1975). This suggests that there are multiple populations of alcoholics, each with a different relationship to criminality.

An issue that has been neglected in this literature is the comparison of career patterns among criminal and noncriminal alcoholics. Pittman and Gordon infer the role of alcoholism in one type of criminal career by trac-ing arrest patterns over time. Comparable analyses of the role of alcohol-ism in noncriminal careers could also trace changes in significant career points.

Summary and Conclusions

Research on the relationship between crime and alcohol use is divided into three major categories: (1) the role of alcohol in the criminal situation, (2) the prevalence of alcoholism among criminals, and (3) the criminal history of alcoholics. This chapter discusses how problems in each step of the research process—hypothesis formation, sample selection, definitions of alcohol use and crime, and data analysis—affect study results in these three areas.

The vast majority of studies in the alcohol–crime literature have been carried out in the absence of clearly defined hypotheses. Because studies are usually couched in terms of bivariate models, they are usually inadequate in addressing such questions as: What differentiates criminal events where alcohol is merely present from those where it plays an active role in the crime? What factors distinguish the vast majority of drinking situations that do not culminate in a crime from those that do? Does alcoholism exert an effect on the criminal event independent of excessive drinking at the time? What roles do alcohol use and alcoholism play in the criminal career?

The major source of sample bias is the selection of criminals or alcoholics that have been identified as such by an agency of social control. Prisons are the most frequent source of samples for studies of the use of alcohol in the criminal event; this biases findings in favor of more serious crimes. Prison samples may also underestimate the prevalence of alcohol use in the criminal event because of the apparent weeding out of alcohol-related cases in the criminal justice process.

Prison samples are used almost exclusively in studies of alcoholism among criminals. This is likely to result in an overestimation of alcoholism among criminals. Alcoholic criminals have a greater probability of appearing in prison samples than do nonalcoholic prisoners, owing in part to higher rates of recidivism and greater probability of arrest and conviction.

The extent of criminality among alcoholics is highly dependent on the nature of the sample used. Alcoholics selected from prisons or chronic police case inebriates have higher rates of criminality than those selected from psychiatric hospitals or mental health clinics. The evidence suggests that there are a number of different populations of alcoholics, each with a different level and pattern of prior criminality.

There is considerable variability in definitions of alcohol use and alcoholism in the alcohol–crime literature. This makes it difficult to compare results among studies. The evidence on alcohol use in the criminal event suggests that when alcohol is present, it is present in both the victim and the offender, usually to the point of drunkenness. Unfortunately, most studies do not distinguish between drinking and drunkenness, and typically measure consumption for only one of the two parties. Thus, they are unable to examine the structure of interaction that precedes the crime, of which alcohol is only a part. Defining alcohol use by blood or urine alcohol concentration yields the most uniform results. However, it overestimates the alcohol factor when used for offenders, perhaps because intoxicated offenders are the most likely to be immediately apprehended. Studies defining alcohol use by police reports are difficult to interpret because the criteria for determining drunkenness are not well specified, and police reports are a conglomerate of several sources of information. Studies using offender self-reports yield lower estimates of alcohol involvement than do studies using police reports because the former usually use prison samples. Offenders in alcohol-related crimes seem to be selectively weeded out of the criminal justice system prior to imprisonment.

Virtually no two studies of the prevalence of alcoholism among criminals use the same definition of alcoholism. In addition, they often do not specify the criteria used to identify individuals as alcoholics. The inclusion of alcohol-related arrests in measures of alcoholism in prison populations tends to increase prevalence estimates.

Studies of the criminal history of alcoholics that define alcoholism in terms of social or legal problems related to drinking yield higher proportions of prior criminality than those defining alcoholism in terms of physical problems. It is important for studies to specify type of crime in the criminal history of alcoholics because drinking-related crimes comprise a large proportion of prior offenses.

Data analysis in much of the literature is confined to a simplistic bivariate model. In examining the role of alcohol in the criminal event, at least four sets of factors should be considered as possible control variables: drinking patterns, personality characteristics, contextual effects, and norms relating to the frequency and acceptability of drinking among various race, sex, and economic groups. Over one-third of the studies in this area failed to control for any of these factors.

Three of the major analysis issues in the study of the prevalence of alcoholism among criminals are the delineation of the role of chronic alcoholism versus acute excessive use in the criminal event, the selection of appropriate comparison groups, and the analysis of the role of alcoholism in the criminal career. This last is also an important issue in the study of criminality among alcoholics. The career perspective has received relatively slight attention in the study of both alcoholism among criminals and criminality among alcoholics.

In conclusion, there are many challenges to future research in the alcohol–crime area in view of the existing methodological problems. We would like to suggest a few general directions for further methodological development. First, relevant theories relating to the effect of alcohol on human behavior must be more firmly integrated into future research. Testable hypotheses or models could then be constructed. This would provide a much needed guide for the selection of appropriate samples, definitions of crime and alcohol variables, and inclusion of control variables.

Second, utilization of more than one type of data collection technique should be considered, for example, examination of police records in combination with a general population survey of drinking patterns and problems, and an ethnography of social interaction in taverns. This would not reduce the biases inherent in each technique, but it would allow "weight of the evidence" statements to be made based on multiple data sources.

Third, the general alcohol literature that deals with definitions of alcohol use and abuse could be more carefully examined for its utility in alcohol–crime studies. This literature could be used for the specific dimensions of alcohol use that are most relevant to a given research question in the alcohol–crime area. Finally, research should be designed in such a way that the end result is a set of conditional statements on the role of alcohol in the criminal event or a typology of ways in which alcohol and crime are interrelated throughout the life course.

3 Violence, Alcohol, and Setting: An Unexplored Nexus

RICHARD H. BLUM

Introduction

The topic addressed here is the interrelationship among alcohol, violence, and environmental events. The specific question is, What is known about the role of situational factors which refines one's understanding of that violent human conduct which simultaneously appears associated with alcohol? Implicit is the assumption that situational factors do play a role in violence per se, and that when alcohol is also present, they continue to be influential. Just how?

Violence in this context is to be understood as that physically harmful behavior (one person to another) which is criminal. Our interest here excludes traffic criminality. The "presence" of alcohol is defined both immediately and as an antecedent; that is, alcohol present in the body, alcohol being used in the situation, or a history of alcohol consumption that is sufficient to have warranted a person's tagging (e.g., an alcoholic). Situation or environment means immediate influences on conduct, which are matters of setting, context, specific stimuli, or (phenomenologically) meanings attached thereto. We are forewarned by the definitions: What might appear at first glance as straightforward is a barrel of worms, slippery wigglers typical of the human sciences of our times; we are dealing with specificities imposed on general structures, common language manipulated in the hope of finding a cohesive referent somewhere therein, determinants bravely designated and quickly transformed into something more than an operational event. It is the curse of current criminology.

This chapter does not itself offer a review of that growing literature independently dealing with violence per se, with alcohol as an influence on conduct, and it but illustrates stimuli known to affect aggressive behavior. With respect to the role of alcohol in violence generally, attention is called to reviews which summarize the state of knowledge and perplexity.

RICHARD H. BLUM. American Lives Endowment, Portola Valley, California.

With respect to an early and general review of the violence literature, refer to the Report of the National Commission on the Causes and Prevention of Violence, *Crimes of Violence* (Mulvihill & Tumin, 1969; Mulvihill, Tumin, & Curtis, 1969); Volume 12 concerns explanations of individual violence, and Volume 13 comprises appended reports, including Good (1969), McClearn (1969), Ervin (1969), Megargee (1969), and Chodorkoff and Baxter (1969). A work which also reviews, arguing the sociological perspective, is Wolfgang and Ferracuti's *The Subculture of Violence* (1967).

Dealing specifically with the relationship between alcohol and violence, or necessarily alcohol and aggression, since much that is inferred about violence derives from work traveling under aggression's auspices, are several praiseworthy works. Nathan and Lisman (1976) succinctly inspect behavioral determinants of drinking and, conversely, alcohol's effects on aggressive behavior. Pernanen (1976) examines the relationship of alcohol to crimes of violence, including thoughtful analyses of problems of logic and design. J. Roizen and Schneberk (1977a) also review the alcohol-crime relationship. Each of these is a solid piece of work cognizant of situational variables, those that receive but minor attention in that much more extensive literature which neither alludes to nor elucidates the situational context. The reader interested in the alcohol–crime relationship will attend to these reviews as well as to Tinklenberg's (1973) work.

Premises

Basic to an examination of the role of situational factors in alcohol-associated violent criminality is a biological precept. That precept, treated as fact, constitutes an essential feature in the definition of living matter. That which is alive is irritable. It responds to changes in its external environment. It, conceived now in terms of levels and locales of organization, responds to changes in its inner environment. Much of that responsiveness is adaptive, that is, facilitates survival in itself or, teleologically, furthers life itself, including those activities which are or become aspects of being alive. This is a Darwinian, functional premise.

Any environmental event may be considered as having possible stimulus qualities, that is, eliciting some change within the organism. All environmental events, given dynamic field theory, will have effects on living matters, even though these effects may not be responses as such; that is, they may not involve an organized, "planned" reaction, being adaptive or directing. Simultaneously, granting field theory, the organism by its presence and reactions is both part of and affects its environment. Life and its environment are, then, to be viewed contextually, or in a more partist mode, in dynamic interaction.

Be this so, there will be for humans engaged in criminal violence no conduct which is not environmentally influenced and sustained, or without its own environmental effects.

Drugs

Drugs are defined as chemical agents which affect living protoplasm. Such changes necessarily affect the capacities of organisms to detect, organize, and generate responses to the environment (internal and external), and to changes in that environment. Since environments are changed or constant depending upon temporal and structural criteria employed in the judgment, drugs affect response to stimuli and, in interaction, affect the environment. The drug is an element in the environment–organism context necessarily affecting that context, with its action, in turn, being affected. Alcohol is but one such chemical and can be expected, when present in an alcohol-sensitive organism, to affect all events occurring therein. Applied to human violence, the theory disallows any violent behavior not affected by the element of alcohol present in that context.

Focus and Measures

The foregoing theory, as perspective, is neat. Tests and measures of it are not, nor is empirical knowledge advanced if one but meditates upon contented gestalts or field theory unifications. One is moved instead to specificity, that is, to explicit levels of organization and events, and to the identification of overt and inferred variables therein. Yet there are dilemmas inherent in specificity, in application of scientific method (much of it borrowed from physical models) to the human condition. As specificity increases—for example, through operational definitions and controlled observations—one tends toward reductionism. As observations are made upon substrates, the capacity to generalize to higher orders of integration is impeded. One solution is to entertain only limited observations made at various levels of focus, not assuming that knowledge is better served by either the more reductionist (partist) or holistic, higher-level conceptual schemes.

Because levels of interests have themselves generated loyalties to subsets of scientific ideology, disputes about knowledge have arisen which offer differing conceptions of truth. Applied to the multiple and disparate phenomena of violence, there appears a current commitment to several foci which, although sometimes argued as such, are not exclusive and incompatible. If one assumes that knowledge can arise from (or indeed consists of) several levels of observation, that empirical verification derives from intuitive insights, and that, contrariwise, insight as integrative schema evolves from an empirical process, one does not exclude as data about the world any abstractions arising from various sources and kinds of observations. With respect to violence, such diversity is the current state of knowledge. Certainly systematization now for the purposes of "closure" is premature.

Psychopharmacological Premises

Because of the limited data in the alcohol field, and because of the tendency of psychopharmacology and alcohol studies to be separate, it is well to derive some general principles from the former, more general field to illustrate what may be found in the latter, which is a subdiscipline—in theory but not in practice.

One begins with general premises, probabilities, as follows. Any compound which affects the central nervous system (CNS) affects response capabilities for complex social behavior. Drug action affects specific neurohumoral subsystems differentially and thus the social behavior which they may mediate. No psychoactive drug itself is a "cause" of complex human behavior; yet any drug is likely to modify that complex behavior, although such modification need not be constant over time, since processes of adaptation, sensitization, interaction, and the like occur. Insofar as drugs are administered which allow "normal" behavior to continue, the role of a compound is necessarily but one element affecting that behavior; as dosage increases such that visible limitations on the behavior repertoire occue (e.g., motor decrement, reduced information processing, sedation, coma, death), the contribution of the drug is seen to be the greater. These instances of decreased functional capability are generally of least interest to social/behavioral scientists. In consequence the observer interested in complex events, as, for example, interpersonal violence, will have the task of identifying and measuring more modest effects, those that interact with neurophysiological processes as well as social behaviors.

Illustrative Findings

Measures of aspects of performance that can fluctuate readily, such as mood, tend to be psychoactive drug sensitive. Relatively stable aspects of performance, such as IQ or personality, are more drug resistant. The nature of the task will be differentially related to drug impact (e.g., speed is more drug sensitive than accuracy). Delayed feedback tasks are more sensitive than are immediate feedback tasks. Complex tasks are more sensitive than simple ones (Joyce, 1971). Drug effects vary with motivation and incentives (Hills, Belleville, & Wikler, 1957). Drugs act differentially on motivation–incentive systems. Persons self-administering may select drugs compatible with ongoing or preferred arousal states. These preferences, selections, and states may, in turn, be culturally imposed (Carstairs, 1954). Specific psychoactive drugs may then be selected to be ego syntonic because of their known specific and expected nonspecific effects. Even so, the results may be damaging rather than ego syntonic.

A gross category of behavior—for example, aggression—may be altered by a drug or drugs acting differentially on mediating events or subsystems. For example, a drug may trigger aggression, check already triggered acts, alter responses to trigger stimuli, or change levels of arousal or (otherwise measured) aggression levels (Welch, 1969).

Further, the behavior of one person under study can be affected by drugs taken by any others present, whether or not the subject is him/herself experiencing drug administration (Joyce, 1965; Nowlis & Nowlis, 1956; Starkweather, 1959).

Settings affect response. Subjects given LSD in a laboratory showed more unusual behavior than when doing errands around town (Vojtechovsky, Safratova, & Havrankova, 1972). An unusual drug response may occur primarily because of social conditions interacting with a subject trait.

Psychoactive compounds, be they exogenous or endogenous, tend not to trigger specific emotional states but affect levels of arousal and associated readiness systems. A person's interpretation of these nonspecific effects is, in turn, affected by nondrug factors such as expectations, learning, environmental cues, and the like (Schachter, 1964; Schachter & Singer, 1962; Schachter & Wheeler, 1962). Cognition of drug effects in the situational context may be central to the self-definition of drug-related emotions and to emerging behavior.

Judgment in a situation, upon which subsequent interpretations of drug nonspecific effects and emerging social behavior depend, may itself be enhanced or impaired by a drug's specific effects (Gillis, 1975), and task structure itself is important in determining the effects a psychoactive drug has. Interpersonal judgments—for example, estimates of what another person will do—are differentially affected by different drugs, even though these drugs may have other similar specific effects, and are simultaneously affected by the predrug consistency of the person's approach to problems (Zachariadis & Varonos, 1975). Thus, those judgments affecting social behavior arise from stable and unstable cognitive styles, and from the kind of drug present.

Specific drug effects are, generally, a function of dosage, of dose–response curves over time, frequency and manner of administration, and concurrent psychological and physiological status of the subject. For some functions and some drugs, curves of performance are other than straight line (e.g., biphasic, reversing, and so forth). Alcohol has a number of nonlinear effects.

The nature of the experience reported by a subject as drug related can vary strongly with the setting; meanings and perceptions can vary as a function of the drug's specific effects and as a response to meanings imposed by a situation—for instance, instructions from others, proposed interpretations of nonspecific effects, mood-affecting physical surroundings, and the like. The opportunity for more varied behavior under novel drug conditions appears to increase (become less predictable) when the setting is less structured. Contrariwise, the more institutional the setting— clear roles, evident authority, traditional meanings, restricted opportunities for alternative interpretations—the more likely is drug-associated behavior to be predictable (R. H. Blum, 1969b; R. H. Blum & Associates, 1964).

While there are no social conduct outcomes—acute or chronic—of psychoactive drug use which are not influenced by the salient social environment, it is also the case that drug-related responses depend upon individual characteristics, enduring or transient. These range from matters of neuropathology to personality and delinquency, to interests or cognitive styles. Such neurophysiological and personality variables are, in turn, the product of genetic, developmental, social, and other forces. From drug interactions themselves, through (inferred) neurohumoral status (e.g., endogenous depression), to traits such as anxiety or hostility, there are relatively consistent individual factors which operate to affect drug responses in predictable ways. These predetermining, consistent, or "predisposing" individual features are not to be viewed as creating (as long as a varied response repertoire is available) a passive subject. Humans, when self-administering drugs, select their environments for drug use, select drugs with preferred effects, select stimuli or cues to which to respond as part of the imposition of meanings on situations, plan their strategies for living to include drugs, and may "choose" their drug responses. The presence of a drug may, in turn, impede, alter, or enhance any of these individual selective actions. Selection presumes anticipation, of which learned cues are a part. Learning, then, affects drug choices and drug reactions.

Implications for Alcohol and Violence

The foregoing suggests that the following "principles" will apply to the role of alcohol and setting in violent behavior.

Under no circumstances will alcohol be a sole "cause" of violence. Alcohol may alter perceptions, cognitive performance, moods/emotions, and response capabilities and preferences. Less adaptive solutions, such as violence, can occur with decrements in judgment. Violence may also be adaptive, or perceived as such. Meanings imposed on the environment may change. Violence variability may be a function of cues that are subliminal to the observer but are notably altered perceptions within the person. One expects that violence will occur when both preexisting and situational factors stimulate, facilitate, or permit it. Violence in association with alcohol may vary with dosage and, in turn, with pharmacologically specific effects including arousal levels, cognitive deficits, and psychological reactions to such changes (e.g., anxiety). Variability in the form, target, and frequency of violence is thus to be expected.

Interaction Effects

Genuine interaction effects (drug with person and setting) are to be distinguished from nondemonstrable attributions, as for example, when alcohol is used to justify or excuse behavior which occurs independent of any pharmacological drug effect. The symbolic functions of drugs can be paramount in conduct which is itself strongly invested with symbols and emotions, as violence is. Alcohol's specific effects will be dose related, although dosage effects vary within and among individuals; but nonspecific effects, including social behaviors, need not be dose related. (Two sets of social behaviors which should be dose related are those which rest upon state-dependent learning and drug-specific reactions in others present in the situation.) Since violence is symbolically laden, one does not expect violence to show a regular relation to dosage, although extreme dosages should prevent, because of ataxia, any effective perpetrations of harm on stronger targets.

Individuals tend to show fairly consistent conduct styles (dependent on age epochs, roles, personality), but at the same time people experience a variety of situations. Therefore, the measure of intraindividual consistency in violence is not simply a temporal one but must look for constancy in settings, their meanings, self-generated or imposed. Since violence is a rare event, even among violent individuals (whereas drinking is common), one expects the stimuli to violence to be rare combinations of inner states, outer stimuli, contexts, and meanings.

Alcohol Settings and Violence

There is no reason to search for situational factors associated with alcohol and emergent violence unless one is convinced that an association between alcohol and violence itself is demonstrated. Further, granting that alcohol is never the "sole cause of violence," one wants to know, before searching for setting variables, that violence itself is in part situationally (and variably) precipitated. One then asks but a few refining questions. Does alcohol really play a role in violence, or does violence occur in response to situational or other forces, where the presence of alcohol is but coincidental (i.e., correlative but not an active necessary antecedent)? If alcohol does play an antecedent (causal) role, is it independent of or does it interact with situational variables? If both, has one been able to disentangle them, or is it wiser to examine contexts rather than variables teased from contexts and observed artificially by experiment? Pernanen (1976) wisely has discussed such relationships more formally and elaborately in terms of explanatory models, speaking of direct-cause, conjunctive, conditional, interactive, and common-cause relationships, and of intervening variables. Siu's (1979) proposal is not to be taken lightly: that all pharmacological *in vitro* studies should include a statistical inference not only on the probability of chance, p_c (e.g., $p_c < .05$), but on the probability of irrelevancy, p_i, which is defined as the likelihood of being accurately generalizable to real life. What is the p_i of the studies we are reviewing here?

First, with reference to alcohol and violence, where do we stand? Certainly there is a long history of observation. The earliest records, those of Pharaoh's Egypt, attended to those psychomotor consequences of drinking which increased susceptibility to others' violence (drunks, being unable to defend themselves, were robbed) or decreased to ability to be violent effectively (Pharaoh's soldiers were prohibited from drinking before going into battle) (R. H. Blum, 1969b). Only recently has alcohol's role as the, or in the, violent offender become a dominant concern.

That concern is, with strong qualifications, justified. Pernanen (1976), taking stock, has offered the following conclusions:

1. Alcoholics may have a greater risk of being apprehended by the police. . . .

2. Due to the higher risk of acute use of alcohol at any time, alcoholics are at a higher risk of displaying violent behavior, whatever the appropriate causal models of a situational nature.

3. Prolonged excessive alcohol use may be connected with predispositional attributes that increase the probability of aggressive behavior in connection with acute alcohol use. . . .

4. Prolonged excessive alcohol use may . . . give rise to predispositional changes in the individual, which outside of any alcohol use situations, increase the probability of violent behavior. An example is brain damage, especially of an epileptiform character.

5. Prolonged excessive alcohol use may be conjunctively [not causally] connected with alcohol use patterns that also in nonalcoholics may give rise to states of the organism that increase the likelihood of aggressive behavior. Poor nutritional habits when drinking may lead to hypoglycemia and binge drinking may lead to REM-sleep deprivation. Both conditions by themselves increase

the likelihood of violent behavior. In addition, there may be an interactive effect with alcohol use.

6. "Alcohol use" may indicate different variables for alcoholics and nonalcoholics, so that alcoholics . . . display alcohol use . . . that could show a comparatively strong relationship to violent behavior.

7. Prolonged excessive users of alcohol may, due to developmental or genetic factors, belong to a subpopulation that through a common cause, such as early childhood experiences or affective disorder, shows a higher probability of antisocial behavior and among these, violent behavior.

8. A large proportion of excessive alcohol users are subjected to societal and interpersonal reactions . . . [forcing them] into subcultures where violent behavior is condoned, expected, or technically necessary for functioning. (pp. 435–436)

Alcohol, as Pernanen sees it, is implicated in violence—but causally so only in interaction with personal predispositions to aggression, as sources of neuropathology that are in turn conducive to violent outbursts, possibly in interaction with life-style-association physiological substrates which produce irritability, and because the drinker may be precipitated into violent subcultures. Pernanen rejects a simple, direct-cause relationship, for example, as an aggression disinhibitor.

J. Roizen and Schneberk (1977a) have focused not on violence but on crime, although violent acts figure strongly in the crime statistics in which, in turn, alcohol plays a visible (even if uncertain) role. They argue that the number of scientists arguing for direct and simple relationships between alcohol and crime has decreased as the complexity of logic and the sophistication of designs and statistical inference have increased. Roizen and Schneberk hold that—given the complexity of the phenomena, the neglect of theory, the wealth of data, and the confounding interrelationships— one is forced to "multifactorial, complex explanations of the relationship between drinking and crime." They observe:

The presence of alcohol in homicide events appears . . . to be related to weapon use, degree of violence and victim precipitation. . . . Determining the interrelations among these contextual variables is not possible with available data. (p. 359)

Factually:

Victim precipitation is much more prevalent in the alcohol-present homicides than in the alcohol-absent homicides. . . . Effects related to the time of day, the actions of the victims, the presence of alcohol, all appear to play a role in criminal events. (pp. 362, 364)

They infer that there are crimes where the offender "commits the act with knowledge of the increased risk coming from having been drinking"

(p. 369). That risk, presumably, is related to demonstrable alcohol effects—impaired performance, decreased judgment, intensified moods (e.g., anger), or possible "dyscontrol" ("pathological intoxication") associated with brains abnormality. And, overall:

> That some kinds of criminal activity are partially or wholly a function of, or exacerbated by, the presence of alcohol in the situation is not disputed. . . . What is at issue is determining the amount and kind of criminal behavior that is a tangible consequence of drinking alcoholic beverages. (p. 292)

To this point, then, relying on the reviewers (including Blum, 1969b), one does conclude that alcohol can play a role in violence. In some instances it is directly implicated as one of the multiple antecedents, but explication of when and how and how much is incomplete. As Sobell and Sobell (1975) note, "Research exploring the relationship of drinking to violent crimes is . . . neglected."

Toch (1969) studied violent people by studying violent incidents, constructing a typology of violent men. Alcohol is frequently present, for example, among those assaulting policemen. The state of mind prior to the incident may well feature anticipation, planning of the forthcoming action, particularly among those who have learned that violence is a successful form of self-expression, defense, or exploitation. Toch holds that alcohol's importance varies situationally, and that typically it leads to exaggerated responses, produces risk by making the drinker more conspicuous to others, reduces accuracy of judgment of the risks in being violent, and/or augments the joy in impulse and aggression (cf. Neitzsche and Ruth Benedict's Dionysian modes, or the barroom brawls on television). Toch views his violent-prone sample as psychologically defective persons predisposed to react to particular triggering situations. Alcohol serves as one contextual element, generally one that increases violence risk.

Alcohol and Aggression

Attention to alcohol and violence concerns real drinkers in the real world of crime, given impetus by researchers such as Wolfgang (1958) and Virkkunen (1974). In experiments, convention has it that the violence equivalent is aggressive behavior. Attention to that experimental literature brings us one step closer to the alcohol–setting–violence relationship, elucidating at least experimental elements. One must be warned that aggression measures may not intercorrelate, that there is no simple referent for the clinical and experimental concept of aggression (Antons, 1970).

Nathan and Lisman (1976) offer a lucid presentation of that literature, beginning, appropriately, with the conclusions of conflicting earlier reviewers. Carpenter and Armenti (1972) found for the role of alcohol as precipitating aggression; Bennett, Buss, and Carpenter (1969) did not. Nathan and Lisman found the literature (to that date) equivocal. They cautiously accepted evidence to the effect that distilled spirits, blood alcohol levels, are associated with increasing aggression, but that expectations play a powerful role. They concluded that laboratory aggression measures are unsure and noted that blood alcohol levels achieved are often so low that they shed no light on conduct by heavy consumers, among whom alcoholics are presumed to be numbered.

When blood alcohol content (BAC) is very high (Nathan, Titler, Lowenstein, Solomon, & Rossi, 1970), alcoholics on an observation ward "usually" became psychotic and violent; marked psychomotor deficits (ataxia), however, vitiated any harm that could be done to others. Unfortunately, and typically, one does not know if under other environmental conditions violence may not have emerged. The two identified conditions here, solitary and group, did not differentially affect violence.

Feldman (1977), concluding his overview, is also cautious, suggesting that expectations and the drinker role are demonstrable links to aggression and acknowledging that alcohol may "potentiate an existing aggressive response." He doubts that it creates a response not already at hand predispositionally.

Aggression Per Se

The laboratory literature, extant in psychology since the introductory studies of the "frustration–aggression" theory, rarely provides studies attending simultaneously to alcohol and situational variables in aggression.

One does learn that by varying environmental stimuli, one alters the appearance or expression of aggression. These demonstrations fortify the expectation that alcohol and settings may together—in interaction, conditionally, separately but additively—facilitate that which is in fact incapable of experimental, adjudicated study, namely, criminal violence.

We find, for example, that aggression is affected by learning. A person seeing an earlier aggressive model copies that; if one is emotionally aroused just prior to seeing such an aggressive model, response levels are increased (Hicks, 1965; Nelson, Gelfand, & Hartmann, 1969). Further, such learning is a function of success; Bandura (1973) has shown that aggressive modeling follows the successful aggression of the example (see also R. Epstein, 1966). Further, when the aggression can be justified by reference to the actions of someone else, it is more likely to continue (Bandura, 1973). Modeling effects (copying) are lessened if there is an already high level of anger or when there is risk of retaliation (Baron, 1971; Baron & Kepner, 1970). When a weapon is present it will be a more powerful stimulant when emotional arousal is already obtained (Berkowitz, 1974). Arousal itself—an impetus to action as well as to learning (Cofer & Appleby, 1964)—is, in turn, induced by the observation of fighting (Zillmann, 1971); and that, in turn, augments aggressive responding, so that a reverberating process, escalation, obtains (Tannenbaum, 1972). The sympathetic nervous system arousal levels rise directly with overt aggression (Geer & Buss, 1962; Taylor, 1967).

Additional studies adduced by Geen and Berkowitz (1966) are confirmatory, suggesting that aggression itself is a stimulus to further aggression, that prior arousal facilitates the priming process, that successful aggression (by others) feeds new aggression, and that the action of others available for justifying aggression stimulates it more intensely. Aggression by others directed at a subject, by provocation or intended hurt, induces counteraggression, and this increases with the intensity of the attack received or perceived as intended. The response process is, however, mediated by personality variables so that persons rated ordinarily as overcontrolling are less aggressive than undercontrollers.

Both situational and trait factors affect aggression (Kaufmann & Marcus, 1965). When an experimental companion is characterized as similar to subjects with valued traits, as contrasted to being dissimilar, aggression is higher toward the unlike person. At the same time, subjects rated as characterologically more hostile show the greater aggression. Berkowitz and Geen (1967) also showed that the target's "cue value" is a situational influence. Berkowitz (1964) holds that anger arousal does create a readiness to act, which, in the presence of suitable cues, will be expressed. If expression is externally constrained temporarily and then constraints are removed, aggression will be stronger than if not inhibited. For aroused subjects, aggression in the absence of costs is rewarding.

Berkowitz (1974) has identified experimentally demonstrated situational cues which increase aggression levels: the presence of a gun; facilitating or constraining explanations of the experimental situation; provocation by insult; stimulation by viewing media violence; noise levels; when the victim is seen as a justified target in terms of his/her role (a boxer vs. a student); when previously neutral stimuli have become conditioned, through reward, as stimuli for aggression; when there is approval for the aggression; and when there is feedback information showing that the aggression is producing intended (and increasingly greater) pain in the target. Baron (1971) showed that increased pain in the target may inhibit aggression when anger levels are low and the target is similar to the subject. The victim's suffering, then, can be (but is not always) a reinforcing component of aggression. Chronic delinquents usually increase their aggression as evidence of the victim's suffering is forthcoming. Successful aggression, after arousal—with anger and as habit—is its own reward. Keep that in mind.

There are other illustrative findings. Milgram (1974) made famous aggression by instruction, seemingly independent of the victim's pain but with implicitly authoritative approval. Expected retaliation or its absence plays a role (Feldman, 1977). Threat of retaliation greater than the subject is able to inflict constrains aggression. "Threat" here implies anticipation. How a subject perceives the antagonist's intention can play a strong role in influencing aggression levels. Common sense tells us the same.

Be mindful that an experiment is always a specific situation whose "controlled" variables are but subcomponents. One therefore expects considerable variation in outcomes as a function of experimental design and milieu. Even so, experimental findings are consistent enough to support the quite sensible generalization that aggression varies with emotional arousal, set, preexisting traits, and social history, and, unquestionably, as a function of the situation, with a range of elements implicated. One must not retreat, in the face of much behavioristic methodology, to stimulus-response models, for it is evident that how the subject perceives the situation, his or her meanings and anticipations, governs aggression.

Whether aggression is a "release" or an invoked "response" remains a basic dispute in theory. The dispute relates to the value question of whether humans are born "good" or "bad." Are we biologically predisposed to aggression as expression and reward, or is aggression's emergence, initially at least, a defensive response capability to threat? Do not rely on the experimental literature today for an answer to this question.

Personality and Alcohol

Since our concern is with alcohol and situational variations in aggression, it will be useful to illustrate some of the personal variables which may be related both to extreme forms of alcohol conduct and to situational response. Implicit is the expectation that if people with special alcohol habits or histories do show aggressive responses to particular situations that are different from others (either other types of extreme drinkers or those without drinking problems), one of the mediating variables may be subsumed under personality. We are not concerned here with the search for the "alcoholic personality" as such, or for its more elusive predecessor, the "pre-alcoholic personality" (see Barnes, 1979; E. M. Blum & Blum, 1969;

Sutker, Archer, Brantley, & Kilpatrick, 1979). We do not attend to aggression in alcoholics in violent subgroups among alcoholic populations, and to processes demonstrable within alcoholics, particularly subgroups, which appear to make violence more likely as an outcome of personality-setting interaction.

Let us consider some of the trait candidates. Renson, Adams, and Tinklenberg (1978) found that alcoholics with a history of violence scored higher on the Buss–Durkee Inventory measures of hostility, assault, irritability, and resentment than did alcoholics without violence histories. In a case history study of 2300 excessive drinkers, Wanberg (1969) found only two "drinking symptoms" common to most of his populations—drinking to relax, and being ashamed—but over 80% expressed resentment of others. One wonders if the common resentment has one of its roots in chronic rebelliousness. Alexander (1965) learned that adolescents drinking without situational sanction (i.e., under norms of abstinence) were rebellious, measured by emotional distance to the father and by frequency of disobedience to parents. These teenage drinkers, who drank when their friends and father did not, drank more often and more excessively than teenagers whose parents and/or friends were drinkers. As distance and disobedience to parents increased, drinking increases. This antinormative drinking is, then, symptomatic of parent-oriented rebellion and occurs independently of social group support. One infers that the drinking is itself an aggressive act and, further, that the teenager so beginning a drinking career is rebellious toward and hostile to parents, as well as less responsive to his or her own peer group norms.

Social drinkers, after drinking heavily in a competitive setting, will be the more aggressive if they have a history of argumentativeness and aggressivity, and if they score low on socialization, self-control, and responsibility. Furthermore, the degree of aggression increases with the amount of alcohol consumed (Boyatzis, 1975). It is known (Wolfgang, 1958) that violence between spouses during drinking is a frequent prehomicidal condition. It is of interest, then, to learn (Hope, 1969) that trait hostility is greater in and between alcoholics and their spouses than among controls.

Both motor and cognitive impairments are well known as consequences of drinking per se; further cognitive impairment may be found in heavy drinkers in the absence of alcohol. Story (1968) has shown that such impairment, in this instance regression to primary process modes, varies with the nature of the cognitive material. When sober alcoholics are faced with thinking tasks which involve oral conflict materials, they show greater decrement than for nonoral material, and oral conflict stimuli have a greater effect on the thinking of alcoholics than of controls. One may infer that the alcoholic brings to a drinking setting conflicts about drinking which express themselves in poorer, more primitive cognitive performance. There is also a subgroup of alcoholics whose irrational behavior precipitated by alcohol, which may include violence, appears to be a function of preexisting neuropathology, for example, an epileptiform syndrome or "pathological intoxication" with confirming electroencephalogram evidence (Maletzky, 1976). Maletzky's sample had no history of sober violence or psychosis; their aggressive conduct under intravenous injection is described as in response to "imagined threats," being "dysfunctional," and "blind rage." Maletzky's findings differ from those of Bach-y-Rita, Lion, and Ervin (1970) and may be attributable to the larger dosages given by Maletzky. While Bach-y-Rita *et al.* regarded stress as necessary in inducing pathological intoxication, Maletzky described his experimental setting as nonstressful (except for injected alcohol itself and its consequences).

A series of studies suggests that both locus of control and cue dependency vary between alcohol populations and others. Locus of control, in turn, may vary with hostility. C. B. Williams and Vantress (1969) reported that those scoring higher on external control (what they do depends on the environment, is influenced more by others) are also higher on resentment, suspiciousness, and irritability. O'Leary, Donovan, Freeman, and Chaney (1976), in turn, showed that alcoholics are to be subdivided into groups depending on felt locus of control. Those with external locus (what happens to one is not under personal, inner control) showed the highest levels of psychopathology on the Minnesota Multiphasic Personality Inventory (MMPI). (See also Goss & Morosko, 1970; O'Leary, Donovan, & Hague, 1974.) Alcoholics with external locus of control are also found, in these studies, to be less well defended, more anxious, alienated, and self-critical. Donovan and O'Leary (1975) reported that alcoholics measured on a scale of experienced social control say they experience less control over stressful stimuli. Inner locus of control is, in turn, correlated with experienced (perceived and immediate) social control.

In the 1976 study by O'Leary *et al.*, psychopathology (the MMPI measure implies lack of care for others, amorality, opportunism) was the greatest among those alcoholics with both felt external locus of control and least levels of experienced social control. The contradiction arising from earlier findings of internal locus of control among alcoholics (e.g., Distefano, Pryer, & Garrison, 1972) is resolved by the findings of O'Leary *et al.* (1976). Identified is one psychopathic subgroup with very low felt inner and perceived social control. It is this group which O'Leary *et al.* described as having a more limited repertoire of adaptive behaviors. Insofar as this group may also have the field-dependent, "here-and-now" (stimulus-bound) perceptual–cognitive traits often reported among alcoholics, then the coping of this alcoholic subgroup will be limited indeed (see Pernanen, 1976).

G. Goldstein (1976) has discussed the extreme field dependency found among alcoholics; this was equivalent to that found among the brain damaged and some classes of schizophrenics. Given Linton and Graham's finding that field dependency predicts suggestibility, one would expect greater external dependency and lower autonomous control in situations by alcoholics—except for drinking behavior itself, which relies on internal cues associated with maintaining blood alcohol levels. Goldstein, reviewing the neurologists, cited Halstead to the effect that impaired abstract reasoning—associated with the neuropathic field of dependency or stimulus-bound "forced responsiveness" of the alcoholic—is a defect in biological intelligence. Goldstein argued that as situational demands increase in complexity (requiring abstraction and problem solving), the alcoholic will be less able to respond adequately. It can be argued that these limited perceptual capacities, coupled with impaired abstraction and other response abilities, mean that more social situations are stressful for alcoholics. For them, more situational events become conditioned as stress or aversive stimuli; with drinking, in a vicious circle, even less adequate social coping occurs.

Implicit in such speculations may be "theories" of drinking as stress related and perhaps (not necessarily—one can invoke assertiveness just as well) escapist, and theories of aggression (when it occurs as part of an inadequate response) as related to frustration or poor coping. Aggression may just as well be explained as a more primitive mobilization of resources under conditions of arousal, which is enhanced insofar as power fantasies are involved. Should power displays be adaptive, as they might be, the aggressive response of the alcoholic may also show some short-term situational mastery, compensating for other deficits.

The foregoing studies, intended to be an illustrative rather than an exhaustive review, are taken to show that there are neurological and personality differences among subgroups of alcoholics. At least two subgroups are identified as having high chronic levels of hostility, rebelliousness, resentment, irritability, and the like. In these people, when both felt lack of and absence of imposed personal control exists, existing psychopathology expresses itself in conduct detrimental to others. Further, given cognitive deficits and stimulus-bound responses as a function of alcohol excess (acute or chronic) such that realistic perceptions are jeopardized, the ensuing immediate social adjustments that are made are likely to be less than adequate. Under these conditions, violence is more probable. Given that anger, low self-esteem, and the general phenomena of need-determined and habitual perceptions, coupled with the aggressive conditioning of neutral stimuli, the perceptual world of one subset of alcoholics will include sensitivity to slight and threat, these serving as provocations to violence. Insofar as the situation does not contain real constraints against violence, or the drinker does not perceive these as present, then violence risks are enhanced.

One does conclude that alcohol has differential effects on, and that its meanings are responded to differently by, various alcohol problem subgroups. Among several of these, given particular settings, the risk of violence is increased. Unfortunately, there is no epidemiological work to show the distribution of subgroups among the larger alcohol problem population, nor any incidence or setting counts which tell us how often violence-eliciting settings are encountered in daily life. With that data on hand, one might ask the question, Given all the factors present favoring violence, what are the heretofore hidden factors which still constrain it? For the ordinary citizen or applied scientist, that is the question which holds promise for violence control.

At this point one comes to assumptions about the inner world of the potentially aggressive drinker; that world of feelings, perceptions, and meanings which defines and selects available responses. Observers trained experimentally make that move cautiously and piecemeal, sometimes disavowing "black box" ascriptions in obedience to behaviorism. Others begin with a person's personal history portrait to understand situational responses from a clinical or individualistic standpoint. When enough people have been seen, typologies are created and similar inner worlds for a group are assumed, and a phenomenological basis for predicting response is created. The clinical or phenomenological approach is predicated on the assumption that existing personality will "express itself" in situations, not that situations dominate to create roles or determine responses. Refer to Chotlos and Goldstein (1966) for a sensitive clinical picture of "the alcoholic," what his/her situations are, seen from the inside, and how, by implication, some situations demand aggression if that inner world is to be maintained and served. The weights assigned in research design and explanation can discriminate psychiatrists from sociologists—with the psychologists more likely among the piece-at-a-time group.

Drinking and Situational Factors

As situational variables are implicated in aggression per se, so they are in drinking. It is important to realize that in the alcohol–situation–aggression (or violence) nexus, drinking and aggression can be independently affected by situational components. Further, just as relatively enduring characteristics (personality, attitudes, neurological status) brought to the situation affect aggressivity, these same kinds of variables appear also to affect drinking behavior. Rohan's (1975) admonition to attend to drinking as what a person does rather than something a person has—with variations in frequency, magnitude, and conduct as a function of varying circumstances—is good advice when examining drinking as situationally influenced. Keep in mind that drinking, in turn, affects moods and perceptions, thus altering the drinker's definition of the situation.

Allman, Taylor, and Nathan (1972) have shown that drinking in chronic alcoholics varies with stress and companionship. When stress was combined with being with other drinkers, in contrast to isolation, drinking increased. Stress alone brought on anger, tension, and depression; alcohol independently enhanced levels of depression and anxiety. Coopersmith (1964) had shown earlier that alcoholics compared to others showed greater arousal to certain emotional communications, but that arousal was lowered by their drinking. Stress effects varied by person. It was also observed that irritation increased with continued drinking.

Higgins (1976) found that stress as an environmental feature was less important than prior drinking history; consumption is best predicted by being an alcoholic or not. Nevertheless, one may identify features that induce drinking. These include threats to self-esteem, insult to heavy drinkers, and requirements for self-assertiveness in difficult social situations. Drinking varies with the drinking conduct of others in the situation. Nathan and Lisman (1976) concluded that additional setting variables affecting alcohol intake include the drinking conduct of the group leader (see also Goldman, 1974), interpersonal difficulties between family members, group versus individual drinking decisions, and being alone or with others.

Glatt (1976), in a clinical commentary, noted that triggers or restraints in drinking situations include the ease or tension in the social setting, the kind and amounts of drinks available (and how available these are) and the presence or absence of controlling others. How family dynamics affect drinking is illustrated by Davis, Berenson, Steinglass, and Davis (1974), who showed that drinking may aid coping and adaptiveness, augmenting appropriate assertiveness under the guise of a drunken role approved by family members. Such role taking facilitated by drinking more is consistent with the findings of Deardorff, Melges, Hout, and Savage (1976), showing that within the family context, feelings of power derive from drinking. Thus, in situations requiring assertiveness (Miller, Hersen, Eisler, & Hilsman, 1974b) or autonomy, alcoholics' drinking may increase. These observations are consistent with McClelland's (1975) thesis that drinking enhances power fantasies, and they are compatible with findings that power-inducing social suggestion increases consumption among male social drinkers.

Incorporating the Coopersmith and Woodrow (1967) finding that alcoholics do not have lower tolerance for social stress than others, Miller *et al.* (1974b) suggested that the uniform response to stressful situations by alcoholics is drinking. Other people have a greater variety of adaptive responses available.

The interpretive scheme which posits social stress and nonadaptive overdrinking for alcoholics as limited choice is compatible with Bowman, Stein, and Newton's (1975) finding that volume consumed relates inversely to postdrinking adaptive social behavior over 6 months. Volume, in turn, may be relatively invulnerable to situational sensitivity to the cues to which social drinkers respond. Nathan and O'Brien (1971) and Miller, Hersen, Eisler, Epstein, and Wooten (1974a) concur that an internal stimulus, decreasing BAC, is associated with increased consumption, not with typical social setting cues. (See also Mello & Mendelson, 1973.)

Expectations influence drinking. Maisto, Lauerman, and Adesso (1977), reviewing earlier studies (Marlatt, Demming, & Reid, 1973; T. K. Williams, 1970), noted that alcoholics told they were being given alcohol (and receiving it) reported more "craving" after drinking than those not so informed. Furthermore, information indicating that a drink is alcoholic led to more actual drinking among alcoholics than among social drinkers. Reexamining Williams's data, Maisto *et al.* showed that the craving effect is long lasting, confirming that cognitive facts—in this instance, expectations induced by information, true or false—are associated with reported desires for alcohol and actual drinking. Marlatt, Kosturn, and Lang (1975) examined both frustration and provocation among students who were drinking. Demonstrated in this experiment, and consistent with findings of Higgins and Marlatt (1975), is that drinking increases following provocation with no retaliation opportunity, but that presumed anger provocation alone is a lesser stimulus for drinking among students.

One concludes that situational factors do affect drinking, but that both the number of operating cues and variety of responses to these setting variables are greater among social drinkers than among alcoholics, for the alcoholics' consumption is strongly dictated by internal cues associated with BACs. Certain features do affect how much an alcoholic drinks in a given setting: availability; work requirements; speed of gratification; expectations; instructions; the presence, significance, and importance of others; and the kinds of social interaction with special importance for stressful, threatening interactions. Insofar as alcohol is, in turn, directly or indirectly related to violence, then such situational variables should themselves be consequential to violence prediction.

Alcohol's Effects on Mood and Emotion

Probably how a person responds to interpersonal events depends in part on his or her feelings at the time. Moods, emotions, and set affect what stimuli are noted, how they are interpreted, and how ready a person is to offer a response. If alcohol itself increases the probability of some moods or particular states being present and these are, in turn, preconditions for violence, then a sequence of setting variables is implicated in the history of a violent incident. Particular stimuli increase drinking, the drinking produces a mood, and the mood is a selector for social stimuli and their meanings, so that, for example, if an event occurs which is seen by the drinker as a threat, or it evokes a power display, then, especially when aggression-facilitating setting influences are present, violence may emerge.

The literature is fairly consistent concerning the effects of alcohol on mood, although some of the observed effects may, in fact, depend upon an alcohol–group interaction. Hartocollis in 1962 observed that alcoholics given alcohol intravenously in groups were more emotional (elated, aggressive, boisterous) than those injected under solitary conditions. Only those in a group expressed hostility. Coopersmith (1964), in a review, found that moderate doses of alcohol led to feelings of relief or ease (i.e., lower arousal levels) in the CNS. Threshold levels were increased, but reactive selectivity to affective material was decreased with alcohol. For this (student) group, alcohol reduced physiological arousal and inferred psychological distress; controls were the more defensive when exposed to affective material presumed to be threatening. The concept of perceptual vigilance is invoked. Coopersmith interpreted his findings to show that modest doses of alcohol in normal subjects cushion threatening emotional material, allow detachment and subsequent reduced defensiveness, contribute to individual variability, and prevent distress. Pollack (1966), comparing alcoholics and others, measured "coping" (to threat) by a projective method weighted with sexual and aggressive (sentence completion) themes. Judged adequacy of coping improved for the normal under the alcohol condition and deteriorated for the alcoholics. In a student social drinker study, Warren and Raynes (1972) reported that student drinking in a group showed the greatest mood changes, including reduced friendliness. Those drinking alone became less anxious. All drinkers, compared to controls, became more angry.

Among alcoholics, mood improvement is not the rule. Goldman (1974) observed that in a when-to-drink decision setting, alcoholics became, as consumption increased, more psychiatrically bizarre, reported more physical ills, and had mood changes. Alterman, Gottheil, and Crawford (1975) have argued that unhappy mood changes occur as alcohol levels in alcoholics increase. But the discomfort is also attributable to deciding to drink (in a treatment setting where abstinence is the approved mode of conduct) rather than drinking itself. Tension preceded as well as followed the decision to "fall off the wagon." Mello and Mendelson (1971), in their review, concluded that alcohol independently, when consumed over time, produces dysphoria. This need not be a function of BAC, for, with reduced food intake, reverse tolerance occurs; small amounts of alcohol can produce greater intoxication. Alcohol also affects sleep, including, as Pernanen (1976) noted, rapid-eye-movement sleep disturbance, which can, in turn, affect mood and responsivity.

Nathan and Lisman (1976), in a review, showed that anxiety and depression increase as drinking among alcoholics continues. Nathan, Titler, Lowenstein, Solomon, and Rossi (1970) found that anger as well as depression and anxiety rises, particularly soon after a nondrinking phase, an effect limited to men. As alcoholics' blood levels increased, they became more anxious, depressed, and hostile, as well as less vigorous. Before drinking, subjects had not forecast these effects on and in themselves.

Tamerin, Weiner, and Mendelson (1970), studying alcoholics' predrinking expectations, observed that subjects anticipated that during drinking they would feel better and more sociable; they did not anticipate the increased aggression actually occurring when they drank. Contrary to their predictions, dysphoria, sexuality, and feelings of closeness also increased; they did correctly predict increasing irresponsibility. An important paradoxical effect was observed: Men who became violent did not recall aggressivity; it was recollected by those who had not become violent. The authors suggested that drinking may be undertaken in order to regress, rebel, and release repression.

Implicit is the assumption that, if violence is latent and repressed, the to-be-violent alcoholic will deny that risk but will simultaneously set out to employ alcohol instrumentally to create a setting for its release. That same alcoholic state can provide an excuse for what has occurred and also gives justification for forgetting it all afterward. The unconscious is not to be disregarded in alcoholic violence.

Vanicelli (1972) found that some alcoholics showed increased anxiety, while it decreased in others, leading to the suggestion of alcoholic subtypes characterized by differing alcohol effects on mood. Higgins (1976, citing Korman, Knopf, & Austin, 1960; Williams, 1970; and Kissin & Hankoff, 1959) proposed that alcohol has a "normalizing" effect, reducing extreme sympathetic reactivity among alcoholics, and reducing anxiety and depression among social drinkers. Among alcoholics, the already noted increase in anxiety and depression may express previously absent (suppressed?) emotions, being expressed as hostility, guilt, and resentment.

Higgins cited Mendelson, La Dou, and Solomon (1964) to the effect that psychopathic aggression and sexuality are displayed as alcoholics drink over time, and that control over conduct deteriorates. Nonalcoholics do not show such changes. Self-esteem also deteriorates during drinking episodes. Non alcoholics show greater social interaction when drinking; alcoholics may become more withdrawn even if they claim, as many do, that drinking is a social lubricant. These and other studies, particularly on tension reduction, led Higgins to emphasize, in agreement with Pliner and Cappell (1974), that the experimental setting itself plays a powerful role in influencing the emotional response to alcohol. Thus, while alcohol has an effect on moods—one which differs both among and between alcoholics as contrasted with normals—that effect appears to depend upon not only the quantity consumed but also upon the experiment qua setting. Some of the setting variables are the experimenters, whose own interactions with subjects may produce uncontrolled emotional effects. Nevertheless, among alcoholics, the predominant moods observed in drinking are unhappy ones and can include anger.

Alcohol, Setting, and Aggressive or Violent Conduct

We now turn to those observations that help elucidate the role of setting variables which, in association with alcohol, determine aggressive or violent responses. The experimental work derives for the most part from the observations of an association between alcohol and violence, and from the common sensical data which place the violent event in particular circumstances. Case history studies such as those of Gerson (1978), Pittman and Handy (1964), Shupe (1954), Sila (1977), Virkkunen (1974), and Wolfgang and Ferracuti (1967) have amply shown that particular kinds of people (spouses, acquaintances), places (homes, bars), times (weekends), sequences (argumentative interaction between drinkers with violent histories, including "victim precipitation"), and opportunities (weapon availability) do characterize the violent situation. Pernanen (1976), considering the data and defining situational variables as those which vary within individuals over time, lamented the paucity of studies per se and in particular, those in natural studies with (acute) alcohol versus nonalcohol conditions compared. Furthermore, there has been little systematic variation of a number of setting variables, of which alcohol is but one.

Pernanen implicated the following as features in alcohol settings likely to be related to violent outcomes:

1. interpersonal interactions
2. aggressive power fantasies

3. concurrent moods

4. culturally determined power structures in the drinking situation

5. the here-and-now, temporally limited and field-dependent perceptions of the alcoholic or alcohol influenced person

6. escalating insult or threat as an interpersonal process

7. sleep-deprivation-related irritability and aggression

8. the more masculine (macho) self-conception of heavier-drinking men

9. greater actual muscularity–masculinity among heavy drinking males

10. psychological conflict or other stress

11. safe or facilitating environments (homes, taverns) and

12. the interpretation of another's act as intending aggression, or the inability to cope with another's aggression because of alcohol-related inabilities to abstract, to solve the problem, to engage in verbal reasoning, or to have available alternative responses derived from general, prior, or out-of-the-setting (as opposed to physically and temporally immediate) reactions.

Pernanen also considered as operative:

1. the demonstrated liability of conduct under the influence of alcohol

2. the narrowing of the perceptual field

3. the attribution of arbitrariness to others' perceived aggression

4. deterioration in an abstraction capability under alcohol which would provide other than a hostile attribution to others

5. culturally imposed definitions of the drinking setting as free of normal restraints (i.e., "time out" or as encouraging risk taking)

6. the culturally imposed lack of restraint in emotional expression among intimates

7. failure to understand strangers' intentions

8. the absence of strong institutional sanctions controlling behavior in the alcohol setting (e.g., ritual authority, norms, the self-selection of aggressive people to alcohol settings), so that there are aggression-permissive or aggression-demanding individual and group norms

9. alcohol-related predispositional variables such as psychomotor epilepsy and susceptibility to "pathological intoxication," nutritionally related hypoglycemia and irritability, and low frustration tolerance in alcoholics.

Finally, and here Pernanen cited DeVito, Flaherty, and Mozdzierz (1970), people with acting-out (impulse-releasing characterological defects) tendencies may choose to drink to facilitate those tendencies. Implied by De-Vito's observation is that the drinker's own expectation that alcohol makes for or allows aggressivity is a self-fulfilling belief. As already aggressive people select alcohol (e.g., as justification, opportunity and pharmacological arouser, or mood enhancer), their actions follow their "plan." That the "plans" of alcoholics are often antisocial is consonant with the high prevalance of "psychopaths" in the chronic alcoholic population (Sutker *et al.,* 1979).

The Cultural Context

A series of cross-cultural, anthropological, and sociological studies attests to differences within and between cultures as to how drinking is done and what conduct ensues. As Child, Bacon, and Barry (1965) concluded, "a high rate of consumption does not necessarily mean that alcohol is disruptive of social life." There are also data showing that as consumption increases within a society, alcoholism and associated problems increase, indeed, at a logarithmic rate. (See Bruun, Edwards, Lumio, Mäkelä, Pan, Popham, Room, Schmidt, Skog, Sulkunen, & Österberg, 1975.) We shall not reconcile these two views here, noting only that we believe that the key is the comparison of populations on the degree of integrated drinking, before examining consumption and risk data.

Sadoun, Lolli, and Silverman (1965) showed, comparing France and Italy, that although Italy has a higher rate of alcohol consumption per capita, France has the higher alcoholism rate. Within the United States, certain ethnic groups (Jewish, Italian, Greek) demonstrate "integrated" drinking where drinking conduct is institutionalized and initially ceremonial, such that high variability in behavior or the investment in alcohol of idiosyncratic symbolic or emotional loads does not occur.

Irish-American or Yankee drinking takes a different pattern, not being learned within an authoritative family structure but rather among unsupervised peers with different and more extravagant norms for expected or accepted behavior operating. Pearce and Garrett (1970), for example, found that 25% of nondelinquents, but 69% of delinquents, first drank without parental permission; that delinquents began and continued drinking with peers; and that nondelinquents first drank in the home and continued that pattern. A cultural case study of a peasant community with integrated drinking, where drunkenness and violence are rare, is presented by R. H. Blum and Blum (1963). A contrasting picture of violent settings is offered by Wolfgang and Ferracuti (1967). Coupled with the additional observations of Jellinek (1960) and Leake and Silverman (1966), there is convincing evidence that cultures as a whole impose on personality, on alcohol, and on drinking settings and conduct, those values, roles, and standards which are for that culture its expressive style. These determine not only variability associated with alcohol use but some of the emotions, meanings, and roles which the drinker expresses. The incidence of violence is mediated by these conditions. One must not claim, however, that violence as expressive behavior is solely determined by cultural factors, for within even small homogeneous societies deviant conduct occurs, be that neurological or psychologically based.

An excellent study by Cinquemani (1975) compares two Central Mexican Indian tribes, both of which drink to extreme intoxication. (See also Bunzel, 1940.) One group, the Los Pastores, shows a good deal of unpremeditated violence while drinking. Drinking is done by males outside of family settings. The belief among the Los Pastores is that men are forced to violence by mescal, their destiny, or by the victim. It is also believed that if mescal is available, men will inevitably become drunk. For neither the drinking nor the violence is an assumed motive, nor is personal responsibility assigned; fatalism is the rule. Nevertheless, ritual, ceremonial occasions are also heavy drinking ones, but here no violence ensues. Within Los Pastores, then, one distinguishes two settings which dictate violence or no, the violent cantina and the nonviolent ceremonial (e.g., religious or festival) occasion.

Compared to the Los Pastores are the Mixtecans, who also drink heavily. The Mixtecans do not associate alcohol with violence. Their intoxication is not boisterous, although they drink to unconsciousness at fiesta occasions. Mixtecan group drinking appears to express and enhance group superiority; assaults do not mar that belief or function.

There is a third group, the Maxenos of Chichicastenango, where violence sometimes occurs, but here men are held responsible for their drunken actions, punishment being severe. The Maxenos, also observed by Bunzel (1940) and less systematically by the Blums (E. M. Blum & Blum, 1969), use drunkenness as a means for communicating with departed spirits, which is a desired capability (i.e., a valued role attribute in religious practice and one that serves ancestral and family cohesion). Intoxication for spirit communication is nonviolent, whereas in group situations where intrakin animosity operates, violence occurs. Some Maxenos, to avoid the latter, refuse to drink with kinsmen or others to whom they are hostile.

Work such as Cinquemani's offers a satisfying description of variables at the whole cultural (tribal) level which allows the prediction of violence prevalence under specified conditions (cantina, religious festival, hostile kinsmen) and for one versus another tribal society. One can learn beliefs and values, observe behavior, easily estimate BACs (in all three groups, men drink until they pass out), and conclude that one has indeed shown how the expression of violence is a cultural phenomenon.

These cross-cultural studies are not helpful in accounting for individual deviance (e.g., the rare murderous Mixtecan or the "Ferdinand the Bull" among Los Pastores), nor indeed for the expression of violence itself, even under facilitating conditions such as among Los Pastores. One wants to know, beyond incidence data, more about the individuals and specific events present when violence among Los Pastores occurs and does not occur in the cantina (or other nonceremonial) setting. Even though Los Pastores claim that drinking and violence are both inevitable, the latter is not inevitable on every drinking occasion. There is greater difficulty when one seeks to apply the cultural paradigm (easily applied to small, autonomous, homogeneous societies) to groups within a larger hetereogeneous society, as Wolfgang and Ferracuti (1967) have sought to do. As disputes among the several delinquency theories in sociology make clear, it may be more an act of semantics than science to describe a subgroup, as for example, professional thieves or skid row drunks, as a "subculture." As groups they certainly have identifiable life-styles, but people move in and out of these and other social groups as a function of age, drinking, or other status, self-selecting and being assigned; and they do not transmit over the generations a symbolic and material heritage differentiating the subgroup and creating positive attraction and cohesion. To the contrary, the subgroups share much with the larger society, being part of it but self-disdaining and disdained, and one cannot be sure that membership is not a function of neuropsychological deficit (i.e., being the place where the losers or the lost go—and where the predators seek them).

The minor questions in cross-cultural studies become major problems when one seeks to account for alcoholic violence "subculturally" within a Western society. It is not that parameters such as cultural beliefs or roles are not applicable, it is that they are less concise. In the face of data at the group, situational, or psychological and psychopharmacological level, a narrower focus seems helpful; for example, a focus on coherent groups, particular occasions, and comparative individual behavior.

Group Structure and Events

The literature concerned with alcoholic aggression is remarkably devoid of studies of group processes, dynamics, and interactions as such. Social psychology as a discipline has not touched alcohol–violence studies. Yet it is at this group level that analyses one step lower than the cultural or subcultural level are readily conceived. The best approximation is that work which deals with the one group which has been of interest to alcohol workers, the family. There are dozens of clinical studies bearing on family dynamics, many of which attribute to roles, feelings, and processes within the family a causative role in the creation of alcoholism or other addictions, or which show how events in the family lead to violence. (For reviews, see Janzen, 1977; Satir, 1967; and Steinglass, 1976.) Indeed, the case history method of Wolfgang and others—which shows how violence emerges out of sequential situational events (e.g., family quarrels) or is victim "precipitated"—is a kind of epidemiology of group process and the violent incident.

Bruun (1959) did address himself directly to group effects, using the data generated by Takala, Pihkanen, and Markkanen (1957). He observed that reactions were a function of group position. Central persons (giving and receiving more communications) accounted for an increase in aggressive interpersonal reactions. Similarly, individual factors, the acceptance of expressed aggression, also positively related to actual aggression.

Bennett *et al.* (1969) demonstrated that aggression in a "teaching" situation did not occur as a function of increased alcohol dosage but rather increased over time under circumstances where the victim (an experimental accomplice) was also believed to be drinking. Their data indicate that aggression in a situation where punishment is sanctioned during a task, occurs in the presence of a drinking subordinate peer. This experiment illustrates that there is a social context—roles, task, and drinking conduct—in which aggression emerges, and, further, that the experiment is itself a social milieu, the circumstances of which produce (or in other experiments, do not produce) an aggressive response when alcohol is administered.

There is a paucity of experimental work attending to small-group (primary or secondary) variables affecting violence. More observations exist of a clinical nature bearing on family dynamics. Some of the most exciting observations are in-place, naturalistic ones of drinking milieus, for example, in Samuels's *The Negro Tavern* (1976). Clearly, more work on the small group in its milieu is needed before the emergence of violence becomes understood as an interactional process.

Interpersonal Challenge

A number of animal and human studies, which have explored alcohol-induced aggression, have measured varying BACs to learn if subsequent levels of aggression vary. Consequently, investigators have created experimental conditions (including means for expressing aggression, typically a "shock box" of one sort or another) which are believed to be stimuli for aggression. Setting stimuli are then introduced which are considered likely to be provocative. The challenges have included insult, example instruction, threats, competition, storied criminal opportunities, and frustration.

Taylor and Gammon (1976) offer one of the very few studies in which the design not only allows for an experiment as the social setting but also compares two social situations. Using subjects intoxicated and sober in a reaction-time competition, there were two social conditions: one with an observer who was silent, and the second with an observer who sought to persuade the subject to administer less intense and less frequent shocks to the unseen competitor. Intoxicated subjects initiated more painful shocks than sober ones. Shock intensities were reduced among intoxicated and sober subjects when the observer argued for that policy. Shock intensities increased over time. Shock varied reciprocally (i.e., with shock intensities delivered to the subject by the imaginary competitor). Sober subjects were much more governed by reciprocity. There were strong differences among subjects. Ratings of the competitor were the more favorable among intoxicated subjects under the persuasion condition; sober subjects' ratings were the more favorable under the silent-observer condition. There were also interaction effects. The investigators, faced by the failure of intoxicated subjects to be reciprocally sensitive (i.e., to lower shock levels as their competitor/opponent did so), invoked McClelland, Davis, Kalin, and Wanner (1972) and McClelland (1975), and noted Boyatzis's (1974) observations of greater baiting and defying among intoxicated subjects. They suggested an effort among intoxicated subjects to gain/retain ascendancy.

Important for the evaluation of situational effects, one sees in this experiment that levels of aggression do vary with several of the setting variables. Alcohol does play a differentiating role in producing response.

Taylor and Gammon (1975) further examined alcohol and aggression, varying the drink (bourbon or vodka) and measuring interpersonal judgments as well. Using the same shock competition design as the 1976 study, the investigators found that aggression (shock) levels were dependent upon the subject's own shock experience at the hands of the (imaginary) competitor; that is, they were reciprocal. There was an interaction effect between alcohol and reciprocity. Bourbon and vodka drinkers differed, with vodka drinkers the more extreme and the less reciprocal. High-dose vodka subjects attributed more hostility to their competitor than did low-dose vodka subjects or bourbon subjects. Self-ratings of anxiety, amount of alcohol consumed, and desire to win also varied with drink and dose. The investigators considered their findings in the light of their own supporting earlier study (Shuntich & Taylor, 1972), in contrast to that of Bennett *et al.* (1969) where, with a nonretaliating (helpless) opponent, alcohol levels did not correlate with aggression. They concluded that a situation where the competitor is not helpless and retaliates is an aggression-facilitating situation, one in which alcohol dosage levels do influence outcomes. They noted, with reference to vodka versus bourbon, that vodka has fewer congeners therein, and that BACs increase at a faster level. Boyatzis (1974) had earlier shown some of the effects in a natural setting, which Taylor and associates elaborated. There, too, the type of drink differentially affected aggression in a situation where leaders "encouraged" games competition, with distilled spirits (various) associated with more aggression than beer, although BACs were the same.

The 1975 study by Taylor and Gammon shows how, in contrast with Bennett *et al.*, the experiment is, itself, a situation in which alcohol–aggression outcomes are dependent upon the social situation produced by the experimental design. It is also shown that experienced discomfort—call it provocation, punishment, or competition effect—is a situationally produced variable which, with alcohol, determines aggressive response. Further, one sees that emotional and attitudinal features covary with alcohol and aggression levels, attributed hostility, strength of the competitive motive, and felt absence of anxiety—which are all strongest in the high-dose vodka, aggressive group. The Taylor and Gammon studies are model experiments. One would next like to see how alcoholics with violence histories, versus those without, respond to challenges under varying restraint conditions where some violent outcome is allowable.

In another study, Taylor, Gammon, and Capasso (1976), again using students drinking vodka and the reaction-time/competition design, controlled for threat or intention on the part of the competitor. Competitors were portrayed via a (bogus) tape message to the subject indicating whether or not the competitor would administer shock to the subject even if the competitor won, thus providing threat and no-threat conditions. Under threat conditions, the intoxicated subjects administered higher-level shock than did sober subjects; under nonthreatening conditions, sober ones did not differ from intoxicated students. The study demonstrated once again that alcohol is a variable associated with greater aggression, but here only under conditions of threat reciprocity. In contrast, Taylor, Schmutte, and Leonard (1977) challenged vodka-drinking students with a puzzle presented as an intelligence test. Following either frustration or success on the puzzle, students then participated in the reaction-time/competition shock of earlier experiments. Drinking men set higher shock intensities, but the prior experience of frustration (or success) had no effect on either group. The experiment failed to support a frustration–aggression theory of alcohol-related aggressivity.

Laboratory aggression studies suffer from not being proofs of stimuli to criminal violence, however sensible and suggestive the findings. We have not been able to uncover any much-needed study of violent offenders under varying alcohol and situational conditions—whether in a natural or laboratory environment. But consider as a beginning the study by Nicol, Gunn, Gristwood, Foggitt, and Watson (1973). Ninety prison inmates were subjects and were asked to imagine their conduct in nine criminal life-style situations. Subjects had been rated for violence histories. They were then given cards describing a range of possible reactions and were asked to rank the cards in order of their own likely response. Focusing on those responses which gave a priority to violence or drinking, the authors compared this self-selecting sample against criminal records (about half had been convicted of violent crimes). Although there were more men diagnosed as alcoholic in the violence-self-description group, and more younger men, the men with violent histories did not select more violent responses in the story situations. Men with violent histories did more often select drinking responses.

Had Nicol *et al.* focused on methods sensitive to possible repression (recall Tamerin *et al.,* 1970), the faking of goodness (as psychopaths and others do), and mental state compartmentalization, and had they provided alcohol (and placebo) with aggressive opportunities, response choices might have been brought out that are not only associated with real histories but also give insight into situational triggers. (As to individual histories, the study by Boyatzis, 1974, does show a correlation between the measure of aggression and prior violence history.)

Individual Reactions

Given the near absence of studies bearing directly on the environment–alcohol–violence relationship, it is presumptuous to impose refined classifications by levels of focus. Thus, the foregoing studies, while invoking variables which may be conceived as common to a group (i.e., interpersonally general, such as "competition," "insult," "common social situations"), provide individual stimuli, and one finds considerable individual response variation. Only a few studies examine those reactions to setting which focus primarily on individual processes.

Lang, Goeckner, Adesso, and Marlatt (1976), for instance, studied heavy social drinkers with an eye to how expectations about alcohol might affect aggression. Half of the subjects were told they would receive vodka and tonic; half, only tonic. Half of each group actually received vodka; half, only tonic. They were then assigned to a provocation situation with an insulting partner, or had an amiable partner, again on a 50:50 basis within each of the four alcohol or placebo groups. Partners then became learners in a word-association experiment in which subjects had an opportunity as "teachers" to shock the former partner. Conversations between the two were recorded and rated for verbal aggressivity. The results showed that those told they would receive alcohol believed they had received alcohol, although actual alcohol recipients estimated the greater consumption. Even so, expectations accounted for half the variance of all main effects.

Verbal aggression occurred in the provoked group but not in the unprovoked group. Intensity of shocks administered to provoking partners was higher for those told they would receive alcohol than for tonic-expecting subjects. Actual alcohol and actual provocation (vs. no alcohol and no provocation) had no effect on the shock measure. Thus, differences in levels of aggression among heavy social drinkers were primarily, in this setting, a function of seeing oneself as having drunk alcohol. The authors suggest that alcohol may be used to justify aggression to oneself, even when there has been no provocation and no real drinking. It is also the case that assuming the role of the drinker may induce the personal expectation of expressive aggression. One regrets the absence of clinical debriefings after the experiment to elucidate further how drinking expectations or self-concepts of the drinking role played their role in producing experimental aggression. Such debriefing might also have illuminated subject's perceptions of what the experimenters had intended to be "insult."

One reflects further on Tamerin et al. (1970) to the effect that there are strong incongruities among the before, during, and after drinking states in violent alcoholics. The presumed intertwining of drug, set, role, and psychodynamic features—these differentially operating as a function of setting—thus remains a major inquiry area. A pharmacological agent such as alcohol certainly generates altered sensations, including nonspecific effects subject to interpretation, some of which is learned from others (see Becker, 1963). Meanings are derived from inner states and projected onto external events, just as, conversely, external meanings are imposed upon the individual, becoming his/her own beliefs. Insofar as alcohol alters that which is sensed and provides, as an alternate state, an occasion requiring new meanings, these can well be ascribed to the environment. As we saw in the study by Taylor and Gammon (1975), attributions occur, and they are the more hostile as the subject is hostile him/herself. It is imperative, therefore, to examine environments, natural or experimental, not for meanings the experimenter attaches to stimuli that he/she injects and names, but for the stimuli actually acting on the subject and the significations the subject attaches thereto. Clearly, the research worker must appreciate the phenomenology of violence during the acute alcohol states as well as before and after them. It is up to us to resolve the contradictions inherent in what presents itself superficially as the inconsistency of the violent drinker or the "erratic" nature of alcohol-related violent crime.

Conclusion

There is little systematic work on the setting–alcohol–violence nexus. There is none which uses another drug besides alcohol as a control along with the placebo. There are fine naturalistic observations but no natural experiments. There is respectable experimentation but little concern with phenomenology and certainly no marriage of experimentation and psychodynamics in the same set of studies.

The literature does tell us, common-sensibly, that some environmental features elicit aggression and that alcohol does play a role. That role is a mix, at the very least, of psychopharmacology, prior physiological/anatomical effects, the drinking context, learning, arousal, and expectations. The separate studies on stimuli to drinking, on the special psychological and neurological features of subgroups of heavy drinkers, on stimuli to aggression per se, and the statistics and available case studies on violence are all instructive. They confirm, albeit with qualifications and cautions, that alcohol is *not* an incidental feature, although it may be a contextual one not easily capable of separate, partist analysis. The work to date also confirms that situational variations do influence drinking, psychological states, and aggression and violence.

Over the long run, the research task is a matter of elucidating the most common elements that elicit and prevent violence in drinkers, and ordering these in some sort of hierarchy of probable presence and effects. There is also the question of pertinent research methodologies, in particular, how to find violent validations (i.e., real crime) for aggressive experimental design. Further, how does one encourage research at various levels —cultural, group, and individual—and in several settings—natural, quasi-natural, and experimental? In the latter, one should also keep in mind that the experiment *is* the setting, its nice inner design perhaps not as consequential for dependent outcomes as the milieu variations implicit.

As for criminology: Advances in scientific criminology do not occur at a rate faster than in its basic disciplines, from genetics and neurology through anthropology. Criminology itself has not been an experimental science but a descriptive one, and its descriptions have delivered insight infrequently. It is, and will probably remain, a "poor relative," so that such research encouragement as is warranted must be addressed to members of the basic disciplines interested in alcohol and violence, or to those few criminologists with basic training in the appropriate sciences, and to the interdisciplinary eclectic.

There is in criminology, as in alcohol studies, an eminently practical thrust, and a moral one. The history of that practice seems more successful for alcohol research than for criminology, for the latter has been forced to address an immense variety of behaviors having in common a social–political–moral process, the criminal law, rather than being derived from empirical entities (i.e., constructs of the sort useful in science). The focus in violence at least narrows the field and may indeed allow us the luxury of addressing a set of natural behavioral entities.

While the argument for stamping out crime, in this instance violence, is certainly justified, it is unwise to claim that the social sciences are strong contenders for providing tranquility and public safety. It will be much easier to learn about alcohol, situational stimuli, and violence than it will be to do anything about stopping crime.

To learn about ourselves as humans must be the sufficient near-term reward. To appreciate the stimulating complexity of things heretofore thought of as simple (alcohol "causes" violence) is cautionary and instructive. The longer-term practical goal, violence prevention, will be harder to come by. Nevertheless, such facts as are adduced, when communicated as part of public education, may at least retard multiplying evils born of ignorant public policy. Certainly, it is worthwhile to do research on situational variables in the alcohol–setting–violence nexus, but with the proviso that, but for an occasional happy surprise, the merit is a contribution to basic knowledge not the promise of any immediate program of violence prevention or control.

4 Situational Factors in the Relationship between Alcohol and Crime

PAUL M. ROMAN

Introduction

Despite the considerable literature on the relationship between the consumption of alcohol and the occurrence of criminal behavior reviewed throughout this volume, there are essentially no studies which provide empirical evidence about the situational settings most conducive to the dual presence of drinking and crime. This may be seen as a challenge to research within the paradigm of social epidemiology: The agency of alcohol and the human actor as host who commits criminal acts are specified, but the environment wherein agent and host become linked has neither been specified nor studied. Put somewhat differently, the overwhelming number of events in which both alcohol and criminal behavior are present would lead to the compelling surmise that alcohol is the causal factor through its "disinhibiting" effects on the actor. But equally, if not more, significant is the datum that criminal behavior does not occur in the overwhelming number of events in which alcohol is present.

This chapter is an overview of a number of hypotheses stemming from several bodies of published literature, prepared to determine the "state of the art" linking situational factors to drinking and criminal behavior. Since there is an absence of literature bearing directly on the topic, it might be concluded that there is no basis for a review; on the other hand, given a broader goal of extending research on alcohol and crime, there is justification for establishing frames of reference within which such essential research could be conducted.

This overview begins with a definition of the parameters of "situational factors linking alcohol and crime," which is followed by an examination

PAUL M. ROMAN. Department of Sociology, Tulane University, New Orleans, Louisiana.

of two interrelated frameworks within which these situational linkages can be conceptualized: anomie and cultural norms. The methodological and contextual perspective labeled "situational ecology" is then outlined, together with potentially relevant structural features of settings in which alcohol use and criminal behavior are concomitant events. Finally, there is a concluding statement.

Delimiting the Parameters of the Research Problem

An immediate difficulty in any analysis of the relationship between alcohol use and criminal behavior lies in the definitional ambiguity attending both concepts. Thus we here suggest conceptual parameters for "alcohol use" and "criminal behavior" which may facilitate the generation of research hypotheses as well as serving as guides in empirical measurement.

It is an empirical fact that the number of drinking events known to be concomitant with criminal behavior is miniscule relative to the total number of drinking events. Although not quantified empirically, a considerable number and range of acts of deviant behavior accompany drinking events, ranging from improper sexual advances to homicide. Deviance in this instance is defined as those behaviors likely to elicit social sanctions by members of the group in a nondrinking situation but less likely to elicit such reactions in a drinking situation. This highlights the implicit definition of most drinking situations as partial "time outs" from normative proscriptions.

A psychological element relevant to this formulation is that the effects of ethanol consumption are in most instances some form of disinhibition, with the accompanying proposition that disinhibition increases with increases in ethanol levels in the body. It then follows that the likelihood of deviance increases with increasing ethanol consumption. An alternative conceptualization of disinhibition is aggression, which is a social psychological rather than a psychological construct. The widely accepted and partially established notion that alcohol consumption produces disinhibition again points to a normative quality of drinking occasions wherein "different" behavior is expected and to some degree tolerated. We suggest that aggressive acts can be placed on a lengthy continuum, and that this continuum includes most of the "different" behavior occurring concomitantly with alcohol consumption. At one end of the continuum we find persons who talk more frequently and more loudly after consuming alcohol. Such behavior may be seen as invasions, however mild, of others' social space. Further, alcohol consumption in bars or at cocktail parties accompanies conversations with persons one would not likely converse with except for the presence of alcohol; again, this may be seen as a very mild form of aggression.

Moving along the continuum to interaction between persons of the opposite sex, drinking is frequently accompanied by what might be viewed as verbal negotiations which may lead to physical contact and perhaps ultimately to sexual intercourse. Here the aggression concept is more clearly illustrated, although the analysis of such interaction vis-à-vis alcohol consumption is usually clouded by use of the narrow concept of disinhibition.

Finally, the more potent examples of aggression concomitant with alcohol consumption are well known and are discussed in detail elsewhere in this volume. These, of course, include forcible rape, assault, and homicide.

It is suggested, therefore, that an understanding of the role of situational factors in linking alcohol and crime would be facilitated by extending the frame of reference to include those events which are usually not viewed as problematic, but which may be morphologically similar to those problematic events which include both alcohol consumption and felonious crimes.

"Crime" constitutes a set of definitional constructs that may be imposed upon deviant acts at some point following their occurrence. This imposition may be attempted by laymen who observe the deviance or by "imputational specialists" (Lofland, 1969) such as police, who either directly or indirectly obtain information about the event, with the ultimate decision about the appropriate labeling of the event resting with judicial authority. "Crime" is a relative definition that is not bound to social time or space. Returning to the continuum of aggressive behaviors, it is significant to specify the conditions under which acts of aggression concomitant with alcohol consumption become socially translated into "crimes." In other words, when does the invasion of social space become "assault," the verbal aggression become "slander," and the sexual advances become attempted or forcible "rape"?

Thus it is proposed that ethanol consumption is disinhibiting and usually occurs in normative circumstances in which controls are relaxed in anticipation of the disinhibition; that a range of forms of aggression is likely to accompany drinking events and increase in frequency with the blood alcohol concentration obtained; and that through a series of systematic social reactions, some proportion of these deviant acts subsequently comes to be defined as criminal behaviors.

It is also important to look at drinking within conceptual limits. The delimitation of this chapter focuses on alcohol consumption per se, without attempting to specify excessive drinking, deviant drinking, alcohol abuse, drunkenness, or alcoholism. The reasoning here is that all of the latter definitions are inclusive of deviant acts; that is, drunkenness usually connotes aggression or other socially offensive behavior. The delimitation to consumption alone avoids psychological conditions and personality traits as intervening variables between drinking and deviance; this is to maintain the focus within a sociological perspective. The delimitation attempts to avoid causal imputation and alternatively views drinking as a risk factor in the commission of criminal acts. The delimitation leaves the parameters of the definition of criminal behavior open, although published literature would lead us to assume that this behavior is principally aggression against persons and property.

It might be possible, but seemingly less feasible, to specify application of this frame of reference to the occurrence of deviant and criminal acts among problem drinkers and alcoholics. Bacon (1963), for example, suggests that criminal acts frequently accompany the progression of alcoholism and the "desocialization" of the alcoholic. The evident difficulties here are the immediate contaminations of definition, with deviant and sometimes criminal acts included in the definitions of alcoholics and problem drinkers. In the latter instance particularly (Cahalan, 1970; Cahalan & Room, 1974), trouble with the police can be a defining characteristic of a problem drinker. Furthermore, the definition of alcoholism is practically impossible for research within the framework of social epidemiology, other than limiting the definition to those cases formally defined as alcoholics by physicians, with this definition again likely contaminated by a record of notably aggressive and/or criminal behavior.

Thus the delimitation offered is both broad and narrow, broad in the sense of encompassing a continuum of aggressive behavior and all drinking events but narrow through avoiding intervening variables of a psychological nature and avoiding differentiation of drinkers. The delimitation anticipates the direction of the subsequent discussion, which first focuses on the structure of norms as it may affect the linkage between alcohol consumption and criminal behavior, and then turns to actual normative content. This sets the stage for a discussion of situational ecology.

The Structure and Strength of Norms: Degrees of Anomie

The concept of anomie has long been central to sociological analysis of deviant behavior. It can refer to the absence of normative structure, the disintegration of preexisting normative structure, or the absence of metanorms to guide selection between conflicting normative prescriptions. It is the latter usage which is most appropriate to the present concern. The penetration of the term "anomie" into the popular culture has diluted this subtle sociological distinction: While knowledge of a variety of normative orientations abounds in most situations, anomie marks the absence of meta-norms to determine the resolution of contradictory prescriptions. Regardless of how the notion of anomie is operationalized, its basic assumption is essentially negative; that is, deviant behavior results from an absence of norms and social controls. For present purposes, "anomie" is specified as the absence of structures to elicit sanctions toward aggressive acts and excessive drinking.

An anomic explanation is implicit in much of the published literature on alcohol and crime. The use of this approach in framing issues relative to situational factors in the alcohol and crime relationship might include a dual focus on the effects of weak(ened) social controls on patterns of drinking behavior and the effects of such controls on criminal behavior. Further, one could examine the effects of such weak(ened) structures on the escalation of deviant acts and the decision-making transactions which ultimately produce labeled criminal behaviors.

There is empirical and theoretical literature on the relationships between anomie and drinking (Snyder, 1964), and between anomie and crime (e.g., Gibbons, 1976), but empirical studies which approach a concern about the relationship between alcohol consumption and crime are rare—with the exception of the comprehensive study reported by R. Jessor, Graves, Hanson, and Jessor (1968), and in that instance the research did not extend to felonious acts.

It is predicted that research would reveal anomie to facilitate the occurrence of aggression concomitant with alcohol consumption. To this end, the measurement of anomie would be most significant at the group rather than the societal level. For example, normative conflict and the relative absence of meta-norms would be expected under conditions of rapid social change, migration, and interactions characterized by the presence of individuals or groups from variant backgrounds of socialization. The neighborhood could be the unit of analysis within which the degree of anomie could be specified. The presumed mechanisms of consequence are that both aggressive behavior and alcohol consumption would occur relatively unchecked in anomic settings.

The Content of Cultural and Subcultural Norms

In the determination of the relationship between alcohol and crime, the content of normative structures vis-à-vis aggressive behavior and alcohol consumption is of considerable importance. Normative content interacts with the degree of anomie, and the effects of normative content are either muted or accentuated by the degree of normative structure in particular situations. MacAndrew and Edgerton (1969) have argued that cultural norms define the typical behaviors that accompany drinking situations; they bring substantial anthropological evidence together which demonstrates the cross-cultural diversity in behavioral reactions to ethanol consumption and are especially concerned with rejecting the stereotype that aggressive and antisocial behaviors are inevitable consequences of heavy drinking in human groups. This general proposition points toward the possibility of subcultural variations in drinking norms within American society. Such variations in behavioral expectations may account for variations in the association between alcohol and crime across different subcultural and ethnic groups. In other words, aggressive behavior which follows alcohol consumption, and which comes to be defined as criminal, may be a function of normative traditions which may act as self-fulfilling prophecies. Such a surmise is based on the assumption of substantial subcultural diversity across American society, encompassing social-class and regional differences as well as those based on ethnicity.

Levine (1977) has documented the changes in American attitudes toward the relationship between drinking and crime and violence, implying that normative variations in behavior may have been a consequence of different belief systems which were altered over time. Levy and Kunitz (1974) have considered differences in drinking norms and patterns within various American Indian tribes, and an extensive review of empirical evidence confirming the presence of various symptomatic drinking-related behaviors among American Indians has been reported by Leland (1976). In a classic study, Snyder (1958) considered the origins and social supports for Jewish drinking practices, wherein routine and ritualized alcohol consumption has minimal social consequences, especially in terms of expected aggressive behavior. Fallding (1974) has attempted to derive the drinking norms governing behavior in a middle-class New Jersey community. Stivers (1976) has traced the transformation of drinking customs in rural Ireland, where maximal consumption with minimal aggressive consequences was normative, to the case of Irish-Americans and their at least partial acceptance of a "drunkard" subcultural stereotype, with consequent changes in expected behavior.

It is likely that normative structures act to reduce risks and insulate group members against aggressive behavior associated with drinking occasions, which in turn may be translated into definitions of such behavior as criminal. There is no doubt that expectations and tolerance of aggressive behavior likewise vary by age, social class, and ethnicity. Such variations in the content of norms regarding both alcohol consumption and aggressive behaviors point toward the research possibilities of examining covariation. This could provide for developing a matrix of hypothesized interrelations among these two categories of variation in normative content, further including consideration of the possible effects of degrees of normative structure or anomie, as discussed in the previous section.

Situational Ecology

The foregoing conceptual frameworks could provide the basis for hypothesis construction within a methodological and contextual approach that we here summarily label as "situational ecology." Such exploration could build upon research on deviant behavior that has proceeded within the somewhat ambiguous approach known as ethnomethodology, social psychological experimentation focused on the genesis and escalation of deviance, and studies which specifically examine the physical ecology of settings in order to predict the behavior likely to occur in those settings.

One of the oldest and most influential hypotheses regarding the linkage between alcohol and crime is within the framework of situational ecology; namely, that the 19th-century saloon in America was a setting which both permitted and promoted excessive alcohol consumption and attendant aggressive acts. N. Clark (1976), among other historical scholars, has argued that the saloon per se rather than alcohol was the primary object of concern in the Temperance movement. While Prohibition succeeded in eliminating most "saloons," there has been minimal subsequent attention to the relationship between drinking environments and crime, aside from descriptions of behavior in isolated examples of contemporary "saloons" which are included in the contribution by Roizen (Chapter 6, this volume).

Lofland (1969) has provided a conceptual framework within which hypotheses about situational factors linking drinking and crime might be fruitfully organized and reviewed. Lofland proposes that deviant acts are of two general types: defensive deviance and adventurous deviance. Most of his attention is devoted to the former category, and he postulates a series of events labeled "threat," "encapsulation," and "closure" which lead to the defensive deviant act. Of significance to the situational ecology framework is his postulation of intervening factors involving the actor and his/her socialization, others present in the situation, and available "hardware" as differentially facilitating the commission of a defensive deviant act. He proceeds further to consider the possible role of these facilitating factors in the escalation of deviant behavior, which in the terms of the present framework includes focusing on the social transformation of aggressive acts into criminal acts. These factors may affect the likelihood of excessive drinking, of aggression, and of the labeling of aggressive behavior as crime.

This approach provides a focus for considering several substantive aspects of drinking environments relative to the potential for aggressive behavior which is subsequently translated into criminal behavior, of which the following are examples:

1. Other actors in the drinking environment
   a. Drinking alone
   b. Drinking with relatives
   c. Drinking with acquaintances
   d. Drinking with unknown others
2. Other drinkers in drinking environment
   a. Drinking in presence of other drinkers
   b. Drinking in presence of nondrinkers
3. Role relationships vis-à-vis expected aggressive behavior
   a. Dominant relationships in which aggression is expected from drinker
   b. Submissive relationships in which aggression is not expected from drinker
   c. Equal-power relationships in which aggression may be directed or received
4. Mobility
   a. Drinker remaining in drinking environment
   b. Drinker moving from drinking environment to new environment
5. Definition of drinking situation
   a. Drinking for escape/drug effects
   b. Recreational/"time-out" drinking events
   c. Ceremonial drinking events
6. Drinking environment
   a. Drinking in home
   b. Drinking in private nonhome setting
   c. Drinking in tavern/bar
   d. Drinking in open space
7. Facilitating hardware
   a. Absence of aggression-related hardware
   b. Drinker or other's possession of aggression-related hardware
   c. Copresence of aggression-related hardware
8. Labeling agents
   a. Absence of labeling/social control agents
   b. Presence of labeling/social control agents

The procedure in utilizing such a framework would be to develop situation-based hypotheses within multivariate matrices. These in turn could be embedded in matrices from the guiding theoretical constructs of the structure and content of norms prevailing in these situational contexts.

Conclusion

This overview offers the observation that there is a minimum of specific literature describing the empirical relationships between situational contexts of drinking and occurrence of criminal behavior. The fundamental importance of this issue in considering the alcohol and crime relationship does, however, provide justification for developing hypotheses that might be subject to eventual empirical test. In this chapter we have delimited the problem as centered upon the occurrence of aggressive acts in drinking situations and the escalation of such acts to criminal behavior through processes of social definition. The perspectives of the structure and content of norms are offered as sources of concepts to guide consideration of possible empirical relationships. Situational ecology is offered as a contextual perspective within which several sets of hypotheses could be organized as a step toward developing a research agenda for the study of situational effects.

5 Alcohol Careers and Criminal Careers

JAMES J. COLLINS, JR.

Introduction

Perspective of the Chapter

This chapter, as well as the others in this volume, is concerned with the relationship between alcohol consumption and and criminal behavior. Specifically, the covariation between drinking and serious crime, as these behavioral categories covary over time in individual careers, is the focus of this discussion. A "careers" perspective toward the alcohol–crime relationship is appropriate for related empirical, methodological, and theoretical reasons.

It is clear from previous research on drinking and crime patterns that age regularities characterize each of these two classes of behavior. The frequency and volume of drinking change by age; the seriousness and types of drinking problems show systematic age variations. The number of individuals who are active in criminal behavior and the types of such behavioral involvement also vary by age. Further, as is shown later, the young adult years are especially notable for both drinking problems and serious crime problems. This finding suggests that age should be an organizing dimension in the consideration of the alcohol–crime relationship.

Age variations in the relevant variables also suggest the appropriateness of longitudinal data and research designs. The ideal research approach is one that follows individuals over time and looks at questions of onset, patterning, and changes in drinking and crime. Such research exists only for selected aspects of the alcohol–crime relationship. Alcohol careers and criminal careers literatures are essentially separate bodies of research and theory, and each is examined independently. We report on this previous

JAMES J. COLLINS, JR. Research Triangle Institute, Research Triangle Park, North Carolina.

work with emphasis on that which uses a longitudinal or quasi-longitudinal approach. Longitudinal designs speak most directly to the age–crime patterns of interest here. Literature that focuses on both alcohol and crime as they covary in individual careers is also examined. Because this literature is very limited, an important goal of this chapter is to sort out relevant findings from the separate literatures on drinking careers and on crime careers in a way that augments the sparse literature that deals with both together.

There are also theoretical reasons for a career perspective toward the alcohol–crime relationship. Past attempts to explain the etiologies of drinking problems and crime recognize the relevance of age to those explanations. A variety of psychological and sociological concepts—such as stress, dependency, masculinity, anticipatory socialization, opportunity, and power—have been used in the past to help explain drinking and/or crime problems. These concepts derive explanatory power, in part, from their variation along an age dimension. General theories of human behavior that focus on such things as psychological development or socialization also acknowledge the importance of age.

Thus a career perspective provides an appropriate orientation for considering the alcohol–crime relationship. Past findings and theory indicate this, and the powerful longitudinal methodology is suggested by the nature of the explanatory problem. This chapter then, uses a career perspective to examine the sequence and patterns of drinking and illegal activity as they develop over age or life stages.

The Age Variable

Our use of the age variable in this chapter requires some clarification. As indicated earlier, we have been led to consider age as important by the empirical regularities indicating that it varies systematically and in similar ways with the two major variables at issue here: alcohol use and criminal behavior. But age as a variable can be relevant in different ways. In this discussion, it is used as a simple classificatory variable around which to organize and analyze data, "as an orientational focus around which facts can be assembled" (Klausner, 1973, p. 87).

Age can also be interpreted as an explanatory variable; potentially this is a more important use if explanation is to follow description. There is a need to locate those conceptual elements embedded in the measure of time or human development operationally defined as age that may have explanatory power. Later in this chapter, a potentially fruitful theoretical perspective is suggested.

In addition to classificatory and explanatory uses, the age variable may be useful from a public policy perspective. Ultimately it is hoped that more complete explanation of the alcohol–crime relationship will result in knowledge with the capacity to inform public policy. The organization of this knowledge around the age variable may facilitate policy implementation. Policy makers are acclimated to consider the relevance of age to policy formulation. Public policy is often developed to apply differentially to age groups.

Methodological Problems

The definition and measurement of problem drinking is itself problematic. Problem drinking can be defined in terms of frequency or amount of drinking. The definition can be based on indicators of psychological state or social adjustment; problem drinking can be defined clinically (as in a diagnosis of alcoholism), or multidimensional scales of problem drinking can be used. The judgment of social workers or probation officers can be used to indicate that an individual is a problem drinker. The definition and measurement issues are complex. They are not dealt with separately or at length here; more attention is paid to these issues by Greenberg in Chapter 2 of this volume. When a definition–measurement problem is relevant to a discussion or critique of particular findings it is discussed. The general strategy is to accept an ecletic and "problem"-oriented view of deviant drinking. The multidimensional approach used by Cahalan and Room (1974) is preferred; it allows analysis to consider multidimensional aspects of problem drinking but yet is a definition that is also specific and narrowly construed in its particular ingredients.

The definition and measurement of crime is also problematic, since the word "crime" can be interpreted in a number of ways. One position is that crime is a legal concept and should only include events that are officially recorded as illegal acts, or even that only offenses formally confirmed by a conviction should be considered crimes. This strict interpretation is not followed here. Neither are behavioral criteria applied to classify crime on the basis of undimensional and generic behavior categories. Any attempt to define crime in a way that is consistent with both legal criteria and with human behavior categories, while also meeting the demands of valid measurement, is characterized by unresolvable tensions between legal and scientific demands. Crime is broadly and heuristically defined in this chapter. Estimates of criminal behavior that include both officially recorded and unrecorded crime are preferred, but they are infrequently available. Methodological problems of definition and measurement of crime are dealt with in this discussion only to the extent that they impinge on particular research findings or interpretations.

Serious crime is the focus of this chapter. Offenses such as homicide, rape, assault, robbery, burglary, arson, fraud, and embezzlement are of interest; nonserious offenses like public drunkeness, vagrancy, gambling, and disorderly conduct are considered only to the extent that they may be pertinent to the discussion of criminal careers. Suicide and traffic offenses (including driving while intoxicated) are arbitrarily excluded from consideration.

Overview of Balance of the Chapter

The next section of this chapter contains a discussion of the relevant literature for analysis of drinking patterns and drinking problems as they vary and develop over lifetimes. Following that, criminal behavior patterns are examined as they change over offender lifetimes. Then, drinking and criminal patterns are discussed together. Finally, conceptual, policy, and future research issues are discussed.

Throughout the chapter the age dimension is important; both drinking and illegal behavior vary systematically by age. The chapter concentrates on empirical research that deals systematically with the age/time dimension, but relevant biographical and autobiographical data are also introduced. A number of biographical sources were consulted, and although these kinds of data have limitations, they can be used to generate insights and as the basis for comparison to other empirical findings.

The chapter focuses on males. This is largely a function of previous research and writing. Virtually no systematic work has attempted to look at the alcohol and serious crime relationship among females. Past work that has considered the alcohol–crime connection for women has focused on prostitution or, more recently, on family violence. Prostitution is not of interest here due to its nonserious nature; the family violence literature is discussed by Hamilton and Collins in Chapter 7 of this volume.

Alcohol Careers

Drinking Patterns

Alcohol consumption is widespread in the United States. Survey results indicate that 68% of the U.S. adult population drinks at least once a year. The percentage of drinkers is higher for men (Cahalan & Cisin, 1968).

Drinking patterns vary systematically along a number of dimensions. Those who live in the inner-city are more likely to drink than those who live in rural areas; religious affiliation affects alcohol consumption patterns; race and socioeconomic status are related to drinking patterns (Bahr & Caplow, 1973; Cahalan & Cisin, 1968; Cahalan & Room, 1972; L. N. Robins, Murphy, & Breckenridge, 1968; Room, 1972). Developmental background and psychological makeup have also been shown to be related to drinking patterns (Jessor & Jessor, 1975; McClelland, Davis, Kalin, & Wanner, 1972; Rachal, Williams, Brehm, Cavanaugh, Moore, & Eckerman, 1975; L. N. Robins, Bates, & O'Neal, 1962; A. F. Williams, 1976).

It has also been estabilshed clearly that age is systematically related to drinking patterns. Drinking normally begins in adolescence or before; according to surveys of three student cohorts from the seventh, eighth, and ninth grades which were followed over 4 years, 83% of males and 79% of females have begun to drink by the 12th grade (Jessor & Jessor, 1977). In another survey of 13,122 students in grades 7 to 12, 80% of the adolescents reported having had a drink, and 74% reported having drank two to three times or more (Rachal et al., 1975). This survey also indicated that boys drank more often than girls and that 23% of both sexes drank at least once a week. The Jessor and Jessor survey indicates that after 4 years in college, 95% of the subjects in their survey had begun to drink.

Among adults one has to look at the specifics of drinking patterns by age to describe adequately age–drinking variation. Frequency of drinking and amount drank per drinking occasion need to be considered. Older men drink more frequently than younger men, but younger men tend to drink more on any particular drinking occasion (Hartford & Mills, 1978; Robinson, 1976; Vogel-Sprott, 1976). As old age approaches, the percentage of drinkers classified as heavy drinkers decreases (Cahalan & Cisin, 1968).

Spontaneous Remission

To help understand the covariation of alcohol consumption and criminal behavior, drinking patterns need to be characterized as they vary over drinking careers. The patterns appear to change considerably; as already mentioned, there are differences in frequency of drinking and amount drank per drinking occasion between younger and older men. Survey results for representative population samples also show that problems associated with drinking tend to vary over age. Research on special populations like those in treatment or those with criminal convictions also shows that problems associated with drinking, once developed, are not necessarily continuous and permanent: "available evidence clearly indicates that many people change their drinking behavior markedly over a span of time. . . . Many people evolve or mature out of their drinking problems" (Cahalan & Cisin, 1976b, p. 103).

In a probability sample of American men, ages 21 to 59, Cahalan and Cisin (1976b) reported that compared to men who reported having a current problem as a result of drinking, twice as many reported having had a problem with drinking at some time. In a follow-up from a college student sample, Fillmore (1975) reported similar results. Data were originally collected in the period 1949–1952 from 17,000 students in 27 American colleges and universities; in 1971–1972, follow-up data were collected from a stratified random sample of 206 of the original respondents. There were sex differences in changes in problem drinking from Time 1 to Time 2; but as Fillmore (1975) summarized the findings: "Among both men and women there was a trend to shift toward nonproblem drinking" (p. 826).

The research of Robins and her colleagues on special populations also indicates that problem drinking is not a consistent, continuous phenomenon. In a study of a former patient population of a child guidance clinic some 30 years after contact with the clinic, there is evidence of remission of heavy drinking (Robins, Bates, & O'Neal, 1962). In a comparison of the drinking behavior of black and white subjects, Robins, Murphy, and Breckenridge (1968) also found that the percentage of those who are currently heavy drinkers is lower than this percentage when *ever* being a heavy drinker is the criterion. Goodwin, Crane, and Guze (1971), in a follow-up of 223 convicted male felons after 8 years, concluded that alcoholism tends to disappear with increasing age. Hoffman and Nelson (1971), in an examination of intelligence and personality characteristics in 148 alcoholic patients, concluded that "there are fewer differences between alcoholics and nonalcoholics than between alcoholics of different ages" (p. 145). Clearly, drinking careers are characterized by variety and inconsistency.

R. Roizen, Cahalan, and Shanks (1978) examined the literature concerning spontaneous remission of problem drinking and conducted a careful analysis of longitudinal data gathered during two national surveys. The longitudinal results for the surveys are reported in Cahalan and Room (1974). The R. Roizen *et al.* (1978) article reports that past research indicates about a 25-point spread in estimates of spontaneous remission—between 15 and 40%. The surveys by Cahalan and co-workers (Cahalan, 1970; Cahalan & Cisin, 1968, 1976b; Cahalan & Room, 1972) show that there is roughly a 30-point spread in problem drinker remission rates between Time 1 and Time 2. The remission rate goes from 24 to 55% and depends to a large extent on the standards that are applied to define problem drinking. The rate of remission is virtually zero if abstinence is the criterion; the overall range of improvement is between 11 and 71% depending on definition criteria (R. Roizen et al. 1978).

R. Roizen, Cahalan, and Shanks demonstrated the complexity of the age–problem–drinking relationship by conducting a sensitivity analysis under different definitions of the dependent and independent variables for different sample subgroups. The relationship of age to problem drinking is important, given the focus of this chapter, and the relevance of age depends in part on how the dependent variable is defined. If the magnitude of the Time 2 drinking problem score is the measure of the dependent variable, age is positively associated with drinking problem score: beta equals .168. If the dependent variable is defined as improvement in the problem drinking score between Time 1 and Time 2, the relationship is inverse: beta equals −.160. If the dependent variable is measured in terms of a raw change in the problem drinking score between Time 1 and Time 2, age does not enter the regression. In this latter case, age is found to be unrelated to problem drinking. R. Roizen et al. (1978) interpreted the findings as follows:

> The relationship between age and each of the outcome variables is particularly noteworthy: low age predicts high time 2 problem scores but also high improvement, and age does not enter the regression on raw changes at all. Clearly, studies of prognosis would come away with quite different impressions of the effect of age, depending on their scoring of the dependent variable. Contrary to the picture of problem drinkers created in clinical studies—where the median age of alcoholics is most often in the mid-forties—cross-sectional, general population surveys repeatedly have shown that drinking problems are largely a young man's game. . . . In a sense this finding merely is replicated in the positive association between youth and time 2 problem levels. Youth may also emerge as a predictor of improvement because of its influence on initial position in the full sample, an influence that provides younger, rather than older, respondents with more opportunity to remit because of the generally higher mean problem scores of younger men at time 1. The disappearance of age in the regression equation for raw change suggests, however, that young men are more likely than older men both to acquire and to lose drinking problems. The association between age and raw change is curvilinear, which eliminates age from the regression equation for raw changes. By extension, the positive association between youth and remission becomes a by-product of the fact that youth predicts greater *instability* in drinking problems over time. (pp. 212–213)

We have quoted at length here for related substantive and methodological reasons. The important substantive points are: (1) age and drinking problems are related; drinking problems tend to be most serious for young men, and (2) drinking problems are not stable through lifetimes; they tend to be episodic and transitory. The important methodological points are: (1) the age–drinking relationship is a complex one, and (2) research findings tend to be sensitive to definitional and measurement decisions.

Drinking Career Problems

It will be useful at this point to discuss how our examination of drinking careers fits into the overall goal of this chapter—to examine the relationship of alcohol careers and criminal careers. We are not concerned with the entire range of problems associated with alcohol consumption. Excessive or problem drinking can create physiological, psychological, and social problems. Cirrhosis of the liver, mental disorders, and job-related problems are examples of common outcomes associated with problem drinking. Alcoholism, however defined, is typically estimated to afflict 5–10% of the drinking population. As serious as alcoholism problems may be, they are not the subject of this discussion. On the other hand, in our analysis of the alcohol–crime relationship, we do not wish to define "crime" too narrowly.

Although our focus is serious crime, the occurrence of a serious criminal event often depends on chance factors. A fight between individuals in one set of circumstances may not be viewed as a serious problem but in another set of circumstances may become an aggravated assault or homicide. Our purpose, then, is to select a wide range of problems associated with drinking without eliminating consideration of behaviors that are, potentially if not technically, criminal. As we show later in this chapter, serious crime is predominantly attributable to youthful and young adult offenders. Drinking problems of the kind that are relevant here are also most common in younger age groups. On the surface, the similar age patterns of drinking and crime problems suggest that careful attention needs to be paid to the young adult years.

There has been a tendency in the literature to examine age variations in both drinking and crime careers in three approximate age range categories: adolescence (< 18), young adulthood (18–25), and later adulthood (> 25). There are several reasons for using age 18 to delineate adolescence and adulthood. This age is legally important; the law has come increasingly to recognize age 18 as the point where changes in privilege and responsibility status take place. Eighteen-year-olds can make contracts and vote, and are subject to the adult justice system rather than the juvenile justice system. Individuals under age 18 can be tried in adult courts, and although some offenders over 18 are handled under special "youthful offender" programs, in general age 18 separates juveniles and adults. Past research has also tended to use age 18 as the boundary between adolescence and adulthood.

Separation of the young and later adult years is also justified by consistently observed empirical regularities and by past conventions. Drinking, problem drinking, and crime patterns are distinct in younger and older adult years. It may not be easy to locate the age which best divides younger and older adults, but age 25 seems a reasonable choice.

Problem-Drinking Patterns of Juveniles

We define juveniles as individuals who have not reached their 18th birthdays. Earlier we indicated that the vast majority of older teenagers have consumed alcohol at least once. In strict terms the consumption of alcohol by individuals who are less than 18 years of age is usually, itself, illegal. Whether one tends to view teenage drinking as illegal and deviant or whether one views it as normative depends on perspective. A juvenile court judge may be inclined to see teenage drinking as deviant behavior, whereas teenagers may view their peers' drinking as harmless, routine behavior. The aspect of any alcohol–crime relationship in the juvenile years of interest here is not that having to do with the illegal nature of the drinking behavior itself, but rather whether or not the drinking appears to stimulate or "cause" other, more serious, forms of illegality.

Three general points are made here. First, a significant percentage of juveniles either drink frequently or are classified as engaged in problem drinking. The national survey of high school students referred to earlier indicates that 24% of boys and 18% of girls in the 9th to 12th grades are classified as moderate to heavy or heavy drinkers (Rachal et al., 1975, pp. 40–42). Jessor and Jessor (1977) have reported that 42% of 12th-grade males and 33% of 12th-grade females are engaged in problem drinking. Problem drinking is operationally defined to include a measure of drinking frequency and negative consequences associated with drinking.

Second, research findings indicate that there is an association between teenage drinking and other forms of antisocial behavior. Juveniles who are delinquent, or who engage in deviant behavior, appear to drink more than juveniles not officially classified as delinquent; 88–90% of one delinquent population reported using alcohol (Friedman & Friedman, 1973). This percentage is higher than that for a "normal" population. Wirt, Winokur, and Roff (1975) found a "strong association" between antisocial behavior and drinking. Rachal et al. (1975) found a direct relationship between drinking and marijuana use. Jessor and Jessor (1975) found "strong support for the relation of drinking onset to other possible transition or problem behaviors'' (p. 45). The interpretation of Mandell and Ginzburg also supports the finding that deviant youth drank more than nondeviant youth, but they hypothesized that this deviance–drinking association does not indicate a causal relationship:

> The data do support the hypothesis that youth who behave in unacceptable or delinquent ways do drink more than other youth. But even they do not commit as much delinquent behavior while under the influence of alcohol. This has led to the hypothesis that alcohol use among youth may serve as an alternative to other unacceptable behavior. (Mandell & Ginzburg, 1976, p. 184)

In this comment and in later discussion, Mandell and Ginzburg suggest that teenage drinking and teenage deviance have a common set of "causal" factors. It appears clear that there is no simple causal relationship between juvenile drinking and juvenile delinquency. The same is true of adult drinking and crime.

Pernanen (1976, Chapter 1, this volume) has provided an excellent discussion of the variety of ways that alcohol consumption and aggressive behavior may be related. Any relationship between alcohol and crime is almost certainly complex and interactive. (The manifestation of "pathological intoxication," that is, eruptive violent behavior as an apparent direct result of ingesting alcohol, may be an exception. However, it appears this condition is rare [Mark & Ervin, 1970, p. 126; Moyer, 1976, pp. 80–96; Skelton, 1970].) We conclude that, while it is true that drinking and delinquent behavior can be shown to vary together, it is not possible to make the claim that the former causes the latter. In fact, a hypothesis suggesting that both problem drinking and juvenile crime derive from a common set of factors seems best supported by available evidence.

The third point made here about alcohol, crime, and juveniles is that alcohol problems later in life appear to be related to juvenile antisocial behavior patterns. "The data from these recent retrospective studies indicate that there may be characteristic adolescent personality and adaptional patterns associated with adult alcoholism" (Mandell & Ginzburg, 1976, p. 194). Truancy, school failure, and juvenile court appearance each have power to predict alcoholism in adulthood (Robins et al., 1962, 1968).

Drinking Problems during Adulthood

Drinking Problems during Young Adulthood. The literature and research on drinking practices and problems among young adults (aged 18–25) is uneven. Good-quality general-population survey data are available for drinking patterns and drinking problems in the U.S. male adult population between ages 21 and 59 (Cahalan & Cisin, 1968, 1976b; Cahalan & Room, 1972, 1974). Comparable data for females and for males between the ages of 18 and 21 are not available. There is a large body of literature that describes the drinking practices of college students and drinking by those in military service (Blane & Hewitt, 1977). For our purposes here, the value of research that focuses on a college or military population is limited. The generalizability of findings from college and military populations is problematic. Samples from such populations are biased, and the character of the criminal behavior engaged in by these groups is not typical. College students are only rarely involved in the kind of serious crime of interest here. College students tend to have a higher socioeconomic status than noncollege youth and also tend to be academic achievers. Both higher socioeconomic status and school success are related to low rates of serious crime. Military personnel show a relatively high rate of problem drinking compared to the general population and for this reason would be of interest for this discussion (Blane & Hewitt, 1977). But the research on problem drinking in the military does not focus on criminal aspects of problem drinking behavior, and, in addition, the military services have their own justice systems. Offenses committed by military personnel are generally dealt with by military justice processes. The existence of unique military offense categories and of a separate justice process makes it difficult to integrate this research with research on civilian populations.

According to Mandell and Ginzburg (1976), the 18- to 20-year-old group has the highest proportion of the population with some drinking problem and is also the age of heaviest drinking; one of three 18- to 20-year-olds report having had a problem as a result of drinking. Blane and Hewitt (1977) have reviewed approximately 80 surveys that deal with drinking and drinking problems among college age youth and conclude: "The 18- to 24-year-old group has the highest level of intoxication experience and problems of all age ranges" (pp. iv–13). A National Institute of Alcohol Abuse and Alcoholism (NIAAA) report states: "The highest rates of problem drinking occurred among men in the 18–20 age group—21 percent" (NIAAA, 1978, p. 11). Cahalan and Cisin state: "Heavy drinking and all types of drinking problems are at their height among men in their early twenties" (1976b, p. 104). Unless one focuses on physiological aspects of drinking problems or on marital and job problems from drinking, there is little doubt about available evidence. Younger men are most likely to have drinking problems.

Drinking Problems among Men Aged 21–59. An important distinction is made between "problem drinking" and alcoholism. Problem drinking is associated with a host of problems: heavy intake of alcohol, family or financial problems, health problems, problems with the police, etc. Alcoholism, as it is usually defined, is a condition that is almost always a result of many years of heavy drinking and is accompanied by withdrawal symptoms when drinking is interrupted. The presence of alcoholism is sufficient to result in drinking problems. The reverse is not true.

The Cahalan *et al.* surveys (Cahalan, 1970; Cahalan & Cisin, 1968, 1976a; Cahalan & Room, 1972) measure problem drinking in a way that allows specific evaluation of the kinds of problems associated with drinking at various ages. Cahalan and his coauthors, in each of their publications, discuss their perspective toward problem drinking or drinking problems and emphasize that the precise terms are actually *"problems associated with the use of alcohol or problem related drinking"* (Cahalan 1970, p. 12). Cahalan prefers the definition of Plaut (1967) as one that is heuristically appropriate: "Problem drinking is a repetitive use of beverage alcohol causing physical, psychological, or social harm to the drinker or to others." Use of this definition requires that one acknowledge that the demonstration of "causality" is scientifically problematic (Cahalan, 1970, pp. 12–27). The Cahalan *et al.* publications focus on three drinking-problem categories, which are relevant for our purposes: binge drinking, belligerence, and police problems. These problems tend to be most common at earlier rather than later ages and are the kinds of problems most likely to be defined as or result in a crime problem.

Binge drinking is defined as being intoxicated for more than one day at a time on more than one occasion, or for at least several days at one time on one occasion. Police problems include trouble with the law and accidents caused by drinking where personal injury is involved. A belligerence problem refers to respondents who express aggressive behavior after drinking, although not necessarily in an overt physical manner (Cahalan, 1970). The Cahalan surveys measured a variety of other problems, but these three have been selected for consideration here because they are directly or potentially relevant to the alcohol–crime relationship.

Binge drinking may be related to violent behavior through nutritional factors or through rapid-eye-movement (REM) sleep deprivation. There is evidence that hypoglycemia may elevate the probability of aggressive behavior in individuals. Although prolonged (binge) alcohol consumption does not itself cause hypoglycemia, there is some likelihood that a nutritional deficit would result from poor diet or fasting during binge drinking. Pernanen (1976) has reviewed this literature and has noted that hypoglycemia can develop in normal subjects after 42 hours of fasting. There is also evidence that some alcoholics have a metabolic disturbance that is related to hypoglycemia. Binge drinking is of interest here because of its intervening relevance to the condition of hypogylcemia and the increased likelihood of violence arising from that condition. Binge drinking is also likely to disrupt REM sleep patterns, and this disruption can lead to psychotic reactions and violence (Pernanen, 1976).

Police problems as a result of drinking and the tendency to become belligerent when drinking are included here because these categories describe outcomes that may indicate involvement or potential involvement in serious criminal behavior.

The various drinking problems measured by Cahalan and Room (1974) were categorized by whether or not a current problem existed or whether subjects had ever had a particular problem. A current problem was defined as one that occurred in the last three years; a past problem was one that occurred at any time. The existence of a drinking problem was also examined in terms of accession and remission rates; the accession rate was taken as the proportion of those who had a current problem who had developed the problem in the preceding 3 years. The remission rate was the proportion of those who did not have a current problem who had had a problem at any time prior to 3 years ago. Comparison of accession and remission rates allows appraisal of: (1) amount of turnover and (2) the tendency of accession to predominate over remission or vice versa, and hence the prevalence variation (Cahalan & Room, 1974).

Table 5.1 indicates that binge drinking, belligerence, and police problems vary systematically by age in the same general way. Binge drinking is a current problem for 10% of those in the 21–24 age group. The percentage of those who have a current binge drinking problem drops to 3% in the 25–29 age group and remains low across all of the remaining age groups to age 59. Binge drinking has a fairly high remission rate; two-thirds of those who have had a high past binge drinking problem do not have a problem during the last 3 years. The low accession rate and the relatively high remission rate indicate a variable pattern for binge drinking but suggest clearly a problem drinking pattern that is most common in the younger adult years.

Belligerence is also most common in the youngest age category. Fifteen percent of males aged 21–24 report having this problem. The percentage of individuals in each age category with this problem decreases gradually until the age 35–39 category, after which it remains relatively stable. The accession rate for belligerence is low—only 12%—and the remission rate is also on the low side in comparison to remisson rates for other drinking problem types (55%). Belligerence as a result of drinking is a problem that apparently tends to develop early and to persist. In comparison to other drinking problems, belligerence is stable.

Police problems as a result of drinking have a pattern very similar to the one for binge drinking. The problem is most common in the youngest age group; 10% of those in this age group are classified as having a current "police" drinking problem. The problem drops off to 4% in the 25–29 age category and remains low and stable. Relatively high accession and remission rates (33 and 72%) indicate considerable movement in and out of this

TABLE 5.1. Percentages of Individuals with Binge Drinking, Belligerence, Police Problems, and Overall Problem Score as a Result of Drinking, with Accession and Remission Rates for These Problems (by Age Category)[a]

Problem	Number with high current problem	Age group (years)[b]									Accession rate	Remission rate
		21-24 (147)	25-29 (204)	30-34 (186)	35-39 (216)	40-44 (226)	45-49 (201)	50-54 (199)	55-59 (182)	Total (1561)		
Binge drinking	50	10	3	3	3	1	2	4	2	3	29	66
Belligerence	128	15	12	10	8	7	8	6	2	8	12	55
Police	47	10	4	2	2	2	2	4	1	3	33	72
Current overall problem score	67	40	22	20	21	17	17	17	11	20	—	—

[a]From Tables 6 and 7 in Cahalan and Room (1974).
[b]The number of subjects in each age group is given in parentheses.

problem category over time. The category "police problems" does not distinguish different kinds of problems. Presumably, arrest for homicide or for disorderly conduct would be reported by respondents as a police problem. Nonetheless this problem category is suggestive of the behavior under consideration here.

Drinking problems which have a variable pattern over age, as measured by accession and remission, present a different problem of interpretation than do those which have a stable pattern. As Cahalan and Room (1974) noted, problems which tend to be periodic and occasional can be expected to appear later than habitual problems "simply because, by definition, they are less likely to appear at all" (p. 60). For this reason, the consistent finding of an age-prevalence relationship for binge drinking and police problems is noteworthy. The research design itself creates some tendency for high problem scores to be evenly distributed by age. In the face of this design effect, the finding that binge drinking and police problems cluster at one age category would appear to be a significant finding. Later in this chapter we discuss this finding systematically from theoretical and policy perspectives. The finding that belligerence is a drinking problem that remains fairly stable over age categories suggests that age may not be as important a variable in the explanation of belligerence.

Cahalan and Room (1974) also examined the order of precedence and the order of succession of pairs of drinking problems so that the temporal ordering of drinking problems can be specified—at least for drinking problem pairs. The three problems being considered here—binge drinking, belligerence, and police problems—tend to occur earlier in time than most of the other problems. Job problems and problems with family, relatives, and friends, for example, tend to occur after binge drinking, belligerence, and police problems.

Cahalan and Room (1974) also examined the predictive power of past problems for explaining current problems. Partial correlation coefficients indicate that past problems are not strong predictors of current problems. Predictive power is moderate if a past problem in the same area is used in the equation to predict a current problem in the same area. Multiple correlation coefficients for binge drinking, belligerence, and police problems, regressed on each of the other problem categories when a past problem in the same area is included, are .50, .56, and .42, respectively. When a past problem in the same area is excluded from the regression, the multiple correlation coefficients are reduced to .34 for binge drinking, .35 for belligerence, and .20 for police problems. Past problems in the same area are better able to predict current problems in that area than are past problems in other areas.

Attempting to explain the findings for the relationship between age and drinking problems, Cahalan and Room (1974) used the life cycle concept, which integrates the combined effects of age, marital, and dependent status. The authors looked at problem drinking rates by age category for each of three family status categories: living with wife and children, living with wife and having no children, and living with neither wife nor children. The survey results indicate there is a family status effect over and above the effect of age. Binge drinking and police problems are highest for individuals who are living with neither spouse nor children. This outcome holds for each of these two problem types across all four age categories: 21-29, 30-39, 40-49, 50-59. Belligerence results are not so consistent. In the 21-29 age group, equal percentages (14%) have a current high belligerence problem in two categories: living with wife and children, and living with neither wife nor children. Ten percent of the 21-29 age group have a high current belligerence problem in the living with wife and having no children category. These data also indicate that within the family–dependent status categories, there is no even progression toward a lower percentage of individuals who have high current belligerence problems as age increases. The variables of age and status interact with each other in the belligerence problem category.

Social position also has an independent effect on rates of drinking problems. "Those of lowest position have much higher rates of drinking problems than do others, and they tend to get into trouble over drinking out of all proportion to the frequency with which they drank heavily" (Cahalan & Room, 1974, p. 109).

In their summary of findings in this valuable book, Cahalan and Room noted that problematic intake, personality variables, social differentiation, and life history variables all have the capacity to explain some of the variation in problem drinking. Drinking environment, like community or neighborhood characteristics, is also correlated with drinking problems. The relevance of these factors and the complex ways they are related to each other require both sophisticated empirical data and theoretical models to explain the relationship.

Summary—Alcohol Careers

The discussion in this section can be summarized in three major points:

1. The kind of drinking problems that are likely also to be "crime" problems are most common among younger men,
2. Many young men mature out of crime-related drinking problems,
3. Research findings in the drinking problems area are sensitive to how problems are defined.

In the following section the relationship between age and crime is examined. Following that, an examination is made of the current knowledge about the alcohol–crime relationship as it varies over age. Finally, theoretical and policy issues are discussed.

Criminal Careers

Introduction

Data about crime in the United States are plentiful. The Federal Bureau of Investigation (FBI) manages the official crime-reporting system and collects local reports from almost all jurisdictions around the country for crime recorded by the police. In addition, national and city crime victimization surveys conducted by the Law Enforcement Assistance Administration (LEAA) through Bureau of the Census probability samples provide a great deal of information about the total incidence of serious crime—not just crime recorded by the police. A large body of research provides still more data about crime, criminals, and the criminal justice system. But much of these data about crime are methodologically flawed or not useful for this chapter.

Methodological Problems

The present discussion focuses on the criminal behavior of individuals as it varies by age. Estimates of the frequency and type of criminal behavior come from two main sources: official records and self-reports of criminal activity. Most research uses either one or the other; a few studies use both kinds of data. Victimization survey data are also a valuable resource for research on crime. However, their use is only recently expanding. The national victimization surveys were begun in the early 1970s, but a large volume of usable data has only been available in the last few years.

The Shortcomings of Official Crime Data

Official crime data are deficient in two major ways. They are incomplete, and they are biased. Official data are incomplete because not all crimes are reported to the police, nor are they always recorded by the police if they are reported. Since the advent of victimization surveys, the magnitude of unrecorded crime, or the "dark figure" of crime, has been better understood. Skogan (1975) has shown, from a comparison of official and victimization survey data, that only 28% of the offenses of forcible rape, aggravated assault, robbery, burglary, larceny, and auto theft are reported to the police, and that reporting rates vary by crime type. Official crime data are also of limited utility for research purposes because the official reports do not systematically gather much detailed information about offense, offender, and victim characteristics. The presence of alcohol in offender, victim, or both, for example, is not routinely recorded by police and reported to the FBI.

Self-Reported Offense Data

Use of interviews and questionnairs to gather information from individuals about their own illegal behavior has become a frequent research technique over the last two decades. This approach has the advantage of avoiding the incompleteness and biases of official crime data. Self-report data have their own set of methodological problems but are superior to arrest data in some respects. Official crime data are gathered to support law enforcement operations, that is, for organizational purposes (Kitsuse & Cicourel, 1963). Instruments for self-report data can be designed to produce data of maximum validity; data consistency and reliability can be controlled. There is also a potential to control bias in the data by use of probability sampling procedures in the selection of respondents. The detail and scope of self-report data collected can be maximized through careful design of data collection instruments.

On the negative side, there are problems of recall and distortion with self-report crime data. Individuals who are reporting retrospectively about their past behavior may forget events and details or may remember inaccurately. Some individuals will also distort their responses; they may exaggerate the extent or seriousness of their criminal activity, or they may neglect to report relevant events or details. The latter failure to report is probably the more serious problem for serious criminal behavior.

It is not possible to be precise about the magnitude of the inaccuracies of self-report data. Methodological evaluations have been undertaken through use of the polygraph (J. P. Clark & Tifft, 1966), use of informants (Gold, 1970), and comparison of arrest records and self-reports of offenses committed (Petersilia, Greenwood & Lavin, 1978; Wolfgang & Collins, 1978). Taken as a whole, the results of these and other methodological evaluations suggest that the use of self-report data for research is justified. These data should not be viewed as providing precise estimates of the behavior at issue, but carefully collected self-report data are a valuable supplement to or replacement for arrest data. The Wolfgang and Collins (1978) report, for example, found that although correlation coefficients were low between self-reports and arrest data, the relationships between these two measures of crime were similar within the same offender categories.

The Prevalence of Criminal Activity among Males

The proportion of individuals in the population who are arrested at some time in their lives is substantial. In longitudinal research for a 1945 Philadelphia male birth cohort sample, 47% of the subjects had at least one officially recorded police contact for a nontraffic offense by age 30 (Collins, 1976). Research carried out in three phases for a 1945 Philadelphia birth cohort of males is referred to frequently in this chapter. Some previously unpublished findings from data on a sample of 10% of the original cohort are reported here. This data set and the history of research on this cohort is described in Wolfgang, Figlio, and Sellin (1972) and in Wolfgang and Collins (1978).

Shannon's research on two birth cohorts (1942 and 1949) from Racine, Wisconsin, indicates that 67% of the males from the 1947 cohort had at least one recorded nontraffic police contact by age 33, and that 71% of the males from a 1949 birth cohort had at least one recorded nontraffic contact by age 26. Between 15 and 26% of these recorded contacts for the three Racine cohorts were for "suspicion" or "investigation," making the percentages of males with police contacts where specific acts of illegality were indicated very similar to the 47% found in the Philadelphia cohort sample (Shannon, 1977a, 1979).

West and Farington (1977) found that 31% (120 of 411) of a sample of males from a working-class area of London had been convicted of an offense by the time the group reached young adulthood. The sample members were born between 1951 and 1954, and convictions occurring up until 1975 were counted; the ages of the sample members at the end of data collection were between 21 and 24. A 31% conviction rate for individuals of these ages appears to approximate the "police contact" rate for the older subjects in the Wolfgang and Collins and Shannon research. Police contacts are more frequent than convictions; not all arrests are followed by prosecution, nor do all prosecutions result in conviction. As the subjects in the West and Farington study grow older, more of them may be convicted. In addition, juvenile status offenses like truancy were not included in the "convictions" of the West and Farington sample; these offenses were counted in the Philadelphia and Racine cohort.

The percentages of individuals who have official records for serious offenses are lower than the figures just given. The Philadelphia data indicate that 24% of the cohort had official contacts for the more serious index offenses. (Index offenses are those classed as Part I offenses in the FBI's Uniform Crime Reports: homicide, forcible rape, aggravated assault, robbery, burglary, larceny, and auto theft.) In the Shannon data (1979), 12% of the 1942 male cohort and 13% of the 1949 male cohort had recorded contacts for felonies.

Based on self-reports of illegal behavior, the prevalence of individual criminal behavior is much higher. Over 90% of those interviewed in the Philadelphia cohort sample reported committing illegal acts. Even if all minor offenses (like the juvenile status offenses, public drunkenness, vandalism, etc.) are eliminated, and if some of the more serious offenses (like drug sales and weapons offenses) are not included, 65% of juveniles and 39% of adults between the ages of 18 and 26 reported committing an offense included in the Uniform Crime Reports as a serious index offense. It is also true, however, that the serious criminality of most individuals is infrequent and temporary, and never comes to the official attention of the police. But virtually everyone, on the basis of self-reports about their own behavior, is at risk of becoming an official crime statistic.

Offense Frequency and Age

Official data indicate that the majority of arrested offenders are adult males under the age of 25. Uniform Crime Report (UCR) estimates indicate that 57% of all those arrested for any offense in 1976 were less than 25 years of age; 74% of those arrested for the serious index offenses were less than 25 years of age. Males made up 84% of all arrests and 80% of those arrested for index offenses. The UCR data also indicate that at age 13 there is a notable increase in arrestees. Of all arrestees, 5.6% are age 13 or 14. Between ages 15 and 19 the percentages of all arrestees that are arrested at each age ranges between 5 and 6%. Arrestees at each of the ages (15, 16, 17, 18, and 19) represent between 8.2 and 5.9% of those arrested for the more serious index offenses (Federal Bureau of Investigation, 1977).

Most research findings also indicate that official offense frequency, as measured by arrest or conviction, increases precipitously in the 13-to-15 age period, peaks in the 16-to-18 age period, and diminishes thereafter. Some research shows that arrest and conviction frequency increases again for offenders in their 30s, but such increases are typically for nonserious offenses. For serious offense categories, the rapid increase, peak, and subsequent decline in offense frequency that take place during adolescence and young adulthood are consistent findings.

Table 5.2 provides age-specific offense information from age 14 to age 30 for the Philadelphia cohort sample, based on official data. The peak age

TABLE 5.2. Numbers of Official Offenders, Offenses, and Index Offenses, by Age (Philadelphia Cohort Sample)[a]

Age (years)	Number of offenders	Number of offenses—all categories	Mean number of offenses	Number of index offenses
13 and under	—	216	1.5	70
14	98	147	1.5	33
15	139	224	1.6	65
16	170	292	1.7	72
17	117	183	1.6	50
18	96	126	1.3	46
19	96	139	1.4	36
20	88	127	1.4	36
21	69	116	1.7	39
22	56	81	1.4	32
23	63	97	1.5	50
24	62	113	1.8	45
25	54	95	1.8	41
26	47	85	1.8	33
27	43	74	1.7	36
28	31	51	1.6	25
29	33	53	1.6	24
30	17	39	2.3	19

[a]Unpublished data; see Collins (1976) for a discussion.

for numbers of offenders and offenses is age 16. There are more officially recognized offenders at this age, and these offenders are charged with more total offenses and more index offenses than at any other age. Age 15 has the next highest numbers of offenders and offenses. The numbers decrease rapidly after age 16, but it should be noted that the more serious index offense category remains relatively high to age 24 or 25. The mean numbers of offenses reported in Column 4 do not vary over a wide range. This suggests that the offense frequency of active offenders varies within a narrow range—at least as indicated by these arrest data. Thus, the attribution of a substantial percentage of crime to younger age groups is explained largely by the existence of more active offenders rather than by the offense frequency of active offenders. In fact, in their early 20s, this sample of offenders were charged with more per capita offenses than were the offenders who were arrested in their middle teens.

Shannon's (1977a, 1977b) findings for two Racine, Wisconsin, birth cohorts indicate that 6- to 17-year-old males from both 1942 and 1949 cohorts had higher mean index offense rates than did males in the 18–20 age group. These mean rates were computed by dividing the total number of cohort members into the total number of index offenses officially recorded against the cohorts. Means are for all cohort members—not just active offenders. The mean number of police contacts for index offenses for males in the 1942 cohort is .28 for 6- to 17-year-olds and .07 for 18- to 20-year-olds. In the 1949 cohort, 6- to 17-year-old males had a mean index police contact rate of .50; 18- to 20-year-olds had a rate of .10. These findings may on the surface appear to be inconsistent with the data in Table 5.2. However, the offense means in the Shannon research were computed with all of the cohort members included in the denominator, not just active offenders, as in the Philadelphia data reported in Table 5.2. If the means were computed with only the number of active offenders in the denominator, it is likely that the findings would be similar to those from the Philadelphia cohort.

Findings derived from official records of serious offense activity by age in the Philadelphia and Racine cohorts show that juvenile and young adults are responsible for a large disproportion of serious crime. The evidence also suggests that those who are active offenders during young adulthood are notable because they tend to be more seriously involved than active juvenile offenders.

Interviews were completed with 58% (564 of 971) of the Phildelphia cohort sample. During the interviews, which were conducted when the cohort members were age 26, individuals were asked to self-report about offenses committed for which they were never arrested. Interviewees were asked how many times before age 18 and how many times after age 18 they had engaged in 30 different kinds of crime and deviant behavior.

Table 5.3 displays selected self-reported offense behavior for juveniles and young adults in two ways. Columns 1 and 2 compare reported offense frequency for juveniles and young adults. Only in three offense categories (serious assault, auto theft, shoplifting) do juveniles report committing substantially greater per capita numbers of offenses than young adults. In three offense categories (robbery, larceny from person, threaten with weapon), young adults report higher offense frequency than juveniles.

Columns 3 and 4 indicate the percentage of offenders in the two age groupings who reported committing any offense of the types indicated. Comparison of juveniles and young adults on this basis shows that in six of the nine offense categories, juveniles were much more likely than young adults to be active offenders. There is very little difference between juveniles and adults for the offense of rape, and in the categories of threatening with a weapon and bad check writing, young adults were more likely than juveniles to be active offenders.

TABLE 5.3. Mean Self-Reported Offense Activity and Percentage of Offenders Reporting Any Offense Activity for Juvenile (< 18) and Young Adult (18–26) Periods[a]

Offense	Mean offenses reported		Percentage reporting any offense	
	< 18 yr	18–26 yr	< 18 yr	18–26 yr
Rape	.2	.1	6	5
Serious assault	3.2	1.5	31	22
Robbery	1.4	3.8	15	9
Larceny from person (no threat or force)	4.1	6.8	33	17
Threaten with weapon	.5	.6	25	8
Burglary	1.7	1.3	27	14
Auto theft	2.0	.6	25	8
Shoplifting	10.8	4.9	68	24
Passed bad check	.03	.3	2	7
TOTAL	23.9	20.0	65	39
			(any index offense)	

[a]Responses derived from interviews with 236 offenders. The number of valid responses for the offense categories ranged between 224 and 233.

Consideration of these self-report results in the light of official statistics also clearly suggests the major reason why juveniles are officially charged with a high percentage of the serious crime rate: *There are many more active offenders in the juvenile years.* Most of the disportionate involvement of juveniles in comparison to young adults may be explained by the fact that more juveniles are committing offenses rather than by the offense activity rate of active offenders.

An important difference between juveniles and young adults is suggested by the robbery and larceny from person categories. These offense categories are especially notable because they are acquisitive crimes that also involve actual or potential personal injury. These offenses also have a high potential for creating a fear of crime in communities. In these serious offense categories the young adult years may represent the more serious age period. Even though fewer young adults are active offenders than are juveniles, the frequency of their offending is considerably higher than that of juveniles.

The distinction between offense rate and the number of active offenders is important and has not been made clear by much past research. Theoretical and policy interpretation of crime data will depend in part on the number of different offenders committing a given volume of crime. The incapacitative effect of incarceration, for example, will depend on such individual offense rates.

Changes in offending patterns of different birth cohorts or changes in arrest practices over time also complicate interpretation of age-specific offense data. There is evidence that recent birth cohorts are more likely to be arrested than older cohorts (Blumstein & Cohen, 1978; Shannon, 1977a). It is difficult to establish how much of the higher arrest rates for later birth cohorts is a result of more criminal behavior on the part of cohort members and how much of the higher arrest rates may be an artifact of an increased police tendency to arrest or to record illegal behavior. In any case, interpretation of the age–criminal-behavior relationship is complex because official data may reflect one or a combination of the following factors:

1. Changes in police arrest or recording practices
2. The same proportion of individuals in given age categories who are active offenders, but who commit more offenses
3. A greater proportion of individuals in one or more age categories who are active offenders
4. Changes in the age composition of the population, for example, proportionately more individuals in the 18–25 age category

Data for different birth cohorts and use of official and self-report data for the same individuals help to interpret the meaning of official statistics. For our purposes here the major point is the distinction between the size of the offender population and the offense rate of active offenders. As age increases, the proportion of individuals in a given age category who are active offenders appears to decrease, while the offense rate of those who remain active appears to increase.

Age-Offense Patterns from Research on Prison Populations

Recent research on prison populations has also examined offense activity by age, and these findings, apparently, are inconsistent in some ways with the findings already discussed. Petersilia *et al.* (1978) reported on interviews with a systematically selected sample of 49 offenders, and based on self-reported offenses, the authors have developed offense rate estimates for three age periods: the juvenile period, the young adult period, and the adult period. It needs to be emphasized, as the authors themselves stated, that generalization from their sample is not justified. The size of the sample is small, and each member was selected from a California prison population based on the fact that the current incarceration was for at least one count of armed robbery and the fact that each subject had served at least one prior prison term (Petersilia *et al.,* 1978). These sample selection criteria guaranteed that only individuals with serious criminal histories would be included in the research. The average age of the sample was 39. This also suggests that individuals in the sample were indeed "serious and habitual" offenders. The offenders in the Philadelphia and Racine cohorts cannot be described in this way. Many of the offenders in the Philadelphia cohort did not have serious criminal careers; less than one-third (32%) had five or more official police contacts by age 30.

Petersilia *et al.* (1978) segmented the three career periods of the individuals in the sample based on the criteria of either age or "landmark" incarceration. For example, the juvenile period was delineated by age 18 or the first juvenile incarceration. Data were gathered for the offenses of auto theft, purse snatching, theft over $50, burglary, robbery, aggravated assault, forgery, drug sales, and forcible rape.

Table 5.4 provides offense rate estimates for nondrug offenses for three career segments and for the total career. These rates have been adjusted to reflect time at risk; the annual rate reflects an adjustment to take account of time incarcerated. The juvenile rate is more than 2.5 times higher than the young adult rate. The magnitude of this age difference is much higher than that indicated by the arrests and self-reports from the Philadelphia cohort sample. The Philadelphia self-reports suggest more per capita offense activity in the juvenile years than in the young adult years, but the difference between juvenile and adult years does not approach this difference for the California prison sample. According to the retrospective self-reports of this group of serious offenders, their juvenile years were characterized by high levels of serious criminal behavior, and these years

TABLE 5.4. Serious (Nondrug) Offense Rates, by Age Period[a, b]

Age period	Annual offense rate[c]
Juvenile period	28.4
Young adult period	11.0
Adult period	4.6
Entire period	11.9

[a]From Petersilia *et al.* (1978, p. 27).
[b]Based on self-reports.
[c]Monthly nondrug offense rate multiplied by 12.

were followed by a precipitous dropoff in offense frequency. Assuming that the reports of the California sample reflect true differences in their behavior over age, the difference between them and the Philadelphia results may be explained by the differences in individual subjects. As previously mentioned, the California prison sample represents an older group of individuals who had demonstrated long-term, serious involvement in criminal behavior. The offenders in the Philadelphia sample include many individuals who had short-term, nonserious criminal careers. If the age–offense-rate difference is explained by such a difference in sample, the interpretation of data for criminal behavior needs to pay close attention to the characteristics of offenders for whom that behavior is measured.

Petersilia *et al.* (1978) examined the offense patterns and attitudes of the offenders in their sample, and separated interviewees into one of two categories: the intensive or the intermittent types. The first type engaged in more sustained criminal behavior and were more rational in their criminal pursuits. The intermittent type tended to be involved in crime less systematically and in a more opportunistic/irregular way. The intensive type saw themselves as professional criminals, at least for part of their careers; the intermittent type did not view themselves as professional criminals, and they tended to realize small gains from their offenses. When the offense rates of the intensive and intermittent types are compared, the differences are dramatic. Over the entire career, the offense rate of the intensive is 10 times that of the intermittent. When drug sales are eliminated from the offense rates, the rate for the intensive offenders is still seven times higher than that of the intermittent. This is a further indication that offense rates are widely variable, depending on offender characteristics, and that even within serious offender categories there is considerable variation in amount of criminal activity.

Peterson and Braiker (1978) have reported on the results of a survey of the California prison population. The survey was drawn to be representative of the entire system population but is biased toward older, more serious offenders due to sample attrition and response rate. The survey instrument collected a variety of demographic, behavioral, and attitudinal data from 624 subjects; self-reported offense data were gathered for 14 types of serious criminal behavior committed in the 3 years prior to the current incarceration.

The Peterson and Braiker (1978) inmate survey examined the variation in offense rates by age. Their findings are consistent with the Petersilia *et al.* (1978) survey. Younger offenders commit more per capita offenses. The authors also examined the effect of prior record on offense rate and controlled for this past record effect in the analysis of age effect. They concluded: "Both age and prior record are significantly and independently associated with the amount of crime that offenders commit. Younger offenders commit more crimes no matter what their prior record; offenders with prior felony records commit more crimes no matter what their age" (p. 75).

Peterson and Braiker also examined the annual offense rates for high-rate and low-rate offenders. Offense rates are highly skewed. The authors divided offenders into two groups on the basis of the median number of offenses reported. The offense rate disparity, both within offense category and overall, is dramatic. Active armed robbery offenders in the low-rate category reported committing .7 robberies a year; active high-rate armed robbery offenders reported 9.4 such offenses a year. Low-rate active burglary offenders reported 1.1 burglaries a year; high-rate active burglary offenders reported 27.7 such offenses. Overall the total nondrug offense rate for high-rate active offenders is 12 times higher than the same rate for low-rate active offenders. These large differences are comparable to the findings of Petersilia *et al.* for intensive and intermittent offenders. It appears that within serious offender categories there may be a separate core of very serious offenders.

Age and Offense Seriousness

Thus far in the age and crime section of this chapter, we have concentrated on age variation in offense type and frequency. There are other age-related aspects of offense patterns that are relevant; one of these is age variation in offense seriousness. It is important to know, for example, whether or not the offenses committed by young adults are more serious than those committed by juveniles. Crime control policies and programs may be shaped in part by these findings.

Petersilia *et al.* (1978) developed a measure of crime seriousness that combined frequency of reported criminal behavior and seriousness of that behavior. The offense seriousness weight is based on the amount of incarceration time served by California offenders for different offense types. Comparison of crime seriousness indices across juvenile, young adult, and adult periods indicates that results are skewed by the scores of some very active offenders. The results do suggest that the young adult period is the age span during which criminal activity is most serious. Results also indicate that in the later adult period, offense seriousness diminishes. Shannon (1977b) also examined the relationship between age and seriousness of police contacts; in this research, seriousness was measured by offense category. He found that there was a gradual rise in seriousness with age for males.

Results from the Philadelphia cohort sample also indicate an increase in offense seriousness with age. The number of officially recorded police contacts for the Philadelphia cohort sample is 2261; 93% of these offenses have been scored for seriousness using the Sellin–Wolfgang scoring system (Sellin & Wolfgang, 1974). Seriousness scores were developed for this system from surveys of individuals' judgments about offense ingredients. Respondents assigned scores to offense ingredients based on their perceptions of seriousness. Characteristics of offenses like the presence and extent of injury to a victim, the presence and extent of property loss or damage, and the presence of a weapon during the commission determine the seriousness score of a particular offense. Thus, a robbery where the victim was injured has a higher seriousness score than one where there was no injury; a burglary where the amount of property loss is $1000 has a higher score than one where the loss is $100. All of those offenses for which sufficient information was contained in the police narrative were scored for seriousness based on offense ingredients. These scores provide a basis for describing the seriousness of offenses and offender careers that do not depend simply on counting the number of occurrences and classifying the occurrence by legal category.

Table 5.5 provides mean offense seriousness scores by age for two offense groupings. In Column 1 it is clear that offense seriousness is directly associated with age. Based on the dimensions of injury, property loss, weapons use, etc., offenses committed by older offenders are more serious than those committed by younger offenders. The differences between juvenile and adult years are quite large, and the age–seriousness relationship is evident up to age 30.

In the case of index offenses, the juvenile–adult difference is again clear. Index offenses committed by young offenders tend to be less serious than those committed by adult offenders. However, the steady increase in seriousness scores with age that was evident when index and nonindex offenses were included in computations is not observed. In fact, index offenses committed at ages 20 and 21 develop the highest seriousness scores. The dropoff in seriousness found by other research in the later adult period cannot be observed here. This may simply be because this decrease in the seriousness of offenses committed by older adults does not occur until after age 30.

Age and Offense Specialization

Until recently, there has been a tendency to characterize the continuing offender career as one that becomes more rational and specialized as the career advances. Criminals were viewed as learning the crime trade during the juvenile and young adult years. Those who continued to offend, it was

TABLE 5.5. Mean Offense Seriousness Scores for Philadelphia Cohort Sample Offenses: All Offenses and Index Offenses

Age (years)	All offenses[a]		Index offenses[a]	
13	139	$(84)^b$	239	(29)
14	112	$(135)^b$	282	(33)
15	125	$(198)^b$	249	(65)
16	112	$(259)^b$	269	(70)
17	124	$(177)^b$	244	(48)
18	258	(116)	576	(35)
19	273	(127)	619	(37)
20	277	(118)	826	(28)
21	398	(108)	766	(32)
22	382	(71)	561	(22)
23	396	(85)	504	(39)
24	367	(98)	582	(32)
25	486	(77)	509	(25)
26	444	(74)	579	(24)
27	582	(60)	643	(23)
28	530	(45)	532	(22)
29	567	(36)	593	(14)
30	447	(28)	450	(10)

^{a}The number of offenses in each category is given in parentheses.

^{b}Juvenile status offenses (truancy, incorrigibility, running away, and curfew violations) have not been included in seriousness score computations. Inclusion of these offenses would have overstated juvenile–adult differences because status offenses have very low seriousness scores and are not offenses that can be charged against adults.

believed, would specialize and become more proficient as they acquired experience. This veiw was apparently the result of popular characterization and evidence from a limited number of offender careers. Now there is little evidence from empirical research that most offenders "specialize" in the sense that they become bank robbers or burglars.

An early attempt to examine this issue was provided by Frum (1958), who examined 319 inmate files from two Indiana prisions. Frum claimed to have discovered "striking uniformities" in the development of offense patterns. However, the "uniformities" that emerged are quite heterogeneous, and a substantial percentage of careers cannot easily be fit into any uniform pattern. Juvenile offense histories were not complete for the individuals in his study because juvenile offenses very often did not become a part of official adult files. Inclusion of more juvenile offenses would likely have increased the heterogeneity of individual offense careers further, because juveniles are known to commit a wide variety of illegal acts.

Much more attention has been paid to the subject of offense specialization and career offense patterns in recent years. The evidence is not conclusive but suggests three things: (1) offense specialization that does emerge is most accurately characterized by generic rather than particular offense types (e.g., robbery rather than bank robbery, property crime rather than burglary); (2) age is related to the specialization issue (i.e., juvenile offense patterns tend to differ from adult offense patterns in the same individual career); (3) a small percentage of older individuals who have serious criminal careers also have homogeneous or specialized later career offense patterns. Point three should be viewed as a speculative statement or hypothesis for future testing; it is not well supported by data.

There is a little ambiguity in findings on the offense specialization question for the juvenile years. Researchers have consistently found that juvenile offenders do not specialize or have predictable offense patterns (Hindelang, 1971; Robin, 1964; Wolfgang et al., 1972). The Wolfgang et al. findings resulted from an analysis using a Markov process approach to look for stable patterns in the accumulation of additional offenses for individual offenders. Examination of probability coefficients from transition matrices for offense transitions indicated almost no power to predict the type of future offenses from the pattern of previous offenses. Thornberry and Figlio (1978) have extended the Markov chain analysis for the Philadelphia cohort sample to age 30. The finding of independence of offense type between offense transitions is again affirmed even though 12 years of adult offenses have been added to the analysis.

Offense patterns are likely to change after the juvenile years, so that on the issue of comparative offense patterns, juveniles and adults differ. There is an elevated tendency for juvenile offenders to commit property offenses in comparison to adults, and for adults to commit personal offenses in comparison to juveniles (Glueck & Glueck, 1937; Petersilia et al., 1978; West and Farington, 1977). However, these overall juvenile–adult differences in propensity toward a disproportionate involvement in property and personal crime do not translate into specialization. There does appear to be a tendency for the number of different offense types to diminish in later age periods. Petersilia et al. (1978) showed that, based on the self-reports of the 49 offenders they interviewed, the number of different types of crime engaged in goes down in the young and later adult periods. In the juvenile period, 74% of the offenders committed two or more offense types. That share goes down to 69% in the young adult period and 48% in the adult period. The findings displayed in Table 5.3 also support this interpretation. Higher percentages of juveniles than adults report involvement in all of the offense categories except three, and the differences are small for these three offense types. Peterson and Braiker (1978) summarized their findings on this point as follows:

> As offenders age, they reduce the number of different kinds of crime types that they commit. However, in general, older offenders do not appear to commit their active crime types at significantly lower crime rates than do younger offenders. Thus, age appears to be associated with narrowing one's range of criminal activities. It is important to emphasize, however, that this does not mean that older offenders tend to be specialists. Older offenders are still likely to commit a variety of different kinds of crimes so that it is perhaps more appropriate to regard them as selective offenders, rather than as specialists. (p. 75)

General Criminal Career Issues

Before discussing the evidence which simultaneously addresses the issues of both alcohol careers and criminal careers, some final points about criminal career findings need to be made. Age-related career issues of a more general nature have theoretical and policy relevance; they involve questions about age of onset, career length, recidivism, and incarceration periods.

Empirical evidence shows that the earlier the age of onset of criminal activity, the more serious the future criminal career is likely to be (Hamparian, Schuster, Dinitz, & Conrad, 1978; Olson, 1978; Robin, 1964; West, 1973; West & Farington, 1977; Wolfgang et al., 1972). However, much of this evidence was developed from research on samples of younger offenders where data collection was truncated at age 18 or another relatively young age. In the case of such research, the inverse relationship between age at first arrest and the number of total arrests may be largely a function of the artificial upper age limit on the possibility of arrest. However, Peterson and Braiker (1978) also found an inverse relationship between age of onset of criminality and seriousness of offense career. As already indicated, this age effect was found to be independent of prior criminal record.

The relationship between age of onset and career seriousness is only one of several relevant questions. Other important questions are: (1) how long does the criminal career last? and (2) how are age of onset, length of career, and offense patterns related over time? A great deal of attention has been focused on age of onset and later offense patterns, but little is known about criminal career length and its relation to other career characteristics.

Good estimates of career length require a longitudinal or quasi-longitudinal research design, and such designs require a large investment of time and resources. Evidence from the existing longitudinal research that has attempted to estimate the length of criminal careers suggests that the magnitude of the career length estimate is largely a function of how long subjects are followed in time. Wolfgang and Collins (1978) followed individuals to age 30 and estimated career length for chronic offenders at 9.3 years. In research by Petersilia *et al.* (1978), the average age of the subjects was 39, and median career length was estimated at 18 years.

If one is interested in the length and characteristics of a criminal career so that policy options can be examined, it is not sufficient to have independent data about career offense patterns or career length. In order to be useful for policy purposes, criminal career data should locate accurately the offense patterns within particular career segments. With such data, policy options and probable effects of different options can be estimated. The argument has been made, for example, that present incapacitation crime control policy is inefficient due to a tendency to incarcerate offenders after the most serious phase of their criminal career. The view argues that younger offenders should be the target of incapacitation policies because they commit more offenses (Boland & Wilson, 1978).

Some past research has estimated the likelihood that individuals will recidivate, that is, the probability that one offense will be followed by another. The longitudinal data sets from both Philadelphia and Racine indicate high probabilities of recidivism. After the third official contract, approximately an 80% chance exists that an individual will have an additional police contact (Shannon 1977a; Wolfgang & Collins, 1978). While these findings do not explicitly deal with the relationship of age and recidivism, they do indicate a high and stable likelihood that those who have more than two officially recorded offenses will continue to come to the attention of the police for criminal offenses.

On the other hand, these recidivism probabilities can be used to illustrate how attrition takes place in offender populations over time. The Philadelphia data show approximately an .8 probability of an additional police contact after the third contact. These data also indicate that the time between contacts decreases with each contact, to less than one per year by the ninth contact. The time between the second and third contacts is 1.5 years; the time between the third and fourth contacts is 1.1 years (Wolfgang & Collins, 1978). If we combine these two findings with an .8 probability of recidivism, and use an estimate of 1 year for the expected time between official contacts, then we can illustrate how attrition may affect a recidivist offender population. Over a 5-year period, 100 offenders would be reduced to 33 offenders (100 × .8 × .8 × .8 × .8 × .8 = 32.8).

The pool of offenders from a given population segment also has new members entering it over time; as some offenders are ending their careers, others are just beginning careers in crime. There is a tendency for serious offenders to begin their offense careers at a young age, but a significant percentage do begin later. Collins (1976) noted that 13% of the chronic offenders (minimum of five officially recorded police contacts) in the Philadelphia cohort sample had no officially recorded police contacts during their juvenile years. The percentage of recidivists (two to four offenses) who never had an official contact in their juvenile years was 24%. Alternately, some who begin serious criminal careers at a young age also desist early. In the Philadelphia cohort, 11% of those who had five or more official police contacts as juveniles never had another contact during the 18–30 adult years. These findings suggest that while there may be systematic variations between age and criminal behavior, there are also considerable departures from the common patterns.

Most serious offender careers are interrupted by periods of incarceration. Although Mack (1972) found that 7% of a group of "able criminals" were never incarcerated, there is very little evidence showing that many persistent offenders are able to avoid arrest, conviction, and incarceration. Further, as an active criminal career progresses, the likelihood that it will be interrupted by incarceration is increased. Wolfgang and Collins (1978) found that the average length of time served for each index offense committed by the Philadelphia cohort sample was generally higher for older offenders, and chronic offenders were more likely than less serious offenders to be arrested, convicted, and incarcerated. Petersilia *et al.* (1978) found that arrest, conviction, and incarceration rates increased between each of the three career periods: juvenile, young adult, and adult.

It should be obvious that the variations and discontinuities in individual criminal careers are considerble. This implies that attempts at theoretical integration of findings and use of these findings to direct public policy will require complex and probabilistic theoretical and policy models.

The Biographical Perspective

In this section, biographies and autobiographies for a number of serious and repetitive offenders are examined. Biographical material is used to address some of the same questions which were addressed in previous sections. It is almost certain that the individuals whose personal histories are considered here are not representative of offenders in general. The fact that they are the subjects of books, and in many cases the authors, itself suggests that they are not typical. The value of using these sources derives from the detail and depth of the data provided by them. (Allen, 1977; Braly, 1976; Brown, 1965; Klockars, 1974; Martin, 1952; Parker & Allerton, 1962; Shaw, 1930, 1931; Sutherland, 1937; Sutton, 1976). The scope and richness of the information provided goes beyond that which is possible when records and interviews are used to gather data.

The picture of delinquent and criminal careers that emerges from an examination of these 10 books describing the lives of serious offenders is generally consistent with the empirical evidence cited earlier. The individuals described in these books started committing their offenses at an early age; several were active offenders by the age of 10. However, the pattern is not uniformly consistent. Braly (1976), for example, after some early delinquency, had a fairly successful and conforming adolescence. He began to commit burglaries when, as a young man, he worked as a newspaper reporter. The criminal careers described in these books also tend to span many years although this is not true for every case. Brown (1965), according to his own story, made a decision to stop committing serious criminal offenses at age 16 and even moved from Harlem to facilitate his withdrawal from criminal activity. Shaw (1930) indicated that "Stanley's" delinquent activities had not recurred for 5 years after his release from a penal institution as a juvenile. The other subjects described in these books continued active criminality into middle age and beyond. Allen's (1977) career was interrupted after he was paralyzed in a gun battle with the police.

The offender careers described in the biographical sources generally started with property offenses like burglary or larceny; most individuals later began to commit robberies. The degree of specialization that appears to exist in the accounts of these books is greater than that found in the systematic empirical research. However, an examination of the official records that are provided for several of these offenders does not confirm the degree of specialization that is suggested by their own accounts. There are examples of two "specialists": the professional fence described by Klockars (1974) and the commitment of Willie Sutton (1976) to bank robbery. In each of these cases, almost absolute consistency in illegal behavior categories may be noted; however, this absolute consistency in offense type does not apply to the other subjects.

A statement by Martin (1952) may reflect a major reason why offense specialization is not apparent when particular offense types like burglary or robbery are used as the dimensions along which "specialization" is measured:

> When you're stealing, you can't just be a burglar, you've got to be a burglar, stickup man, twenty different things. Burglary in the long run is safer. You'll get away with a hundred burglaries where you'll get away with five stickups. But if there's a place over here where there's a lot of money and the only way to

get it is go in and stick him up, you're a hell of a thief if you don't stick him up.
(pp. 54–55)

Narrow specialization is apparently a luxury that must give way to the demands of opportunity. But there may be greater specialization than is apparent from official records. If offense specialization is viewed broadly—for example, as covert property crime (burglary, robbery) or manipulative property crime (conning, forgery)—then specialization may be characteristic of many offenders. By their own accounts, most of the offenders engaged in a variety of illegal behaviors, but for those individuals for whom official records were also available, it appears that the records overstate the variety. Most past research on the offense specialization question has relied on official records. It would appear from the combined evaluation of empirical research and biographical accounts that some specialization is typical of criminal careers, and that specialization is more likely in adulthood.

The biographical case study data contained in the examined books suggest escalation in offense seriousness with the advancing career. Consistent with the earlier empirical findings, escalating seriousness may only continue into the late 20s or early 30s for most offenders.

The descriptions in these biographies also confirm that serious, persistent offenders do not continually avoid arrest and incarceration. The exception from these books is "Vincent," the professional fence (Klockars, 1974). Both the juvenile offenders referred to who ended their careers early were incarcerated as juveniles on multiple occasions. The same is true of the adult years. Willie Sutton, in spite of his proclaimed ability to avoid detection and to escape from prison, spent well over half of his adult life in prison.

According to the biographical accounts in these books, some of the motivations for beginning and ending criminal careers are apparent. In the juvenile years the importance of challenge and excitement seems clear. This motivation was clearly a factor in each of the careers that began at a very young age (Allen, 1977; Braly, 1976; Brown, 1965; Martin, 1952; Parker & Allerton, 1962; Shaw, 1930). "It wasn't that I craved for anything. It was more the excitement than anything else" (Martin, 1952, p. 16). The importance of excitement and thrill in motivating delinquent behavior has also been noted in the scientific literature (Peterson & Braiker, 1978).

Individuals appear motivated to end or to alter their patterns of serious criminality in later adult years for similar reasons. As discussed earlier, there is a tendency for serious crime to desist as age increases. Often this desistance may be best described as a movement from serious criminal activity to arrest for public order offenses like public drunkenness. The psychological and social processes that may explain the pattern have not been adequately dealt with in the scientific literature. The drugs-and-crime literature has addressed the issue for heroin addicts, and it is hypothesized in this literature that heroin addicts mature out of their addiction because of the demands of their addiction. Its requirements for high daily income create a life-style that is too physically and psychologically demanding for older adults.

In the biographical accounts examined here, for individuals whose careers continued into later adulthood, there are apparently two sets of factors that influence changes in later criminal career. First, physiological and psychological concomitants of the aging process appear to combine to reduce the efficiency and confidence necessary for daring criminal activity. Second, the risk of serious criminal sanction is increased as the continuing offender accumulates a more serious criminal history (Martin, 1952; Parker & Allerton, 1962; Sutherland, 1937).

Summary—Criminal Careers

Although substantial percentages of individuals in the general population are arrested for nontraffic criminal offenses before middle age, it appears that only 12–24% are ever arrested for serious "street" crime. Offenses committed by young adults are more serious than those committed by juveniles, and overall offense frequency decreases with age. The majority of those arrested for serious offenses do not go on to have lengthy, serious, criminal careers, although the probability of recidivism increases to about 80% after three police contacts. Shannon has suggested that these findings indicate that a small percentage of serious offenders emerges: "It appears that the high probability of continuation after any given contact, is a consequence of the rapid development of a 'hard core' of continuers" (1977a).

Much of the research on criminal careers has relied on the study of incarcerated populations. Incarcerated individuals likely represent the "hard core," and the offense patterns of this group differ from those who are surveyed outside prison. Available evidence also suggests that within chronic offender categories, there is a smaller percentage who are responsible for a grossly disproportionate volume of serious crime. Criminal careers tend toward diversity rather than toward narrow specialization.

The young adult age period should be a focus for theoretical effort and policy attention; this age span is particularly notable for serious criminal activity. However, considerable variation is noted in age-related offense patterns. Some begin to offend early and desist early; others apparently to begin late and continue for a long time. Still others begin early and have uninterrupted and extended criminal careers. More data on nonincarcerated samples is required so that criminal careers can be charted in ways which allow the relationships of offense onset, type, intensity, and career length to be specified. This will require longitudinal or quasi-longitudinal research designs.

Alcohol Careers and Criminal Careers

Recent Review of the Alcohol–Crime Literature

Considerable evidence indicates an association between alcohol consumption and serious criminal behavior. We do not refer here to "alcohol defined or alcohol related crime" (J. Roizen & Schneberk, 1977a, p. 299). Alcohol-defined or alcohol-related offenses include public drunkenness and illegal consumption or sale of alcoholic beverages. Obviously the correlation between public drunkenness and alcohol consumption would approach unity. We are interested in alcohol consumption and serious offenses, and considerable evidence suggests that alcohol is often present in or before criminal events, and that a disproportionate number of criminal offenders have alcohol problems.

J. Roizen and Schneberk (1977a) divided their review and critique of the alcohol–crime literature into three categories: alcohol in the criminal event, drinking problems of criminal offenders, and criminal careers of labeled alcoholics. A large number of research studies were reviewed in each of these categories. The event-centered literature showed that most commonly, if alcohol was present, both offender and victim had been drinking. For the offenses of homicide, assault, and rape, one may note that substantial percentages of all such events have drinking offenders and victims.

A review of 21 studies of incarcerated offenders showed that the percentages of these offenders who are reported to have been drinking before their incarceration offense varied widely, and that there was not a clear difference in the percentages for personal and property crimes (J. Roizen & Schneberk, 1977a). In this regard, the findings from research on prison populations differ from research on arrested population and from analysis of offense events. In the case of data for events, alcohol is typically found to be related to the personal injury offender and offense, not to property offenders and offenses. Research on prison samples indicates significant alcohol involvement for property offenses as well.

Interviews of approximately 10,400 inmates in state correctional institutions show that the percentage of offenders who reported they were drinking at the time of the offense for which they are currently incarcerated is as indicated in Table 5.6. Percentages are highest for arson, homicide, sex, and assault offenses; and lowest for robbery, burglary, larceny, motor vehicle theft, and forgery. Although the percentages are generally highest for personal offenses (arson excepted), substantial percentages of property offenders report alcohol involvement. Findings were also found to vary by recidivism and race. The data on reported drinking at the time of the offense from this survey indicate that recidivists are more likely to report drinking than nonrecidivists, and that White inmates are more likely than Blacks to report drinking at the time of the present incarceration offense (J. Roizen & Schneberk, 1977a).

Other Evidence

Research on those labeled alcoholic or problem drinkers indicates that a disproportionate number have criminal records (Goodwin *et al.*, 1971; Guze, Tuason, Gatfield, Stewart, & Picken, 1962; Lindelius & Salum,

TABLE 5.6. Percentage of State Prison Inmates Who Reported Drinking at the Time of the Offense for Which They Were Currently Incarcerated[a]

Offense	Percentage of offenders who reported drinking at the time of the offense
Homicide	53
Sex	57
Assault	61
Robbery	39
Burglary	47
Larceny	38
Motor vehicle theft	46
Forgery	38
Arson	67
TOTAL (all crimes)	43

[a]From a survey of state correctional inmates conducted by the Bureau of the Census (BOC) for the Law Enforcement Assistance Administration (LEAA) in 1974, as reproduced in J. Roizen and Schneberk (1977a, p. 30).

1973). Incarcerated offenders are disproportionately classified as alcoholic or as having alcoholic problems. Other research finds that problem drinkers are more likely to recidivate than are those without drinking problems (Edwards, Kyle & Nicholls, 1977; Institute for Scientific Analysis, 1978; National Institute of Alcohol Abuse and Alcoholism, 1978; J. Roizen & Schneberk, 1977a). Such findings suggest that problem drinking is causally related to criminal behavior. It has been common to theorize that drinking problems "cause" the criminal behavior. However, "the majority of criminal offenders do not have drinking problems and the majority of alcoholics have not committed serious crimes" (J. Roizen & Schneberk, 1977a, p. 396). In spite of the coexistence of drinking problems and criminal careers within the same individual lifetimes, the nature of the link between the variables is not clear. In fact, Roizen and Schneberk suggest that "if there is a causal connection, it is crime causing chronic inebriety rather than the other way around" (p. 399). This statement is not justified by past work but is based on findings that indicate that serious crimes usually occur prior to middle age, and that alcoholism problems are usually manifested at about middle age. Furthermore, as we have indicated, the kind of drinking problems which appear to be most analogous to illegal behavior, or which seem most likely to lead to crime, are most common in the young adult years.

Pittman and Gordon (1958) examined the criminal career patterns of 186 individuals incarcerated for public intoxication. The number of total arrests for the sample and the number of arrests for public intoxication depended on age; those under age 35 had substantially fewer arrests than those over 35. The average age of the sample was 47.7 years. Although 31% of those in the sample had never been arrested on any charge except public intoxication, 37% had serious criminal arrest records; this percentage is higher than for the general population. The authors described the careers of these offenders as "biphasic." Serious offenses tend to occur early in the career and to cease after age 35: "The criminal career is generally divided into two distinct phases. The first covers the earlier years of life, generally when the man is under 40 years of age, and is marked by arrest and incarcerations for offenses that are seemingly unrelated to excessive use of alcohol" (Pittman & Gordon, 1958, pp. 263–264). The research of Glueck and Glueck (1937) also indicates that the predominant offense pattern for offenders over age 35 is drunkenness. In a sample of 404 prisoners and former prisoners, Gibbens and Silberman (1970) found that heavy drinkers tended to be convicted at an older age, and that they were best described as "polycriminals" because of the mixture of their offenses. There is considerable evidence that young and later adult offense patterns are different from each other.

Age and the Presence of Alcohol in Offenses

Table 5.7 displays findings for a survey of more than 10,000 state correctional inmates. Age variations may be noted in the percentage of offenders who reported drinking at the time of the offense which resulted in the current incarceration. For crimes against the person, there is a direct relationship between age and drinking at the time of the offense. Thirty-nine percent reported drinking in the under-age-20 category; by the age span 26–30, 48% of offenders reported they were drinking at the time of the offense. The percentage increases to more than 50% between ages 31 and 35, and remains relatively high.

There is not so clear a relationship between age and drinking at the time of a property offense. After age 30 the percentages of offenders who report drinking increases and remains high relative to younger ages, but the relationship is not as strong or clear as with personal offenses. Data from the Peterson and Braiker (1978) survey of California inmates are fairly consistent with these findings. Alcohol is present for substantial percentages of offenses—especially assaultive offenses. Although the Peterson–Braiker data do not show a clear increase in the presence of alcohol for personal offenses with age, there is some trend in this direction.

The respondents in the Peterson and Braiker survey of California correctional inmates were also asked to report whether and how many times they "got drunk and hurt someone." Twenty-four percent reported at least one such incident during the 3 years prior to the current incarceration; 3%

TABLE 5.7. Percentages of Inmates Who Reported Drinking at the Time of Their Incarceration Crime, by Age[a]

Age (years)	Crimes against person	Crimes against property
< 20	38.6	36.4
21–25	41.7	33.4
26–30	48.2	33.8
31–35	53.6	38.4
36–40	53.8	40.5
41–45	57.8	41.6
46–50	61.4	37.7
> 50	58.7	39.9

[a]From BOC-LEAA survey; see note to Table 5.6.

TABLE 5.8. Percentages of Inmates Who Reported They "Got Drunk and Hurt Someone," by Age[a]

Age (years)	Number of times[b]		
	0	1	2
<21	71	16	13
	(104)	(24)	(19)
21–25	68	21	11
	(100)	(31)	(17)
25–30	76	17	7
	(84)	(19)	(8)
>30	80	15	5
	(91)	(17)	(6)

[a]From a survey of California correctional inmates: See Peterson and Braiker (1978). Data provided by Mark Peterson of the Rand Corporation, Santa Monica, Calif.
[b]The number of respondents in each age group is given in parentheses.

reported committing such an offense more than five times in the 3-year period. There are age variations in the reports of this offense. Table 5.8 indicates that younger offenders are more likely to report one or more of these offenses, and that in the 21–25 age category, almost one of three offenders report they "got drunk and hurt someone" in the 3 years prior to the current incarceration.

On the surface, the age–alcohol–offense patterns of Tables 5.7 and 5.8 are inconsistent. The data from the Bureau of the Census (BOC) state correctional inmate survey indicate that alcohol is more likely to be present in the offenses (especially the personal offenses) of older offenders. Table 5.8, which reports responses from a sample of California inmates, indicates that those under 25 are more likely than older inmates to report having gotten drunk and hurt someone during the 3 years prior to their current incarceration. These findings are not necessarily inconsistent with each other. Two speculative explanations are offered here that may explain the discrepancy.

The phrase "got drunk and hurt someone" may elicit positive responses for aggressive behavior that is not likely to result in arrest, conviction, and incarceration. Getting drunk and hurting someone may describe a fight between peers or intrafamilial attack. Such assaultive behavior generally has a low likelihood of resulting in incarceration because it is less likely to be reported to the police and less likely to be prosecuted even if an arrest takes place. The inmates who report drinking at the time of the incarceration offense have been incarcerated for all kinds of personal offenses, not just offenses described by the phrase "got drunk and hurt someone." If this is the case, then the age differences in the findings for the two inmate surveys may be explained by differences in offense type.

A second possible explanation for the apparent inconsistency in the age–alcohol–offense findings for the two inmate samples may derive from a differential age tendency to use alcohol as a deviance disavowal or denial mechanism. Older offenders who are incarcerated for personal offenses may be more likely to see such illegal behavior as personally discrediting. In such a case, alcohol use in connection with criminal offense may be reported as a way of deflecting responsibility for such behavior onto the effects of drinking.

In any case, the data from both the BOC inmate sample survey and the California inmate survey suggest that alcohol consumption is an important element in criminal behavior. It is not possible with these data to be specific about how alcohol may be influential, nor is it possible to separate real criminogenic effects from deviance disavowal responses. Such answers need better data on the issues and further theoretical development in the alcohol–behavior relationship.

Offender Perceptions of the Importance of Alcohol

The Rand study of 49 criminal careers directly addresses the question of the influence of alcohol in criminal behavior (Petersilia *et al.,* 1978). It will be recalled that this research divides the careers of this group of serious offenders incarcerated for the offense of robbery into three phases: the juvenile period, the young adult period, and the adult period. Findings from this small and biased sample are not generalizable, and the alcohol influence data are limited. Nonetheless, the research is notable because it allows comparison of the perceived effect of alcohol as it varies by career phase. The influence of alcohol and drugs is confounded in some of the findings because interviewees were asked, in some of the questions, about the influence of drugs or alcohol; in these cases it is not possible to discuss separately the effect of drugs and the effect of alcohol. In some other questions, the separate effects of drugs and of alcohol were inquired about (Petersilia *et al.,* 1978).

Petersilia *et al.* (1978) asked interviewees to provide the main reason and contributing factors for engaging in crime during each of the three career periods. In the juvenile period, 10% said their main reason was to get money for drugs or alcohol. In the young adult and adult periods, the respective percentages that gave this as the main reason were 30 and 29%. The reported use of the money gained from crimes roughly paralleled the responses for the "main reason" for engaging in crimes. Twelve percent of juveniles, 30% of young adults, and 24% of adults reported that they used their monetary gains for drugs and alcohol (Petersilia *et al.*, 1978). In the juvenile period, 24% said that "being under the influence of alcohol or drugs" was a contributing factor. In young adult and adult periods, "being under the influence of alcohol or drugs" was viewed as a contributing factor for 25% and 31% of the offenders, respectively. Thus, in the perception of these offenders, drugs and alcohol play important roles in the motivation of criminal activity. It is not possible to separate the effects of drugs and alcohol in these findings.

Interviewees were also asked to report on the influence of drugs and alcohol during the commission of criminal acts (as opposed to the career influence previously discussed). Table 5.9 indicates a rough consistency in the perceived influence of alcohol over the career periods. About one in four judged alcohol as influential in each period. But 63% in the juvenile period and 41% in the two later periods judged neither alcohol nor drugs as influential. Interestingly, this group of offenders judged alcohol use as a more important criminogenic factor than drug use. Overall these offenders perceived drugs or alcohol as influential factors. Similar findings resulted when individuals were asked to judge whether drugs or alcohol were influential during the three career phases. Forty-six percent believed drugs or alcohol were an influence in the juvenile period. Two-thirds believed drugs or alcohol were influential in the two later periods.

Based on interview data, rap sheet information, and inmate files, offenders from the Petersilia *et al.* (1978) survey were classified on the basis of their use of alcohol and drugs. The authors classified the 49 offenders in this research as being drug involved (25%) alcohol involved (29%) involved

TABLE 5.9. Influence of Drugs or Alcohol during Criminal Acts[a]

| | Percentage | | |
Influence	Juvenile period ($n = 40$)	Young adult period ($n = 44$)	Adult period ($n = 42$)
Alcohol	25.0	29.6	26.2
Drugs	10.0	20.5	23.8
Both drugs and alcohol	2.5	9.1	9.5
Neither alcohol nor drugs	62.5	40.9	40.5

[a]From Petersilia *et al.* (1978, p. 81).

with both (18%) and involved with neither (29%). The offense rates and patterns of each category were then examined and the authors concluded: The drugs–alcohol involvement was poorly predictive of individual offense rates. Offenders classified as being involved with both drugs and alcohol had the highest offense rates; offenders classified as alcohol involved had the lowest offense rates (Petersilia *et al.*, p. 83). Examination of median number of crimes against the person for young adult and adult periods also indicates that the lowest rate is for alcohol-involved offenders—a rate even lower than that for offenses classified as being involved with neither alcohol nor drugs.

The authors compared the likelihood of being arrested, convicted, and incarcerated for the four drugs–alcohol-involved offender groups. Alcohol-involved offenders were more likely than the other groups to be arrested for offenses they committed and were more likely to be convicted if arrested. The disparity in arrest likelihood was substantial; the percentage of offenses resulting in arrests was 2.9% for drug-involved offenders, 3.3% for offenders involved with both drugs and alcohol, 2.1% for offenders involved with neither drugs nor alcohol, and 12.1% for alcohol-involved offenders. This disparity, if it also applies to other arrested offender populations, has important implications. It suggests that offenders who are involved with alcohol are more likely to be arrested than are offenders who are not so involved. Therefore, alcohol-involved offenders may be overrepresented in the criminal justice system.

The 624 inmates surveyed by Peterson and Braiker were asked to self-report on the importance of 15 reasons to their own criminal behavior. They were asked about such influences as losing a job, revenge, excitement, and the effect of drugs or alcohol on the crime committed most often. As in the smaller California survey just discussed, it is not possible to separate perceived drug and alcohol effects. Respondents noted the reasons for engaging in criminal behavior as "very important," "somewhat important," "somewhat unimportant," and "not important at all." The respondents were asked to rate the importance of their offenses "because of drugs or alcohol." An earlier question in the series asked how important a reason "getting money for drugs" was, so that presumably the "because of drugs or alcohol" question would be interpreted by respondents to refer to direct effects of drug or alcohol use on their criminal behavior, and not to the income need created by regular use of expensive drugs. Thirty-one percent of the respondents reported that drug or alcohol effects were "very important"; an additional 16% reported drugs or alcohol were "somewhat important." These two response categories total 47%; approximately an equal percentage (45%) said drugs or alcohol were "not important at all" (Peterson & Braiker, 1978, Table 6.1).

Biographical Evidence

Existing research provides a great deal of evidence suggesting a relationship between alcohol consumption and criminal behavior. Most of the research is associational—it looks for the coexistence of drinking and crime in the same event, time frame, lifetime, or life segment. The research frequently confirms the coexistence, but only rarely can it demonstrate probable cause. In the preceding sections we have examined the empirical evidence and found it suggestive. Some serious criminal behavior probably occurs that would not occur in the absence of drinking.

The biographical accounts of offender careers were also examined for evidence of a relationship between alcohol and crime. These sources do not provide strong evidence one way or the other. In fact, in these accounts, drinking is not viewed as an important factor in the early etiology of criminal behavior for any of the subjects of these books. Braly says about himself at age 18: "Not only had I never been laid, I also had never been drunk" (1976, p. 69). Neither does it appear from their stories that the later criminal behavior of the subjects was caused by alcohol consumption, at least not in the sense that drinking itself provided a direct impetus toward a criminal career. The fact that alcohol is not causally connected to criminal careers in the view of these individuals does not mean that drinking does not sometimes have an influence on the occurrence of crime—that is, on certain events within the career.

As indicated by the account of an assault on a girlfriend by Martin, these individuals may fail to recognize or be explicit about the role of alcohol in their criminal behavior. Martin (1952) tells of an occurrence late in his criminal career that could be classified accurately as an aggravated assault:

> So after fixing the light cord, we sit down and we're talking about this and that, and we wound up getting pretty drunk. And uh, the windup of it was, I still don't know how it happened, we got into some kind of an argument or something down on the second floor landing and I, uh, wound up knockin' her down the stairs. (p. 258)

The subject of this assault was hospitalized with her injuries. It seems apparent that this incident in the life of one individual committed to a "career" in crime was influenced by drinking, but there is no indication that alcohol exerted an ongoing influence on his criminal activities, nor is there any explicit recognition on the part of the author about the influence of alcohol in the offense.

The discussion of Claude Brown about the violence that characterized Saturday nights in Harlem suggests the same attitude. Brown (1965) without explicitly saying that alcohol "caused" the routine and recurrent violence in Harlem, implicitly suggests a close connection between the drinking and violent activities. Violence was endemic to Brown's Harlem and much of it occurred on Saturday night:

> Saturday night. I suppose there's a Saturday night in every Negro community throughout the nation just like Saturday night in Harlem. The bars will jump. The precinct station will have a busy night. The hospital's emergency ward will jump.
>
> Cats who have been working all their lives, who've never been in any trouble before, good-doing righteous cats, self-respecting, law-abiding citizens— they'll all come out. Perhaps it'll be their night in the bar, their night in the police station, maybe their night in the emergency ward.
>
> They tell me that young doctors really try hard for a chance to do their internship in Harlem Hospital—it offers such a wide variety of experiences. They say it's the best place in the city where a surgeon can train. They say you get all kinds of experience just working there on Saturday nights. (p. 312)

The close association of drinking and violence on Saturday night in Harlem does not necessarily mean that the physiological or disinhibiting effects of alcohol explain the relationship. In fact, based on Brown's description, the interpretation of MacAndrew and Edgerton (1969) seems best able to explain Saturday night violence in Harlem. These authors suggest that drunkenness often results in untoward behavior, not because of alcohol's direct effects, but because drunkenness sometimes occurs under "societally sanctioned freedom from the otherwise enforceable demands that persons comply with the conventional proprieties" (p. 89); drunkenness is sometimes a "time out" period.

There is some evidence from the biographical material that heavy drinking among professional criminals is common, but that drinking and criminal activities should be kept separated. Criminal offenders typically drink a great deal, but drinking and crime activities should be separated in the interest of avoiding detection or maintaining a high level of efficiency:

> A person who is a professional thief may cease to be one. This would generally result from a violation of the codes of the profession or else from inefficiency due to age, fear, narcotic drugs or drink. (Sutherland, 1937, p. 215)

> Tommy's weaknesses are the usual weaknesses of thieves: booze and broads. (Sutton, 1976, p. 3)

In these views, alcohol consumption is often a part of a criminal lifestyle, but drinking is also something that may make one susceptible to failure.

There is further suggestion in a case study illustration from Petersilia *et al.* (1978) that part of the alcohol–crime connection is explained by the effect of alcohol on arrest vulnerability. The criminal career of "Ken" is described. He is an individual with an acute dependence on alcohol and frequently commits offenses while intoxicated:

> I went to a bar and started pouring down the booze—this was the first time in nearly three months. This other guy and I sat getting drunk and talking about how shitty life was. Then we went outside and stopped a cab and got in. After the cab started up, I grabbed the driver by the neck and told him to drive out of town. After he did that we made him get out, I beat him up and the other guy took his wallet. I didn't have a weapon, but I'm pretty big and I was so mad I had to take it out on someone. I think the other guy had a knife on him, though. We went back to his place and I stayed a week. I didn't go back to work, so I guess I was fired by that time. Then I went back to my wife. We argued all the time. She went on welfare and I lived off that money, spending a lot of time drinking in bars. I'd almost forgotten about the cab job, but three months later the cops came to the house and arrested me. My buddy had ratted on me when the cops grabbed him for something else. I was identified by the cab driver and ended up doing four years of prison time before I escaped. I escaped with this guy I had gotten close to in prison, who was getting some help from his girlfriend. We got outside and the other guy got away clean, but as usual I got caught again. Because of that escape, I did about seven years of time for that cab robbery. (p. 105)

One thing seems clear about the alcohol–crime relationship—it does not seem accurate to characterize drinking as an important influence in the etiology of a criminal career, but drinking does appear to contribute to the occurrence of particular criminal events. It may do so through the effects of alcohol on motivation or perception, either directly or in interaction with other factors. Apparently the excessive consumption of alcohol, aside from any effect it may have on criminal behavior, is more common among individuals who are likely to commit crime. In the criminal careers biographical literature examined here, it seems accurate to say that while alcohol is not etiologically important, at times drinking has something to do with the occurrence of crime. Reports of those from prison samples who responded to questions about the role of alcohol also suggest that it may be an important factor. Future research needs to examine questions of criminal career etiology and criminal event etiology separately.

Summary—Alcohol Careers and Criminal Careers

Some offenders believe, or say they believe, that alcohol is an important cause of their own offenses. A large volume and variety of empirical research indicates an association between alcohol and crime. Some of this evidence suggests a causal association. It is difficult to integrate the effect of age into what is known about the alcohol–crime relationship, although there appears to be a different kind of relationship in younger and older male offenders. It is difficult to find much direct evidence for a systematic relationship between alcohol consumption and criminal behavior at young ages. Young men clearly have more serious behavioral problems as a result of drinking than do older men, but past research has not looked in detail at the alcohol–crime connection during that age period. Alcohol may be more important in the criminality of older men, either in its effect on the occurrence of the criminal behavior or in an elevation in the probability of arrest for older offenders, or both.

Some evidence suggests that alcohol-involved serious offenders commit offenses at a lower rate than non-alcohol-involved serious offenders. Evidence also suggests that alcohol-involved offenders are more likely to be arrested for serious offenses than are those who are not involved with alcohol. It does not appear that alcohol is a causal or precipitating factor in the origin of criminal careers. The effect of alcohol appears to be most relevant for only some criminal events within offender careers. Because serious offense activity is concentrated in the late adolescent–young adult years, research attention needs to be focused there.

Some portion of the empirical relationship between alcohol consumption and criminal behavior is also likely an artifact of deviance disavowal. Separation of alcohol as an excuse from alcohol as a genuine effect, either a physiological effect or as an influence on the structuring of norms or context, is not possible from current theory and data. It is likely that disavowal, physiological effect, and social definition are all important to the alcohol–crime relationship. Until the relationships are better articulated, it is difficult to examine how age may contribute to explanation.

Finally, it is clear that future research should: (1) focus on nonprison populations, (2) use multiple levels of data and data sources (like self-reports of drinking and illegal activity and official records) to measure criminal behavior, and (3) develop data which are descriptive of the criminal event itself and of the personal interactions of individuals who may have participated in the event. This last category of data is crucial if empirical findings are to provide the power to infer "causality."

Conceptual and Policy Directions

Conceptual Interpretations

In this chapter alcohol problems, crime patterns, and the relationship between these behavioral categories have been examined as a function of age. It has been argued that the young adult period should be the focus of future conceptual and empirical work. During the young adult years, serious drinking and crime problems are most frequent. It is not certain whether or how these separate problems during the same age span are interrelated. However, the focus on young adults and their problem behavior is likely to be fruitful. Even if it were found that alcohol and crime problems in young adulthood are not directly related to each other, it is unlikely that they would be found to be independent of each other. It has been observed here and elsewhere that the more likely explanatory role for alcohol as a factor in criminal behavior is an indirect one—perhaps in what Pernanen has called a "conditional or interactive relationship." Alcohol in such relationships has no main effect but depends on other conditions or interactions (Pernanen, 1976). Research and theory to spell out alcohol–crime connections in finer detail are needed. Because the empirical evidence directs us to the young adult years, focus there is likely to be fertile. However, these empirical regularities require a systematic conceptual scheme if explanation is to follow description.

Most theoretical attempts to explain delinquent and criminal behavior focus on the adolescent years and on delinquency. They do not integrate empirical findings and interpretive schemes into the adult years. The young adult period has been a neglected area for social psychological theory. Rappaport (1972) has made the same point about the psychological development literature. The assumption in the criminological literature apparently is that adult criminal behavior has its roots in adolescence, and that understanding of the early development process will provide the basis for understanding adult criminality. The age variable is not systematically integrated into criminological theories beyond adolescence.

Some previous theoretical work has emphasized the importance of social learning and exposure to attitudes favorable to the violation of law (Akers, 1973; Sutherland & Cressey, 1974). Other work has emphasized the importance of opportunities to achieve stature and material reward through legitimate channels (Cloward & Ohlin, 1960; Merton, 1968). The influence of peers, achievement, and socialization is emphasized by others (Hirschi, 1969). Some other theoretical constructions give priority to psychological concepts like self-concept (Reckless, 1967), reaction formation (A. K. Cohen, 1955), or hypermasculinity (McCord & McCord, 1962; Zucker, 1968). Age and the developmental process is not systematically integrated into these attempts to explain delinquency and crime.

With regard to the relevance of age, the general sociological and psychological literatures give more direction than specific theories of crime and deviance. The sociological literature has long recognized the relevance of age as a normative criterion (Nardi, 1973). Age-related expectations are connected with behavior, roles, and sanctions; societal norms are structured in part around age-graded criteria.

Although the psychological literature on emotional and cognitive development deals mainly with the adolescent years, there are exceptions. Kohlberg (1973), reversing his earlier position, maintains that there are adult stages of moral development. Piaget's (1932/1948) final stage of "formal operations," reached between the ages of 12 and 15, has been viewed by most as the final development stage. The formal operations stage undergoes refinement and development but has been viewed in most of the cognitive development literature as the final, qualitatively unique stage of moral development. According to Kohlberg, his longitudinal research indicates that there are two unique stages of adult moral reasoning: the social contract utilitarian orientation and the universal principles of justice orientation. Of special interest here is the finding that individuals who have attained the formal operations stage do not move in an uninterrupted progression to stabilization of this stage or to a new adult stage. There appears to be a "retrogression" or transitional phase during which young adults revert to moral interpretations which may appear to be based on early-stage thinking. Whether or not the observed hiatus is a retrogression or a transitional phase between a lower and higher moral stage of development is not the issue here. What is of interest here is that there appears to be a unique orientation in moral development that manifests itself around age 20. This "irregularity" on the moral development dimension coincides with the ages during which problem drinking and serious crime are also significant problems.

It is clear that consideration of the relationship between age, alcohol, and crime requires the conceptual mapping of complex relationships between a number of variables. If past theoretical work has demonstrated anything with certainty it is that alcohol effects interact with and are often mediated through other influences on behavior (Pernanen, 1976). The mapping of the alcohol–crime relationship must be multidimensional.

A comprehensive theoretical framework is required to deal with the alcohol–crime relationship. The work of Jessor and Jessor (1977) provides an example of a comprehensive social psychological framework for the systematic description and explanation of deviant behavior. This theoretical integration breaks each of three "systems" (sociocultural, personality, socialization) into subsystems or structures with each system. The socialization system, for example, is broken down into the parental reward structure, the parental belief structure, and the parental control structure. Ultimately, a comprehensive explanatory framework such as that proposed by Jessor and Jessor is required to deal with the relationships which are relevant in the alcohol–crime connection. However, recognition of the need for a comprehensive model does not require exclusive use of a comprehensive approach. Knowledge development is an incremental process; narrow perspective, with its focus on selected facts or aspects, has value.

This approach can fill in pieces of the total mosaic. In fact, this chapter might be viewed as one describing the "mosaic age," and it is intended to be a beginning in the integration of age with other variables in the mosaic field.

Methodological Issues

In an earlier section of this chapter, we referred briefly to our use of the variable "age." It is important that a distinction be made between use of the age dimension as a classificatory variable and use of age as an explanatory independent variable. Wohlwill (1970) has discussed this at length and suggests that age, as it is used in much research, should not be considered a variable in the scientific sense. Wohlwill further suggests that age is meaningful only if it is at least used to denote a continuum along which individual development is charted. The measure of time we call (chronological) age is appropriate for use as a classificatory variable but, as such, has no explanatory referent. Wohlwill would argue that this use is not theoretically meaningful, and, while one may disagree with this position, it is nonetheless important to be clear about the scientific meaning of the age variable. The use of age as a variable, therefore, in this chapter and in the literature and research reviewed here, does not rise above the classificatory level. Age has not been an analytically meaningful variable but has merely been used as a time dimension along which we have organized empirical findings. This use is scientifically appropriate, but we also wish to consider age in a more substantively relevant way. If age is to have explanatory value, its social and psychological relevance must be clarified and made explicit.

The conceptualization of the life cycle as being made up of three distinct dimensions of time may help to clarify the different modes of meaning and use for the age variable. Neugarten and Datan (1973) break the life cycle down into "life time," "historical time," and "social time." Life time is chronological age and refers to the chronological dimension, but it may also include the development aspects of age that are analytically meaningful. Historical time refers to the unique social and cultural context and events which coexist for a discrete number of individual lifetimes. Social time refers to the unique system of age norms and age grading that is characteristic of a society within which a given number of lifetimes are lived.

The distinction between life times and historical time is important because it points to a distinction that needs to be made between age effects and cohort (historical) effects (Riley & Waring, 1978). Stated in different terms, there is a need "to separate ontogenetic from generational change components" (Woodruff & Birren, 1972, p. 252). The use of longitudinal cohort research to measure development and change over time in individual lives is a powerful research approach. But this method does not control for unique cohort effects, that is, the particular historical events and context that influence individuals.

Woodruff and Birren (1972) developed a design to separate age and cohort change and found that the cohort effect was substantial. A group of college students who had taken the California Personality Inventory (CPI) in 1944 were retested on the same test in 1969. In addition, separate samples of college and high school students were administered the CPI in 1969. The actual differences in score on the CPI for the indivduals who took the test in 1944 and again in 1969 were small, although the perceptions of the group when they were asked how they thought they had performed in the earlier testing indicated that they perceived themselves as performing more poorly than they actually had. When the scores of the present students were compared to the scores of the 1944 students, there were substantial differences. The authors concluded:

> Taken as a whole, the results of this study confirm what has been suggested by the discrepancy between cross-sectional and longitudinal literature on personality test scores. The slight differences which occur in personality test scores for the same individuals over long periods of time indicate that objective age changes in personality are small from adolescence to middle age. Larger age differences resulting from cross-sectional studies suggest that objective cohort differences in personality may be great. (p. 258)

These findings are important in two ways. First, they suggest that research designs and interpretation of findings must attempt to separate age and cohort effects. Second, given the age variations in drinking problems and crime, it may be fruitful to locate the specific psychological characteristics that do vary by age.

Conceptual Summary

Even though comprehensive conceptual frameworks that explain deviant behavior variations between youth and adulthood were not found, we have discussed some findings and approaches that seem applicable or promising for our purposes.

A finding that recurs in several places deals with neurosis and psychosis as those classifications vary by age (Eysenck & Eysenck, 1969). In an evaluation of MMPI profiles for law offenders in six different age groups, there was evidence that neurotic scales go up with age, and that psychotic scales go down: "The findings show partial support for both hypotheses of a gradual increase in 'neuroticism' associated with age as well as a gradual decrease in 'psychoticism' with age" (McCleary & Mensk, 1977,

p. 165). In other research it has also been found that sociopathy wanes later in life (Goodwin *et al.,* 1971).

It is not clear how these findings may relate to the major issues of interest here, but there does appear to be a tendency for the psychotic–psychopathic diagnoses to occur in younger adults where alcohol and crime problems are also more likely. These findings and those of Kohlberg (1973) on the "slippage" in moral development which occurs in young adulthood suggest that more research needs to be done on emotional and cognitive development in these years. This research may shed light on the reasons for the concentration of drinking and serious crime problems during those ages.

There also appear to be age-graded differences on other psychological characteristics such as reflectiveness–impulsiveness, optimism–pessimism, and extraversion–introversion (Coyne, Whitbourne, & Glenwick, 1978; Kogan, 1973; Kogan & Wollack, 1961). These psychological age variations may also be related to the drinking and crime problems.

It is not easy to specify the sociological and psychological literature which may be relevant for interpretation of the finding that drinking and crime problems are most common in the young adult years. It is clear that social norms are age graded and that social control activities are also structured by age. On the one hand, this points toward the relevance of age aspects of the socialization process, but it also indicates that the social control reaction process is important. It may be, for example, that the age-graded empirical regularities for crime data reflect, in whole or part, differences in the definition and recording of offenses for juvenile and adult offenders, and not differences in actual criminal behavior for juveniles and adults. The existence of separate juvenile and adult systems of justice provides some support for this interpretation. It is not likely that the bifurcated justice systems simply mask behavioral similarities. Self-report data clearly indicate juvenile–adult behavioral differences. However, it is likely that the social reaction process itself has some effect on the official crime data, and this effect needs to be separated from actual behavioral differences.

There are also likely to be other kinds of interactions that influence age–alcohol–crime relationships. Within different subcultural contexts, socialization and behavioral expectations about drinking and crime may differ. Some cultures may be more tolerant of alcohol-related violence than others, and there may be age-specific expectations in this regard.

In summary, it is clear that, given the importance of the young adult stage in drinking and crime problems, the most promising theoretical orientations to pursue are those that attempt to explain emotional and cognitive development and those that examine the age variations in social expectations, sanctions, and beliefs about the effects of alcohol consumption.

Policy Implications

The attempt to understand the age effect in the alcohol–crime relationship demands a high level of scientific rigor. Sampling, measurement, and analytic issues must be considered carefully; conceptual clarity is mandatory. However, the demands of scientific rigor can be relaxed if social science findings are to be interpreted for social policy purposes. There is no substitute for careful and rigorous social science. But, given the likelihood that total understanding in most areas of human social behavior is likely to remain rudimentary for a long time, and given the desire to make use of what social science insights may be available to inform current social policy, research findings can be interpreted from a policy perspective. Klausner (1973) has distinguished two separate orientations to the interpretation of facts: the analytic and the applied. The former is what would be called the scientific; the latter could be called policy interpretation. Obviously, the orientations are not independent; there are links between the two.

We have noted earlier a distinction in the nature of the age variable. It can be used as a classificatory or explanatory variable. A third use of that variable is also possible—one that has a reference frame in the policy sphere. Social policy needs to be constructed around criteria that are easily available and useful as indicators for delineating options; age is such an indicator. Age can be used as a heuristic variable around which policy choices can be arrayed. An age range can delineate a segment of the population to be the subject of education, prevention, or intervention activities.

Historically and legally, age has been used as a fundamental defining policy criterion. In both drinking and crime areas, age has been the basis for social control; it has defined when drinking becomes legal and it has been used to separate the "delinquent" from the "criminal." The pursuit of scientific understanding of the influence of age on alcohol, crime, and the relationship between the two will also facilitate the policy use of age. One advantage of pursuing such understanding is that findings are more easily transferable into social policy because the linkage between the scientific and policy variables is easier to make.

Conclusion

Existing evidence does not allow definitive statements about the relationship between alcohol consumption and criminal behavior over the life cycle. Both drinking and crime problems clearly vary by age, but few inferences about the causal processes associated with this covariation are possible. Indeed, it is not certain that the similar empirical regularities of drinking problems and criminal behavior in the young adult years have any systematic causal relationship to each other. These two phenomena may each be independently explained by other factors. We do not think this is the case but are hard pressed to provide a conceptual integration of the empirical regularities. We have, however, suggested a developmental research approach to address questions about alcohol and criminal careers.

Future work should address the issues in two ways. Research should focus on the young adult years in a way that deals specifically with alcohol consumption patterns and their behavioral implications. Future research should also focus on the criminal behavior of young adults and work back from that behavior to determine whether alcohol has played a role. This future work should attend carefully to the measurement of drinking behavior and criminal behavior.

Future research should be carried out in general population samples—not just on problem drinkers or criminal populations.

Finally, future work needs to include consideration of attitudes and beliefs about drinking. There is good reason to believe that behavioral effects of alcohol derive in part from the reinterpretation of normative expectations and from altered evaluations of behavior that accompany alcohol's presence. When alcohol is present, social psychological reality is modified. This modified environment needs to be described as part of future research on the relationship between alcohol consumption and criminal behavior.

If future research attends to these points, the interpretation of findings can be meaningful and can provide a basis for both theoretical development and public decision making.

6 Alcohol and Criminal Behavior among Blacks: The Case for Research on Special Populations

JUDY ROIZEN

Introduction

Of the 2 million most serious felony crimes committed in the United States in 1977, 34% were committed by Blacks. Estimates of the proportion of offenders drinking immediately before or at the time of the crime vary from one- to two-thirds of Black offenders. This chapter explores the role of drinking in the commission of criminal acts for a single, special population: Blacks, primarily Black men. We are mostly interested here in drinking during criminal events rather than criminal careers. However, the two are not unrelated. Offenders with drinking problems are significantly more likely to have been drinking prior to crimes they commit, and recidivists are more likely to have been drinking and to report drinking problems than are first-time offenders. Despite an increasingly large body of empirical knowledge, the nature of the involvement of alcohol (specifically) or drinking behavior (generally) in criminal events and criminal careers is not well established. In part, the elusive nature of these relationships is a function of the increasingly common use of alcohol across class, status, and age groups. Distinguishing the presence of alcohol from its involvement in criminal events has proven to be a complex task.

The value of looking at these relationships in special populations is twofold: (1) it moves the focus away from the relationship between drinking and crime generally—a focus which has not been particularly productive in the past; (2) it becomes possible to link what is known about alcohol and criminal behavior to other research on the population concerned. The

JUDY ROIZEN. Brunel University, London, England.

danger, however, is in the potential loss of general theories about the social determinants of crime. For example, the class determinants of criminal behavior can be lost in the search for ethnic correlates. Similarly, chronological age can be mistaken for historical cohort effects. Boys aged 16 in 1968, for example, may have drinking patterns more similar to those of men who were 30 in 1968 than boys who were 16 in 1945.

These problems, while serious, do not outweigh the advantages of looking at populations separately. Demographic specificity allows for turning up the "magnification" on social processes—making it possible to combine, for example, survey data from general population studies with ethnographic data from a single community or status group.

As an example: drinking rates (i.e., quantity and frequency) for Black and White men are comparable when social class is controlled. Ethnographic data suggest, however, that drinking contexts may differ across status groups. A close look at specific social contexts, such as ghetto taverns, will help distinguish which among the various aspects of drinking situations affect criminal behavior.

Wolfgang (1958) outlined the need for demographically specific analyses two decades ago:

> Such differences [between the races with respect to the presence or absence of alcohol in the homicide situation] have a meaning only when the races [or sexes] are compared to each other. This comparison, of course, leaves unanswered the much larger question of the relationship between drinking and homicide. In order to discuss this latter question, the researcher would have to possess information about the drinking norms within each race [or sex] group, and then compare these drinking norms with the sample which persons involved in homicide could then be said to represent. The drinking mores of males and Negroes—the two groups that appear to be most significantly associated with homicide and the presence of alcohol—may be such that a larger share of the male and Negro population in general compared to the female and white population is engaged in social interaction involving alcohol ingestion at any time. Hence, the higher incidence of alcohol present in males and Negroes among persons involved in criminal homicide may simply be a reflection of the higher incidence of drinking among these two groups in the general population. Analysis, however, must proceed on the basis of frequency distributions of victims and offenders in whom alcohol was present. Such distributions do not, of course, tell us what the chances are of killing or being killed while drinking. The relative amounts of time spent drinking, where, when, with whom and under what circumstances are data about the general population not presently available, but these factors probably vary by race, sex, age, and other social attributes. (pp. 139–140)

In the last decade a good deal of empirical research on the drinking behavior of Blacks has been carried out. This chapter reviews some of this research, its adequacy and its relevance to understanding criminal events and criminal careers.

State-of-the-art papers tend to be eclectic (e.g., see Pernanen's discussion in Chapter 1, this volume), and this chapter is not an exception. There is no defined literature on the relationship of drinking and crime for Blacks. Therefore, we have drawn extensively from the theoretical literature, the empirical literature on drinking rates and patterns, event-based studies of individual crimes (Wolfgang-type), and surveys of incarcerated offenders. We also review here several general studies of delinquency and problem behavior, and two ethnographies of Black taverns.

This chapter is organized to answer several questions:

1. What contributions can the study of special populations make to understanding the role of alcohol in criminal behavior?
2. What is the empirical evidence for an "alcohol explanation" of criminal behavior among Blacks?
3. Do available data and theories support subcultural or demographic explanations? If so, which populations deserve special status and for what reasons?
4. Where are the gaps in existing literatures on drinking patterns and criminal behavior of Blacks as well as the literatures asserting a putative relationship between the two?

Defining the Variables: Crime and Drinking

In a large part, a review of this type is dependent on how other investigators have defined both the dependent and independent variables. Some of the studies reviewed here have looked at general deviance; others, at aggressive behavior; still others, at arrests and convictions. Noninstrumental crimes have been much more thoroughly reviewed than instrumental crimes—even though noninstrumental crimes account for only a small proportion of all crimes. Homicides, crimes which have received the most research attention, are a small proportion of all crimes. All violent, interpersonal crimes taken together account for less than 5% of all crimes committed in a year in the United States (U.S. Department of Justice, 1977).

The relationship between alcohol and criminal behavior has also received much more attention for noninstrumental than instrumental crimes. Some reviews are restricted only to these crimes (e.g. Pernanen, 1976). In our view, the evidence does not warrant this restriction. While studies based on arrest records have shown greater proportions of homicides, assaults, and rapes to be alcohol involved as compared to instrumental crimes, the data from prison studies have not shown this to be the case. However, the largest and most recent prison study carried out by the Law Enforcement Assistance Administration (LEAA) (the 1974 census of prisoners) shows between one-third and one-half of all crimes to have been committed by drinking offenders. Therefore, this review is not limited to noninstrumental crime or to the general problems of aggression but includes all serious crime (i.e., felony crime for adults or any arrest for youth) for which data are available. At the same time, we have had to be mindful of the fact that a large data-based review of secondary sources, such as ours, is constrained by the available evidence.

In an earlier work (J. Roizen & Schneberk, 1977a), the methodological issues involved in defining and measuring criminal behavior using secondary sources are outlined in some detail. These include, for example, biases due to the large proportion of uncleared crime, biases in prison samples toward long-term offenders, the absence of data on white-collar crime, and delays involved in arresting offenders for many types of crime.

Defining an appropriate alcohol variable also is not without difficulty. In the early work (J. Roizen & Schneberk, 1977a), we argued that the relationship between drinking and crime is, in fact, a number of different relationships depending on which aspect and effect of alcohol is being looked at and from what perspective: event-centered (i.e., situationally defined) or person-centered. There we argued:

> Most research on the relationship between drinking and crime has failed to acknowledge the difficulty in delimiting and defining criminal events, as well as defining the diverse roles alcohol can play in these events. Alcohol can be involved in forming intent for a crime, in aggravating the course of a criminal event once it has begun (e.g., by excess violence) or it can affect the apprehension of a suspect for a crime already committed. Different *aspects* of alcohol (e.g., BAC, alcoholism, drunkenness) can be involved in criminal events; as can different *effects* of alcohol (e.g., loss of concentration, drunkenness, sensorimotor incapacity). Alcohol can play a causal role in the event or simply be present without effect. Alcohol can affect a criminal career and never be a factor in particular criminal events. (p. 293)

Broadly, what is argued is that different aspects of alcohol constitute the elements of different theories: for example, drunkenness in an event as compared to the contribution of drinking careers to criminal careers. Even from an event-centered perspective, the presence of alcohol can be explained by several theories simultaneously, that is, each one explaining a variable proportion of the alcohol presence and requiring a different alcohol measure.

As an example, assume a population of homicide offenders in which 30% had been drinking. Logically:

1. Twenty-five percent of the cases can be a result of drunkenness in which the offender unintentionally uses excessive violence.

2. Another 25% could be best explained as the result of abusive behavior on the part of a drunken victim: a victim from a subculture in which norms around drinking permit a "letting go" of conventional behavior.
3. Ten percent of the cases may be explained by the fact that unemployed men spend a large part of their day in a drinking setting (e.g., a tavern) in which the norms around social interaction are loosely defined and the level of violence is high. Joblessness explains the presence of these men in a tavern. Tavern norms account for the behavior once there.
4. In 15% of the cases alcohol may be present but play no role.

In all of these cases alcohol is present. In some it directly affects the outcome of the situation (e.g., Number 1), in some it indirectly affects the situation (e.g., Number 3), and in some cases alcohol is present without effect.

From the perspective of trying to develop coherent social policy, the hope is always that single causes of social problems (e.g., a single alcohol theory) can be discovered. Yet it is unlikely that behavior as motivationally and socially complex as criminal behavior has any single underlying cause, or that the cause could be assumed to be a substance as commonly used as alcohol.

The important question, for our purposes, is whether and to what degree alcohol should play a part in complex explanations of criminal behavior. Arthur Stinchcombe, writing on social theories, has argued that the crucial question to ask with respect to alternative strategies in constructing theories is not "whether a theory is true but whether it is sometimes useful" (Stinchcombe, 1968, p. 4). We do not argue here that alcohol is a major "cause" of crime. Rather, we argue that looking at the relationship between drinking and criminal behavior is a sometimes useful strategy for understanding the environment in which criminal behavior takes place. It is unlikely that alcohol will be found to be more important as a determinant of crime than unemployment, failure in school, or family disorganization. However, within a broader environment of poverty and institutionalized racism, crimes take place at specific times and in specific places. This chapter explores the role of drinking in these events in as much detail as the data allow.

Under what circumstances can we say that alcohol-specific theories are "useful"? Historically, it has been more useful to ground the causes of deviant behavior in the individual rather than in the society. In so doing, drink has been one source of moral and psychological failing to which other failings, such as criminal behavior, have been attributed. Much of our thinking about drink still takes the form of temperance thinking, which includes "a specific vision of man's character in which self-mastery, industry and moral consistency are prized virtues. . . . Sobriety is a cornerstone of this ethic because it ensures the cardinal quality of self-command" (Gusfield, 1963, p. 31). Gusfield has cogently argued that temperance activities provided both a pathway of assimilation for lower-class converts and an avenue of social distance from those who had not yet "seen the light." Drink has been one form of social excuse for the deviant behavior of the poor and disreputable. By putting blame "on the bottle," social conditions which otherwise probably would have been held responsible for deviant behavior have been less likely to be examined. If this review is to move beyond engaging in "status" politics by multiple attributions of deviance (e.g., criminal behavior and aberrant drinking) to those of marginal status (Blacks), these social functions of alcohol theories need to be acknowledged.

In this context, Room (1979) has argued recently that "much modern literature on drug policies has emphasized the denial of drugs to subject populations as a means of maintaining moral hegemony over them" (p. 3). He noted that the use of alcohol and tolerance of drunkenness have been "the prerogative of statuses with full citizenship rights in a society—or to put it the other way, alcohol [has been denied] to slaves, women, servants, native populations, prisoners, children and other such subservient estates" (p. 3). In American society, Blacks are a low-status group, maintaining certain status characteristics of "subservient estates." The danger is that drinking (especially heavy or problem drinking)—which is widely tolerated in those of higher status—will be made the scapegoat of other forms of problem behavior in those of lower status.

As a scientific explanation, rather than a social one, the utility of alcohol theories is a function of the extent to which alcohol as an explanatory variable makes comprehensible disparate social facts, that is, the extent to which an alcohol focus brings order into an otherwise disorderly domain. If alcohol theories/explanations of deviant behavior are to be more than societal "excuses," the complexity of these explanations as scientific theories needs to be acknowledged.

With an eye to this problem Pernanen (1976) has argued:

At this state of knowledge . . . the formal methodological designs of empirical studies . . . largely determine the substantive findings. . . . this fact can best be brought forth by this formal approach. . . . an explication of the logic of explanation is needed to fit previous empirical findings into a cumulative body of knowledge and to guide research. . . . If these aspects are not taken into account, we will be deluged with one or two factor theories making exaggerated claims of explanatory power and the research carried out will be limited to bi-variate analyses and "direct cause" thinking. . . . We will then also have to be content with logical non-concepts such as "plays a causal role" or "has explanatory potential." (pp. 382, 387)

Continuing, he argued that in a "study that investigates the situational determinants of violence in connection with alcohol use, the contribution of
predispositional or other long-term variables will be ignored" (p. 382).

Pointing to similar problems in research on crime generally, Gibbons
(1971) noted:

> The lack of progress on etiological questions has been the result of inordinate
> attention to motivational formulations and genetic processes. Although both
> genetic and situational factors are implicated in crime . . . the latter may well
> be more important and more frequently encountered than many criminolo-
> gists have acknowledged. (p. 275)

The case is made for "value-added" theories of crime causation—that
is, staged theories in which each stage is a necessary condition for the occurrences of the next stage. Smelser (1963) has defined this as follows:

> Every stage in the value-added process, therefore, is a necessary condition for
> the appropriate and effective addition of value in the next stage. . . . The suf-
> ficient condition for the final production, moreover, is the combination of
> every necessary condition, according to a definite pattern. (p. 14)

Gibbons (1971) offered the following example:

> A value-added conception of homicide would assert that the experience of
> growing up in a subcultural setting where violence is a common theme is a pre-
> condition for violent acts, but that specific instances of aggression and homi-
> cide do not occur until other events transpire, such as a marital dispute while
> drinking (p. 272)

Shoham, Ben-David, and Rahav (1974) argued in their more general
work on violence that biological, psychological, psychoanalytic, and sociological aspects of violence are less relevant to the explanation of violence
than the actual chain of events leading up to the violent act. A violent act is
the end product of an escalating series of provocative acts, each a response
serving as a stimulus to the adversary. The role of the ambiguity of some
acts in this series, especially the initial ones, is also built into an explanatory scheme.

Alcohol Theories: The Need for Complexity

Value-added theories are necessarily complex, combining, for our purposes, developmental and situational characteristics of criminal and
drinking careers, within a demographically defined population. To illustrate the complexity of (demographically specific) value-added theories
and to create a standard against which to measure the limitations of exist-

ing empirical data, we offer the following outline of two examples of complex alcohol theories. They are distinguished by the different *aspects* of alcohol (e.g., blood alcohol level as compared to drinking norms) and its *effects* (e.g., changes in mood and cognition and disinhibited behavior).

Alcohol and Cognition

Changes in both cognitive and emotional states after drinking have been noted in a number of studies. Recent experimental work suggests that alcohol has an effect on enhancing as well as altering moods after drinking (Marlatt & Rohsenow, 1979). Several studies have demonstrated a diminished capacity for abstract conceptualization (Kastl, 1969; Tarter, Jones, Simpson, & Vega, 1971). Jellinek and McFarland (1940) long ago noted, "after alcohol ingestion, associations are impoverished and follow a path of least resistance" (p. 358). Washburne (1956) is quoted by Pernanen as arguing that "a narrowing of the time dimension is the most important factor associated with role-playing situations involving the use of alcohol" (p. 108). Parker (1977) has argued that cognitive impairment occurs even among social drinkers. All of these alcohol-related effects are mediated by social learning, social learning in turn being subculturally bound. Each suggests a lessening of resources to cope with complex situations.

Recent work by Moskowitz and DePry (1968), from the drinking/driving literature, suggests a strong relationship between drinking and inability to perform complex tasks. This research is especially important in understanding stress situations which have the potential for violence. As social analysts of specific crimes have noted, the probability of violence is bound up with the offender's sense of control over the criminal event. A drinking offender is less likely to interpret external cues in the same way as a nondrinking offender, focusing instead on internal cues in a psychological environment where mood is intensified with drink.

Two examples are illustrative: Einstadter, (1969), in his account of the social organization of robbery, has argued:

> The successful completion of a robbery depends mainly on the coordination of various tasks that must be completed. Through coordination and specialization of roles of participants in the robbery, the robbery group not only assures more protection to itself but adds the measure of efficiency and shock in quickly overtaking the victim by a show of disciplined force. . . . no matter how many robbers participate in a robbery and no matter how functionally differentiated the partnership might be, the element of surprise and momentary domination of the scene must be maximized if the robbery is to be successfully completed. (p. 74)

The likelihood of violence is increased substantially when disorganization and loss of control by the offender(s) occur, and both are more likely if the offenders (or victim) have been drinking. To take another example, the scene of most domestic violence, the home, is typically situationally complex. A domestic argument is likely to occur at a time when the television is on, family and friends are present, and domestic activities are underway. A drinking actor may misread cues and focus on his/her own embarrassment or awkwardness rather than on attempts by a coactor to extract him/herself from the situation. As we have written elsewhere, "situations with the potential for violence are inherently complex—having several actors, disagreement over fact or values, and often several observers. The narrowing of perceptual field that results from drinking . . . the decremental changes in ability to process new information . . . limit the ability to act on several cues at the same time" (J. Roizen & Schneberk, 1977a, p. 423). These limitations on information processing are likely to be strongly mediated by other types of learned behaviors—much of which is determined by the individual's place in the social structure.

Alcohol and Social Expectations

Several experimental studies have shown that the effects of alcohol are strongly mediated by social expectations. These studies have shown that the belief that one is drinking alcohol is as powerful in explaining alcohol-related acts of aggression as is the level of alcohol ingested (Lang, Goeckner, Adesso, & Marlatt, 1976; Marlatt & Rohsenow, 1979). The same level of alcohol has been shown to have differential effects on performance in experimental settings, as a function of cognitive factors, personality factors, and prior drinking experience.

Of all forms of alcohol theories, those based on social expectations may be the ones most easily made demographically specific. Wolfgang (1958) has noted:

The significance of a jostle, a slightly derogatory remark, or the appearance of a weapon in the hands of an adversary are stimuli differentially perceived and interpreted by Negroes and whites, males and females. Social expectations of response in particular types of social interaction result in differential "definitions of the situation.". . . A male is usually expected to defend the name and honor of his mother, the virtue of womanhood . . . and to accept no derogation about his race (even from members of his own race), his age, or his masculinity. . . . Quick resort to physical combat as a measure of daring, courage, or defense of status appears to be a cultural expression, especially for lower socioeconomic class males of both races. (p. 153)

Definitions of situations which are the product of a machismo ethic among lower-class men, in a setting in which the social expectation is that alcohol disinhibits or diminishes responsibility, appear to lead frequently to violent outcomes (Samuels, 1976).

MacAndrew and Edgerton (1969) have effectively argued:

> In the course of socialization persons learn about drunkenness whatever the society presumes to be the case. . . . comporting themselves in consonance with what is thus imparted to them, they become the living confirmation of their societies presumptions. . . . if we are ever to understand drunken comportment, we must focus on the shared understandings of the nature of drunkenness that obtain among men living together in societies. (p. 171)

Unfortunately, social norms around drinking—and their variation across social groups, drinking occasions, and contexts—are relatively unexplored in social research. In our view, however, this is an essential area for understanding the relationship between alcohol and crime in specific populations.

Little research on drinking and criminal behavior is organized around the kinds of theories outlined here. The purpose of this theoretical exercise is to demonstrate the complexity of alcohol theories and to provide a theoretical baseline against which to measure the empirical research. The justification for research on special population depends on the specification of theories such as these for the populations under study. Both cognitive and normative alcohol theories are likely to be especially important in explanations of the relationship between drinking and crime for the population in which we are interested. For example, among Blacks it has been suggested that the norms around drinking in certain settings (e.g., taverns) provide a context which is highly tolerant of abusive and violent behavior (Samuels, 1976; Silberman, 1978). Thus, specification of the "disinhibiting" effects of drinking among Blacks would provide the theoretical focus needed for new research, as well as the better integration of data which now exist.

Without theories of this sort—theories which are carefully specified as to causal locus, and which account for situational predispositional factors—we are left with any number of studies which report alcohol presence and little else.

The Demography of Criminal Behavior: Ethnicity and Class

Looking closely at deviant behavior in any ethnic or class group is likely to invite criticism and accusations of blaming the victim. However, while Blacks make up only about 12% of the population, they are responsible for a dramatically greater proportion of serious crimes. In 1977, 55% of robberies, 46% of rapes, 51% of murders, and 39% of assaults were committed by Blacks. Arrests for serious crimes by ethnicity for those over 18 are reported in detail in Table 6.1. The proportion of Black arrests is even higher in cities than in the country as a whole (see, for comparison, U.S. Department of Justice, 1977).

No other ethnic group shows the same level of serious criminal involvement as Blacks—although other ethnic groups (e.g., Puerto Ricans) are as urban and as poor, and are even less well educated. In an important analysis cited by Silberman (1978):

> According to an analysis of police statistics . . . 63 percent of the people arrested for violent crimes in the period 1970–72 were black—and only 15.3 percent were Hispanic. Relative to population, blacks were arrested for a violent

TABLE 6.1. Total Arrests for Serious Crimes, by Ethnicity, 1977[a, b]

Crime	Percentage		
	White	Black	Others[d]
Total	70.4	26.8	2.8
Criminal homicide			
1. Murder and nonnegligent manslaughter	45.9	51.2	2.9
2. Manslaughter by negligence	77.6	19.9	2.5
Forcible rape	51.5	46.1	2.4
Robbery	43.1	54.8	2.1
Aggravated assault	58.6	39.3	2.1
Burglary	65.9	32.4	1.7
Larceny/theft	63.6	34.1	2.3
Motor vehicle theft	65.3	32.3	2.4
Violent crime[e]	53.2	44.6	2.2
Property crime[f]	64.3	33.5	2.2
Subtotal for above offenses	61.4	36.4	2.2
Other assaults	64.2	33.5	2.3
Arson	71.7	26.4	1.9
Forgery and counterfeiting	65.3	33.6	1.1
Fraud	67.2	31.6	1.2
Embezzlement	75.8	22.9	1.3
Stolen property, buying, receiving, and possessing	62.9	35.8	1.3

[a]From U.S. Department of Justice (1977).
[b]Subjects aged 18 and over.
[c]Because of rounding, the percentages may not add to total.
[d]Less than .1%.
[e]Violent crime: offenses of murder, forcible rape, robbery, and aggravated assault.
[f]Property crime: offenses of burglary, larceny/theft, motor vehicle theft.

crime more than three times as often as were Hispanics, and for robbery, nearly four and one half times as often. Although the disparities vary from crime to crime, they remain consistently large. (p. 120)

Class and Race

The debate on the relationships of class and race to criminal behavior has a long history, one that is not reviewed here. In general, the evidence suggests that police discrimination against minorities notwithstanding, Blacks commit serious crime more frequently and Black youth commit more serious delinquent acts more frequently than whites, independently of social class.

Wolfgang, Figlio, and Sellin (1972), in their study of a full youth cohort, have analyzed these relationships in detail. This is one of the few studies in the literatures reviewed here to analyze both class and race effects. Of the nearly 10,000 cohort subjects, 35% had had one or more contacts with the police. Among whites, 37% of the delinquents were defined as low SES (socioeconomic status), compared to 27% of nondelinquents. Among Blacks, 89% of delinquents were low SES, compared to 79% of nondelinquents. Controlling for both race and class, this study found that 53% of the non-White low-SES subjects were delinquent as compared to 36% of the White low-SES subjects; of the higher-SES non-Whites, 36% were delinquent, compared to 26% of higher-SES Whites. Thus, race was found to be related to delinquency independently of class.

Race differences were found to be greatest for the most serious crimes, both personal and property. Non-Whites in this cohort are "13 times as high in rape, 20 times as high in robbery, over 10 times as high in aggravated assault" (Wolfgang et al., 1972, p. 70). The most important comparisons, however, are between one-time offenders and recidivists. Of White delinquents, 55% were one-time offenders, compared to 35% of Blacks. Non-White repeaters were responsible for most of the serious offenses involving bodily injury, with respect to seriousness of offense (using a weighted rate based on seriousness):

1. There are no significant race differences within each respective SES level for one-time delinquents . . .
2. Significant race differences appear among recidivists . . .
3. The greatest difference is not between the races or between the SES levels, but between nonwhite one-time offensivity and nonwhite recidivism. The weighted rate [weighted by seriousness of offense] differential for nonwhite lower SES boys shows recidivists 22 times as high as one-time offenders and that for nonwhite higher SES boys shows recidivists 26 times as high as one-time offenders. (Wolfgang et al., 1972, pp. 79–80)

These authors further noted:

> Once again our attention is mostly drawn to the delinquency status difference rather than to race or SES differences. The sheer size of offenses of bodily harm committed by nonwhite lower SES boys who are recidivists is alone a measure of the importance of promoting some kind of intervention as a basis for prevention. The 787 offenses of injury committed in this category alone constitute 56 percent of all 1,388 such offenses. (pp. 79–80)

Sex

Men account for between 80 and 90% of all those arrested and convicted of serious crime in the United States (Ward, Jackson, & Ward, 1969). This review focuses predominantly on men. However, the drinking practices literature shows Black women to be especially vulnerable to alcohol problems, and the literature on women's crime shows non-White women to commit crimes significantly more frequently than White women. Thus, where data are available we have noted them.

In the next sections of the chapter, we review, in relation to Blacks, the literature on drinking and criminal behavior, and the literature on drinking practices and problems. The primary issue here is not whether alcohol plays a role in criminal events among Blacks but whether there is evidence to suggest that alcohol plays a different role or roles or is significant in a greater proportion of cases for Black offenders than for Whites. The absence of theory, especially demographically specific theory, leaves a patchwork of evidence rather than a coherent picture of the role of drinking in criminal events or criminal careers.

Blacks: Drinking and Crime—A Review of the Empirical Research

In an often-cited analysis of alcohol and crime among Blacks, an authority on Black drinking problems has argued that "a number of studies support the hypothesis that alcohol plays a crucial role in influencing crime in Black America" (Harper, 1976; p. 129). The argument, not atypical of those found in the literature on alcohol and crime, is constructed as follows (the bracketed numbers refer to points in our critique):

> Shupe (1954) notes that crimes of physical violence are definitely crimes of alcohol influence [1]. For example, a study by Robins et al. (1968) reports that young black men of urban St. Louis tended to get into trouble with the law while drinking and that many of the men had established police records of offenses committed while drinking [2]. In a similar study, King et al. (1969) con-

clude that alcohol abuse among black men is associated with their social problems and problems with the law. Grigsby's (1963) report of black inmates reveals that one-third were under the influence of alcohol at the time they committed their crimes [3]. While Guze and Associates (1969) found 51 percent alcoholics in a followup study of black male felons [4]. In regards to criminal homicide, Wolfgang and Strohm's (1956) study of offenders and victims of homicide indicates that alcohol was present in 70 percent of black men and 67 percent of black women involved as compared to 50 percent of white men and 44 percent of white females. They also note that the greatest number of alcohol-related homicides occurred on Saturday and the fewest number on Tuesday.

The high incidence of alcohol-related homicide and criminal acts in Black America is influenced by a number of socioeconomic and psychological conditions that interact with alcohol abuse. One of the most salient conditions is the phenomenon of stress. . . . Racism, unemployment, anxiety, physical illness, summer heat, loss of loved ones, extreme poverty, and crowded inner cities are some examples of the stress that stimulates heavy drinking which serves as a catalyst in releasing explosive violent behavior [5].

These studies suggest that alcohol abuse among lower social-class blacks accounts for a significant proportion of criminal behavior. . . . The literature of mental health . . . shows that lower social-class blacks are more likely, than middle-class in general, to act out aggressively. Therefore, the catalyst of alcohol along with the predisposition to act out can often lead to argument, assault, and homicide. (Harper, 1976, pp. 129, 133–134)

A closer look at these data shows that:

1. Shupe (1954) has little or no bearing on issues related to Black crime and is, indeed, one of the most methodologically flawed studies in this literature. (For a review of this study, see J. Roizen & Schneberk, 1977a.)
2. Robins's research shows that among both Black and White groups, drinking is associated with a large number of heavy childhood and adult social problems.
3. In Grigsby's study, fewer Black offenders than Whites were drinking at the time of the crime.
4. Guze finds fewer Black alcoholics than Whites in his follow-up.
5. No evidence is presented here that supports these arguments or explains how these situational determinants differ for Blacks as compared to the urban poor generally.

Drinking behavior and drinking problems among Blacks may or may not be associated with serious crime. The responsibility of alcohol-linked behavior for criminal behavior must necessarily be determined by the empirical evidence rigorously reviewed.

We reviewed the available literature with five questions in mind:

1. Do data on incarcerated populations show more or less drinking at the time of or immediately before crimes committed by Blacks when compared to Whites?
2. Are there specific crimes which are more or less likely to be committed by Blacks under the influence of alcohol?
3. Is there evidence that the characteristics of Black criminal offenders or the crimes they commit differ from White offenders or crimes—when alcohol is present?
4. Do Black criminal offenders report having had more or different alcohol problems when compared to White offenders?
5. Where differences between Blacks and Whites exist, are the samples controlled for social class (i.e., net of social class)? Are there differences by ethnicity in the characteristics of offenders or crimes?

As we shall see, the data from arrest records, prison records, and interviews do not generally support the view that Blacks are more likely than Whites to have been involved in a crime with alcohol present. What this suggests is that when Blacks with serious social and personal problems—such as those found among Black prison offenders—are compared to similar Whites, they are less likely to have drinking problems or to be heavy drinkers than Whites. This evidence, then, does not support the view that drinking plays a greater role in the etiology of criminal behavior among Blacks than Whites.

The empirical study of drinking and criminal behavior has a long history. As early as 1845, surveys of American prisons were conducted to explore the relationship between drunkenness and crime. However, as Figure 6.1 shows, these studies present no clear picture of the extent of alcohol's responsibility for crimes—nor, indeed, of its responsibility for any other serious event. For crime, as for other serious events, estimates of alcohol involvement cover a very wide range, when estimates are compared in different studies. As Figure 6.1 shows, estimates of alcohol presence in criminal events range from low estimates of less than 10% to high estimates of 80–100%. This range in estimates does not differ from other serious events such as suicide or accidents. In part, this variation in estimates of alcohol's presence is explained by differences in measures of drinking behavior from study to study, but it is also explained by the fact that few, if any, of these studies are based on theories of deviance and drinking which are specified adequately enough to provide an orientation for measurement. In our earlier work (J. Roizen & Schneberk, 1977a) on this problem we argued:

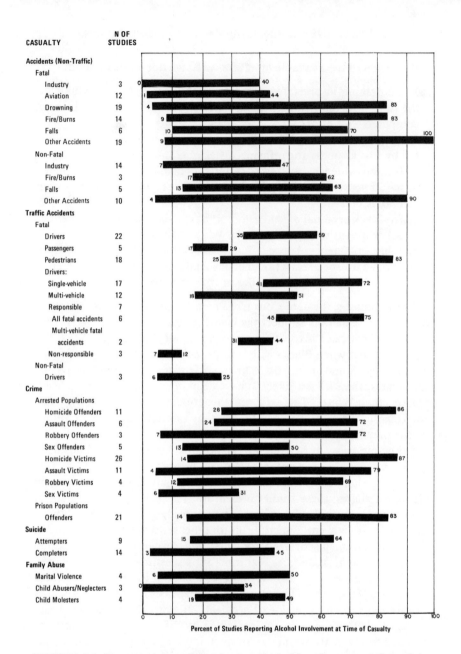

CASUALTY	N OF STUDIES
Accidents (Non-Traffic)	
Fatal	
Industry	3
Aviation	12
Drowning	19
Fire/Burns	14
Falls	6
Other Accidents	19
Non-Fatal	
Industry	14
Fire/Burns	3
Falls	5
Other Accidents	10
Traffic Accidents	
Fatal	
Drivers	22
Passengers	5
Pedestrians	18
Drivers:	
Single-vehicle	17
Multi-vehicle	12
Responsible	7
All fatal accidents	6
Multi-vehicle fatal accidents	2
Non-responsible	3
Non-Fatal	
Drivers	3
Crime	
Arrested Populations	
Homicide Offenders	11
Assault Offenders	6
Robbery Offenders	3
Sex Offenders	5
Homicide Victims	26
Assault Victims	11
Robbery Victims	4
Sex Victims	4
Prison Populations	
Offenders	21
Suicide	
Attempters	9
Completers	14
Family Abuse	
Marital Violence	4
Child Abusers/Neglecters	3
Child Molesters	4

Percent of Studies Reporting Alcohol Involvement at Time of Casualty

FIGURE 6.1. Summary of studies reporting alcohol involvement at time of the casualty (in %). From Aarens *et al.* (1977, p. 23). "Other accidents" include, for example, poisoning, food asphyxiation deaths (choking), frost injuries, and deaths. The studies used measures such as BACs, police reports of drinking, witness reports, and self-reports.

222

The absence of a general theory or theories of alcohol-involved social problems has been a serious constraint on diversity in the collection of data about criminal events. The disease theory of alcoholism, theories of drinking problems, and theories of deviance should bring different organizing frames to research on crime problems. But these controversies in the alcohol literature have been ignored, by and large, in contemporary research on drinking and crime. This is especially true with respect to data on the event . . . itself.

The contemporary empirical research on drinking and crime is associational research. There is active restraint on making causal claims, although causal claims are often implicit in the structure of the research design. With few exceptions, the research is organized around neither an alcohol theory or theories nor a crime theory. (pp. 320–321)

The studies of alcohol and crime reported in this chapter are studies of arrested populations and prison populations. Both types of study have been used frequently for research and administrative purposes. Neither, however, has been used to any degree to study ethnic variation in the relationship between alcohol and crime. Arrest record data provide the most extensive and accurate data about criminal events; these data make it possible to link drinking data, when available, to other characteristics of persons and situations. Studies of prison populations usually gather fewer data, tend to use self-reports, and often reflect some theoretical focus, even if limited. Each type of study limits the kinds of questions that can be asked of the data. Arrest record studies are useful when the focus is on the criminal event and the immediate role of alcohol. Prison-based studies are more likely to be person centered. Typically, little data are gathered about the event, but data may be gathered on multiple social and psychological problems. These studies are particularly useful in exploring the cumulation of social problems in certain individuals. In this section, we look at studies of both types.

Few of the studies of prisons make up the literature on drinking and crime use ethnicity as a stratifying variable. We have included all the major studies that do so in this analysis. Four of the 15 prison studies reviewed reported event-based drinking data by ethnicity. These studies show a smaller proportion of Black male offenders as compared to White offenders to have been drinking at the time of the crime. Grigsby (1963) found that 26% of Black male offenders in Florida were intoxicated at the time of the crime, compared with 32% of Whites. Mayfield (1972) found that 53% of Blacks in North Carolina were intoxicated, compared with 60% of Whites. The 1974 LEAA survey (U.S. Department of Justice, LEAA, 1975) found 37% of Blacks drinking at the time of the crime, compared with 50% of Whites. The single study of women (Cole, Fisher, & Cole, 1968), a study of women homicide offenders only, reports a larger proportion of Black women drinkers (56%) compared to White women

(45%). Four of the studies are of single prisons and one is a national sample of prisoners. While prison studies of this sort are not useful in distinguishing the many roles alcohol can play in criminal events, they do provide an overall measure of the presence of alcohol.

The largest of the prison studies is the 1974 national census of prisoners (U.S. Department of Justice, LEAA, 1975) referred to earlier. Because of the number of crimes covered and the large number of offenders sampled (about 10,000), this survey is especially important.

It shows that Black men were considerably less likely than Whites to have been drinking at the time of the crime. Table 6.2 reports the proportion of Black and White men by the most serious present offense for which they are currently incarcerated. There are some noteworthy differences by ethnicity in these tables. Overall, Whites show a high and fairly stable proportion of drinkers across type of crime, while Blacks show considerable variation by type of crime. Fifty-five percent of the White offenders incarcerated for homicide and 53% of White offenders committing robbery reported drinking at the time of the crime. Comparable proportions for Blacks are 50% and 30%.

TABLE 6.2. Percentage Drinking at Time of Crime, by Most Serious Present Offense[a]

| | Percentage drinking at time | | | |
| | White males | Black males | Total males | |
Worst present offense	(%)	(%)	n	%
Murder	54.8	50.1	10,811	52.8
Attempted murder	61.3	38.9	2,088	48.4
Manslaughter	60.6	51.4	4,260	55.1
Kidnapping	60.6	39.2	1,220	55.2
Sex	62.9	49.3	6,919	57.0
Aggravated assault	71.7	50.6	3,311	62.2
Assault, simple and undetermined	58.5	55.5	1,781	58.8
Robbery with weapon	52.9	30.3	11,113	38.9
Robbery without weapon	55.8	32.0	5,504	40.5
Burglary	51.7	38.0	16,241	46.8
Larceny	40.6	30.9	4,491	37.5
Auto theft	52.6	26.7	1,564	46.0
Forgery	44.2	24.1	2,887	38.0
Arson	70.2	52.9	647	66.7
Other	33.9	22.7	8,254	29.9

[a]From reanalysis of the 1974 national prison survey (U.S. Department of Justice, LEAA, 1975).

Controlling for factors associated with drinking—previous convictions and age—partially explains these differences. Taking robberies as exemplary, 33% of robberies committed by whites were committed by offenders with three or more previous convictions. This compares to 20% of robberies committed by Blacks. Given the greater propensity of men with prior convictions to have been drinking at the time of the crime, we would expect a larger proportion of White than Black robbery offenders to have been drinking. However, even when we control for number of convictions within a single crime category, Blacks are considerably less likely than Whites to have been drinking at the time of the crime.

In Table 6.3, using data from the same survey, property crimes and crimes against persons are reported separately by age and ethnicity. Fewer offenders in each group who have committed property crimes, as compared to those committing crimes against the person, were drinking at the time of their present offense. The differences between Black and White samples in proportions drinking diminish dramatically with age for both broad categories of crime. Black property offenders over 40 are only slightly less likely than Whites to have been drinking. Among those having committed crimes against the person, older Black offenders are about as likely as Whites to have been drinking. However, among young offenders—who are overrepresented in prison populations—Blacks were less likely than Whites to have been drinking at time of the crime. This survey also asked about level of drinking at the time of the crime. Again, Blacks were less likely than Whites to have been drinking heavily.

Black drinking patterns, the smaller proportion of Blacks who drink, and the smaller proportion of Black drinking offenders in the prison population may be in part a function of the relative poverty of Blacks. Black youth, especially, are less likely than whites to be employed. They are, therefore, less likely to have legitimate access to money for alcohol. However, the relationship of income, employment, drinking, and crime is a complicated one. Unemployed men are more likely than those who are employed to need to commit crimes for money (Gibbons, 1971). They are also more likely than employed men to have the time to spend in drinking settings, when they have money to do so. They are, however, less likely than those who are employed to be able to drink frequently, because they lack the money. As we show later in the section on drinking contexts, unemployed men make up a large part of the clientele of the ghetto tavern. The ghetto tavern, we argue, is an important context for the planning and carrying out of criminal activity. However, unemployed men have to find the price of admission to a tavern (i.e., the price of a drink). Among both Black and White groups, unemployed men were less likely to have been drinking at the time of the crime than those who were employed. A larger

TABLE 6.3. Crimes and Percentage of Drinkers by Age and Ethnicity (Men Only)[a]

	Whites		Blacks	
Age	% drinking	n	% drinking	n
Crimes against property				
Under 20	42.8	3369	26.2	1305
21–25	38.1	6257	25.8	2604
26–30	40.8	4098	26.1	1870
31–35	41.1	2454	34.4	1374
36–40	42.3	1475	37.8	851
41–45	44.5	1271	37.0	655
Over 45	44.7	1559	31.5	574
Crimes against persons				
Under 20	55.5	1955	29.8	2025
21–25	55.4	5588	34.6	6744
26–30	58.5	5619	39.7	4662
31–35	57.2	3662	49.1	3179
36–40	57.2	2672	49.0	1683
41–45	63.5	1978	50.1	1172
Over 45	62.8	2965	57.0	2523

[a]From reanalysis of the 1974 national prison survey (U.S. Department of Justice, LEAA, 1975).

proportion of Black than White inmates were unemployed prior to incarceration. However, independent of labor force status, Blacks were less likely than White offenders to have been drinking (see Table 6.4).

Another measure of the relationship of drinking and crime is the prevalence of reported drinking problems in prison populations. Unfortunately, there has been little analysis of the relationship between "chronic" and "acute" drinking problems. The studies which have compared the two types of measures show a correlation between the two—problem drinkers are more likely than other offenders to have been drinking at the time of the crime (California Department of Public Health, 1960; Mayfield, 1972). When roughly comparable measures of drinking problems in a prison population are compared to those in the general population, the incidence of drinking problems is considerably higher in the prison population. Table 6.5 compares drinking problems in general and drinking problems in prison populations. If we compare Black drinking practices and problems with those of Whites within prison populations, however, we find, again, that Blacks are less likely to be drinkers and to report drinking problems.

Four studies, all of males only, report drinking measures. Grigsby (1963) found in Florida that 43% of White offenders were "regular drinkers," compared with 30% of non-Whites; Globetti et al. (1974) found in Mississippi that 56% of Whites compared with 34% of Blacks were "regular drinkers." Guze et al. (1962) found that 47% of White offenders in Missouri were labeled alcoholics, compared with 27% of Blacks.

The 1960 State of California survey of drinking problems of newly committed offenders, the largest of these studies, reports twice as many White as Black offenders with drinking problems. In an extensive analysis of problem drinkers and those without drinking problems, these investigators found substantial differences in the two groups. Comparing White with Black offenders, however, yielded few differences on social or criminological characteristics. In a noteworthy analysis, it is shown that the distributions of crimes in both the problem- and non-problem-drinking group are similar for both Black and White groups. For example, 12% of the Whites in the problem-drinking group were imprisoned for robbery, compared with 32% of the Blacks, while the proportions of robbers among the nonproblem groups were much the same. Only 5% of the Black drinkers' offenses were for "forgery and checks," compared with six or seven times that number for Whites; again the proportions were much the same for the nondrinkers of both races. This suggests that no type of offense was particularly likely to be committed by problem drinkers—White or Black. The non-drinking-problem group included a larger proportion of drug offenders, more of whom were Black. Removing these offenders

TABLE 6.4. Percentage of Drinkers by Employment Status and Ethnicity[a]

Employment status	Whites		Blacks	
	% drinking	n	% drinking	n
Employed full time	51.8	31,353	39.1	21,172
Employed part time	51.8	2,810	38.5	3,087
Unemployed, looking for work	41.6	5,176	31.7	3,192
Unemployed, not looking for work	40.9	8,354	27.1	3,909

[a]From reanalysis of the 1974 national prison survey (U.S. Department of Justice, LEAA, 1975).

TABLE 6.5. Comparison of Drinking Problems in Two Prison Samples with Drinking Problems in a National Sample of Men[a]

Prison samples	General-population samples of men
North Carolina Prison (Mayfield, 1972)	
37% of the sample had one or more indications of problem drinking	2.5% labeled self alcoholic or problem drinker[b]
13% labeled self excessive drinker, problem drinker, or alcoholic	2.5% labeled self as ex-alcoholic or problem drinker[b]
5% received treatment for alcoholism	4% yes to "Have you ever been tested or had counseling for any drinking problem?"[c]
25% had been convicted of drunkenness or DWIL	28% yes to "Were you ever arrested for drunk driving?" or "Have you ever gotten into any other kind of trouble with the law because of anything connected with drinking or with alcohol (aside from drunk driving arrests)?"[d]
	14% yes to "Did drinking ever cause you to have an accident or injury of some kind—either at work, at home, on the street, or someplace else?"[d]
Mississippi Prison (Globetti, 1974)	
40% had three or more personal and social complications as a result of drinking	29% had high current or high past problems (respondent reported relatively severe problems in at least two of a dozen problem areas, or in seven or more mild problems associated with drinking on the Cahalan–Room "Overall Problem Score" (see Cahalan & Room, 1974, p. 27)[b]

[a]From J. Roizen and Schneberk (1977a, p. 382).
[b]R. Roizen (1974).
[c]Cahalan and Treiman (1976, Table 20).
[d]Reanalysis of the 1967 San Francisco sample: men only, aged 21–59; described in Cahalan and Room (1974).

from the base of the calculations for the nonproblem group makes the distribution of crimes in the two groups (problem vs. nonproblem drinkers) even more similar.

Jail-based studies present a somewhat different picture of drinking patterns, ethnicity, and criminal behavior when compared to prison studies. The arrest data show a strong relationship between seriousness of the crime and alcohol involvement, a relationship not found in prison studies. Studies based on arrest record data show 7% of robberies (Normandeau, 1968), 24% of rapes (Amir, 1971), 24% of assaults (Pittman & Handy, 1964), and 55% of homicides (Wolfgang & Strohm, 1956) to be alcohol involved. Comparable proportions based on prison data (U.S. Department of Justice, LEAA, 1975) are 39%, 57%, 60%, and 53%, respectively. The prison data also reveal that a large proportion of burglaries (47%) and car thefts (46%) are alcohol involved.

Differences in the patterns of relationships found in arrest records as compared to self-reports (prison studies) may be due to unreliability in the alcohol measure, differences in the sample of offenders, or both factors. Given the substantial delay in clearance for most crimes, reconstructing the role of alcohol in the event from arrest records may involve considerable ambiguity and error. Additionally, recent analysis of the national data on prison offenders suggests that processes of selection in the prison population toward offenders with longer criminal records, more serious offenses, and longer sentences are in the direction that would show a greater proportion of offenders who are drinkers.

Several jail studies have analyzed the ethnicity of victims; and several, both victims and offenders. Homicide studies are the most numerous of these. While Blacks commit homicides at a rate greatly in excess of that expected by their proportion in the population, these homicides are not necessarily more likely to be alcohol involved. Table 6.6 presents the data from several studies on alcohol involvement by ethnicity and sex of victim. Looking first at male victims and at those studies which report alcohol in the victim only (i.e., Baltimore, Atlanta, and Cleveland), only small differences are found in the level of alcohol involvement in the two ethnic groups. About half of the White male victims in the three studies had been drinking, as compared to about 60% of non-White male victims. Female victims, generally, were less likely to have been drinking; however, a larger proportion of non-White female victims than White had been drinking.

The two other studies shown in Table 6.6 (Philadelphia and Chicago) report alcohol involvement in the event (victim, offender, or both). Logically, this should increase the amount of alcohol involvement. However, when compared to victim-only studies, the differences found in the two types of data are not dramatic. When the two event-based studies are compared to each other, they each tell slightly different stories. Comparing the Philadelphia data to those from Chicago shows significantly higher levels of alcohol involvement in events involving Black men but less in events involving Black women.

The most comprehensive data on homicide events were reported by Wolfgang (1958). Summarizing the presence of alcohol in victim and offender, he reported several significant race-related associations:

1. *Alcohol in the homicide situation and race of the offender:*
Alcohol was present in the situation in 67% of cases which involved a black offender, 58% of cases involving a white offender.
2. *Alcohol in the homicide situation and race of the male victim:*
70% of cases when a black man was killed.
50% of cases when a white man was killed.

TABLE 6.6. Alcohol Presence by Race and Sex of Victim

	Alcohol present (% of subjects)[a]				
	Philadelphia, 1956[b]	Chicago, 1968[c]	Baltimore, 1967[d]	Atlanta, 1974[a]	Cleveland, 1974[f]
Non-White males	62 (331)	54 (223)	54 (333)	65 (167)	58 (220)
Non-White females	47 (96)	61 (84)	30 (103)	48 (47)	38 (52)
White males	43 (118)	46 (67)	44 (102)	58 (62)	54 (69)
White females	32 (43)	47 (20)	32 (38)	3 (19)	27 (21)

[a]The number of subjects in each group is given in parentheses.
[b]From Wolfgang (1958).
[c]From Voss and Hepburn (1968).
[d]From Criminal Justice Commission, Baltimore (1967).
[e]From Chief Medical Examiner, Atlanta (1976).
[f]From Gerber (1974).

3. *Alcohol in the homicide situation and race of the female victim:*
67% of cases when a black woman was killed.
44% of cases when a white woman was killed.
4. *Alcohol in the offender (offender only or both victim and offender) and race of the offender:*
58% of black offenders.
72% of white offenders.
5. *Alcohol in the victim (whether victim only or both victim and offender) and race of the victim:*
58% of black victims.
40% of white victims. (p. 138)

Alcohol was also more likely to be present in victim-precipitated homicides, which, in turn, were more likely than others to have involved a Black man or woman. Additionally, a significant relationship was found between day of week, presence of alcohol, and homicide.

Turning to another event-based study, Amir (1971) in his comprehensive study of rape found no difference in the presence of alcohol in the situation during intraracial rapes (the greatest numbers of all rapes). Thirty-four percent of Black/Black (race of male/race of female) and 32% of White/White rapes showed alcohol to be present. A very large proportion of White/Black rapes showed the presence of alcohol, but the number of these was small (n = 17). Alcohol was present in 42% of the cases involving a White offender and 24% of the cases involving a Black offender. Blacks were no more likely than Whites to have met their victims in a bar or in front of a bar. As with homicide, rape was more likely to be committed on Friday and Saturday than on weekdays; again, times when drinking is greater.

These event-based studies yield a great deal of information on characteristics of crimes; unfortunately, they tell us little about alcohol involvement. We do not know how much the alleged offenders and victims had been drinking or in what circumstances. Because there is no standard reporting of drinking behavior, we do not know if differences found in alcohol involvement from study to study are because of poor measurement, regional variation in drinking behavior, or some other factor. For crimes which have delayed clearance, the quality of the alcohol depends particularly heavily on the jurisdiction's interest in collecting them. While there are some apparent ethnic differences in reported alcohol involvement in these data, the only consistent difference is found among women homicide offenders.

On balance, then, the prison data show less alcohol involvement among Blacks when compared to Whites for almost all crime categories. The data on arrested populations (predominantly studies of homicide) show alcohol involvement to be comparable for Black and White groups.

One explanation of these differences by type of study is that stratifying offenders by type of crime and most recent offense may fail to distinguish offenders on salient grounds. All of the studies reviewed here have characterized men and women by a single offense. The argument has been cogently made that studies which fail to characterize criminal actors by their criminal histories combine into analytic categories men and women who may have little in common except their most recent offense (Irwin, 1970; Roebuck & Johnson, 1962). Roebuck and Johnson noted that "offenders, utterly unconcerned with criminological research, show some variability in their offense . . . calling a man an 'armed robber' on the basis of his most recent crime, even though he has a long previous history as a con man is unlikely to lead to . . . useful knowledge" (p. 29). In a study of 400 black offenders from a Virginia prison, these authors developed a typology of criminal offenders based on criminal histories. A comprehensive comparative analysis of one criminal type—drinking assaulters—shows this group to be significantly different from other Black offenders on a large number of characteristics. Unfortunately for our purposes, no Whites were included; thus, whether these differences are ethnic, class, or criminological is undetermined. Comparing this group with others in their sample, the authors reported that the drinking assaulters were less likely to have been reared in a slum environment, more recently arrived from other parts of the South, and more often from rigid patriarchial homes in which the supervision was harsh or erratic. As a group, they were better adjusted as adults than were other offenders. The exception to this is that they were more frequently gamblers and problem drinkers, although their parental homes had "frowned on gambling, drinking, card playing and dancing." Roebuck and Johnson (1962) argued:

> They evinced a preoccupation with physical courage; and they mentioned again and again the necessity for fighting and violence as a method of self-preservation. Readiness to fight was a masculine proclivity, a necessary element in the temperament of every "real man." The possession of a knife at all times was a must. In a sense, they may be viewed as juveniles, as street and playground "warriors." The necessity of defending themselves, as well-dressed, "good" boys, from their more delinquent peers at school provided a socially useful, rewarding outlet for aggressive impulses that could not be vented in the home. . . .
>
> Most of their fighting which led to assault charges took place in bars, with male drinking acquaintances, and in gambling games with their peers. . . . they all carried knives, which were the weapons of their choice. They displayed little respect for the policeman, who to them was "the man" who snooped into their private lives—a "kill-joy."
>
> The arrest records of this group were comparatively long (mean average ar-

rests per man, 15), but few property charges were evident. Rather, intoxication and assault charges appeared with regularity and often concurrently. There was no evidence of criminal progression. (pp. 32–33)

For our purposes, this study is of particular interest: (1) it shows drinking and criminal behavior in a richer social context; (2) it suggests the wide variety of criminal and drinking histories found in an incarcerated population; and (3) it breaks some of the stereotypes which accompany explanations of deviance among Blacks (e.g., these offenders were more likely than others to come from stable, intact families). A wide range of variables are employed to explain the relationship between drinking and crime, and an attempt is made to link situational and predispositional factors.

Black Drinking Patterns: A Review of the Empirical Research

Given the limited drinking data in these studies of offenders, we turn to the drinking practices literature to explore in more detail the social correlates and consequences of drinking. As noted, what is essential to understanding the relationship between drinking and criminal behavior is some knowledge of "the relative amounts of time drinking, where, when, with whom and under what circumstances." Trying to infer the relationships between drinking and criminal behavior by the conjunction of studies of offenders with clinical and general population data has its own limitations. The risk is especially great of making the kind of ecological mistakes that are commonly made in these literatures, for example, the assumption that relationships found in the aggregate explain individual behavior. In the absence of more comprehensive drinking data on offenders, however, we turn to clinical samples, general population studies, and ethnographics for the insights they offer on drinking patterns among those most "at risk" of criminal activity: young, lower-class, Black men.

Sterne and Pittman (1972) noted in their review of the research on American drinking behavior: "In the course of reviewing existing research on American Negro drinking behavior at the start of this study, we were struck by the paucity of systematic inquiries into what constitutes normal drinking behavior for this ethnic minority, and by the relative abundance of studies concerned with alcoholism or alcohol-related problem behaviors among Negroes" (p. 2). On the basis of these studies of the "pathology-oriented" literature, they concluded that "Negroes are a high risk group for the development of problems associated with drinking" (p. 2). This conclusion is based on several factors: (1) the overrepresentation of Blacks in the "pathology-oriented" studies; (2) the belief that the sociocultural milieu in which Blacks, especially lower-class Blacks, live is conducive to the development of alcohol pathologies; and (3) the putative, social, and personal functions which alcohol is perceived to serve for Blacks. These authors noted several themes in their review of the literature:

1. A pattern of weekend drinking—partly linked to pay day but also linked to the fact that Saturday, historically, has been a day for relaxation, visiting, and drinking.
2. The importance of the tavern in the Black community. Taverns are especially numerous in lower-class neighborhoods and serve as social centers and social clubs.
3. The utilitarian and escape functions of drinking among Blacks.

The relationship between ethnicity and social class has received some attention in the drinking practices literature, but with inconsistent results. Survey studies, especially, have failed to show significant differences between Black and White drinking practices, and the net of differences explained by social class; while ethnographic studies and studies of small samples (e.g., L. N. Robins, Murphy, & Breckenridge, 1968) have shown marked differences. Several studies from the drinking/driving literature show the complexity of analysis of this kind. They are cited here because they measure both drinking behavior and drinking consequences; they are commonly cited to demonstrate Blacks' greater risk of negative consequences of drinking. M. M. Hyman (1968), in a study of nearly 20,000 drivers, found a clear negative relationship between social status and "accident vulnerability." Blacks, however, were more "vulnerable" than Whites at every status level and were more likely than Whites to have been drinking heavily. Black males were found with blood alcohol concentrations (BACs) above .10 almost five times as frequently as White males. Cosper and Mozersky's (1968) study of drivers found no class difference in the proportion of drinkers, in levels of BAC, or drinking problems. However, this study found a larger proportion of heavy drinkers among non-Whites than Whites, at the same time finding that non-Whites were, on average, less likely to be drinkers. A large survey of DWI offenders reported by Fine, Scoles, and Mulligan (1974) reported that Blacks have more serious drinking problems than Whites.

Zylman (1972), in an analysis of collisions and a control sample of drivers, concluded:

1. Nonwhites were involved in collisions about one-third more often than would be expected from their representation in the control group.
2. When unskilled whites of a given age class were compared with unskilled nonwhites in the same age class, the collision experience was similar; therefore,

the significance attributed to excess of nonwhite collision involvement should be attributed to socio-economic class instead.

3. Nonwhites comprised about 14% of the low social class but provided 45% of the BACs of 0.11% and higher for that class.

4. Low status nonwhites represented just 4.6% of the total population-at-risk but provided 21% of all BACs of 0.11% and higher.

5. Driving after heavy drinking is primarily a characteristic of the lower status drivers, but

6. among those drivers it is more likely to be the nonwhite than the whites who engage in that activity. (p. 81)

These studies tend to show that fewer Blacks than Whites drink; that when Blacks drink, they drink more heavily and have greater negative consequences; and that net of social class effects, ethnic effects remain. Taken together, studies of this type suggest that social status and race are equally important variables in explaining drinking behavior and negative consequences. Unfortunately, there are no comparable studies of other serious events, such as criminal behavior, which match the driving studies in analytic complexity.

Clinical populations offer another "window" on ethnic differences in drinking rates and problems, and they, too, give some support to the position that Blacks are more likely to have drinking-related problems. A number of studies of treatment and hospital populations show a significantly larger than expected proportion of Blacks among alcoholics. Malzberg (1947), Locke, Kramer, and Pasamanick (1960), and Locke and Duvall (1974) showed higher rates of alcoholic psychosis, while Bahn and Chandler (1961) showed more alcohol-related disorders. Barchka, Stewart, and Guze (1968) reported that Black males showed symptoms of alcoholism significantly more frequently than Whites. A Maryland survey (Gorwitz, Bahn, Warthern, & Cooper 1970) of admissions to psychiatric facilities showed Black men to have considerably higher per capita rates of alcoholism than White men.

The skid-row research, however, does not necessarily support the evidence from clinical populations. Levinson (1970) has argued that while the number of skid-row Blacks has increased in the past decades, the vast majority are not alcoholics. Rather, they are homeless, out of work, and often migrants. They are, on average, younger and in better health than White skid-row men.

Research on street-corner life, such as Liebow's *Tally's Corner* (1967), further supports a view of street drinking that makes it an artifact of problems in work and home life rather than personal pathology.

Looking further, we find that a number of studies show that Blacks either begin drinking earlier or become heavier drinkers at an earlier age than Whites. Among these are Robins *et al.* (1968) and Viamontes and

Powell (1974), and Vitols (1968). Several studies also show that Blacks end up in alcoholism treatment at a younger age than Whites (Nathan, Lipson, Vettraino, & Solomon, 1968; Vitols, 1968).

However, in counterpoint, a number of studies of youth drinking show that Black youth drink less than White youth. This research shows both higher levels of abstention and less heavy drinking (see especially Rachal, Williams, Brehm, Cavanaugh, Moore, & Eckerman, 1975).

As this overview shows, the data on Black drinking practices and problems present contradictory findings. The findings from clinical studies are particularly difficult to interpret. In part, this is because of the many possible explanations for finding disproportionate numbers of Blacks in treatment populations. Young Black men are especially likely to end up in treatment populations for reasons that have more to do with their relationship to the larger society than with their personal pathology. In the absence of a supportive welfare or incomes policy, alcoholism treatment is an "acceptable" form of social deviance and dependence. Further, given the many social problems of lower-class Blacks, "the bottle" may provide a comfortable form of explanation for what is perceived by many Blacks as personal failure. Only in the past two decades has any serious research attention been given to ethnic, class, and sex variation in drinking patterns. Assessing ethnic and class differences is still difficult because general population surveys include relatively few members of each ethnic group.

In the following section we review several studies of drinking practices and problems in more detail and then turn to several ethnographic studies.

Drinking Practices

Surprisingly, given the evidence of many of the clinically based studies, most general studies show only small differences between Black and White men in rate of drinking. Looking first at the study by Cahalan, Cisin, and Crossley (1969), a national sample of both men and women, we find no substantial differences among men in drinking rates: 29% of all White drinkers are "heavy" drinkers and 24% of Black drinkers. Among women, however, the differences are dramatic. A larger proportion of Black women are both abstainers and heavy drinkers. Looking only at the proportion of men and women who are heavy drinkers (as a percentage of all drinkers), Black women outnumber White women three to one (a finding corroborated by Sterne & Pittman, 1972).

The Cahalan *et al.* (1969) study also compared Blacks to all low-SES men (most of whom are White in the national sample). Again it shows little difference between Blacks and Whites (Table 6.7). In fact, we find that

TABLE 6.7. Drinking Rates of Black Men Compared to Men of Low Socioeconomic Status [a]

Group	Drinking rates				Percentage heavy drinkers of all drinkers
	Abstain	Infrequent	Light to moderate	Heavy [b]	
Men					
Black (full sample)	21	13	47	19	24
Age 21–39					
All races (lowest SES) [c]	25	6	44	25	33
Age 40–59					
All races (lowest SES)	27	12	38	23	31

[a]Adapted from Cahalan *et al.* (1969, Tables 3 and 20).
[b]"Heavy drinkers": defined in this survey as those who drink nearly every day, have five or more drinks per occasion once in a while, or have five drinks per occasion at least once a week.
[c]SES is a varient of the Hollingshead Index of Social Position; see Cahalan *et al.* (1969, pp. 23–24).

slightly more men from the lowest socioeconomic group are heavy drinkers, compared to Black men generally.

The Robins *et al.* (1968) study of young Black men in St. Louis makes the strongest case for ethnic differences in drinking rates. Drinking behavior was studied is 223 Black men, aged 30–36, who were raised in St. Louis and sampled from school records. Interviews and official records were located for 95% of the sample. All respondents were in their early 30s at the time of interview. Thirty percent of the Black men, compared to 18% of Whites, reported heavy drinking (seven or more drinks per week and seven or more per occasion or four daily). Sixty-one percent of the Blacks were heavy drinkers at some time. This study also shows substantial drinking problems in this population (see later discussion). The sample for this study, however, is not a random sample of school attenders but includes a disproportionate number of men who, as children, had school and/or family problems.

Sterne and Pittman (1972), in a reanalysis of data from Knupfer's California study, (Knupfer & Room, 1970), reported no "significant differences between San Francisco Negroes and Whites in either abstaining or amount of drinking when the comparisons are limited to persons of the same social status level" (p. 423).

Several studies show drinking patterns among lower-class Blacks, and lower-class men and women generally, which are at variance with practices in the general population. Binge drinking and weekend drinking are the more frequent styles of drinking among lower-class drinkers, generally, and especially among Blacks (Cahalan & Room, 1974; Lewis, 1955; Sterne & Pittman, 1972; Strayer, 1961). Insofar as negative consequences of drinking are likely to occur at relatively high BACs, periodic heavy drinking is likely to be an implicative style of drinking.

Drinking Problems

Turning to problems associated with drinking, we find a higher level of reported problems among Black and Whites. Given the association between heavy drinking and drinking problems, this is not easily explained. The level of drinking problems suggests a much higher rate of heavy drinking than is found in these samples. Cahalan and Room (1974) observed. "Many studies of drinking problems . . . have found that problems are more prevalent among the poor than among the remainder of the population, even though drinking at all (and in some contexts drinking fairly regularly and heavily) is more prevalent among persons of higher social status" (p. 89). There are several possible explanations for this discrepancy between rates and problems. One is that Blacks, and lower-class respondents generally, may be more likely than Whites to attribute problems to drinking. Further, Blacks may drink less, on average, but drink heavily when they do drink, making the usual measures of quantity/frequency less sensitive for this population. Additionally, quantity/frequency questions may be harder for Blacks and low-status respondents to answer, both because they are particularly demanding of respondents' ability to average their drinking and because they are most easily answered by drinkers who consume regular amounts of alcohol every day.

As Table 6.8 shows, young men and men with the lowest social status (those men most likely to commit crimes) report the highest consequences of drinking. Moreover, as shown in Table 6.9, low-SES men, generally, have higher levels of specific problems, and twice as many score high on overall problems independent of age. Cahalan (1970), in his analysis of problem drinkers reported: "The highest rate of having both interpersonal problems and implicative drinking behavior was in the group of young men of lower social status in the largest cities, and the lowest rate was in the group of older men of higher status in the small and medium-size towns" (p. 57). This early national survey shows that Blacks, compared to all other "ethnoreligious" groups, experience the highest rates of social consequences from drinking (i.e., problems with family, neighbors, friends, job, police).

Cahalan and Room (1974) have shown the same general relationship between drinking problems (high consequences) and ethnicity. Among Black men in this sample, 31% showed "high consequences" (a high score on "tangible consequences"—the same measures indicated in the previous paragraph, with health and finances added). This was higher than any other ethnoreligious group except Latin Americans, was several times the proportion found in most groups, and was more than twice the proportion in the sample as a whole (14%).

In both surveys, drinking problems were associated with a number of important social psychological variables. "Tangible consequences" was correlated with "psychiatric symptoms" (.27), "intrapunitiveness" ("does things he regrets," "did not give up hope of amounting to something") (.36), "alienation" (.30), and "impulsivity" (.28) (Cahalan & Room, 1974). Cahalan and Room also reported that "problematic intake" was associated with "impulsivity" and "tolerance of deviance." They noted: "The strongest predictions of tangible consequences of drinking, then, are made by variables indicating a disadvantaged status: under and unemployment, low status, and disadvantaged ethnic groups. In spite of their relatively high intercorrelations, each contributes separately to the prediction of tangible consequences" (p. 124).

TABLE 6.8. Drinking Problems of Young Men by Ethnicity and Socioeconomic Status (%)

	Robins et al.[a]		Cahalan[b]		Cahalan[b]	
	Blacks	Whites		Low SES	High SES
Heavy drinker[c]	30	18	Frequent intoxication[d]	17	25
One or more medical problems[e]	23	NA	Health (doctor said to cut down)	8	4
Social problems					
Arrests	15	NA	Problems with police, accidents	3	2
Job difficulties	4	NA	Job problems[f]	6	2
Violence	6	NA	Belligerence[g]	18	5
Complaints by family	35	5	Problems with spouse, relatives[h]	22	11
One or more social problems	42	14	Current overall problems	32	13
			High consequences[i]	33	13

[a]Robins et al. (1968, Table 3, p. 666).

[b]Cahalan (1970, Table 5, p. 46).

[c]Seven or more drinks per week; either seven or more drinks per occasion or at least four drinks daily.

[d]Minimum of 5 or more drinks at least once a week; or 8 or more drinks on one of the most recent two drinking occasions and twice in the last 2 months; or 12 or more drinks on one of the last two occasions and twice in last year; or currently by getting high or tight at least once a week. [e]Includes tremulousness, psychoses, hospitalization, liver disease, fits, gastritis, injury while drinking, suicide attempts, neuropathy, poor nutrition/anemia, and ulcer.

[f]Lost or nearly lost job because of drinking, people at work suggested he cut down, or self-report of drinking interfering with job or employment opportunities.

[g]Respondent felt aggressive or cross after drinking, or got into fight or heated argument.

[h]Spouse getting angry or threatening to leave over drinking, or any two of the following: spouse concerned over drinking, spouse or relative said cut down, or self-report of harmful effect of drinking on marriage or home life.

[i]All above measures, plus problems with friends and financial problems (taken from Cahalan & Room, 1974, p. 91, for men aged 21–29).

TABLE 6.9. Selected Drinking Problems by Socioeconomic Status and Age[a, b]

Prevalence of drinking-related problems	Percentage with specific problems	
	Age 21–29	Age 30–39
Frequent intoxication		
High SES	17	13
Low SES	25	20
Binge drinking		
High SES	2	1
Low SES	9	6
Symptomatic drinking		
High SES	21	6
Low SES	18	11
Psychological dependency		
High SES	11	5
Low SES	19	4
Problems with spouse, relatives		
High SES	11	5
Low SES	22	9
Problems with friends, neighbors		
High SES	—	1
Low SES	4	4
Job problems		
High SES	2	3
Low SES	6	4
Problems with police, incidents		
High SES	2	—
Low SES	3	—
Health		
High SES	4	3
Low SES	8	7
Financial		
High SES	—	3
Low SES	7	8
Belligerence		
High SES	5	8
Low SES	18	5
High current overall problems		
High SES	18	13
Low SES	32	20

[a]Adapted from Cahalan and Room (1974).
[b]Men under age 40 only.

Although the Cahalan and Room studies show Blacks as having high levels of drinking problems, Robins *et al.* (1968) have reported drinking problems and negative consequences of drinking among Black men which are far greater than those reported in other studies. This study of urban men reports both the highest level of drinking-related problems in a Black population and the highest rate of drinking. A summary of the results of this study is given in Table 6.8. This study shows dramatic differences between Black and White respondents. However, when these data are compared to roughly comparable data controlled for class (Table 6.8), the differences are much less dramatic. As Table 6.8 shows, urban Blacks still report higher levels of drinking problems of most types than low-status men do generally.

For our purposes, the relationships between negative consequences and level of drinking are especially important to determine. It is noteworthy that the relationship between quantity/frequency and drinking problems, especially social consequences, is stronger for lower-status men than for men generally. In an early work Knupfer and Room (1970) noted the greater likelihood of low-status respondents to incur public consequences (e.g., social and medical consequences) from drinking when compared to higher-status respondents. Higher-status respondents were not without negative consequences but were both better able to manage them and were more likely to convert them to private "intrapsychic" problems. Consistent with this are the data from the national surveys on consequences and social status. While health problems were twice as common among lower-status respondents as compared to upper-status respondents, problems with police, job, friends, and neighbors were three to four times as common (Table 6.9). This suggests that there are more viable mechanisms to diffuse drinking problems among the middle class as compared to the lower or working class. That is, drinking problems are less visible to the public eye.

There are several possible arguments that help bring sense to this rather disordered array of data—especially the contradictory data on drinking rates and drinking problems:

1. It can be argued that special-purpose samples (clinical populations, DWI offenders, hospital samples) are likely to include disproportionate numbers of Blacks and Blacks with serious social and medical problems, because Blacks are highly visible and are more likely to be on the street and live in areas where police work is concentrated. Blacks, as already noted, may "cooperate" in finding their way into treatment populations because they have no alternative strategies for financial and social support. On this view, although Blacks may be no more likely to be arrested for serious criminal behavior (the debate on this topic is en-

lightened by two articles: Black, 1970, and Green, 1970), they may be more likely to be found in other clinical samples. This might explain why Blacks are disproportionately represented in some treatment populations and why Blacks in these samples appear to have more serious drinking problems than either comparably placed Whites or Black criminal offenders. Sterne and Pittman (1972) offer some support for this argument in their analysis of the very high rates of arrest of Blacks for vagrancy and disorderly conduct.

2. It can be argued that general-population samples do not have enough Blacks to be truly representative of the Black population—especially that part of the population which is socially deviant. Offenders, both Black and White, have higher rates of drinking and higher levels of drinking problems than those found among samples matched for sex and class in the general population. Cahalan and Room (1974) have argued that "a distinguishing feature of the institutionalized is the very multiplicity of their problems, so that the proportion of the uninstitutionalized population who can be matched with them in the overall breadth and depth of their drinking may be smaller than is commonly thought" (p. 44). It still must be noted, however, that Blacks in the general population and in the offender populations appear to drink less and to have no greater drinking problems than Whites, when class is accounted for.

3. The style of Black drinking data of the sort which are more subculturally specific may not be captured by either general-population or special-purpose (e.g., clinical) samples. Blacks may, in fact, drink less but have more negative consequences when they do drink.

We turn again to the argument that the data that are needed are data which are subculturally specific; data that test the more complex theories of drinking and behavioral consequences; and data that are measured with considerable attention to situational variation in drinking patterns and drinking norms.

Attitudes, Reasons, and Perceived Effects

Motivations for drinking, like drinking patterns, vary in the general population. While most people give positive (e.g., sociable) reasons for drinking, nearly a third of the men and a quarter of the women in the early national survey gave "escape reasons" for drinking (Cahalan et al., 1969). Heavy drinking is strongly related to escape reasons for drinking among both men and women, but this was especially the case for lower-status young men. Among men under 45, 47% of the escape drinkers were also heavy drinkers, compared to 21% of the nonescape drinkers. Heavy escape drinkers, compared to other heavy drinking men, were also considerably more likely to score higher on scales of neurotic tendencies, alienation, and impulsivity.

Unfortunately, there is little survey analysis of Blacks as a separate population in each of these areas of attitudes, reasons, and effects. In an interesting paper on "effects" of drinking, Buckley and Milkes (1978) showed heavy drinkers to perceive more effects of alcohol—positive and negative. In this study, however, Blacks were no more or less likely to perceive specific effects than other ethnic groups, when level of drinking was controlled. The paucity of data on effects, motives, and attitudes is unfortunate. As we argue in the next section, there is important evidence in the ethnographic literature that the "alcohol" effect in ghetto subcultures is very much a function of the social construction of drinking situations and that this is as important in explaining drinking behavior as the pharmacological effects on the individual.

Drinking Contexts

There are few systematic data on normative expectations around drinking occasions. As Room (1975) has noted:

> There are essentially two dimensions of risk involved in a given drinking-related behavior or demeanor: one is the exposure to risk offered by the behavior or demeanor itself, the other is the vulnerability to tangible consequences which the situation and the individual's social position impose on a given behavior or demeanor. The second dimension is obviously not solely a property of the individual involved. (p. 22)

And as Mäkelä (1976) has observed:

> A further difficulty in making a careful study of the interaction between the social control environment and individual drinking behaviors proper is the fact that changes in behavior depend not only on the alcohol concentration in the blood of the drinker, but also on his experience, tolerance and personality as well as on cultural expectations surrounding him. (p. 12)

The national surveys show an important and strong relationship between drinking context and problem drinking. Cahalan and Room (1974) showed "heavy drinking context" ("a score combining frequency of visiting bars, proportion of friends who drink 'quite a bit' and proportion of occasions in which alcohol is served") to be an important predictor of both "tangible consequences" and "problematic intake."

Survey data, however, give a sketchy and rather inconsistent picture of the role of alcohol problems in the lives of Blacks. In part, the thinness of survey data stems from failure to focus on specific drinking occasions, contexts, and environments. A study of the Pruitt–Igoe housing project in St. Louis shows the greater richness of a survey when confined to a single social and geographical context (Sterne & Pittman, 1972). In this study, youth drinking and adult drinking are compared. Women's drinking is compared to men's. Public and private drinking contexts are described. While the objective measures of drinking behavior are consistent with the data from the national surveys, the anecdotal material and a lengthy description of tavern life show the pervasiveness of drinking problems among project residents and indicate something of its style. Women, especially, are vulnerable to drinking problems. Although a greater proportion of these women than comparably placed White women were abstainers, the drinkers were especially likely to be heavy drinkers.

Drinking begins in the project at an early age and is a common and frequent activity even among adolescents—one that often "disturbs the peace." "Noise, cursing, arguing, usurping of youngsters' play areas, banging on apartment doors, and littering with alcoholic beverage containers" (p. 122) accompany drinking. This behavior is either passively accepted or openly tolerated by parents, project staff, and often the police passing through (Sterne & Pittman, 1972). The object of drinking is to get "high." The style of drinking suggests that there is little else to do.

Public drinking among adults is frequent, although a quarter of the adult respondents reported that they were most likely to drink when alone. While street drinking and "fooling around" are common, taverns are popular places to drink among both women and men drinkers. The tavern is a prominent feature of project life, serving as social club, community center, and drinking locale. The tavern in Black slums plays an especially important part in the everyday life of those most marginal, degenerate, and down on their luck. It is a place to go. For the "regulars," tavern life provides a place and time away from the perceived and actual failures of marital and family life.

The tavern seems no less important in more rural settings. Unlike the urban ghetto, where taverns are densely concentrated, there are fewer of them in small towns. Therefore, in small towns they function even more prominently as black community centers. In his study of life in a South Carolina mill town, Lewis (1955) noted of both the tavern and the church: "Each provides a ready-made pattern of relief from care and relatively unrestricted behavior, each has its regular clientele, and each is run by and for Negroes" (p. 64). Although these taverns are (or were when the study was done) frequently checked by police, "all groups—those who frequent and those who do not—concede the taverns to be 'dangerous' places where the risk of getting hurt or in trouble is high" (p. 64). Said one informant, "I never goes over to [a particular tavern] because I'm going to have to carry me a pistol and as sure as I get my pistol in my pocket, I'm going to have to take it out and shoot some drunken fool" (p. 64).

In spite of this potential for violence in taverns, they are much-frequented places, especially on weekends. On a fairly regular basis men get drunk, get arrested, and get fined. The tolerance for deviance, whether in drinking or in other behavior, is high. Of men who admitted to serious violence, even those who boasted of having killed someone, Lewis reported, "the community shows a certain tolerance for them, they do not lack for association or access to their chosen groups" (p. 252).

Two interesting and underreported ethnographic studies of drinking contexts (Samuels, 1976; Sterne & Pittman, 1972) make the case that lower-class Black taverns provide a social environment markedly different from drinking environments accessible to other parts of the population. While both of these studies make many common observations and come to much the same conclusions, the Samuels study is the longer and more detailed; therefore, we have drawn from it extensively. Several characteristics of the lower-class tavern are especially important for our analysis: the high level of violent and abusive language and behavior, the competition of various activities for the same space, the heavy drinking style; the absence of clear normative expectations around drinking, and the marginal social status of the clientele. These characteristics suggest that while taverns provide a place to go, a place to find people who might know of jobs, and a place to meet friends, they also provide a place for the organization of criminal activity. Much of this activity is petty crime but the suggestion is made that much is not. Thus, the tavern is not only a site where interpersonal violent crime spontaneously takes place but also the site of the organization of other types of crime.

Samuels's study of Milwaukee tavern life provides an excellent detailed description of setting, clientele, and social organization of two taverns. This work is quoted here at some length because of its rich description. The area of the central city, in which 95% of Milwaukee's Black population is resident, has 2 movie theaters, 5 billiard parlors, 12 bowling alleys, 3 club bars, and 354 taverns. "Joy's Inn" is a lower-class tavern and is contrasted to "Brown's," a working-class tavern. The following excerpt (Samuels, 1976) describes Joy's Inn:

The Setting
Joy's Inn was the largest of the three taverns which share the block along with a grocery store, a shoe shine parlor and a carry out. . . .

The outside appearance of Joy's was not markedly distinct from the other taverns or buildings in that vicinity. Externally, they were in an advanced state of disrepair. A bright coat of green paint on Joy's Inn failed to hide the evidence of advancing rot and gave it a garish appearance in an otherwise blighted setting. During summer and winter and at all times of the day and night there was always someone standing or sitting at the entrance of the tavern. Somewhat like a changing of the guard, the tavern stoop was never deserted. . . .

There was a huge heater by the door, which served as a sanctuary where some persons drank surreptitiously from hidden bottles. . . . The television set played continuously even when the juke box was operating. . . . Although a sign over the juke box indicated that dancing is proscribed, single individuals in various states of intoxication were always dancing in the passage between the loungers and drinkers.

The Clientele

Joy's Inn boasted the largest trade in the area. . . . Joy's also functioned as a retail liquor establishment. Consequently, unlike the other taverns in the area, the shelves were always well stacked. At Joy's on any given day, there was a constant flow of activity as patrons came and went. The crowd was rarely smaller than twenty persons. On weekdays between 1:00 p.m. and 3:00 p.m. and on Friday and Saturday nights, the crowd was at its largest.

The clientele consisted primarily of the irregular and hard core unemployed and those on welfare assistance, including a large number of A.D.C. mothers from a nearby housing project. The majority of the patrons were from the rural south, with the exception of the younger adults who were born in Milwaukee. Negro migrants to the city usually gravitated to the St. Francis area where they found their way to the few churches with migrant programs or to taverns such as Joy's. Here information could be obtained concerning housing, day's work, and a variety of other facts about the city. Taverns in this respect served as assimilating institutions by providing migrants with the company of others who were already conversant with the ways of the urban ghetto. . . .

Tavern Interaction: Drinking Rituals

The drinking style at Joy's was generally known as hard drinking. Whiskey was the preferred beverage choice. Some chased their whiskey with beer, others drank it straight. Drinks were not usually mixed and sipped as in other working-class taverns. The shot glass was consumed in one swallow with the wash applied afterwards. This drinking practice was followed equally both by men and women. Drinking at Joy's was on an individual rather than on a communal basis as it was at Brown's. When a patron ordered a half-pint of liquor at Brown's (the working-class tavern), it was understood that the liquor would be shared with a number of friends. At Joy's when an individual ordered a half-pint, the liquor was poured into four shot glasses (double shots) and lined up in front of the person. The wash was placed to the right of this line. The person then methodically drank each of these in turn. . . .

At Joy's, the mutual exchange of drinks between men and women was customary, and on "mother's day," when A.D.C. mothers received their welfare allotment, they did the bulk of the purchasing. In the lower-class tavern, the drinking relationship between men and women in terms of volume, drinking style and rights of purchase, signified the status parity of men and women patrons. . . .

The relationship between the men and women at Joy's was complicated by the presence of prostitutes, who used Joy's as their base of operations, and also, female alcoholics. The availability of cheap sex and the continuous view of women in various stages of debasement, considerably reduced the attractiveness of marriage for the men who attended Joy's on a regular basis. . . .

In the working-class tavern, money could be left on the bar or a coat flung carelessly over a stool to indicate that the place was taken. At Joy's, change or personal possessions left unattended were not viewed as markers, but as free goods to be appropriated by anyone coming upon them. In recognition of this fact, at dances, restaurants, or shoeshine parlors frequented by a similar clientele, hats and coats were not removed from the person.

At Brown's, drunkenness was not sought. Drinks served to facilitate ongoing interactions and the easy flow of conversation. At Joy's it appeared that individuals drink in order to get drunk. In Brown's tavern, public inebriation was rare; at Joy's it was commonplace.

In the lower classes, because everyone was viewed as occupying the same level of desperation, the drinker was freed from expectations of deference and also from expectations of demeanor. Although the norms against public drunkenness were waived in the lower-class tavern, the inebriated person was still regarded as functional and immediately accountable for his actions. The person could indulge himself in all sorts of self-abasements as long as he did not interfere with the other patrons. . . .

It was well known in the tavern that Bill had forced his wife and girlfriend into prostitution, and that Mary had spent time at Wales for attempting to poison her father, and that George had shot his brother over the ownership of a pack of cigarettes, and that Cynthia, after brawling with her drunken boyfriend in the tavern, had dragged him into the streets where he was run over and killed by a car. At Joy's, affective relationships were tenuous at best and even "close" relatives and friends were beyond the pale of easy trust. . . .

Status Arrangements within the Tavern

The Slinger

Different argot titles indicated the various roles individuals played within the ghetto community. In addition to those who used the tavern as a place to get drunk there was a small minority for whom the tavern served as a base for illegitimate operations. In St. Francis such a person was called a "slinger." . . .

Within the ghetto, the slinger was a culture hero. He personified important values in the lower-class subculture, wit, guile, verbal felicity and violence. The slinger was not only "heavy" in St. Francis, he is also a "heavy" in the "man's" world, in terms of the visible attributes of success; an expensive car, expensive clothes and abundant leisure time. He presented a successful career model, that the youths (hoods) who hung around the tavern were already emulating in their adoption of his walk and cheaper versions of his style.

The Scuffler

The scuffler, like the slinger, was also engaged in criminal routines, and used Joy's as a base for his operations. The scuffler was engaged in a series of menial hustles (selling rags and collecting bottles for a deposit). He also functioned as a pimp for the prostitutes using the tavern. There was a close business relationship between the bartender, scuffler and prostitute in the lower-class tavern. Solicitation privileges were allowed on the assumption that the rooms upstairs from the tavern, which were provided for short term sexual liaisons, would be utilized by the prostitutes. Very few lower-class taverns are without this amenity.

The scuffler's career was often short-lived because he had a tendency to become directly involved in petty crimes. Slingers tended to look down on such criminality, believing that they were engaged in by "street niggers," those who had no style (aren't ready). Whereas the slinger had more lucrative hustles and whose daily round involved a number of other commercial outlets, the scuffler's activities were confined primarily to the tavern. Most of his meagre earnings were diverted to drink, which involved the curtailment of the other necessities. This was apparent in the decrepit appearance of the scuffler. . . .

The Hoods

In addition to the slingers and scufflers, the tavern also represented the focus of activities for a number of male juveniles. These individuals were referred to by tavern habitues as "hoods." Drinking among the juveniles occurred in groups. Usually the oldest in the group will go to the tavern and make the purchase, which was usually wine. The drinking was done outside the tavern in a doorway or alleyway. However, even when the group assembled in the tavern and made a collection for a purchase, the order would not be refused. Although tavern keepers knew that their license might be suspended, they would still sell the juvenile liquor. This flowed from the fear that in the event of a refusal, his tavern might be vandalized. . . .

The hoods also worked as part-time pimps for prostitutes and also as homosexual pimps. The more violent among them beat and robbed the drunks as they left the numerous taverns in the area. The hoods also used the tavern to pick up drunken women who were often used to socialize the younger boys into the sexual mores of the group. The hoods were utilized by tavern members themselves as "lookouts" for their dice games which were played in an alley and empty lot adjoining the tavern. The widespread use of the tavern by lower-class Negro youths may be attributed to the fact that the large number of taverns in St. Francis provided them with a wide range of role models for alcohol consumption. (pp. 83–94)

Joy's had the highest level of violence in the area. "A pattern of querulousness pervaded the tavern and the possibility of getting cut or physically assaulted was an ever-present danger at Joy's, even when the patron himself was not directly involved in the altercation" (p. 92). This high level of personal risk, however, made the tavern at one with much of the rest of the ghetto life. Samuels wrote:

One of the most impressive features of the clientele at Joy's was the widespread scarification of both male and female patrons, especially in the face. The multiple wounds on some of the men suggested several battles, and violence as a way of life. Some patrons were known as "bad niggers" because of their propensity for violence. Such a propensity, however, was in terms of degree, because almost everyone in the tavern was armed. To be without a weapon was to be without an essential item of one's attire. In the event where an argument threatened to spill over into violence, invariably the unarmed adversary would hurry home to retrieve his weapon. . . . If during an argument a person exposed a weapon, he invited swift preemptive action. The norm appeared to be "do not expose a weapon if you do not intend to use it." . . . (p. 93)

Samuels noted: "discussions (i.e., toasts and the 'dozens') were also character tests. The focus was on the ability of an individual to sustain verbal attack, make an acerbic response to his adversary, while at the same time maintaining his cool under the stressful condition" (p. 64).

Toasts (long recitations, stories which exhibit struggles for power and show contempt for authority) are an important form of entertainment in bars and on street corners. They extol "badness," violence, sexual prowess, and often cleverness. While extreme in the level of violence exhibited, the Stackolee toast evokes the atmosphere of a lower-class tavern, the trivial nature of conflicts, and glorification of violence. Silberman (1978) wrote, "But manliness and virility are defined as random violence and joyless, indeed affectless sexuality" (p. 146). Stackolee is a "mean man, a purveyor of violence" who "does not hesitate to hurt, taunt, kill if someone offers him the slightest hint of challenge." His violence seems to be an end in itself, for it solves nothing and is aimed at nothing; the bad man is all style—more precisely, perhaps, "all pose and bluster" (pp. 146–147). The setting is a tavern:

And I asked the bartender for something to eat,
he give me a dirty glass of water and a tough-assed piece of meat.
I said, "Bartender, bartender, don't you know who I am?"
He said, "Frankly, my man, I don't give a goddam."
I said, "My name is Stackolee." He said, "Oh, yes, I heard about you up this way.
but I feed you hungry motherfuckers each and every day."
Bout this time the poor bartender had gone to rest—
I pumped six a my rockets [bullets] in his motherfucken chest. . . . (p. 147)

The toast continues through several murders. The story told in this toast can be compared to a murder described by Lewis (1955) in a Kent tavern. A trivial argument develops between two young men who know each other. One man leaves to get a gun. The other stays and waits. He argues that "everyone has to die sometime." The other man returns and kills him.

The ethnographic description of these taverns suggests that among lower-class Blacks, taverns are both the legitimate settings for interpersonal confrontation and violence, and also places which offer freedom from the norms of everyday life. Moreover, they are peopled by men and women with a propensity to violence, who in many cases have little to lose from its occurrence.

Banfield (1968) has argued: "Crime, like poverty, depends primarily upon two sets of variables. One set relates mainly to class culture and personality (but also to sex and age) and determines an individual's *propensity* to crime. The other relates to situational factors (such as the number of policemen on the scene and the size of the payroll) and determines his *incentive*" (p. 159). The probability that a crime will be committed depends on both. The potential of a lower-class tavern for criminal behavior would appear to be great. Of cities, Banfield (1968) wrote: "A city's *potential* for crime may be thought of as the average proneness of persons in various 'sex–age–culture–personality' groups times their number" (p. 159). As a context for criminal behavior associated with drinking, the lower-class tavern should hardly be equaled.

Summary

While it is useful in exploring the relationship of drinking and crime to review the drinking practices of Blacks and lower-class men and women generally, this does not tell much of the story. Drinking, even heavy and problem drinking, is relatively common. Crime is not. Men and women committing serious crimes are a relatively small, statistically and socially deviant population. They are also among those people most likely to elude the survey net. There is little in this research that directly links drinking behavior to criminal behavior. As we have seen, survey data by and large do not show dramatic differences between Black and White drinking patterns, problems, and consequences when social class is accounted for. In general, these data do show that young, lower-class men are greatly at risk of visible negative consequences of drinking and that black women who drink show very high drinking rates. Studies of drinking contexts, such as ghetto taverns, suggest that drinking is relatively common among a significant proportion of lower-class Blacks, and that much of it takes place in an environmental setting in which normative constraints are loosened. As we have seen, however, empirical research on drinking practices has focused less on the environmental determinants of the drinking–crime relationship and more on the characteristics of individual drinkers (e.g., level of drinking and drinking problems).

The evidence, then, is mixed on the relationship between drinking and crime. The empirical data show clearly that criminal offenders drink more and have more drinking problems than those of relatively comparable status in the general population. There is little support, however, from empirical data for the proposition that a disproportionate amount of Black crime is a consequence of drinking. The exceptions to this are the observations gained from tavern studies. Studies of taverns and of the microorganization of drinking behavior are especially important for future research. Ethnic differences in drinking norms are another area in which work is needed. The evidence as it stands does not demonstrate a clear and consistent picture of Black drinking and criminal behavior. Nor do we find support for demographically specific theories of the relationship between alcohol and crime—except, possibly, class-based theories.

It is important in carrying out future research to remember that problem drinking and criminal behavior are both responses to failed lives and a society that has failed to be responsive to them. It is no accident that poor Blacks commit disproportionate numbers of robberies, are disproportionately unemployed, drink heavily when they are able to, or that housing project women become heavy drinkers. The strongest case for the association of drinking and crime, in the absence of better data, is that both are responses to other factors in individual and social life: poverty, family disorganization, and school failure. The utility of an alcohol strategy for explaining social problems must compete with others which make strong prima facie cases.

Acknowledgments

This paper was prepared with considerable research assistance from Candia Smith, Esther Shoenberger, and the library staff of the Social Research Group, University of California, Berkeley. Thanks to Ron Roizen for his contribution to the work on theories of serious events, and to Fred Harper for critical comments on an early draft.

7 The Role of Alcohol in Wife Beating and Child Abuse: A Review of the Literature

CLAIRE JO HAMILTON AND JAMES J. COLLINS, JR.

Introduction

Previous Work

Most researchers and professionals who deal with violence in the family would agree that the consumption of alcohol plays a role, although there would be considerable disagreement among the experts about how frequently alcohol is a factor in the occurrence of such violence. Also, there would be a variety of opinion about how alcohol exerts its influence. This chapter reviews available empirical evidence about the relationship between alcohol use and two specific types of family violence, namely wife beating and child abuse. This chapter also examines proposed explanations for this observed empirical relationship between drinking or problem drinking and the occurrence of violence between family members.

Fundamental methodological problems characterize the family violence literature. Most research is the result of evidence from relatively small samples of "treatment" populations. Typically, families in the process of divorce or treatment make up the study populations. If comparison groups are used, they also tend to be small and often come from populations of unknown representativeness. The major exception to the dual problems of sample size and representativeness in family violence research is a national survey conducted in 1976 by Murray Straus, Richard Gelles, and Suzanne Steinmetz (reported in Gelles & Straus, 1979a, 1979b).

CLAIRE JO HAMILTON AND JAMES J. COLLINS, JR. Research Triangle Institute, Research Triangle Park, North Carolina.

Much family violence research is also characterized by the use of poorly defined and operationalized variables. Even major variables such as "alcoholism" and "spouse abuse" may not be defined. Alcohol use or problem drinking is rarely measured in any but the most general way. The elements of aggressive behavior are often unspecified. In Chapter 2 of this volume, Greenberg discusses in detail methodological problems of the literature on the alcohol–crime relationship, so the same issues are not dealt with at length here. It is sufficient to point out that the methodological shortcomings of the family violence literature are of such a magnitude that it is very difficult to locate findings that can be viewed with confidence.

In addition to methodologically based problems with data on family violence, the interpretation of these data has generally been superficial and unsystematic. The role of alcohol in the occurrence of family violence has not been made explicit. It is typical to find the observation that a given percentage of violent offenders have an alcohol problem or that a given percentage of violent events involve the presence of alcohol, without any discussion of how the drinking problem or presence of alcohol may have been relevant. Alcohol has multiple effects, among them physiological and psychological. Alcohol also alters the rules that govern social interaction, and it shapes the interpretations of social interaction and of individual behavior. In most of the literature, it is difficult to ascertain which of these effect categories or combinations of effects are deemed to be relevant. In a later section of this chapter, a number of different explanations for the role of alcohol are discussed. As we point out there, it is common to find in the literature an attitude toward alcohol that we have called the "malevolence assumption." That is, there is a tendency to see alcohol as blameworthy whenever it accompanies problematic behavior.

In sum, methodological and interpretive problems have clouded the scientific issue of interest here—that is, how often and in what way alcohol consumption directly, indirectly, or in conjunction with other factors "causes" family violence.

Two Distinctions

In thinking about the relationship of alcohol consumption to family violence, it is helpful to distinguish the effects of alcohol as they influence individuals and thereby shape behavior from alcohol effects as they influence events. The person–event dichotomy will not tolerate close scrutiny because the effects of alcohol cannot be isolated as uniquely person or event phenomena. In any given case, alcohol likely exerts an influence on persons and on events in a way that is not compatible with the characterization of alcohol's effects in isolation. However, a conceptual distinction of this order is useful, and most past work can be described as conceiving the effects of alcohol to be either person-based or event-based. The conceptual distinction has methodological and interpretive implications. Emphasis on the person focuses attention on individual characteristics and suggests that individual-level variables will explain the role of alcohol in family violence. Emphasis on the event suggests that characteristics and context of interactions between people are most relevant for understanding the role of alcohol in family violence.

A second conceptual distinction for different kinds of alcohol effects is also useful. Alcohol has both short- and long-term effects. Alcohol has the potential to affect behavior or to shape personal interactions through its immediate and proximate influences. Thus, the distortion in cognitive process that accompanies alcohol consumption or the redefinition of situational norms that may accompany drinking can each shape the outcome of interactions between people and elevate the likelihood of violence. The consumption of alcohol over a long period also has the potential to change the consumer. Most long-term behavioral effects are not well understood, but there has been a tendency in past family violence research to ascribe relevance to the alcoholism or problem drinking of offenders. The literature has not been clear about what changes in the chronic drinker may be related to violent behavior, but it is commonly assumed that if an alcoholic assaults his/her spouse or children, alcoholism must have been a factor.

Apparently the relationship between alcohol consumption and family violence is a complex one that involves multiple factors. Distinctions like those already made may be heuristically appropriate, but real understanding of the alcohol–family violence connection will depend on being able to specify the relations and interactions between multiple variables. Situational details, the psychological characteristics of participants, and the effects of social norms and roles are examples of factors that may have some influence on alcohol consumption and family violence. However, given the rudimentary state of current knowledge, near-term goals need to be modest. Our attempt here is to review existing research so that future study of the alcohol consumption–family violence relationship can proceed from a summary of what is known.

In the next section of this chapter, working definitions of spouse abuse and child abuse are presented. Some general theories of family violence are then discussed, and following that, explanatory attempts that include alcohol are discussed. The discussion then proceeds with sections on the relevant empirical findings that concern the relationship between alcohol use and wife beating and child abuse. Finally, the findings and suggested future research needs are summarized.

Definition of Family Violence and Foci of the Chapter

The definition of family violence must be dealt with at the outset. A precise definition is necessary because it will ultimately determine the topical focus of this chapter. For our purposes, "family violence" refers to overt, intentional (nonaccidental) physical aggression between family members. This definition focuses attention on physical violence within the family, which includes such acts as killing, assaulting, beating, hitting, slapping, pushing, shoving, and throwing objects at one's spouse or children. It is recognized that some of these acts, such as physical punishment to discipline children and slapping one's spouse on occasion, may stretch the meaning of "violence" for some. Nevertheless, the broad definition of violence is retained here, while acknowledging some ambiguity.

Although we have chosen to define family violence in terms of physical violence, we recognize that other types of abuse take place within the family setting. Psychological abuse, verbal abuse, child neglect, and incest are examples of family abuse that occur in significant proportions. However, because we agree with Gelles (1972) and Steinmetz and Straus (1974) that these types of abuse are conceptually distinct from physical violence in the family, we have excluded them from consideration.

The foci of this chapter are marital violence and violence toward children by their caretakers. Marital violence or violence between husbands and wives involves a variety of acts, such as wife beating, husband beating, and marital rape. Because of the paucity of research on husband beating and marital rape, the review in this area centers around the literature on wife beating. The discussion of abuse of children focuses on violence toward children perpetrated by their parents or caretakers. Due to the lack of data on other forms of family violence, such as violence between siblings and parricide, they have been excluded from this analysis.

Explanations of Family Violence

Factors Implicated in Spouse and Child Abuse

Explanations of spouse abuse have traditionally focused on the individual level of analysis, and specifically on psychological characteristics of the spouses. Wife beaters have been characterized as sadistic, mentally ill, alcoholic, and unable to tolerate intimacy (Rounsaville, 1978), as well as suffering from various psychological problems such as morbid jealousy (Hilberman & Munson, 1977–1978) and compulsive masculinity. Some investigators have focused on the victim and have blamed the occurrence and perpetuation of wife beating on masochistic tendencies of wives. Furthermore, wives who are beaten have been described as low in self-esteem, exhibiting intimacy–dependency conflicts, and being in a state of "learned helplessness" (Rounsaville, 1978).

The same emphasis on psychological explanations can be found in investigations of child abuse. Battering parents have been described as suffering from such psychological and personality problems as immaturity, self-centeredness, impulsivity, and depression. They have been described as emotionally crippled, demanding that their children fill their own emotional needs, and expecting behavior from their children that is beyond their capabilities (Fontana, 1971; Spinetta & Rigler, 1972; Steele & Pollock, 1974). Low frustration levels, lack of affect (Fontana, 1971), unmet dependency needs, lack of identity, and rigid and inadequate defenses (Flynn, 1970; Maden & Wrench, 1977) are some of the more specific problems that have been ascribed to these parents. Other child abusers have been found to exhibit psychoses, alcoholism, and drug addiction (Fontana, 1971). Some of these psychological problems are viewed as resulting from early childhood experiences of the parents such as a lack of basic mothering; violent behavior directed against them by their own parents; intensive, pervasive, continuous demands from their parents; and parental criticisms of their inadequate performances (Steele & Pollock, 1974).

Recently, with the work of Straus and his associates, social-structural and cultural factors have been seen as causes of both spouse and child abuse. M. A. Straus (1977–1978) has delineated certain sociocultural factors that contribute to spouse abuse and child abuse: (1) the cultural acceptance of violence in American society and the resultant high level of violence, (2) the cultural norms that legitimate certain levels and types of violence within the family unit, (3) sexual inequality and male domination in American society, (4) the socialization of children in violence, and (5) the high level of conflict that is inherent in the family structure.

Dobash and Dobash (1979) have argued that the explanation of wife beating lies in the domination of wives by their husbands. They discuss the legal, political, economic, and ideological supports for patriarchal domination throughout the history of Western culture and argue that remnants of these supports facilitate the continuation of abuse of wives.

Also hypothesized to contribute to spouse and child abuse have been such social factors as poverty and unemployment (Gil, 1970), status inconsistency (O'Brien, 1971), size of family, and role reversals. These conditions can create stress, tension, and frustration within the family which may erupt into episodes of spouse or child abuse. In addition, factors such as isolation from social support systems (Garbarino, 1977) and a series of life changes for which one is unprepared (Justice & Justice, 1976) may contribute to abuse within the family context.

Theories of Family Violence

Relatively little systematic theory development has been undertaken in the area of family violence. Most investigations have focused on either spouse or child abuse, but few have attempted to offer explanations of both on a family level of analysis (Gelles, 1979a). Some of those who have attempted to delineate a theory of family violence are Goode (1971), Gelles (1972, 1979a), Straus and associates (Gelles & Straus, 1979a; Steinmetz & Straus, 1974; Straus, 1973), and very recently, Mawson (1980) and Burgess (1979). Because the primary purpose of this section is to orient the reader toward explanatory attempts for family violence, our discussion of these theories is not detailed.

Goode's (1971) theory of family violence is called resource theory, but it also contains elements of exchange theory. Resource theory views violence as a resource that may be called upon when other resources are deficient; exchange theory views violence as a result of a breakdown in the reciprocal exchange process involved in social interaction. Goode posits that force or its threat is a fundamental part of all social systems (including the family) because it is one way of obtaining compliance from others. He argues that force is a resource that may be called upon by a family member when other resources for obtaining compliance—such as money, prestige, respect, or love—are lacking or insufficient. Furthermore, when one family member perceives costs to be outweighing rewards in the social exchange process, and when exiting or submission are undesirable alternatives, he/she may resort to violence if these other resources are unavailable.

Gelles's (1972) early work draws attention to social-structural and situational factors that may be implicated in family violence. According to Gelles, such structural and situational factors as the lack of resources for certain people in certain social positions, unemployment, and unwanted pregnancies are at the root of violent behavior between family members. The stress produced by these factors and the ability to cope with stress are differentially distributed throughout the social structure. In addition to these problems, exposure to and experience with violence as a child, which is also differentially distributed in the social structure, constitute training in violence as an appropriate response to stressful stimuli in some situations. Thus, "individuals will use violence towards family members differently as a result of learning experience and structural causal factors that lead to violence" (Gelles, 1972, p. 189).

Straus and associates (Steinmetz & Straus, 1974; Straus, 1973) recognized the need to take into account systemic and cybernetic effects in a theory of family violence. In 1973 Straus presented a "general systems" or cybernetic model of family violence. This model is an attempt to take into account the positive and negative feedback processes involved in escalating or stabilizing the level of family violence and also the processes "which control the operation of the system in relation to its goals" (Straus, 1973, p. 113). Gelles and Straus (1979a) elaborated: "thus a cybernetic feedback process includes gathering and interpreting information about the state of the system, comparing this information with criterion goals or states, and then taking corrective action (in this case violence) to maintain the state or goal" (p. 567).

Steinmetz and Straus (1974) proposed a multivariate system model of family violence. This model includes familial variables such as family organization, family position in the social structure, and values, beliefs, and personality of the family unit. Individual characteristics of family members such as personality traits, psychopathological traits, and occupational roles are also included in the model as well as societal variables such as opportunity structure, societal violence, and harshness/deprivations in the social setting. The model also allows for the relevance of precipitating factors such as perceived unsolvable problems and stressful/frustrating situations. The diagram of this model reflects Steinmetz and Straus's intention to demonstrate that, in the area of family violence, "we are dealing not with one-directional influences but with a whole *system* of mutually influencing and interacting forces, with each part of the system providing feedback to the others" (Steinmetz & Straus, 1974, p. 17).

Recently, Gelles and Straus (1979a) highlighted 15 theories and conceptual frameworks which have been invoked to explain interpersonal violence in general, and which may have some relevance to understanding violence between family members. Gelles and Straus have classified these theories or conceptual frameworks under three levels of analysis: intraindividual, social psychological, and sociocultural explanations. They have attempted to integrate these various theories and different levels of analysis into a theory of family violence. Gelles (1979a) has explained:

> We had hoped that the task of integrating the 15 theories would produce a simplified model from which testable propositions could be drawn. Unfortunately, simplicity was not possible, and we produced a model of key elements of the theory which is long on heuristic value and equally long and complex as a model.

Rather than trying to further simplify the grand integrated model, we chose, instead, to pursue a limited number of theoretical frameworks and use the data from our national survey of family violence to test the adequacy of each explanation. . . . In addition to testing propositions from existing models, we have chosen to try to develop the propositions of a single model we felt was most amenable to providing new insight into explaining the causes of family violence. We have selected exchange theory. (p. 10)

Thus, in an attempt to fully develop one theory of family violence, Gelles (1979a) has demonstrated how exchange theory can be applied to the understanding of family violence. He argued that if reciprocity in rewards during social interaction is not achieved, and interaction cannot be easily terminated, violence may be a consequence. For example, parents of handicapped, ugly, or irritable children may become abusive because they perceive the costs of caring for these children as outweighing the rewards, and they have few alternatives for terminating the relationship. Gelles added: "We see exchange theory as a promising direction because it captures many of the elements of the social psychological theories of violence and because it is well suited to explaining and understanding family relations" (1979a, p. 17).

Two recent theoretical interpretations in the area of family violence are the unusual explanations offered by Burgess (1979) and Mawson (1980). Burgess has applied modern evolutionary theory to the study of child abuse and neglect. He argues that evolutionary theory can help us "understand the long history of child abuse and its generality across species as well as cultures" (p. 12). He presents evidence to demonstrate that the principle of inclusive fitness, or the probability that one's genes will be transmitted to future generations, can be used to help explain child abuse and neglect. That is, the probability of child abuse and neglect is increased as the probability that one's genes will be transmitted is reduced. To support this conception, Burgess points to the higher likelihood that stepchildren and children with disabilities will be abused. Further, because parental investment increased the reproductive potential of their children, Burgess also argues that parents with scarce resources to expend or parents that must incur unusually high costs for parental effort may be more likely to be abusive or neglectful of their children. This is because, in the case of limited resources or high parental costs, inclusive fitness is reduced.

Mawson (1980) believes that interpersonal violent acts can be reinterpreted as expressions of attachment behavior, or contact-seeking behavior, rather than aggression. That is, such acts as wife beating and child abuse can be viewed as the result of the offender seeking intense physical contact with the victim under conditions of stress in conjunction with the offender's predisposition for attachment behavior.

The Role of Alcohol

The focus of this chapter is alcohol involvement in family violence. The discussion of the theories of family violence has so far not dealt with the alcohol factor. This is because the conceptions already cited have not integrated alcohol use into an explanation of family violence. Goode (1971) makes no mention of the alcohol involvement in violence, and Gelles and Straus (1979a) (as well as many others) do not consider alcohol use an important causal factor in family violence. However, Steinmetz and Straus (1974) consider alcoholism as a psychopathological trait, and they included this factor in their system model of family violence. In later works, Straus apparently revises his position to argue that alcohol use does not have explanatory significance for family violence, but that the association observed between alcohol use and family violence may be a function of the "deviance disavowal" or "time-out" properties of alcohol. That is, "some men get drunk to give them an excuse to hit their spouses and children" (Gelles & Straus, 1979a, p. 561).

On the other hand, the family violence literature, especially that which deals with intervention strategies to address the problem, often assumes that alcohol is a cause of violence between family members. This literature is not theoretically satisfying. It is not explicit about how alcohol fits the causal scheme. The characteristics and details of violent events in the family that involve alcohol are not distinguished from those where alcohol is not present. A "malevolence assumption" appears to operate. An offender with a drinking problem or the presence of alcohol in an incident of family violence is assumed to demonstrate that alcohol has explanatory power.

The malevolence assumption has a long history. In the rhetoric of the American Temperance Movement during the 19th and 20th centuries, examples of this view proliferate. Not only are the direct detrimental effects of alcohol emphasized, but all manner of personal and social evils are promiscuously attributed to drinking.

Public debates about policies for the distribution and control of beverage alcohol have long been characterized by moral fervor. Gusfield (1963) and Rorabaugh (1979) have discussed the historical, political, and economic implications of public debate about policies toward alcohol. The moral and political debates about alcohol and its effects have not been confined to the moral and political arenas. These perspectives also have influenced scientific analyses and interpretation. This influence has often been expressed by the following logic: alcohol is destructive and evil, and therefore one is likely to find destruction and evil where alcohol is found. We refer to this as the "malevolence assumption," and it is an implicit attitude in much of what is written on family violence.

One explanation of the relevance of alcohol in family violence has been disinhibition theory. This theory posits that alcohol has a direct and causal relationship to violence because its psychophysiological properties release violent impulses, tendencies, and inhibitions. Many researchers, including Gelles (1972), D. H. Coleman and Straus (1979), and Pernanen (1976), dispute this theory of the alcohol relevance to family violence. They argue that behavior while drinking varies according to the situational context and that this behavior is learned. In addition, D. H. Coleman and Straus's review of laboratory experiments concerning alcohol and aggression concluded that not all subjects who consumed alcohol scored higher on aggression than their nondrinking counterparts (as would be predicted if alcohol is a chemical disinhibitor). Aggression varied with the social setting, and expectations of the effects of alcohol influenced the levels of aggression displayed (D. H. Coleman & Straus, 1979). Furthermore, since not all drinkers are violent, since violence occurs without drinking, and since in some families violence occurs while drinking and nondrinking, violence within the family context must be explained in some way other than as a result of drinking.

Gelles and Straus generally make the argument that the role of alcohol in family violence lies in its use as an "excuse" for deviant behavior. In our society, drinking is considered to reduce an individual's responsibility for his/her actions. Therefore, drinking can act as a mechanism for neutralizing or disavowing the deviance of a family member. All people want to be regarded as normal, or nondeviant, so when a family member commits a deviant act, that individual or the other family members can project the blame onto the effects of alcohol, thus maintaining an image of nondeviancy to themselves and to society. Furthermore, the drinker can use intoxication as a "time-out" period—a period when the individual knows he/she will be viewed by others as less responsible for his/her actions. Thus, it has been hypothesized that a family member may drink in order to be able to carry out violent acts. For Gelles and Straus, this explains the frequent association between drinking and violent behavior. However, D. H. Coleman and Straus's (1979) data revealed that people who drink most heavily display low rates of violence. They attribute this to the pacifying, calming, and depressant effects of heavy alcohol consumption but maintain that those who get drunk from time to time and also have high rates of violence use alcohol as an excuse for their violent behavior. Furthermore, in interviews conducted by Dobash and Dobash (1979), some battered women said that the husbands who were drinking would either deny they had beaten them or would claim that they were intoxicated and therefore were not responsible for their behavior. Dobash and Dobash (1979) also suggest that the battered wife may use drinking as an excuse for a violent husband in order to defer the blame from herself, her husband, or their relationship.

Gelles (1972) and Pernanen (1976) have pointed out that alcohol's contributory role in violence may be in its effects on the escalatory process to physical violence. Gelles says that an argument over a husband's drunkenness may lead to arguments over the husband's other shortcomings (such as masculinity, breadwinning capabilities, sexual abilities, etc.), which in turn may lead to physical violence. Pernanen notes that alcohol may be relevant in the occurrence of family violence in that it may escalate aggression into physical violence through its ability to deteriorate one's conceptual and abstracting abilities. In other words, interpretations of other's actions as hostile or friendly are important in the escalation process. If one's perceptions of cues, conceptual reasoning, and abstracting abilities are reduced through consumption of alcohol, the understanding of another person's behavior and coping mechanisms to deal with stressful situations are distorted or deteriorated. This distortion increases the probability of escalation to physical violence.

Social-learning theory also has the capacity to explain the association between alcohol use and family violence. That is, social norms dictate the appropriate behavior while drinking for various contexts, and, in some contexts, violence while under the influence of alcohol is regarded as acceptable, excused, or, at least, not deserving of condemnation. Certain people who have been exposed to and have learned this lesson may react violently in certain drinking situations. Violent behavior while drinking, in a family context, may be one of these "acceptable" situations.

In many studies of spouse abuse and child abuse, alcohol is not viewed as a cause of these forms of violence, but rather both alcohol use and violence are regarded as symptoms of a pathological condition of the individual. Alcohol use and violence are sometimes viewed as psychopathological traits or symptoms of a socially maladjusted personality. For example, Scott (1974), in his study of battered wives, sees the alcoholism of the battering husbands as a characteristic of a "grossly psychopathic husband" or an exasperated husband who is attempting to escape from an intolerable wife or as an expression of tensions within the marital relationship. R. Straus (1971) says:

Most types of alcoholism are found in association with some form or forms of social pathology. Marital discord, job instability, social alienation, economic strain, and chronic ill health can contribute to and be supported by an alcoholic drinking pattern, and each of these problems tends to interact with the others in a complex clustering of social, psychological, and biological pathology. (p. 251)

There is no explanatory consensus about the role of alcohol in family violence. The explanations offered range from no explanation at all, under the malevolence assumption, to disinhibition theory, to social learning theory, and include the quasi-explanation of the deviance disavowal point of view. In recent years systematic conceptualization has begun to characterize explanatory attempts. As that process continues and is augmented by more and better data about the phenomenon of family violence, the role of alcohol in family violence may be better understood.

Alcohol Involvement in Wife Beating

The examination of spouse abuse presented in this section focuses on wife beating because it has been observed that violence against the wife usually involves more serious aggression than violence against the husband. Furthermore, some current evidence demonstrates that domestic violence is more a problem for women than it is for men (Pernanen, 1979a). Pernanen conducted 933 interviews in a community in Canada to gather information concerning the respondents' last violent incidents. It was found that 60% of the last violent incidents experienced by women occurred in the home; only 17% of the men's incidents occurred at home. Of the incidents reported by women, 51.4% were perpetrated by the spouse; for the men, only 7% of the incidents were carried out by the spouse.

The purpose of this section is to define wife beating, to present evidence of the incidence of wife beating in American society, and then to review the empirical studies that have examined the alcohol involvement in this form of family violence. The findings of these studies are discussed in light of their methodological and theoretical shortcomings.

Definition of Wife Beating

First, it is necessary to define "wife beating" as it is used throughout these studies. In the studies that identify their measures of this form of family violence, it has been noted that wife beating generally refers to serious and/or repeated deliberate assaults by husbands/cohabitees which result in physical injury to the wife. In contrast to most researchers, Straus and his associates have been very specific in their measure of spouse abuse (e.g., Gelles & Straus, 1979b). In their research, a Severe Violence Index of the Conflict Tactics Scale is used to measure wife beating. This index contains the items of kicking, biting, punching, hitting with something, beating up one's spouse, threatening with a knife or gun, and using a knife or gun. Very few empirical studies include psychological or verbal abuse as part of their definition of spouse abuse.

Little research has been conducted in the area of wife beating until recently, and therefore little is known about this form of abuse. The family has traditionally been considered a haven from storm and stress, and an environment of love. Family relations have been viewed as private, and thus violence within the family has not been a visible phenomenon.

Incidence of Wife Beating

In recent years it has come to light that wife beating is more prevalent than was previously believed. It has increasingly become regarded as a serious, frequent, and underestimated problem for American families (Rounsaville, 1978). Furthermore, it has been argued that American cultural norms have made the marriage license a "hitting license" (M. A. Straus, 1976). That is, a certain amount of violence and certain forms of violence within the bonds of matrimony are regarded as appropriate and normal. Recent evidence indicates a surprisingly high incidence of this type of violence.

The Uniform Crime Reports (Federal Bureau of Investigation, 1979, p. 9) indicate that 7.3% of the murder victims during 1978 were either wives killed by their husbands or women killed by their lovers. One of the earliest studies hinting at the incidence of wife beating is Levinger's (1966) study of 600 couples who were seeking a divorce. Of the 600 wives, 37% complained of physical abuse by their spouses. (Only 3% of the husbands complained of physical abuse.) More of the wives had complaints of mental cruelty than anything else (40%), while neglect of home or children ranked second (39%), and financial problems (37%) and physical abuse (37%) ranked third.

O'Brien's (1971) study of 150 families seeking a divorce also indicates that intrafamily physical violence is significant. He recorded spontaneous reports of overt violence in 17% of the cases. Eighty-four percent of these reports were obtained from the wives. In 48% of the families where violence had occurred it had occurred repeatedly throughout the marriage. The remaining 52% of the families had experienced violent episodes only once.

Gelles's (1972) family violence study was based on a sample of 80 families that included 20 social work agency families known to have experienced violent episodes, 20 families from the records of police department calls who were not all known to exhibit family violence, and 40 families who were neighbors of the agency and police families (a comparison group). He found that 55% of the entire sample had experienced physical violence in some form (p. 48). Furthermore, 37% of the neighbor families or comparison group reported violent events (p. 50). While interesting, the findings from the Levinger, O'Brien, and Gelles studies actually tell us little about the incidence of wife beating in the general population because they are based on nonrepresentative samples.

The most informative research on the extent of wife beating is that undertaken by Straus, Gelles, and Steinmetz in 1976. Their study was a nationwide probability survey of 2143 couples. This study was the first of its kind; that is, a study of spouse abuse that can be considered representative of American couples. M. A. Straus (1977–1978) reported that for the year preceding the interview, 3.8% of the respondents admitted to having experienced one or more physical attacks included in the Severe Violence Index. "Applying this incidence rate to the approximately 47 million couples in the United States, means that in any one year, approximately 1.8 million wives are beaten by their husbands" (p. 445). For the couples in the sample who reported violence, the median frequency of these beatings was 2.4 assaults per year. Straus added that there was great variation in the frequency of assaults among the couples: Some couples experienced an assault only once during the year; others, once a week or more.

Data were also gathered on the overall incidence of any violent act, which includes not only the severe violence items but also such acts as throwing things at the spouse, pushing, shoving, grabbing, and slapping. Information was also obtained for violent incidents that had ever occurred in the couples' histories. Based on information on all the violence items for incidents that had ever occurred, it was found that "28 percent of the couples in the study experienced at least one violent incident and 5.3 percent experienced violence that can be considered a beating" (p. 446). With confidence in the representativeness of his sample and underreporting likely to underestimate the incidence of domestic violence, Straus concluded, "the true incidence rate is probably closer to 50 to 60 percent of all couples than it is to the 28 percent who were willing to describe violent acts in a mass interview survey" (p. 447).

Review of Empirical Studies

Only a limited number of empirical studies provide information on the relationship between alcohol use/abuse and wife beating. Table 7.1 lists the small number of studies we found dealing with this topic and summarizes the information obtained from them which is presented in this section. These studies have all been undertaken in the 1970s, reflecting the recent interest in and attention to this phenomenon.

For each study, the last column in Table 7.1 presents the researcher's evaluation of the role of alcohol. This was not always stated explicitly, but in most cases where it was not stated it could be inferred. We indicate in the last column whether the role of alcohol was stated explicitly by the researcher or inferred from the text.

The studies that present data on the alcohol problems or alcohol histories associated with incidents of wife beating suggest that heavy or frequent drinking by husbands plays a role in wife beating. Hilberman and Munson's (1977–1978) study of 60 battered women referred to a clinic for psychiatric evaluation found that 93% of the husbands had alcoholism as a significant problem, according to the wives' reports. Based on the physician reports of 15 battered wives seen in general practice, Dewsbury (1975) reported that 13% of the husbands of the wives in his sample were alcoholic. Rounsaville's (1978) sample of 31 battered women identified in clinical facilities also reported that 45% of their partners were alcoholic. In these studies, the criteria for determining the condition of alcoholism is not reported. These three researchers view the alcohol abuse as a symptom of psychological problems or psychopathology of the husband.

Based on the self-reports of 100 battered women seeking aid, Gayford (1975) found that 74% of the husbands were "frequent heavy" drinkers or "occasional heavy" drinkers. The terms "frequent," "occasional," and "heavy" are not defined. Roy (1977) reported on the cases of 150 battered wives selected at random from 1000 crisis center cases. She found that 85% of the violent husbands had alcoholic and/or drug problems but were very often assaultive while sober as well. In these two studies, the role of alcohol in wife beating is attributed to its disinhibiting effects.

K. H. Coleman and Weinman's (no date) sample consisted of 30 couples who had a history of conjugal violence and a comparison group of 30 couples with no such history. Both husbands and wives were interviewed, and it was reported that more than 50% of the men in the violent group used alcohol frequently, compared with 20% of the men in the nonviolent group. Coleman and Weinman found that both the husbands and wives in the violent sample reported significantly more alcohol use than did the nonviolent couples. Byles (1978) interviewed 130 women and nine men in family court. He found that 68% of all the families represented used alcohol, and that, of these families, 61% involved someone who drank to the point of intoxication. He concluded that violence is more than twice as likely to occur in families with, rather than without, alcohol problems.

TABLE 7.1. Empirical Studies of Alcohol Involvement in Wife Beating

Author (date)	Sample	Alcohol in event (% of cases)	History of alcohol problems (% of cases)	Data source	Role of alcohol
Bard and Zacker (1974)	1388 family disputes; 29% exhibited evidence of assault	•Complainant said second party was both drunk and assaultive in 6% of cases •Police said 21% of assaultive cases involved second party drinking		Police reports and debriefing reports	Family disputes not influenced by alcohol use (stated)
Byles (1978)	130 women and 9 men in family court		68% of families used alcohol; of these, 61% drank to point of intoxication	Reports of those in sample	
Carlson (1977)	101 battered women	Alcohol involved in 67% of incidents which brought them to the agency	•10% of women were alcohol abusers •60% of assailants were alcohol abusers	Women's reports	Disinhibitor (stated)
Chimbos (1978)	34 people who had murdered spouse	In 29%, neither was under influence of alcohol or drugs; in 53%, both offender and victim were under influence; in 18%, offender was under influence		Reports of those in sample	Distorts cognitive skills (stated)

Study	Sample	Findings	Source of data	Theoretical approach
D. H. Coleman and Straus (1979)	2143 American couples	•For husbands "never" drunk, severe violence rate is 2.1 per hundred •For those drunk "very often," rate is 30.8 per hundred •For those who are "almost always drunk, rate is 17.6 per hundred •Similar pattern for wives	•Husbands' self-reports in ½ of cases •Wives' self-reports in ½ of cases	Deviance disavowal at moderate levels of alcohol consumption (stated)
K. H. Coleman and Weinman (no date)	•30 couples reporting conjugal violence •30 couples with no such history (comparison group)	•More than 50% of men in conjugal violence group used alcohol frequently, compared with 20% of men in nonviolent group •Both husbands and wives in violent group had significantly more alcohol use than did nonviolent husbands and wives	Couples' self-reports	
Dewsbury (1975)	15 battered wives	"Alcohol was frequently associated with assaults"	Physicians' reports	Symptom of psychopathology (stated)
Emerson (1975)	1446 family disputes; 70% were between husband and wife	In 46% of all disputes, one or more disputants was under influence of alcohol or drugs; 59% of disputants under influence were husbands, and 26% were wives	Police reports	

(continued)

TABLE 7.1. *(continued)*

Author (date)	Sample	Alcohol in event (% of cases)	History of alcohol problems (% of cases)	Data source	Role of alcohol
Gayford (1975)	100 battered women	In 44% of cases, violence occurred regularly when husband was drunk	•52% of husbands were "frequent heavy" drinkers •22% of husbands were "occasional heavy" drinkers	Women's reports	Disinhibitor (inferred)
Gelles (1972)	20 social work cases, 20 families from police records, and 40 neighbor families (comparison group)	•In only one family was wife violent toward husband and children when drinking •In 48% of violent families, drinking accompanied violence		Interviews with 66 wives and 14 husbands	Deviance disavowal, time-out mechanism; escalates aggression to physical violence (stated)
Gerson (1978)	1790 alcohol-related acts of violence; 23% were marital assaults	Of marital assaults involving alcohol, in 44%, offender drinking only; in 13%, victim drinking only; in 43%, both drinking		Police reports	

Study	Sample	Finding	Finding	Method	Interpretation
Hilberman and Munson (1977–1978)	60 battered women	"Husband was usually drinking at time of the assault, but this was not always the case."	•93% of husbands had problem of alcoholism •7% of women were alcoholics	Women's reports	Symptom of psychological problem (inferred)
Nisonoff and Bitman (1979)	297 people, randomly generated sample of a county	"Alcohol was a contributing factor in 14 (26.4%) of the violent incidents."		Telephone interviews with those in sample	
Rounsaville (1978)	31 battered women	•13% of women were drinking during abusive episode •29% of partners were drinking	•29% of women were alcoholics •45% of partners were alcoholics	Women's reports	Symptom of psychological problem (inferred)
Roy (1977)	150 battered wives	More than 80% of men who drank occasionally were inclined to beat their wives only when under the influence	85% of violent husbands had alcoholic and/or drug problems but, very often, were assaultive while sober	Women's reports	Disinhibitor (stated)

However, it is not clear what is meant by an "alcohol problem." Neither Coleman and Weinman nor Byles give any indication of how alcohol contributes to violent behavior between family members.

Data on the involvement of alcohol at the time of the violent event are scanty and disorganized. Dewsbury (1975) simply states that "alcohol was frequently associated with assaults" (p. 292), and Hilberman and Munson (1977–1978) report that "the husband was usually drinking at the time of the assault, but this was not always the case" (p. 462). Thirteen percent of Rounsaville's (1978) sample of battered women stated that they were usually drinking during the violent episode, and 29% of them stated that their partners were drinking. Gayford (1975) reports that, in 44% of his cases, violence occurred regularly when the husband was drunk. In Roy's (1977) sample, more than 80% of the men who were occasional drinkers were inclined to beat their wives only when they had been drinking. Gelles (1972, p. 111) found that 48% of the violent families he uncovered had drinking accompanying the violent incidents, but in only one family was the wife violent toward her husband and children when she was drinking.

Based on cases identified through police records, Dobash and Dobash (1979) found that 30% of the husbands were intoxicated at the time of the incident. They also reported that 25% of the 109 battered women interviewed said their husbands were often drunk at the time of the beating. Therefore, Dobash and Dobash (1979, p. 118) concluded that most men were not drunk when they attacked their wives.

Nisonoff and Bitman (1979) obtained a sample of 297 people in one county by calling randomly generated telephone numbers. They asked respondents if alcohol was a factor when they were hit or when they hit their spouse. They found that "alcohol was a contributing factor in 26.4 percent of the violent incidents" (p. 135). However, they do not offer an explanation of the role of alcohol. Chimbos (1978) interviewed 34 people who had murdered their spouse, asking them if alcohol or drugs were involved in the homicidal act. In 53% of the cases, both offender and victim were under the influence; in 18%, only the offender was under the influence; and in 29%, neither was under the influence of alcohol or drugs. Chimbos discussed alcohol's tendencies to reduce or distort cognitive skills necessary to stave off violence. In Carlson's (1977) study of 101 battered women involved in a women's aid program, the women reported that alcohol was "involved" in 67% of the incidents which pushed them to seek help, but what is meant by "involvement" of alcohol in the incidents is not specified. Carlson advocates the disinhibition theory of alcohol's effect in their violent events.

Three studies relied on police reports for their alcohol information (Bard & Zacker, 1974; Emerson, 1979; Gerson, 1978). Of the 411 alcohol-involved marital assaults reported by police in Gerson's study, 44% involved just the offender drinking, 43% involved both spouses drinking, and 13% involved just the victim drinking. Because the focus of this report is on alcohol-related violent incidents only, it is impossible to compare the incidents that involve alcohol use with ones that do not or to say what proportion of all incidents involved alcohol.

Emerson's study (1979) of family disputes found that 46% of all disputes involved someone under the influence of alcohol or drugs. Fifty-nine percent of the disputants under the influence were husbands; 26% were wives. On the other hand, Bard and Zacker (1974) concluded that family disputes are not usually influenced by alcohol use. Out of 330 incidents occurring between family members that were judged to be assaults by police, police said that only 21% involved the second party (usually the offender) drinking. In only 6% of the cases did the complainant say the second party was both drunk and assaultive. Furthermore, Bard and Zacker (1974) noted that "the second party was less likely to have used alcohol in assaultive disputes than in those disputes that did not involve an assault" (p. 288). Bard and Zacker's conclusion that alcohol use is not a significant variable in family disputes may be unwarranted given their own finding that in approximately one-third to one-half of all family disputes someone appeared to have used alcohol.

The Straus, Gelles, and Steinmetz nationwide study of over 2000 American couples provides no data on physical violence that occurs while a family member is drinking (Gelles & Straus, 1979a). It provides only data on the level of violence in the home and the frequency of alcohol abuse within the year preceding the interview. These self-report data reveal that for husbands who were "never" drunk, the severe violence rate is 2.1 per 100 couples. For those who were drunk "very often," the rate increases to 30.8 per 100. But for men who are "almost always" drunk, the rate drops to 17.6 per 100 (D. H. Coleman & Straus, 1979, p. 11).

A similar pattern can be observed for the wives in the sample. "Wives who report being drunk even occasionally or more were from 2.5 to six times more likely to have severely abused their spouses than those who report never being drunk during the year. But then the rate drops off for women who were 'very often' or 'almost always' drunk" (D. H. Coleman & Straus, 1979, p. 11). D. H. Coleman and Straus argue that these findings suggest that true alcoholics are anesthetized, but that those who get drunk occasionally use alcohol as an "excuse" for their nonnormative behavior.

The comparability of these studies is minimal, due to the variety and imprecision of the measures employed by the investigators for the major variables of "alcohol use," "alcohol abuse," and "wife beating." For example, many studies do not report the measures used to assess the alcohol use or abuse of their subjects. For example, they simply report findings of "alcoholism" and "alcohol use" based on clinician's assessments or police judgments. In other cases, reference is made to the "frequency" and "involvement" of drinking, alcohol abuse, and alcoholism in violent events and assailants. Nisonoff and Bitman (1979) simply report asking respondents if alcohol is a factor when they are hit or when they hit someone else. Byles (1978) discusses "alcohol problems" but he does not specify what an alcohol problem is. Gayford (1975) classified his sample's husbands (who were heavy drinkers) as "occasional" or "frequent" drinkers; K. H. Coleman and Weinman (no date) classified their sample's alcohol use as "none," "infrequent," "occasional," "frequent," and "often"; while Straus and associates gathered information by self-report on how frequently the respondent "gets drunk" (never, rarely, occasionally, often, very often, almost always).

Comparability between studies is also made difficult through the various measures of wife beating utilized in these studies. The majority of the studies define wife beating as was done earlier—serious and/or repeated deliberate assaults by husbands/cohabitees which result in physical injury to the wife. Rounsaville (1978) defined wife beating more broadly to include physical abuse to any extent; Nisonoff and Bitman (1979) included less serious forms of assault such as slapping in their operational definition of spouse abuse; and Byles's (1978) study of violence included physical assaults on wife, assaults on children, and destruction of property. Gerson (1978) focused his attention on "marital assaults," Bard and Zacker (1974) reported findings on "assaultive disputes," and Emerson (1979) investigated "family disputes," without clearly specifying what is meant by these terms. By far the most precise definition of wife beating is found in the D. H. Coleman and Straus (1979) study. The authors clearly point out that the measure of wife beating is obtained from a Severe Violence Index of the Conflict Tactics Scale, which includes the following acts: kicking, biting, punching, hitting with something, beating up one's spouse, threatening with a knife or gun, and using a knife or gun.

An additional problem in attempting to assess the alcohol involvement in wife beating from these studies is the multiple sources from which the data are derived. Most of the available studies are based on battered wives' reports. Some studies are based on self-reports by either the wife or the husband of a couple or by both husband and wife. The data for other studies are derived from clinicians' and police officers' assessments or reports of men and women seeking divorces. Thus, these studies reflect the different perceptions of reporting individuals concerning the alcohol involvement in violence. This further reduces comparability.

In addition, the overwhelming majority of these studies are based on "captured" samples of small size—either battered women seeking help and treatment for themselves or their husbands, couples seeking help with marriage or family problems or a divorce, or people who commit assaults or murders and become police statistics. Sample compositions such as these make it impossible to generalize the research findings to the general population. Only two studies could be located that have even included comparison groups (K. H. Coleman & Weinman, no date; Gelles, 1972), and only two studies could be found that have attempted to randomly generate their samples (nationwide probability study of Straus, Gelles, & Steinmetz reported in D. H. Coleman & Straus, 1979; Nisonoff & Bitman, 1979).

Most of the studies are purely descriptive in nature; that is, they report percentages of the sample who are "alcoholic," have "alcohol problems," or "use alcohol," or they report percentages of cases where alcohol was "involved" in or "associated" with the violent incidents. These studies do not distinguish the characteristics of the violent incidents that involve alcohol use from the ones that do not.

The investigators who have conducted these studies make the assumption that alcohol use has some explanatory relevance for the understanding of wife beating, yet very few of them specify how or why this might be the case. They seldom make explicit their theory of the role of alcohol in wife beating; in some cases, one can infer or draw out their operating perspective from the tone of the study or the researcher's professional orientation. In a majority of the studies, alcohol is viewed as a symptom of psychopathology or psychological problems (Dewsbury, 1975; Hilberman & Munson, 1977–1978; Rounsaville, 1978). Other researchers believe that alcohol acts as a disinhibitor under which men lose control (cf. Carlson, 1977; Gayford, 1975; Roy, 1977). Still others see the importance of alcohol as lying in its role as a "deviance disavowal" or "time-out" mechanism (cf. D. H. Coleman & Straus, 1979; Gelles, 1972). Gelles (1972) also argues that drinking may serve to escalate marital arguments into physical violence, while Chimbos (1978) and Pernanen (1976) stress alcohol's cognitive distortion effects. And then there are some reseachers who assert that the influence of alcohol has been overstated and is insignificant (Bard & Zacker, 1974).

In the studies that do specify the author's interpretation of the role of alcohol in wife beating, the interpretation is often a post facto explanation for descriptive findings. No theoretically derived hypotheses have been tested. Most researchers would agree that alcohol is not the major causal factor in wife beating. However, most also assume that it plays some role in the etiology or perpetuation of the violent behavior. What that role may be has not been adequately specified to date.

Alcohol Involvement in Child Abuse

The purpose of this section is similar to that of the preceding one—child abuse is defined, some studies of the incidence of child abuse are presented, and finally, empirical studies that provide information on the alcohol involvement in child abuse are reviewed.

Definition of Child Abuse

The definition of child abuse is even more problematic than spouse abuse. Many researchers disagree as to what acts constitute child abuse, and this conflict is reflected in the variety of operational definitions employed in their studies. Most would agree, however, that child abuse involves the use of physical force, willfully inflicted, by a parent or caretaker against a child, resulting in physical injury to the child. This definition excludes accidental injuries and psychological harm to the child. Most researchers would agree that this is justified. But this definition also excludes acts of omission that constitute neglect, which many researchers view as essential aspects of child abuse (e.g., Gil, 1970). Because we agree with Justice and Justice (1976) that there are sharp distinctions between those parents who physically abuse their children and those who neglect them, and because abuse and neglect are conceptually distinct phenomena, we have chosen to separate the two and concentrate our efforts here on intentional physical violence applied to children by their parents or guardians. Nevertheless, the studies which are reviewed here have employed various measures of child abuse. For example, some include acts of neglect, while others do not; and the studies include various levels of severity of physical violence in their measures of child abuse.

Incidence of Child Abuse

During 1978 the American Humane Association (1979) was notified of 614,291 cases of child maltreatment by 50 states, two territories, and the District of Columbia (p. 6). Out of the 66,121 substantiated reports for which information was available, 75.8% of the cases required no treatment; 19.2% were moderately injured; 4.5% were seriously injured and required hospitalization; .2% were permanently disabled; and .3%, or 204 children, died as a result of the maltreatment (p. 35). Of course, these figures reflect only the officially known cases, and they suffer from variations in state laws concerning the definition of child abuse and variations governing reporting procedures. Since it was recognized that estimates of the incidence of child abuse based on official reports reflected only a part of the total number of cases, Gil (1970) conducted a national survey in 1965. He reported that 2.3–3.7% of 110 million adults, or between 2.5 and 4.1 million adults, personally knew families involved in child abuse during the preceding year. This figure represents the estimate of the upper limit of the incidence of child abuse because it is unlikely that each reporting adult knew a different family involved in child abuse. "Light (1973) attempted to control for the possibility that the same case was known by more than one of Gil's survey subjects; he offered a revised estimate of 500,000 incidents based on 1970 census data" (Maden & Wrench, 1977, p. 198).

From the data gathered by the Straus, Gelles, and Steinmetz national survey of 1146 couples who had at least one child between the ages of 3 and 17, Gelles (1979b) found that 8% of the parents reported kicking, biting, or hitting the child with a fist at some time in the child's life; 4% reported beating up the child; and 6% said they had threatened the child with a knife or gun or used a knife or gun against the child. From the data of this same study, Gelles and Straus (1979b) concluded that between 1.4 and 1.9 million children in the United States were vulnerable to physical injury from their parents during the year of their study. They believe that these figures are underestimates because: (1) children aged 1 and 2, who are at a high-risk age for child abuse, were omitted; (2) parents are likely to under-report abusive incidents; (3) the list of possible abuses to which a parent could admit was limited; (4) only one parent was interviewed; and (5) single-parent households, which are a high-risk group, were omitted (Straus, 1979).

Review of Empirical Studies

Many writers on the topic of child abuse assume that there is a significant association between alcohol use/abuse and child abuse. The early findings of Young (1964) suggested that drinking was a primary family problem in 62% of the 300 abusive/neglecting families studied, and that heavy drinking was present, but not the primary problem, in additional families. Mayer and Black (1977) have concluded from studies of the incidence of alcoholism in families with abused or neglected children that a substantial proportion of those families contain an alcoholic parent, but that alcoholism may be somewhat more frequently associated with neglect than with abuse.

The review of empirical studies of the association between alcohol use and child abuse yielded contradictory findings. Some studies find a relationship;

others find that no significant relationship exists. Table 7.2 presents the studies that are reviewed and discussed here. As with the wife-beating research, the interpreation of the sole of alcohol was not always explicit and therefore was inferred where possible.

A few studies dealing with the involvement of alcohol in child abuse have been omitted from Table 7.2 due either to our inability to locate them or to their publication in untranslated texts. Reviews of these studies can be found in T. Epstein, Cameron, and Room (1977); they are only briefly mentioned here. Nau (1967) reported that 34% of his sample of child abusers were under the influence of alcohol at the time of the incident, and that 50% were alcoholics. Grislain, Mainard, and DeBerranger (1968) found that parents in 65% of their child abuse cases demonstrated excessive alcohol use, while Andreini and Green (1975) reported that 24% of their abusive families exhibited alcohol abuse. Twenty-three percent of Gould's (1976) sample of abusive families suffered from stress evolving from problems with alcohol and/or drugs.

The empirical studies we reviewed yield inconsistent findings concerning the prevalence of alcohol problems or alcoholic histories in families of abused children. Some researchers report a significant association between alcohol problems and child abuse. Johnson and Morse (1968) perused a welfare department's case records and questioned the child welfare workers of 101 injured or neglected children who were below the age of 14. They reported that 16 of the injuring parents drank to excess (the total number of parents was not reported). They also reported that one-fourth of the fathers, but only a few of the mothers, drank to excess. "Drinking to excess" was not defined. Simons, Downs, Hurster, and Archer (1966) reported on the cases of 313 mistreated children (abuse, neglect, and accident cases were included) from 293 families identified through legally required medical reports. They found that 10% of the caretakers of these children were alcoholics or drug addicts, diagnosed by psychiatric evaluation. The cases of 42 abused and neglected children who had been treated in a hospital were investigated by Birrell and Birrell (1968). Medical records revealed that in at least 21% of the 39 families represented, alcoholism was present. Kaplun and Reich (1976) studied the postmortem reports, police reports, and child welfare agency reports of 112 cases of child homicide. They found that 29.7% of 61 public welfare families of child homicide victims exhibited the presence of alcoholism before the occurrence of the homicide.

A more recent study was conducted by Behling (1979) of 51 cases of child abuse, including physical abuse, neglect, and sexual abuse. Based on interviews of parents and others involved with the cases, and using medical records, Behling found that 69% of the cases had at least one parent who was alcoholic or who abused alcohol. Sixty-three percent had at least one grandparent who was alcoholic or who abused alcohol, and 92% of the 26 parents who were abused as children were abused by a parent who was alcoholic or who abused alcohol. In sharp contrast to the studies previously mentioned, Behling's study specified the criteria for the determination of alcoholism and alcohol abuse. With some modification, the Family History—Research Diagnostic Criteria (Andreasen, Endicott, Spitzer, & Winokur, 1977; Endicott, Andreasen, & Spitzer, 1975) was used for this diagnosis. This set of criteria includes: (1) a problem with drinking not limited to isolated incidents, and (2) at least one alcohol-related problem in the following areas: legal problems, health problems, marital or family problems, treatment for alcoholism, and social problems. "Alcoholism" and "alcohol abuse" were defined by the presence of certain of these criteria.

In these studies, alcohol abuse is often seen as one factor in the overall social pathology or deviant behavior patterns in the family (Birrell & Birrell, 1968; Kaplun & Reich, 1976), or as a psychological problem or mental health problem of the abusive parent (Johnson & Morse, 1968; Kaplun & Reich, 1976; Simons et al., 1966). However, Behling (1979) does not offer an explanation of the role of alcohol.

On the other hand, several studies have concluded that alcoholism is not a significant problem for the parents of battered children (Baldwin & Oliver, 1975; Scott, 1973; Smith, Hanson, & Noble, 1973; Steele & Pollock, 1974). Smith, Hanson, and Noble's sample consisted of 214 parents of battered babies who had been admitted to hospitals and 76 control parents of children who had been admitted to hospitals for other emergencies. Based on psychiatric, psychological, and social interviews, the authors concluded that "alcoholism and drug dependence were not features among the index cases or controls" (p. 390). Scott (1973) agrees that alcohol use does not play a significant role in child abuse. He analyzed the official records and interviewed 29 men in prison who had killed their child. Only one man had a history of alcoholism. This sample of men was compared to the cases of 78 battered children reported in a previous study. However, the samples were not compared on the alcohol-use variable.

Baldwin and Oliver (1975) gathered information from professional people, written notes, files, and interviews of some parents on 38 cases of severe abuse. They reported that 11.4% of the parents or guardians who were implicated in child abuse had a history of uncontrolled drug or alcohol use, compared to 16.7% of the parents or guardians who were not implicated. They concluded that there was no significant difference between these caretakers on the alcohol-use variable.

Steele and Pollock (1974) studied 60 families in which child abuse had

TABLE 7.2. Empirical Studies of Alcohol Involvement in Child Abuse

Author (date)	Sample	Alcohol in event (% of cases)	History of alcohol problems (% of cases)	Data source	Role of alcohol
Baldwin and Oliver (1975)	38 cases of severe abuse representing 34 families, compared to 22 case reports of a later period		• 11.4% of parents or guardians who were implicated in child abuse had history of uncontrolled drug or alcohol use • 16.7% of parents or guardians who were not implicated had such history	Professionals' reports, written notes, files, interviews of parents	
Behling (1979)	51 cases (physical abuse, neglect, sexual abuse)		• 69% of cases had at least one parent who was alcoholic or who abused alcohol • 63% had at least one grandparent who was alcoholic or who abused alcohol • 92% of 26 parents who were abused as children were abused by a parent who was alcoholic or who abused alcohol	Interviews of parents and others involved with case, medical records	
Birrell and Birrell (1968)	42 abused and neglected children representing 39 families		• In at least 8 families (21%), alcoholism was present • "Alcoholism is frequent . . ."	Medical records	Symptom of family social pathology (stated)

Study	Sample	Findings	Source of data	Form of deviance or pathology in functioning of caretakers (inferred)
Gil (1979)	1380 cases of physical abuse reported through legal channels in 1967 and 1968	"Alcoholic intoxication of perpetrator at time of abusive act" was checked by social workers in 12.5% of cases	Social workers' reports	
B. Johnson and Morse (1968)	101 injured or neglected children	•16 of injuring parents drank to excess •25% of fathers, but only a few mothers, drank to excess	Case records and reports of child welfare workers	Symptom of mental health problem (stated)
Kaplun and Reich (1976)	112 cases of child homicide	Among 61 public welfare families of child homicide victims before the homicides, 29.7% had alcoholism present	Postmortem reports, police reports, welfare agency reports	Represents deviant behavior or psychopathology (stated)
Scott (1973)	29 fathers or substitute fathers who had killed child, compared to sample of 78 battered children of another study	•None significantly intoxicated at time of event •2 men, or possibly 4, had taken some alcohol	Prison records, men's reports	
Simons et al. (1966)	313 children from 293 families (abuse, neglect, and accident cases)	•50% of all caretakers had psychologic difficulties severe enough to require counseling and social services •Of this 50%, only 20% were alcoholic or drug addicts, that is, 10% of total	Psychiatric reports, official records, voluntary agencies' staff reports	Symptom of mental problems (inferred)

(continued)

TABLE 7.2. (*continued*)

Author (date)	Sample	Alcohol in event (% of cases)	History of alcohol problems (% of cases)	Data source	Role of alcohol
Smith *et al.* (1973)	214 parents of battered babies; 76 control parents		"Alcoholism and drug dependence were not features among the index cases or controls."	Psychiatric, psychological, and social interviews with parents	
Steele and Pollock (1974)	60 families in which child abuse had occurred		• "True alcoholism was not a problem except in 1 family; many were total abstainers." • "Among those who did use alcohol, drinking was occasionally a source of marital conflict but bore no significant, direct relationship to episodes of child beating."	Interviews and home visits with families	

occurred. Based on interviews and home visits with these families, they found that alcoholism was not a problem except in one family and noted that many child abusers abstained totally from alcohol use. They concluded that "among those who did use alcohol, drinking was occasionally a source of marital conflict but bore no significant, direct relationship to episodes of child beating" (p. 93). Again, in these studies, it is not clear how the determination of "alcoholism" and "uncontrolled alcohol use" was made.

Only two studies presented here provide any information on the involvement of alcohol immediately prior to or during the abusive event. Gil (1970), who asked social workers to provide information on 1380 cases of physical abuse of children as reported through legal channels in 1967 and 1968, reported that "alcoholic intoxication of perpetrator at time of abusive act" was considered a factor by the social workers in 12.9% of the cases. Scott (1973), however, found that none of the 29 imprisoned men who had murdered their children were significantly intoxicated at the time of the act, but two, or possibly four, had consumed some alcohol.

Mayer and Black (1977) studied 100 alcoholics and 100 opiate addicts who were caring for children under the age of 18. They noted that not all alcoholics seriously abuse or neglect their children, although the majority of them have difficulty with child rearing. But, as D. H. Coleman and Straus (1979) have argued, a majority of any group of parents is likely to experience problems in child rearing. From the Straus, Gelles, and Steinmetz national probability survey data, Coleman and Straus (1979) reported that "fathers who get drunk on more than a rare occasion have double the rate of child abuse as compared to fathers who are never or rarely drunk" (p. 12). The same holds true for mothers, and the rate of child abuse follows the same pattern as that described for spouse abuse— "the rate of child abuse drops sharply for both the fathers and mothers who are most often drunk" (Coleman & Straus, 1979, p. 12). Recall that this drastic rate decline was hypothesized as the result of the anesthetizing effects of extreme intoxication.

It is difficult, if not impossible, to compare these studies and draw any conclusions from their findings because: (1) child abuse is operationally defined differently in various studies (e.g., some studies include cases of neglect; others do not), (2) various and imprecise measures of alcohol abuse are used, and (3) multiple data sources reflect various individuals' perceptions of the alcohol involvement in child abuse.

As discussed earlier, most researchers agree that physical violence intentionally directed toward a child by a parent constitutes child abuse, but some believe that neglect of a child should not be ignored in investigations of child abuse. Johnson and Morse (1968) and Birrell and Birrell (1968) included cases of children injured due to negligence as well as physical violence; Simons *et al.* (1966) investigated cases of both physical violence and neglect, including some cases which were probably accidents; and Behling's (1979) study included cases of sexual abuse. The remainder of the studies shown in Table 7.2 are focused on physical abuse toward children. The Scott (1973) and Kaplun and Reich (1976) studies have employed a very precise measure of child abuse: child homicide by a parent. Baldwin and Oliver (1975) and the Straus, Gelles, and Steinmetz survey (Gelles & Straus, 1979b) have also used precise measures of child abuse. Baldwin and Oliver were concerned with severe abuse cases, operationally defined as cases of death from prolonged assaults; skull or facial bone fractures, bleeding into or around the brain, brain damage, impairment to intellect or senses, or damage to vision; two or more instances of mutilation; three or more separate instances of fracture and/or severe bruising; and multiple fractures and/or severe internal injuries. The national survey conducted by Straus, Gelles, and Steinmetz used the physical violence items of the Conflict Tactics Scale to define child abuse.

The overwhelming majority of these child abuse studies report findings of numbers or percentages of their sample which have a problem of alcoholism. The determination of "alcoholism" comes from various sources: medical records; psychiatric evaluations; social workers' reports; psychiatric, psychological, and social interviews; personal interviews; and interviews in combination with official records. In some studies it is not clear from what source the alcoholism judgment is derived. Other studies focus on "uncontrolled alcohol use" or "drinking to excess," without defining the meaning of these terms. In general, these data are usually derived from social workers' opinions and case records. These various and imprecise measures of alcohol abuse further limit comparability of these studies.

It is evident from the preceding discussion that multiple data sources have been used in these studies. Some studies obtained alcohol and child abuse information from the battering parents themselves; some from psychiatric and psychological tests and evaluations; some from case records of social agencies and social workers' judgments; some from prison records; and some from medical records. The utilization of these various sources and combinations of sources reflects the varying perceptions of the reporting individuals of the extent of alcohol involvement in acts of child abuse.

Like the wife beating studies, the child abuse studies are also based on official or treatment samples of small size. The studies reviewed here are of parents of murdered children or abused/neglected children who have come to the attention of social, medical, or legal authorities. Only one study sampled alcoholics to report on their abusive or nonabusive behavior toward their children (Mayer & Black, 1977). The findings from these studies cannot be generalized to known populations because the samples were not randomly generated; therefore, the findings should only be considered exploratory. Only three of the studies presented in Table 7.2 used a comparison or control group (Baldwin & Oliver, 1975; Scott, 1973; Smith *et al.,* 1973). On the other hand, the research findings from the Straus, Gelles, and Steinmetz study can be generalized to the population; thus, we can place more confidence in the results.

An additional problem in evaluating many research efforts in this area is that alcohol use information is combined with drug use information in the statistics. Apparently, alcohol use is not considered a separate phenomenon from drug use by many researchers of child abuse. Because of this, it is impossible in some studies to distinguish between the involvement of alcohol use and the involvement of drug use in child abuse.

Theoretical interpretation of the relationship between alcohol use and child abuse is virtually nonexistent in the studies reviewed here. No developed theories are presented in these studies; however, most view alcohol abuse as a form of deviance or personal pathology in mental or social functioning which, in some way, contributed to the etiology and/or perpetuation of abusive behavior toward children. On the other hand, a few researchers argue that alcohol plays no significant role in child abuse.

As in the case of spouse abuse, the malevolence assumption toward alcohol is common in the interpretation of child abuse. The presence of alcohol or alcoholism is assumed to be pertinent to the occurrence of violence.

Summary

Given the recency of attention to the family violence area and the lack of methodological rigor in the work that has been done, it is not surprising that the role of alcohol in family violence is not well understood. As discussed throughout this chapter, many serious problems characterize past research in this area; therefore, conclusions inferred from that work should be viewed as tentative. In this section we provide what we believe is a reasonable summary of the empirical evidence concerning the relationship of alcohol consumption to family violence. The following points represent a summary interpretation of the literature.

1. *Alcohol in the event:* Estimates of the percentage of family violence incidents where alcohol was present prior to or during the event ranged from 6% to 67%. This percentage tends to be lower for child abuse than for wife beating. In the case of child abuse, a speculative estimate of the

percentage of all incidents where alcohol was present would be less than 20%. For wife beating, an analogous estimate would be between 25 and 50%.

2. *Alcohol in the person:* Both husbands who abuse their wives and caretakers who abuse their children are more likely than the general population to be alcohol abusers. This conclusion is based on an estimate that 5-10% of the general population has a serious drinking problem. In the research reviewed here, estimates of the percentage of problem drinkers involved in family violence ranged from 0 to 93%. As with the event-based estimates, alcoholism was more likely to be characteristic of wife abusers than of child abusers.

3. The association between rates of family violence and drinking level appears to be curvilinear. The lowest abuse rates are found among those who drink least. The highest rates are found among moderate to heavy drinkers. The heaviest drinkers have higher abuse rates than infrequent or nondrinkers but lower abuse rates than moderately heavy drinkers. It is not clear whether this curvilinearity is a function of dosage level or chronicity of the drinking problem.

4. A few writers deny that alcohol use or alcoholism has any genuine explanatory role in the occurrence of family violence. Those who do ascribe "causality" to alcohol often do so under the malevolence assumption. The best guess appears to be that alcohol is sometimes causally relevant, but very little can be said with confidence about *how* alcohol exerts its influence on family violence.

Conclusion Number 4 leads us to be cautious about attaching explanatory significance to the role of alcohol in the occurrence of family violence. On the one hand, the occurrence of family violence at the same time or among the same people where alcohol, alcohol problems, or alcoholism is present is a consistent empirical regularity. On the other hand, we have noted the serious interpretive and methodological problems that compromise the findings.

Future research studies need to attend to fundamental issues of sampling, definition, and measurement. It seems that the relationship of drinking to the occurrence of family violence is not a simple one. Specific hypothesized relationships need to be examined with data. Research conducted on clearly defined and narrowly focused issues offers the best hope for establishing how alcohol may contribute to family violence.

Future work also needs to attend to the phenomenology of alcohol consumption; we include the deviance disavowal perspective under this rubric. There is evidence that beliefs about alcohol effects exert an influence quite apart from the physiological effects of alcohol. Drinking has a variety of meanings. Drinkers have expectations about how they will be affected by alcohol and how they are permitted to act while drinking. Others, who may interact with someone they know is drinking, will also have a set of expectations about alcohol's effects and the drinker's behavior. The expectations of each will shape interactions and may also influence subsequent interpretation of behavior. Neutral observers of events (like bystanders) or evaluators of events (like social workers or policemen) may also attach meaning to behavioral interactions based in part on the presence or absence of alcohol in the event participants. Finally, the constructions and interpretations of researchers may also be affected by expectations about alcohol; the tendency to ascribe causal relevance to alcohol whenever it is present—what we have referred to as the malevolence assumption—provides ample evidence that scientific observers are influenced by nonneutral constructions of social reality.

The alcohol–family violence literature is muddled by a variety of beliefs and interpretations that make it difficult to map the relationship. Future research needs to specify how normative expectations and behavioral interpretations are influenced by the presence of alcohol. Understanding the phenomenology of alcohol and behavior is crucial to the understanding of the alcohol–family violence relationship.

8 Alcohol Use and Criminal Behavior: An Empirical, Theoretical, and Methodological Overview

JAMES J. COLLINS, JR.

Introduction

Background

This chapter summarizes much of the material covered in more detail in the earlier chapters of the book. Those chapters cover a wide range of empirical, theoretical, and methodological issues. Our summary here is more selective and focuses attention on the social psychological aspects of the alcohol use–criminal behavior relationship; physiological, pharmacological, and medical perspectives are not emphasized here. This chapter also summarizes the results of a research project undertaken to assist the Center for the Study of Crime Correlates and Criminal Behavior of the National Institute of Justice (NIJ) in their program to develop multidisciplinary knowledge about the causes of crime. The final report for that project includes a detailed research agenda for future research on the alcohol–crime relationship (Collins, Guess, Williams, & Hamilton, 1980).

This chapter first describes some of the empirical evidence for an alcohol–crime relationship. The summary is not detailed or exhaustive. The chapters of this book and other recent efforts provide a detailed examination of the empirical evidence (Pernanen, 1976; Roizen & Schneberk, 1978).

After a short overview of the empirical support for an association be-

JAMES J. COLLINS, JR. Research Triangle Institute, Research Triangle Park, North Carolina.

tween alcohol use and crime, there is a review of the theoretical aspects of the association. The consistency and strength of the alcohol–crime empirical association is sufficient to justify the inference that alcohol is sometimes causally implicated in the occurrence of serious crime. Questions of how alcohol exerts its criminogenic influence have not been satisfactorily answered. Explanatory aspects of the alcohol–crime relationship are discussed in the second section of this chapter.

Research on the alcohol–crime relationship involves complex methodological problems. Much past alcohol–crime research has fallen far short of an acceptable level of methodological rigor. In the third section of this chapter, methodological aspects of alcohol–crime research are discussed. In the final section there is a brief discussion of future research needs. These recommendations are both methodological and substantive.

Definitions and Parameters

Reference to an "alcohol–crime relationship" as used here means: the relationship between consumption of beverage alcohol and the occurrence of *serious* criminal behavior. Alcohol consumption is viewed as an independent variable and crime as the dependent variable even though the reverse causal order is a possibility. For example, it is possible that involvement in a criminal career would provide some impetus toward problem drinking. The emphasis on serious criminal behavior in the definition is meant to direct attention to serious personal and property crimes like homicide, assault, burglary, and larceny. The definition excludes less serious offenses like disorderly conduct and gambling; the definition also excludes alcohol-defined offenses like illegal sale of alcohol, public drunkenness, and driving while intoxicated. The issue being considered is: To what extent and in what way does alcohol consumption—directly, indirectly, or in combination with other factors—increase the likelihood of serious personal and property crime.

As consideration of the alcohol–crime relationship developed during the project, the focus on "serious personal and property crime" was further narrowed to an emphasis on *assaultive* crime. The emphasis on assaultive (personal) crime does not imply a judgment that alcohol is irrelevant to property offenses. As will be seen in the next section there is evidence that alcohol use is sometimes associated with property offenses. The emphasis on assaultive crime resulted from: (1) stronger evidence for an alcohol–assaultive crime relationship than for an alcohol–property crime relationship; (2) the likelihood that explanations of alcohol's causal relevance will differ for assaultive and property offenses. Point 2 implies the need for interpretations and research designs developed specifically for investigating either personal or property offense classes; these offense classes involve very different kinds of behavior. Assaultive crime will tend to be expressive behavior; property crime will typically involve instrumental behavior.

A Summary of the Empirical Evidence

The alcohol–crime literature tends to focus either on the offense event or on the incarcerated offender. The event-based literature, usually based on the use of police records, finds that alcohol is present in substantial percentages of the personal injury offenses of homicide, forcible rape, and aggravated assault.

The results of Wolfgang's (1958) research on 588 cases of homicide in Philadelphia for the years 1948–1952 are typical. Using police descriptions of the homicides, Wolfgang found that alcohol was present in either victim, offender, or both in 64% of the cases. In a similar study for homicides in Chicago, Voss and Hepburn (1968) found that alcohol was present in 53% of 370 cases. Amir (1967) found that alcohol was present in either offender, victim, or both in 34% of the 646 cases of rape he analyzed from Philadelphia for the years 1958–1960. In a study of rapes in Winnipeg between 1966 and 1975, Johnson, Gibson, and Linden (1978) found that either offender, victim, or both were drinking in 72% of cases. Rada (1975) collected data from 77 convicted rapists and found that 50% were drinking at the time of the offense. Mayfield (1976) interviewed 307 male inmates convicted of "assaultive" crimes and found that 58% were drinking at the time of the crime. In a study of assaults committed against police, Meyer, Magedanz, Kieselhorst, and Chapman (1978) report that 64% of the assailants were drinking or drunk. In a survey of California inmates, Peterson and Braiker (1980, p. 19) found 24% reported they "got drunk and hurt someone" in the 3 years prior to their current incarceration. Pernanen (1979a), in interviews of a general population of adults from a community in Canada, found that in 52% of reported violent incidents, someone was drinking. In a study of violent crime in Sweden, 68% of the offenders were found to have been drunk when committing their crime (Roslund & Larson, 1979).

Much less attention has been paid to the role of drinking in the offense of robbery and other acquisitive property offenses like burglary and larceny, although there is evidence that alcohol may be an important factor in some property crime. Data from a survey of more than 10,000 inmates in state correctional institutions, conducted by the U.S. Bureau of the Census (BOC) for the National Criminal Justice Information and Statistics Service (NCJISS), show that substantial percentages of individuals serving sentences for property offenses report they were drinking at the time of the offenses.[1] The percentages of inmates who report they were drinking at the time of the offenses for which they are currently incarcerated are as follows for selected property offenses: robbery, 39%, burglary, 47%, larceny, 38%; motor vehicle theft, 46%; forgery, 38%; and arson, 67% (Roizen & Schneberk, 1978, p. 370). In another study of 310 imprisoned male felons, property offenders frequently reported drinking at the time of their commitment offense, and a disproportionate percentage of those incarcerated property offenders were classified as heavy drinkers. Drinking at the time of their offense is reported by 35% of those incarcerated for property offenses; 55% of these offenders are heavy drinkers—this latter percentage is about double the national average for heavy drinking (Institute for Scientific Analysis, 1978, pp. 13, 56). The two inmate surveys referred to in this paragraph also confirm that alcohol and alcohol problems are frequently associated with personal injury offenses. Thus, there is no inconsistency between the inmate survey findings and those discussed earlier; these inmate surveys are notable because they address the alcohol–property crime issue and suggest that alcohol is a relevant factor.

In general, the research already referred to focuses on alcohol's role in behavior explicitly defined as criminal. There is also a body of research that focuses on alcohol's relationship to aggression. Typically, this research is of the experimental or quasi-experimental variety and examines the behavior of humans or animals in experimental conditions. Findings from this research are not conclusive but tend to show that, at least at some dosage levels, the ingestion of alcohol is associated with higher levels of aggression. There are disparate findings, and some results indicate that it is not alcohol consumption per se but type of beverage alcohol consumed or expectations about alcohol's effects that explain increased levels of aggression after drinking. Pernanen (1976, Chapter 1, this volume) and Blum (Chapter 3, this volume) have reviewed this research and it is not reviewed here.

Other research in the alcohol studies area is relevant to the alcohol–crime relationship. For example, examination of the relationship between problem drinking and personality characteristics may also be pertinent to the alcohol–crime relationship. Ultimately, findings from these separate

---

[1]Data analyzing the drinking aspects of this survey have not been published. Descriptive data have been published through the National Criminal Justice Information and Statistics Service (1979). NCJISS is now the Bureau of Justice Statistics (BJS).

literatures should be integrated with the literature that deals explicitly with alcohol use and criminal behavior. We do not attempt that integration here.

Explanation and the Alcohol-Crime Relationship

Asking and Answering the "How" Question

Asking the question *"How* does alcohol use cause crime?" amounts to an attempt at theoretical understanding. A major weakness of most past research on the alcohol-crime relationship has been its largely atheoretical nature or its failure to be explicit about underlying theoretical positions and assumptions. The relative absence of theory in research on the relationship of drinking and crime is partly a function of disciplinary boundaries and specialization. Understanding the behavioral effects of alcohol consumption involves the need to consider physiological, psychological, and sociological factors. Within each of these three substantive orientations, a variety of factors are relevant to the alcohol-crime relationship. In the physiological sphere, factors like the pharmacological effects of different dosage levels, the relationship of hormonal levels to dosage-level effects, and the influence of genetic makeup on the effects of alcohol are examples of questions of interest to alcohol-crime research. The relevance of stress, dependency, and personal power needs are a few of the variables related to alcohol use and crime that have been considered from the psychological point of view. In the sociological sphere, diverse factors such as subcultural or reference group drinking norms, drinking context influences, and the nature of the relationships between drinking event participants have been examined for their power to explain the alcohol-crime relationship. Complexity exists within and across disciplinary boundaries. Theoretical development has been inhibited by the scope of the explanatory problem and by the difficulties of interdisciplinary cooperation.

An Analytic Model

Figure 8.1 illustrates the substantive approaches and the levels of aggregation that may be appropriate foci for analyzing the relationship between alcohol use and crime. The substantive approaches are arranged along a continuum signifying the level of aggregation at which each of the disciplinary orientations typically focuses. The substantive-aggregative foci suggested in the figure are not mutually exclusive. Any given research may involve the use of multiple perspectives and collection and analysis of data at more than one level of aggregation. For example, research whose major perspective is sociocultural might include psychological variables; studies on the influence of cultural attitudes on drinking behavior and violence might also attempt to understand how individual psychological makeup interacts with the cultural influence.

It is our judgment that the alcohol–crime relationship is best understood by complex theoretical models from a multidisciplinary perspective even though there is some evidence that suggests such complexity is not always appropriate. The ingestion of alcohol occasionally appears to be a simple, direct cause of violence. The term "pathological intoxication" describes such a reaction; this term has been used to refer to the occurrence of explosive outbursts of violence after and as a result of drinking (Bach-y-Rita, Lion, & Ervin, 1970; Mark & Ervin, 1970, p. 126; Skelton, 1970). However, in spite of the appearance that alcohol's role in violence may sometimes seem to be manifested in a simple, direct manner, the limited available research suggests that factors other than alcohol are also important. Temporal lobe abnormality measured by the electroencephalogram (EEG) and personality traits are two factors that appear to be related to alcohol-induced explosive violence as described by the pathological intoxication syndrome. Thus, even in the case of pathological intoxication, the need for complex explanatory models of the alcohol–crime relationship is confirmed.

FIGURE 8.1. Substantive–aggregative foci for analyzing the alcohol–crime relationship.

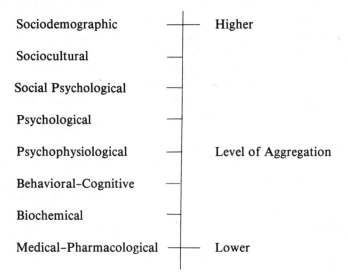

Sociodemographic	—	Higher
Sociocultural	—	
Social Psychological	—	
Psychological	—	
Psychophysiological	—	Level of Aggregation
Behavioral–Cognitive	—	
Biochemical	—	
Medical–Pharmacological	—	Lower

Even though we argue that multidisciplinary theoretical explanations are required to answer the "how" question, we recognize that such comprehensive understanding is difficult to develop. It is unusual to find individuals capable of integrative conceptualization across multiple substantive perspectives. Furthermore, the substantively based structure of the scientific enterprise itself reinforces the tendency to focus attention on narrow substantive ranges. The range of our substantive focus here is also limited. The focus is on social and psychological explanation, that is, on the substantive–aggregative foci in the upper half of Figure 8.1.

Multidisciplinary Theories

There are attempts to systematically organize explanations across the entire range suggested by the figure. Prescott (1980) has summarized a theory of drug and alcohol use that includes cultural, psychological, and biological factors. The somatosensory affectional deprivation (SAD) theory developed by Prescott is founded on a variety of evidence. According to this theory, "the neurobiology of our behavior is not only inseparable from, but is in fact largely shaped by, culture" (Prescott, 1980, p. 286). The shaping of behavior takes place as a result of the sensory and perceptual capacities and characteristics that result from early experiences which are structured by the social, physical, and cultural environment. A need for "neural activation" in humans which is not satisfied by sensory stimulation may be met by the pharmacological stimulation produced by drugs and alcohol.

Prescott claims support for his theory in a variety of findings. One set of findings with relevance for our purposes is the evidence cited from an analysis of violence in 49 primitive cultures. High and low physical violence was successfully predicted in the 49 cultures on the basis of the degree of physical affection toward infants by mothers or caretakers. Prescott claims that deprivation of nurturance and affection causes the occurrence of compensatory behavior to reduce psychological tension. Two of these compensating behaviors are violence toward self and others, and alcoholism and drug abuse.

The level of generality of Prescott's theory, and others of a similar range, make it heuristically inappropriate to our goal of developing a research agenda in the alcohol–crime area. Theories of the "middle range" are most useful for the guidance of empirical research. Such theories involve abstractions but they are close enough to observed data to allow the derivation of propositions for empirical testing (Merton, 1968, p. 39).

The emphasis on social and psychological explanations in this report does not mean that other orientations do not have explanatory power.

Physiological, biological, and pharmacological perspectives have important contributions to make toward understanding how drinking contributes to the occurrence of criminal behavior. Pernanen (1976, Chapter 1, this volume) discusses a number of ways that alcohol may contribute to assaultive behavior through physiological processes. He reviews literatures suggesting that alcohol consumption, especially if it continues over a period of many hours or days, may interfere with REM-sleep patterns or may contribute to nutritional deficiencies. There is evidence that REM-sleep deprivation and the nutritional problem of hypoglecemia may be related to assaultive behavior.

There is also a variety of evidence indicating that there are systematic differences in the physiological effects of alcohol on the basis of age, gender, and race or ethnicity. Although such systematic differences do not necessarily imply that physiologically based explanations are appropriate, there is some evidence that such explanations are valid. Fenna, Mix, Schaefer, and Gilbert (1976) found that Native Indians and Eskimos metabolize ethanol at lower rates than do whites. The authors speculate that physiological changes which have occurred over a long period as a result of dietary habits explain the differences. Goodwin (1980) has interpreted the systematic differences in the human response to alcohol as arising from the interaction of genetic and experiential factors. As we suggest later, age, gender, and race/ethnicity may be variables whose explanatory power comes mainly from their sociocultural roots rather than from their physiological foundations. However, our position in this regard is a judgment; alcohol use may sometimes be causally related to criminal behavior directly, through physiological or genetic influences.

The perspectives listed in the lower portion of Figure 8.1 are not given emphasis in the research agenda of this report because they do not, in a wholistic sense, have a capacity to explain the alcohol–crime relationship. Crime itself is a complex social phenomenon; its definition, both formally and in practice, is a product of the social process. The scientific understanding of the alcohol–crime relationship needs to incorporate social complexity. The search for understanding of the alcohol–crime relationship that is emphasized here embodies a search for explanatory power in the social, cultural, and psychological areas.

Theoretical Models

In two reviews of the theoretical aspects of the relationship between alcohol use and violence, Pernanen (1976, Chapter 1, this volume) proposes a number of explanatory models that may be appropriate for understanding the empirical correlations found between alcohol consumption and crimes of violence. The association of alcohol and violence may be a result of the *direct* effects of alcohol. The association may be explained by a *common-cause* relationship; that is, both alcohol consumption or alcoholism and violence may be caused by the same factor or factors. Prescott's (1980) interpretation of violence in 49 primitive cultures, referred to earlier in this chapter, is an example of a common-cause explanation. Under his SAD theory both alcoholism and violence are caused by early affectional deprivation. The alcohol–violence relationship may be explained by *interactive, conditional,* or *conjunctive* explanatory models. In such explanations, violence results from the consumption of alcohol in some situations, circumstances, or conditions. The condition of alcoholism in an individual, the nature of an individual's socialization experience, and drinking context characteristics are examples of factors that might be included in interactive, conditional, or conjunctive explanatory models. A fourth explanatory model proposed by Pernanen is called the *spuriousness* model. In this model, the association of alcohol and violence is simply associational in the statistical sense, not causal; an example would be the presence of a disproportionate number of alcoholics in prison populations, not because alcoholics commit more crimes but because they are more likely to be arrested and incarcerated when they do commit crimes.

Sociodemographics

The sociodemographic level of analysis for the alcohol–crime relationship attempts to describe and account for systematic variation that occurs on the basis of characteristics that are fundamental bases for human organization. Three of these fundamental organizing (sociodemographic) variables are age, gender, and race/ethnicity. The sociodemographic descriptors themselves are not explanatory independent variables. Theoretical explanation must rely on variables that characterize underlying aspects of the sociodemographics. Age, for example, does not have explanatory power by itself; it is other factors, like the human developmental process or age-graded aspects of social norms, that may have the power to explain the alcohol–crime relationship theoretically. For this reason sociodemographic understanding of the alcohol–crime relationship must be supported by substantively based theoretical conceptions, although observed sociodemographic regularities are useful for directing attention to covariation in need of explanation. Thus the discussion of sociodemographic aspects of the alcohol–crime relationship which follows is supported by explanation based on social and psychological variables.

Age, Alcohol, and Crime

Alcohol consumption and problem-drinking patterns as well as official crime rates differ on the basis of age, gender, and race/ethnicity. Young adult males in the 18–25 or 18–30 age span are especially notable in this regard. In survey data, young adult males have been found to have disproportionately high heavy- and problem-drinking rates (Blane & Hewitt, 1977; Cahalan & Cisin, 1976b; Cahalan & Room, 1974; Mandell & Ginzburg, 1976). It is also clear from official U.S. crime data that young adult males are responsible for a large disproportion of serious crime (Federal Bureau of Investigation, 1978, 1979). A more extensive review of the literature on the relationship between age, drinking, and crime is found in Chapter 5 of this volume. (by Collins)

Very little research has focused on the combined three-factor relationship of age, alcohol use, and criminal behavior. Pittman and Gordon (1958) examined the criminal-career patterns of 186 offenders incarcerated for public intoxication. They found a "biphasic" pattern; serious offenses tended to occur during the younger years; offenses occurring after age 35 or 40 tended to be less serious offenses like public drunkenness. However, it is not clear that this sample of offenders with current alcohol problems also had alcohol problems earlier in their careers when their criminal involvement tended to be more serious.

Peterson and Braiker (1980), in a survey of 624 California prison inmates, found that younger men were more likely to report they "got drunk and hurt someone" than were older men. Thirty-one percent of those under age 25 reported at least one such occurrence in the 3 years prior to the current incarceration; only 22% of those over age 25 reported any such occurrence (unpublished data provided by Mark Peterson of the Rand Corporation).

It is clear that young adult males are disproportionately involved in heavy and problem drinking. It is not clear that the problem drinking is a causal factor in the occurrence of the criminal behavior. The notion of hypermasculinity has been proposed to explain both heavy or problem drinking and criminal behavior—a common-cause explanation in Pernanen's terms (McCord & McCord, 1962; Zucker, 1968). "Macho" behavior frequently includes tendencies toward both heavy drinking and aggression, and seems accurately descriptive of a psychological orientation of many young adult males. In the research of McCord and McCord (1962), the overemphasis on masculinity in the personalities of alcoholics in their sample is a facade. Extreme masculinity was interpreted by the McCords as a mask to cover dependent and passive inclinations.

The notion of personalized power need as conceived by McClelland (1975) and McClelland, Davis, Kalin, and Wanner (1972) to help explain drinking behavior may also be relevant to the alcohol–assault relationship among some young men. According to McClelland's view, men drink in part because alcohol enhances one's sense of personalized power, defined as the power to win personal victories over threatening adversaries (McClelland & Davis, 1972). If this is true, aggressive behavior after drinking may be related to the drinking–power interface.

The source of hypermasculine behavior may also be interpreted from another perspective. During transitional periods of the life cycle, like the transition from adolescence to young adulthood, individuals exhibit an increased tendency toward problem behaviors. This tendency has been noted by Winick (1980) and others. Jessor and Jessor (1977) have developed a comprehensive social psychological theory of problem behavior that pays a great deal of attention to the life-cycle transitions and the problem behavior that often accompanies these transitions. The increased tendency toward problem behavior during life-cycle transitions is not surprising; such transitions are likely to be accompanied by pressures and strains associated with altered social role expectations. The compulsive masculinity observed among young adult males may be a response to these pressures. Whatever the interpretation of the source of hypermasculinity, it appears to have a relationship to deviant behavior for young adult males and may be a fruitful theoretical focus for understanding the relationship between drinking and crime during this segment of the life cycle.

Investigation of moral development also provides a conceptual framework that may be helpful for interpreting the disproportionate involvement of young adult males in problem drinking and crime. Moral development has to do with the assimilation and observation of social norms. Traditionally, moral development has been viewed as complete by late adolescence. Piaget (1932/1948) called the final cognitive development stage "formal operations," and this stage was expected to be complete by age 15. If Piaget's stage theory is accurate, then the high rates of deviance and crime that characterize late adolescence and early adulthood are anomalous. One would expect deviance rates to be higher prior to completed moral development, not afterward. But there is some evidence that moral development may not be completed until young adulthood. Kohlberg (1973) has argued that, contrary to the Piaget conception, there are adult stages of moral development. Further, according to Kohlberg, during the young adult years there is a retrogression, or slippage, of moral development during the transition to principled adult morality. If such a slippage does occur, it coincides with the age span where deviance rates are high, and the slippage may have some capacity to explain the deviant behavior. The investigation of adult moral development may help define the determinants of young adult criminal behavior and describe whether alcohol use is a factor in this behavior. On the surface it seems reasonable to view deviant drinking and criminal behavior as common outcomes of a complex developmental process, perhaps as transitional problem behaviors in the Jessors' terms.

Some evidence from prison inmate surveys suggests that alcohol is more likely to be present at the time of offenses committed by older rather than younger offenders. The 1974 survey of 10,000 state prison inmates showed that older offenders were more likely than younger offenders to report they were drinking at the time of the offenses for which they were incarcerated (unpublished data; see National Criminal Justice Information and Statistics Service, 1979, for a description of this survey and for demographic profiles of the sample). These reports are difficult to interpret causally; the simple presence of alcohol does not indicate that it had any effect on the commission of the offense. Furthermore, prison populations are not representative of offenders generally, and it may be, for example, that older incarcerated offenders are more likely to be drinkers than younger incarcerated offenders. On the other hand, it may be that alcohol is more likely to be causally relevant to the offenses of older offenders as the inmate survey data suggest. The evidence from this inmate survey implies that alcohol use may be important to the criminal behavior of older offenders, and this would appear to contradict our later recommendation that the young adult male should be a focus of future alcohol–crime research. That is not the case. The volume of serious crime is much greater among younger than older ages, and the magnitude of the problem itself justifies special attention. However, it may be that older incarcerated offenders are notable for alcohol-involved crime, or the alcohol–crime relationship may be curvilinear according to age. Such potential complexities can only be understood by additional research.

Gender, Alcohol, and Crime

Females have lower alcohol consumption and problem-drinking rates than males. Females are also relatively unlikely to engage in assaultive crime; official data for the United States indicate that more than eight of every ten arrests are of males. Furthermore, with one possible exception, there do not appear to be conceptual or empirical reasons for paying special attention to the relationship between drinking and serious crime among females. The exception may be the drinking–crime relationship among Black women. Black women who do drink tend to be heavy drinkers, so it may be fruitful to examine the alcohol–crime relationship among Black women. However, we would argue that it is likely to be ethnic characteristics, not gender characteristics, that are most relevant in this regard. Ethnicity as a factor in the alcohol–crime relationship is discussed in the next section. Given our interest in developing a future research agenda, we find no evidence to support a focus on females. The victimization aspects of alcohol's relationship to criminal behavior are another issue. Alcohol appears to contribute to the likelihood of being victimized and may be particularly relevant in the cases of forcible rape and domestic violence, offenses where women are usually the victims. The victimogenic aspects of drinking are discussed later.

Ethnicity, Alcohol, and Crime

There are racial/ethnic regularities in alcohol-use and crime patterns. For example, research in the United States indicates that reported alcohol use at the time of an offense differs for Whites and Blacks. Although the evidence is not fully consistent, alcohol use appears to be more often present during offenses committed by White offenders (Roizen, Chapter 6, this volume). As in the case of gender, we are inclined to interpret observed empirical regularities on the basis of race from a cultural perspective. Recent support for this interpretation is provided by O'Connor (1978). In research that compared the effects of various influences on the drinking patterns of English, Irish, and Anglo-Saxon youth, O'Connor found that ethnic/cultural factors were influential in the explanation of alcohol-use patterns.

Pernanen (1979b, pp. 10–16) and Collins *et al.* (1980, pp. 31–34) have summarized the limited evidence that suggests there is systematic cultural variation in the alcohol–crime relationship. Research in the United States, Canada, Finland, Sweden, Great Britain, and other countries confirms an association between drinking and crime. Methodological inadequacies and the lack of comparability of measures and sampling make it difficult to compare findings for different countries, and the strength of the alcohol–crime association appears to vary by country. This is not surprising; ethnographic research indicates that drinking norms and drinking behavior are specific to cultural context, and such findings support the position that the alcohol–crime relationship will vary by culture. Overall, two inferences are supported: The existence of an alcohol–crime association is generally characteristic of most modern Western societies, and the strength of this association is variable by culture.

The Sociocultural Perspective

It is clear from the literature that cultural factors influence the relationship between drinking and crime; the behavioral effects of alcohol use are shaped by cultural norms. Attitudes toward drinking and rules that govern behavior after drinking are variable across cultures, within the same culture at different times and within particular subcultural components. Blum (Chapter 3, this volume) has discussed a study of Cinquemani (1975) which compares two Central Mexican Indian tribes. Both tribes drink heavily, but only one engages in violent behavior when drinking. Cinquemani attributes this difference to the cultural norms that govern drinking behavior, including the accountability under tribal rules of individuals for their behavior after drinking.

The anthropological research of MacAndrew and Edgerton (1969) also confirms the importance of cultural norms to the behavior that follows drinking. Behavioral standards are sometimes relaxed during what MacAndrew and Edgerton (1969) have called "time-out" periods. Time-out periods are frequently characterized by drinking; Mardi Gras, just before the Lenten season, is a well-known example of a time-out period. Individuals are not expected to follow the same rules that apply during normal times, and time-out periods are culturally specific.

Furthermore, in their examination of the rules that govern "drunken comportment" in several cultures, MacAndrew and Edgerton (1969) pointed out that the notion of disinhibition is theoretically deficient as an explanation of how alcohol causes deviant behavior. Until recent years the disinhibition perspective, explicitly or implicitly, was used as the conceptual foundation for characterizing how drinking caused criminal and deviant behavior. The drug alcohol was assumed to have a pharmacological effect on the human organism that caused the release of baser instincts or the suppression of higher intellectual function; aggression or other problematical behavior was thought to result from this release or loosening. This explanatory perspective has intuitive appeal. Drinking is frequently found to be associated with such activities as revelry, fighting, and reduced control of sexual appetite. Human behavior after drinking often appears to be "disinhibited." While it is often true that different norms apply to behavior after drinking than to behavior when not drinking, MacAndrew and Edgerton showed that drunken-comportment norms exist and that the norms are usually observed. Thus, the disinhibition concept, at least as it refers to the pharmacological power of alcohol to nullify normative mandates, does not appear to be an accurate characterization of the behavioral effects of drinking.

Normative Ambivalence and Ambiguity

Ahlström-Laakso (1976) has discussed the varied characteristics of drinking habits in several European countries. He noted how the social control of behavior after drinking differs between countries. The Irish and Finns, for example, display a recklessness after drinking that is not characteristic of other nationalities and is not explainable on the basis of amount of alcohol consumed. Ahlström-Laakso suggests that the release of aggression through drinking is explained by a cultural ambivalence toward the use of alcohol and an absence of culturally specific informal norms of control over drunken behavior. Countries which have higher rates of alcohol-related aggressive behavior rely on formal legislated mechanisms of control made necessary because of the absence of informal controls.

It is difficult to make explicit connections between norms governing alcohol use and criminal behavior. Heath (1976) has discussed the universality of norms governing alcoholic beverages and noted the difficulty of extrapolating specific aspects of the normative content:

> Alcohol is almost universally subject to rules and regulations like those that pertain to other drinks. Not only are there usually special rules about alcoholic beverages, but the rules tend to have a peculiarly emotional charge. This affective quality relates not only to drinking, but also to drunkenness and drunken comportment. Whether predominant feelings about these are positive, negative, or ambivalent varies from culture to culture, but indifference is rare, and feelings are usually much stronger in connection with alcohol than with respect to other things.
>
> Although feelings run high, and rules are almost universal, there is little consistency—and even considerable contradiction—among human populations with respect to what feelings and rules are appropriate with respect to drinking, drunkenness, drunken behavior, or even the drunken individual. (p. 43)

It is likely that normative expectations and accountability standards are related to drinking behavior in complex ways. The mandates of the rules themselves undoubtedly channel behavior. Less directly, expectations about alcohol's behavioral effects (independent of pharmacological/physiological effects) and the application of standards of accountability to behavior while drinking are also likely to influence behavior while drinking. Lang, Goeckner, Adesso, and Marlatt (1975) showed how the behavior of individuals who believe they have consumed alcohol becomes more aggressive even though they have received a placebo. Similarly, it has been suggested that relaxed standards of accountability that are sometimes applied to the behavior of individuals who have been drinking have a synergistic effect on behavior. Coleman and Straus (1979) have suggested that husbands who are inclined to beat their spouses sometimes drink alcohol so that they will have an excuse to beat their wives. McCaghy (1968) has shown how convicted sex offenders sometimes use drinking as a basis for disavowing responsibility for deviant sexual activity. A contemporary example of the deviance disavowal phenomenon is the attempt of political figures accused in 1980 to blame alcohol for their behavior. Abscam-uncovered corruption and other illegal or scandalous behavior on the part of U.S. congressmen has been attributed to alcohol use.

The use of alcohol to deny or deflect individual responsibility for behavior can also be interpreted from a more general social psychological perspective. The tendency to use rationalization as a mechanism to facilitate deviant behavior in advance has been discussed by Sykes and Matza (1962). These authors developed the notion of "techniques of neutralization" to describe a number of ways that individuals justify their deviant behavior. One technique of neutralization is the "denial of responsibility." In the case of alcohol, this denial entails blaming the effects of alcohol for untoward behavior. Scott and Lyman (1968) have also discussed the human tendency to use excuses or justifications (i.e., "accounts") to avoid the imputation of a deviant identity. An individual might admit that some behavior was wrong but excuse the behavior because it took place after drinking. Alcohol consumption fits well into the socially based human inclination to act as one wishes without accepting negative normative evaluations of such actions.

In summary, sociocultural interpretations have the power to account for some variation in the alcohol–crime relationship. The explanatory power is difficult to specify theoretically or to measure precisely. Norms differ across cultures and subcultures; ambivalence, contradiction, and rationalization characterize the norms. Normative changes that accompany alcohol use sometimes permit or encourage criminal behavior on the part of the drinkier. Such normative effects are direct. Normative influences may also be indirect or synergistic. The attribution of blame to alcohol in any ex post facto manner is an example of the indirect criminogenic influence of alcohol.

The Social Psychological Perspective

Social psychological explanations of the relationship between drinking and crime attempt to integrate some of the complexity that characterizes this relationship. There are a large number of such theories and theory fragments, many not meant to deal simply with the alcohol–crime relationship. Jessor and Jessor (1975, 1977), as inidcated earlier in this chapter, have developed a "problem behavior" theory which is meant to be a comprehensive conceptual scheme for explanation for a variety of adolescent or youthful problem behaviors: drinking, problem drinking, drug use, theft, and aggression. The variables of the problem behavior theory of the Jessors are conceptually organized into: (1) antecedent and background categories like family demographic characteristics and early socialization experience; (2) personality system variables like achievement values, internal–external locus of control, and tolerance of deviance; and (3) social behavior variables like problem drinking and general deviance. While this theory does not make explicit the causal relationship of drinking and crime, it is a valuable guide for systematic conceptual and empirical organization of the issues–especially for the adolescent and young adult years. Jessor and Jessor have found that "the development of drinking is positively associated with an increase in general deviant behavior" (1975, p. 43).

Pernanen (1976, Chapter 1, this volume) has developed a social psychological explanation of alcohol's effect on violent behavior. Pernanen points to the disorganizing effect of alcohol on cognitive function. Drinking reduces one's capacity to perceive, integrate, and coherently process communication cues:

> . . . the model posits a decrease in the perceived number of behavior cues, a narrowing of the perceptual field. The reduction of cues leads to a more random determination of behavior by the situational (environmental and internal) cues present. Intraindividually, this leads to a greater likelihood of affective fluctuations in behavior (and disoriented behavior on the instrumental level). . . . the smaller number of cues determining behavior . . . leads to a greater likelihood of discrepant structurings of the situation and a consequent cognition of the other person's behavior as arbitrary. Perceived arbitrariness of behavior in turn has been shown to lead to aggressive reactions (S. Epstein & Taylor, 1967). (Chapter 1, this volume, p. 28)

There is evidence that abstracting ability and the capacity to use a range of coping devices are reduced by the physiological effects of alcohol on individuals. Pernanen provides a theoretical model to illustrate how alcohol use, through its perceptual and conceptual effects, can increase the probability of interpersonal violence.

The social psychological perspective, especially if the focus is on aspects of interpersonal interactions that may lead to violence, is appropriate for analyzing the victimogenic effects of alcohol use. Empirical evidence suggests that drinking increases the likelihood that one will be victimized or injured more seriously during a victimization. In his work on homicide in Philadelphia, Wolfgang (1958) examined the victim precipitation aspects of this offense and found that victims who contributed to their own victimization were more likely to have been drinking than were victims who did not. Voss and Hepburn (1968) found similar results in Chicago. The research of Leppa (1974) on robbery in Helsinki indicates that the majority of victims were intoxicated at the time they were robbed. When attempts at causal understanding focus on the offense event or the process of violent interaction, alcohol use is one of the factors which appears to have explanatory potential. However, that explanatory capacity might be manifested in the drinking behavior of the victim rather than in the effects of alcohol on the offender.

Roebuck and Johnson (1962) have suggested that there is an identifiable offender type for whom a relationship between drinking and assaultive crime exists that is explainable on the basis of socialization experience. Roebuck and Johnson identified 40 Black offenders (about 10% of their sample) who had arrest histories with a pattern of drunken assaults. This group of offenders had similar backgrounds; they were reared under strong fundamentalist religious demands that emphasize strict control of behavior. Roebuck and Johnson suggested that such individuals are unable to express hostility except after drinking, and that when this expression is facilitated by drinking it tends to be assaultive.

The examples of social psychological explanations included in this section are only a few of those that have potential to explain the alcohol use–criminal behavior relationship. The "hypermasculinity" and "personal power" explanations discussed in an earlier section are social psychological theories and might have been included in this section. Likewise, other theories and theory fragments not discussed here can shed light on the alcohol–crime relationship. The discussion here is meant to suggest several ways that alcohol use might fit a social psychological causal scheme to explain alcohol's effect on criminal behavior.

Given the usual complexity of the relationship between drinking and crime, and given the likely relevance of both psychological and social-level variables to this relationship, social psychological interpretations are appropriate explanatory schemes. In the next section, psychological explanations for the drinking–crime relationship are discussed. The distinction between social psychological explanations and psychological explanations is partly a matter of interpretation; social and psychological factors are not independent of each other. Thus, the discussion of psychological explanations of the drinking–crime relationship in the next section includes factors that are not clearly and simply psychological.

Psychological Perspectives

Past work has shown that individual characteristics influence alcohol's effects on individuals. It is not clear whether these individual differences are physiologically or psychologically based, or to what extent social and cultural factors determine the individually manifested variation. Goodwin (1980), for example, noted how physiological responses to alcohol differ by race, gender, and age, and suggested that genetic and experiential factors interact to shape the effects of alcohol in individuals.

A number of researchers have noted that the condition of alcoholism is associated with responses to the ingestion of alcohol that differ from the responses of nonalcoholics. In a review of the literature on alcohol's effect on the mood of alcoholics, van der Spuy (1972) noted that alcohol's effects on the mood of alcoholics are not as beneficial as these effects in nonalcoholics. In the light of the known empirical association between the chronic excessive alcohol user and crimes of violence (Pernanen, 1976, pp. 422–423; Tinklenberg, 1973, p. 204), the finding that the acute effects of alcohol differ for alcoholics and nonalcoholics suggests the need to establish the basis of the differential effects.

Much of the discussion of alcohol use and its relationship to problematic individual behavior has centered on the issue of the "alcoholic personality." A major debate has been whether or not the psychological attributes typically manifested in individuals defined as alcoholic existed prior to the development of alcoholism. In a recent review of the literature on the alcoholic personality, Barnes (1979, p. 623) has suggested that "an alcoholic personality concept should be broken down into two concepts—the clinical alcoholic personality and the prealcoholic personality." Alcoholics who come to treatment display a common personality pattern, but that pattern is one that has been shaped by the person's drinking history. There do appear to be prealcoholic personality characteristics, but these are not a clearly definable set of features. Those who later become alcoholics tend to be impulsive, gregarious, nonconforming, aggressive, and hostile (Barnes, 1979, pp. 580, 602; Williams, 1976, pp. 250–251). However, it is not clear whether and how these personality features lead to the development of alcoholism and criminal behavior.

Williams (1976) argues that there are two major theories of the alcoholic personality: dependency theory and power theory. McCord and McCord (1962) have been the primary early spokespersons for dependency theory. The hypermasculinity explanation discussed in the previous section of this chapter has roots in dependency theory. "According to the dependency theory, the picture of heightened masculinity including aggression, antisocial behavior and the like seen in prealcoholics is a reaction formation against underlying dependency needs" (Williams, 1976, p. 256). The McCords argue that strong dependency needs characterize alcoholics and that these needs were latent in the prealcoholic personality. The dependency needs were covered up by the apparent self-confidence and assertiveness displayed by the prealcoholic personality. Williams (1976) prefers the power theory explanation of alcoholism because men who have a strong need for personalized power tend to drink excessively and because "the known facts appear to fit the power theory better than they do the dependency theory'' (p. 263).

A number of researchers have also found a relationship between the psychopathic or sociopathic personality and alcoholism. This observed empirical association also amounts to an alcoholism–crime association because psychopathy or sociopathy is partially defined on the basis of repetitive antisocial behavior. In a retrospective longitudinal study of the sociopathic personality, Robins (1966) studied a group of individuals who had been referred to a child guidance clinic as children and compared them to a control group. Seventy-two percent of the sociopaths used alcohol to excess as adults; only 27% of the control group used alcohol excessively. The sociopaths also displayed a variety of other problem behaviors to a disproportionate extent. Seventy five percent of the sociopaths had multiple arrests, compared to 18% of the controls. Fifty-eight percent of the sociopaths were classified as belligerent, compared to 18% of the controls (Robins, 1966, p. 295). Barnes (1979, p. 574) also noted that a number of reports indicate that alcoholics tend to score high on the psychopathic deviate (Pd) scale of the Minnesota Multiphasic Personality Inventory (MMPI).

The relationship between alcoholism, personality, alcohol use, and criminal behavior is difficult to elaborate. Two major problems are: (1) the predominance of individuals who are in treatment in research populations, and (2) the interactive relationships between variables that confound interpretation of findings. It is difficult to know how representative treatment populations are; and attempts to separate the independent effects of alcohol use, changes that have resulted from chronic alcohol use, and personality characteristics present complex analytic problems. It does seem clear that problem drinking and other forms of deviant behavior are associated with certain personality characteristics like hostility and aggression. Further theoretical development is required to describe how these factors are related to each other in a causal sense.

Summary: Social, Cultural, and Psychological Theories

The review of theoretical orientations that have some potential to explain the alcohol–crime relationship is not meant to be complete or comprehensive but suggests those explanatory approaches that have the most empirical support or that offer the best potential for middle-range theoretical development. As indicated earlier, physiological, pharmacological, and medical approaches to the issues have not been emphasized even though such explanations undoubtedly have a contribution to make to the understanding of the alcohol–crime relationship.

Need for a Phenomenological Perspective

Understanding the alcohol–crime relationship theoretically will require a perspective that is sensitive to the phenomenological aspects of the relationship. Human behavior cannot be understood simply in objective terms; behavior is shaped by subjective and objective reality. The processing of stimuli is a dynamic activity that is influenced by the present state and past experience of the stimulus processor. "Perceptions are seen as more than passive receptions of stimuli. They entail cognitive, expressive, and evaluative dimensions" (Singelmann, 1972, p. 416). Social interaction between individuals must also be described as simultaneously meaningful in objective and subjective terms (Singlemann, 1972, p. 423). This phenomenological view of human behavior and social interaction has important implications for research on the relationship between alcohol use and crime.

Measurement of the effects drinking has on individuals is a fundamental variable in the assessment of the alcohol–crime relationship. If one acknowledges, as the phenomenological view suggests, that alcohol's effects include subjective and interpretive aspects, the methodological posture of research is affected. It becomes necessary to include, measure, and integrate both these aspects of social reality in empirical research and theoretical explanation. Past research has confirmed the importance of subjectivity in the behavioral effects of drinking. Earlier we referred to the work of Lang *et al.* (1975), who showed that subjects in an experiment became more aggressive when they were told they received alcohol, regardless of whether the subjects were actually given any alcohol. Apparently beliefs about alcohol's effects have an independent influence on behavior.

The interpretive–cognitive effects of alcohol use are even more relevant to the understanding of interactions between two or more individuals. Inter- and intraindividual subjectivity are both factors. Understanding the effects of alcohol on social interaction will require a capacity to understand subjective aspects of such interactions. Perspectives that focus on factors like the communications process and the situational context of social interaction will have a capacity to improve systematic understanding of how drinking contributes to the occurrence of violent encounters between individuals. Pernanen's work (Chapter 1, this volume) is an example of an interactional perspective which is phenomenologically sensitive.

Social and cultural variables must also be interpreted in a phenomenological sense in the development of theoretical understanding. Alcohol use and its behavioral implications are shaped by rules and interpretations which are rooted in the normative structures of human societies. The MacAndrew and Edgerton (1969) research on drunken comportment in a number of primitive societies, referred to earlier, provides a good example of a phenomenologically sensitive cultural interpretation of behavior after drinking.

The Malevolence Assumption

An additional complicating factor in the theoretical understanding of the alcohol–crime relationship arises from a tendency to view alcohol as a degenerative moral influence. The tendency to ascribe blame to alcohol in an assumptive manner appears to be a general inclination of some societies. The Prohibition Amendment to the U.S. Constitution is a dramatic example. The orientation of the social science literature in this regard is also notable. That literature has tended to ascribe a pejorative influence to alcohol whenever it is present in undesirable events or circumstances. Elsewhere we have referred to this inclination as the "malevolence assumption" (Hamilton & Collins, Chapter 7, this volume). While it is clearly established scientifically that alcohol consumption can have undesirable effects on individual and collective life, it is also apparent that alcohol has been blamed for problems in the absence of sufficient justification. There is a tendency, for example, to assume that the alcoholism of an inmate has caused the inmate status or that the mere presence of alcohol in an assaultive encounter was responsible for the assault.

The individual and general tendencies to blame alcohol are an additional reason why future research should be clear about conceptual matters. If conceptual positions are explicit and precise, inferences are more likely to be made on scientific rather than on value grounds. In sum, a phenomenological view of human behavior and social interaction needs to be incorporated into the design of research on the alcohol–crime relationship. Perception, social interaction, and cultural interpretation are dynamic processes that require understanding of both the objective and the subjective components of reality.

Methodological Issues

Measuring the Drinking Variable

The measurement of the alcohol consumption variable in research on the relationship between drinking and crime has been seriously flawed (Greenberg, Chapter 2, this volume; Roizen & Schneberk, 1978). This deficiency in the literature, by itself, is sufficient to neutralize the inferential capacity of most research findings. In research on the criminal event, alcohol use is typically measured in a "present" or "not present" manner. Information on the amount of drinking by event participants is rare. In past research, where the alcohol problems of individuals constitute the measure of alcohol as an independent variable, terms like "problem drinker" or "alcoholic" tend to be used in a descriptive way. The basis for these classifications is frequently not made explicit.

Ideally, when the acute effects of alcohol constitute the variable of interest, dosage would be experimentally controlled or blood alcohol content (BAC) would be measured through blood, breath, or urine analysis. Unfortunately, only limited aspects of the drinking–crime relationship are researchable in experimental settings, and research using actual offense events or offenders usually takes place a considerable length of time after the criminal event. Thus BAC will not typically be available as the measure of the drinking variable. There are exceptions in past research. Shupe (1954) examined the urine alcohol concentration of 882 persons arrested for felonies in Columbus, Ohio, between 1951 and 1953. Tinklenberg (1973) used Shupe's data to show how higher levels of alcohol consumption were more likely to be linked to violent crime than lower levels, suggesting a curvilinear relationship between dosage and violent crime. Individuals who were arrested for violent crimes tended to have alcohol levels between .10% and .39%. Smaller percentages of these arrested individuals had no alcohol in their urine or less than .1% alcohol. Further, individuals with .4% or more alcohol in their urine were only a small percentage of these arrestees. Tinklenberg interpreted this to indicate that individuals who have very high alcohol levels may be too incapacitated to be physically aggressive.

Further research on the alcohol–crime relationship needs to measure the alcohol variable in detail. Measurement of drinking, minimally, should include type and amount of beverage consumed and, preferably, should include other information such as time spent drinking, food consumed before and during drinking, body weight, drinking history, and other drugs consumed.

Drinking Probability Estimates

Inferences about the alcohol–crime relationship are also limited by the absence of data on the probabilities of drinking for subpopulations and situations. Associational data for drinking and crime are difficult to interpret causally in the absence of baseline estimates of the likelihood that drinking or drunkenness will occur at all. For example, what is the probability that males (females, non-Whites, lower SES, etc.) will drink in the evening (on weekends, etc.)? What is the probability that an individual will drink to intoxication if he/she drinks at all? What is the probability that drunkenness will follow drinking at home versus drinking in a tavern?

There already exist some data that permit baseline estimates of aspects of drinking. There are good estimates of the proportion of the population that drinks (including such estimates for subpopulations like males, non-Whites, etc.). There is also good information about some consequences of drinking and about what proportion of the population is likely to have drinking problems. But more of these kinds of data are needed so that interpretation of research findings are facilitated. To use a simple example, the finding that 25% of an offender population has a drinking problem is difficult to interpret in the absence of valid estimates of what proportion of a sociodemographically similar nonoffender population has a drinking problem.

The collection of drinking data in a way that allows computation of conditional probability estimates requires considerable effort but is worth the investment. Such data provide a capacity for hypothesis testing and inference that is not characteristic of less detailed data. The finding of an empirical association between drinking or drunkenness and crime is difficult to interpret in the absence of an estimate of how likely given types of behavioral configurations (spousal interactions, competition between peers, parties, etc.), which may sometimes include criminal behavior, are also likely to include drinking. If offenses result from a given behavioral configuration 25% of the time and drinking is also present in that type of behavioral configuration 25% of the time, there is no apparent basis for the imputation of causality for the offense to drinking. Of course, if drinking were found to be present in the same events of a given behavioral configuration type as the offenses were, causal inference would be appropriate. However, in research conducted outside experimental conditions, the ability to observe the covariation of particular associational details is limited. Alcohol–crime research will usually be conducted outside the laboratory in natural settings and under conditions where the scope and level of research data detail will be limited. Thus it is difficult to examine events at a level of description which is detailed enough to permit the explicit connection of event ingredients. For this reason, conditional probability estimates can be valuable. If the likelihood of drinking (heavy drinking, drunkenness) is known for some behavioral configurations, inferential capacity is increased.

Alcohol Effects

In most cases the focus of alcohol–crime research is on the acute behavioral effects of alcohol consumption; that is, how does current BAC directly or indirectly affect current behavior? At other times, research might wish to examine alcohol's long-term effects. Some past research has implicitly taken this view. Typically, when alcoholism is considered as the independent variable, it is the long-term, chronic effects of drinking that are at issue. Research needs to be explicit about what effects of alcohol are being examined, at least to the extent of specifying whether acute or chronic effects are the focus. This is no simple task, as much remains to be determined about alcohol's effects on people. As discussed in the section on the alcoholic personality, the acute and chronic effects of drinking may be confounded; the acute effects of alcohol may be shaped by physiological changes that have taken place as a result of long-term, heavy drinking.

Alcohol and Other Drugs

Alcohol is frequently taken with other drugs, both in the sense that alcohol and other drugs may be used in combination and in the sense that alcohol users also use other drugs. Both kinds of polydrug use can have important implications for research which is attempting to determine how alcohol contributes to criminal behavior. The effects of multiple-drug use will likely differ from the effects of alcohol by itself.

Past research which examined polydrug-use patterns tended to look at the multiple use of illicit drugs—not including alcohol. A few studies have included alcohol, and these show that the use of multiple drugs, including alcohol, is common. Tinklenberg, Roth, Kopell, and Murphy (1976) found approximately equal use of alcohol and marijuana in a sample of adolescent delinquents. O'Donnell, Voss, Clayton, Slatin, and Room (1976) found that more than 90% of the alcohol users in a national sample of young men also used other drugs. Preble and Miller (1977) found that the combined daily use of alcohol and methadone was a common pattern among some drug users. Research data collected for individuals entering drug treatment programs show that weekly polydrug use is the predominant pattern, and that alcohol is an element in that pattern in a substantial percentage of cases (Research Triangle Institute, 1980). Research which specifies the particular psychopharmacologic effects of multiple-drug use, including alcohol, on crime is, to our knowledge, nonexistent.

Measuring the Crime Variable

Use of Official Crime Data

Most research on the relationship between alcohol and crime has relied on officially recorded offenses. If official offenses and offenders were an unbiased sample of all offenses and offenders, reliance on official data for research would not be problematic. However, official data are not likely to be a representative sampling of all offenses and offenders. Offense seriousness is directly related to the tendency to report offenses to the police (Elliott, 1977). Offender characteristics such as age and race are related to the probability of arrest (Hindelang, 1978; Peterson & Braiker, 1980; Wolfgang & Collins, 1978). The presence of alcohol in an offense or an offender may further bias the probabilities of arrest, conviction, and incarceration. There is some evidence, for example, that alcohol-involved offenders are more likely to be arrested for offenses committed than are offenders not so involved (Petersilia, Greenwood, & Lavin, 1978).

The alcohol–crime literature also shows that prison populations are often used for research, and prison populations overrepresent more serious offenders. Probably 2–4% or less of all serious crimes committed culminate in the incarceration of an offender. Most offenses are never reported, only about 20% of those reported result in the arrest of an offender, perhaps half of the arrests result in convictions, and only a proportion of the convictions result in incarcerations of the offenders. Those who are incarcerated are those who have committed the most serious offenses and also have the more serious criminal records. Offense seriousness and offender prior record are the major determinants of who is incarcerated. Clearly, research on incarcerated samples focuses on unique individuals. In short, it should be assumed that official crime data are biased. This implies that research which relies on these sources needs to be evaluated accordingly.

Use of Behavioral Criteria

Behavioral rather than legal criteria should be used to define the crime variable. If causal understanding is the goal, explicit examination of drinking and subsequent behavior is required. This is especially true if the causal contribution of alcohol to the occurrence of interpersonal violence is the issue being addressed. Assaults are not discrete events that can be understood in isolation; assaults typically evolve out of personal interactions that may be quite complex. One view of violent interactions between people characterizes this outcome as the culmination of an escalation process (Shoham, Ben-David, & Rahav, 1974). The cognitive impoverishment model of Pernanen (1976, Chapter 1, this volume) described earlier in this chapter, also emphasizes the emergent quality of alcohol-related interpersonal violence. If the influence of alcohol on interactional processes is to be understood, the processes must be described. Gradations of aggressiveness must be measured to that the dependent variable is not simply measured in dichotomous fashion—that is, assault versus no-assault.

This interactional view of alcohol's role in violence seems consistent with the evidence. It seems clear that the effect of drinking is not simple and direct (pathological intoxication may be an exception). Drinking is typically one among a number of factors that determine behavioral outcomes so that understanding the outcomes requires a detailed picture of the process.

At times the influence of alcohol use on property crime or more generally on criminal careers will be the focus of research. In such cases the strategy for measurement of the dependent variable will not emphasize detailed interactional data. However, the level of detail included in the measurement of the dependent variable will be an important determinant of the capacity of the research. For example, detailed offense histories, including offenses that did not result in arrest, will be required if the influence of alcohol use on criminal careers is the focus of research.

Summary: Measuring the Alcohol-Use and Crime Variables

Future research on the relationship between alcohol use and crime should measure the alcohol-use variable in detail. If an event-based analysis is the focus of research, a minimal requirement is the measurement of the presence of alcohol and the amount consumed. If the drinking-problem status of individuals is used as the measure of the alcohol variable, the specific criteria used to classify individuals on the drinking variable need to be made explicit. Use of an existing instrument for the measurement of problem drinking is preferred so that comparison of research results for different data sets is possible.

Research on the relationship between drinking and crime would be best served if detailed drinking history and/or detailed drinking event data were gathered. Ultimately, valid inferences about the causal relevance of alcohol consumption to criminal behavior require conditional probability data for the drinking variable. It is difficult to interpret data which show that offenders in a given percentage of criminal offenses were drinking unless an overall estimate is also available of the likelihood that the offender or the event circumstances would involve alcohol. It is not enough to know that drinking or a drinking problem is coterminous with criminal behavior. Conditional probabilities for the drinking variable are required for valid causal inference. The measurement of the drinking variable also needs to be explicit about whether the acute or chronic effects of alcohol are of interest and whether other drug use may also be a factor.

Careful measurement of the criminal behavior variable will serve future research on the drinking–crime question well. The nature of the detailed measurement will be shaped by the nature of the research questions. At times, detailed interactional data will be required; at other times, measurement will entail description of criminal-career patterns or other aspects of criminal involvement.

Future Research Recommendations

This chapter attempts to summarize the empirical and conceptual state of the art on the drinking–crime relationship. This summary was one of the major goals of an NIJ-funded project to develop a future research agenda for the alcohol–crime area. Five research designs were also developed during the project; these designs address various aspects of the relationship between alcohol consumption and assaultive behavior, and have been detailed by Collins, Guess, Williams, and Hamilton (1980). The following quote from that document summarizes four state-of-the-art judgments that formed the basis for the development of the research designs:

> Past theoretical and conceptual aspects of alcohol/crime research have often been seriously deficient. Future work must improve this state by multidisciplinary work that pays close attention to middle range theory development.
>
> Alcohol's behavioral effects at the individual level have important subjective and interpretive components. This requires that future work attend to phenomenological aspects of the alcohol/crime relationship.
>
> Cultural and scientific attitudes toward alcohol themselves affect interpretations of alcohol's behavioral effects and thus need to be considered in research designs. Cultural factors are also pertinent to the alcohol/crime relationship because norms toward drinking and what behavior is acceptable after drinking are variable across cultures.
>
> Measurement of the alcohol variable and the crime variable needs to be detailed. The alcohol/crime relationship needs to be examined in detail at the micro level of analysis.

The substantive foci of the five detailed research designs were developed in the light of these points and were also based on additional judgments about what particular research questions were most important to address. These judgments led us to recommend future research that: (1) compares national and state (U.S.) rates of alcohol consumption and violent crime at the aggregate level, (2) investigates differences in cultural norms about alcohol use and crime in one or a few communities, (3) investigates the relationship between drinking and marital violence in a survey of couples, (4) focuses on the young adult male to examine the relationship between drinking and assaultive behavior, and (5) explores the effects of setting and context on the alcohol–crime nexus. Details of research designs for these five recommendations are provided in the aforementioned document.

The recommended research approaches and issues are framed in a social psychological perspective. Emphasis on this perspective does not imply a judgment that other perspectives like the physiological and pharmacological do not have a contribution to make to understanding the alcohol–crime relationship. The social psychological emphasis does imply a judgment that other perspectives do not have a comprehensive capacity for dealing with the complex relationships at issue. Crime itself is a complex social phenomenon; its definition, both formally and in practice, is a product of the social process. At this stage in the scientific understanding of the alcohol–crime relationship, it is necessary that future research incorporate this social complexity. The recommended research designs focus on social and psychological factors because this focus is scientifically and heuristically appropriate.

It is our judgment that alcohol use is an important factor in the occurrence of some crime. If we begin to understand how alcohol use exerts its causal influence, the relative importance of alcohol use to the occurrence of criminal behavior can be estimated.

References

Aarens, M., Cameron, T., Roizen, J., Roizen, R., Room, R., Schneberk, D., & Wingard, D. (Eds.). *Alcohol, casualties and crime.* Berkeley, Calif.: Social Research Group, 1977.

Abrahamsen, D. Study of 102 sex offenders at Sing Sing. *Federal Probation,* 1950, *14,* 26–32.

Ahlström-Laakso, S. European drinking habits: A review of research and some suggestions for conceptual integration of findings. In M. W. Everett, J. O. Waddell, & D. B. Heath (Eds.), *Cross-cultural approaches to the study of alcohol.* The Hague: Mouton Publishers, 1976.

Aho, T. *Alkoholi ja vakivalta* [Alcohol and violence]. Selvite Oikeusministerio [Report from Ministry of Justice], Publication 7, D Series, Helsinki, 1976.

Akers, R. L. *Deviant behavior—A social learning approach.* Belmont, Calif.: Wadsworth, 1973.

Alexander, C. N. Alcohol and adolescent rebellion. *Social Forces,* 1965, *43,* 510–518.

Allen, J. *Assault with a deadly weapon: The autobiography of a street criminal* (D. H. Kelley & P. Heymann, Eds.). New York: Pantheon Books, 1977.

Allman, L. R., Taylor, H. A., & Nathan, P. E. Group drinking during stress: Effects on drinking behavior, effect, and psychopathology. *American Journal of Psychiatry,* 1972, *129*(6), 669–678.

Alterman, A. I., Gottheil, E., & Crawford, H. D. Mood changes in an alcoholism treatment program based on drinking decisions. *American Journal of Psychiatry,* 1975, *132*(10), 1032–1037.

American Humane Association. *National analysis of official child neglect and abuse reporting: Annual report, 1978.* Englewood, Colo.: Author, 1979.

Amir, M. Alcohol and forcible rape. *British Journal of the Addictions,* 1967, *62,* 219–232.

Amir, M. *Patterns of forcible rape.* Chicago: University of Chicago Press, 1971.

Andreasen, N., Endicott, J., Spitzer, R. L., & Winokur, G. The family history method using diagnostic criteria. *Archives of General Psychiatry,* 1977, *34,* 1229.

Andreini, M., & Green S., *Statistical description of cases followed by the Anchorage Child Abuse Board, Inc., October 1972–March 1975.* Anchorage, Alaska, 1975. (photocopied)

Antons, K. Empirische Ergebnisse zur Aggressivität von Alkoholkranken. *British Journal of the Addictions,* 1970, *65,* 263–272.

Apfelberg, B. M., Sugar, C., & Pfeffer, A. Z. A psychiatric study of 250 sex offenders. *American Journal of Psychiatry,* 1944, *100,* 762–770.

Bach-y-Rita, G., Lion, J. R., & Ervin, F. R. Pathological intoxication: Clinical and electro-encephalographic studies. *American Journal of Psychiatry,* 1970, *127,* 698–703.

Bacon, S. Alcohol, alcoholism and crime. *Crime and Delinquency,* 1963, *9,* 1–14.

Bahn, A. K., & Chandler, C. A. Alcoholism in psychiatric clinic patients. *Quarterly Journal of Studies on Alcohol,* 1961, *22,* 411–417.

Bahr, H., & Caplow, T. *Old men drunk and sober.* New York: New York University Press, 1973.

Baker, J. L. Indians, alcohol and homicide. *Journal of Social Therapy,* 1959, *5,* 270–275.

Baker, S., Robertson, L., & Spitz, W. Tattoos, alcohol, and violent death. *Journal of Forensic Sciences,* 1971, *16,* 219–228.

Baldwin, J. A., & Oliver, J. E. Epidemiology and family characteristics of severely-abused children. *British Journal of Preventive and Social Medicine,* 1975, *29,* 205–221.

317

Ball, J. C. The reliability and validity of interview data obtained from 59 narcotic drug addicts. *American Journal of Sociology,* 1967, *72,* 650–654.

Banay, R. S. Alcoholism and crime. *Quarterly Journal of Studies on Alcohol,* 1942, *2,* 686–716.

Bandura, A. *Aggression: A social learning analysis.* Englewood Cliffs, N.J.: Prentice-Hall, 1973.

Banfield, E. C. *The unheavenly city.* Boston: Little, Brown, 1968.

Barchka, R., Stewart, M. A., & Guze, S. B. Prevalence of alcoholism among general hospital ward patients. *American Journal of Psychiatry,* 1968, *125,* 681–684.

Bard, M., & Zacker, J. Assaultiveness and alcohol use in family disputes. *Criminology,* 1974, *12,* 281–292.

Barnes, G. E. The alcoholic personality: A reanalysis of the literature. *Journal of Studies on Alcohol,* 1979, *40*(7), 571–634.

Baron, R. A. Magnitude of victim's pain cues and level of prior anger arousal as determinants of adult aggressive behavior. *Journal of Personality and Social Psychology,* 1971, *17*(3), 236–243.

Baron, R. A., & Kepner, C. R. Model's behavior and attraction toward the model as determinants of adult aggressive behavior. *Journal of Personality and Social Psychology,* 1970, *14,* 335–341.

Bartholomew, A. A. Alcoholism and crime. *Australian and New Zealand Journal of Criminology,* 1968, *1,* 70–99.

Bartholomew, A. A., & Kelley, M. F. The incidence of a criminal record in 1000 consecutive "alcoholics." *British Journal of Criminology,* 1965, *5,* 143–149.

Becker, H. A. *The outsiders: Studies on the sociology of deviance.* New York: The Free Press, 1963.

Behling, D. W. Alcohol abuse as encountered in 51 instances of reported child abuse. *Clinical Pediatrics,* 1979, *18,* 87–91.

Bennett, R. M., Buss, A. H., & Carpenter, J. A. Alcohol and human physical aggression. *Quarterly Journal of Studies on Alcohol,* 1969, *30,* 870–876.

Berg, I. A. A comparative study of car thieves. *Journal of Criminal Law and Criminology,* 1944, *34,* 392–396.

Berkowitz, L. Aggressive cues in aggressive behavior and hostility catharsis. *Psychological Review,* 1964, *71*(2), 104–122.

Berkowitz, L. Some determinants of impulsive aggression: Role of mediated associations with reinforcements for aggression. *Psychological Review,* 1974, *84*(2), 165–176.

Berkowitz, L., & Geen, R. G. Stimulus qualities of the target of aggression: A further study. *Journal of Personality and Social Psychology,* 1967, *5*(3), 364–368.

Bett, W. R. Alcohol and crime in Ceylon: A preliminary communication. *British Journal of Inebriety,* 1946, *43,* 57–60.

Birrell, R. G., & Birrell, J. H. W. The maltreatment syndrome in children: A hospital survey. *The Medical Journal of Australia,* 1968, *2,* 1023–1028.

Black, D. J. Production of crime rates. *American Sociological Review,* 1970, *35,*(4), 733–748.

Blane, H. T. Drinking and crime. *Federal Probation,* 1965, *29,* 25–29.

Blane, H. T., & Hewitt, L. E. *Alcohol and youth: An analysis of the literature, 1960–1975.* Springfield, Va.: National Technical Information Service, 1977.

Blum, E. M., & Blum, R. H. *Alcoholism: Modern psychological approaches to treatment.* San Francisco: Jossey-Bass, 1969.

Blum, R. H. Drugs and violence. In National Violence Commission, *Consultants report on the causes and prevention of violence.* Washington, D.C.: U.S. Government Printing Office, 1969. (a)

Blum, R. H. Drugs and violence. In D. J. Mulvihill & M. M. Tumin (Eds.), *Crimes of violence* (Vol. 12). Washington, D.C.: U.S. Government Printing Office, 1969. (b)

Blum, R. H., & Associates. *Utopiates: A study of the use and users of LSD-25.* New York: Atherton, 1964.

Blum, R. H., & Blum, E. M. *Temperate achilles: A study of practice and beliefs associated with alcohol in rural Greece* (Monograph for the Cooperative Commission on the Study of Alcoholism). Stanford University: Institute for the Study of Human Problems, 1963.

Blumstein, A., & Cohen, J. *Estimation of individual crime rates from arrest records.* Unpublished manuscript, Carnegie-Mellon University, Pittsburgh, 1978.

Boland, B., & Wilson, J. Q. Age, crime and punishment. *The Public Interest,* 1978, *51,* 22–34.

Bowman, R. S., Stein, L. I., & Newton, J. R. Measurement and interpretation of drinking behavior: I. On measuring patterns of alcohol consumption; II. Relationships between drinking behavior and social adjustment in a sample of problem drinkers. *Journal of Studies on Alcohol,* 1975, *34*(9), 1154–1172.

Boyatzis, R. E. The effect of alcohol consumption on the aggressive behavior of men. *Quarterly Journal of Studies on Alcohol,* 1974, *45,* 959–972.

Boyatzis, R. E. The predisposition toward alcohol-related interpersonal aggression in men. *Journal of Studies on Alcohol,* 1975, *36,* 1196–1207.

Braly, M. *False starts: A memoir of San Quentin and other prisons.* Boston: Little, Brown, 1976.

Brodbeck, M. Models, meaning and theories. In L. Gross (Ed.), *Symposium on sociological theory.* New York: Harper & Row, 1959.

Brown, C. *Manchild in the promised land.* New York: The New American Library, 1965.

Bruun, K. Significance of role and norms in the small group for individual behavioral changes while drinking. *Quarterly Journal of Studies on Alcohol,* 1959, *20,* 53–64.

Bruun, K., Edwards, G., Lumio, M., Mäkelä, K., Pan, L. Popham, R. E., Room, R. Schmidt, W., Skog, O., Sulkunen, P., & Österberg, E. *Alcohol control policies in public health perspective.* The Finnish Foundation for Alcohol Studies, Vol. 25. Helsinki: Aurasen Kirjapaino Forssa, 1975.

Buckley, S., & Milkes, J. *Contingencies of perceived effects of drinking in a national male sample.* Berkeley, Calif.: Social Research Group, 1978.

Bunzel, R. The role of alcoholism in two Central American cultures. *Psychiatry,* 1940, *3,* 361–387.

Burgess, R. L. *Family violence: Some implications from evolutionary biology.* Paper presented at the annual meeting of the American Society of Criminology, Philadelphia, November 1979.

Byles, J. A. Violence, alcohol problems and other problems in disintegrating families. *Journal of Studies on Alcohol,* 1978, *39,* 551–553.

Cahalan, D. *Problem drinkers.* San Francisco: Jossey-Bass, 1970.

Cahalan, D., & Cisin, I. H. American drinking practices: Summary of findings from a national probability sample. *Quarterly Journal of Studies on Alcohol,* 1968, *29*(1), 130–151.

Cahalan, D., & Cisin, I. H. Epidemiological and social factors associates with drinking problems. In R. E. Torler & A. A. Sugerman (Eds.), *Alcoholism: Interdisciplinary approaches to an enduring problem.* Reading, Mass.: Addison-Wesley, 1976.(a)

Cahalan, D., & Cisin, I. H. Drinking behavior and drinking problems in the United States. In B. Kissin & H. Begleiter (Eds.), *The biology of alcoholism. Vol. 4: Social aspects of alcoholism.* New York: Plenum, 1976.(b)

Cahalan, D., Cisin, I. H., & Crossley, H. M. *American drinking practices: A national study of drinking behavior and attitudes.* New Brunswick, N.J.: Rutgers Center for Alcohol Studies, 1969.

Cahalan, D., & Room, R. Problem drinking among American men aged 21–59. *American Journal of Public Health,* 1972, *62,* 1473–1482.

Cahalan, D., & Room, R. *Problem drinking among American men.* New Brunswick, N.J.: Rutgers Center for Alcohol Studies, 1974.

Cahalan, D., & Treiman, B. *Drinking behavior, attitudes and problems in San Francisco* (for the Bureau of Alcoholism, Department of Public Health, City and County of San Francisco). Berkeley, Calif.: Social Research Group, 1976.

California Department of Public Health. *Criminal offenders and drinking involvement: A preliminary analysis* (Division of Alcoholic Rehabilitation, Publication No. 3). Sacramento: Author, 1960.

California Department of Public Health. *Law violators, probation status, and drinking involvement: A pilot study* (Division of Alcoholic Rehabilitation, Publication No. 4). Sacramento: Author, 1961.

Carlson, B. E. Battered women and their assailants. *Social Work,* 1977, *22,* 455–460.

Carpenter, J. A., & Armenti, N. P. Some effects of ethanol on human sexual and aggressive behavior. In B. Kissin & H. Begleiter (Eds.), *The biology of alcoholism* (Vol. 2). New York: Plenum Press, 1972.

Carstairs, M. Daru and Bhang: Cultural factors in the choice of intoxicants. *Quarterly Journal of Studies on Alcohol,* 1954, *15,* 220–237.

Cassirer, E. *An essay on man.* New Haven, Conn.: Yale University Press, 1944.

Cassity, J. Personality study of 200 murderers. *Journal of Criminal Psychopathology,* 1941, *2,* 296–304.

Chafetz, M. E. Alcohol and alcoholism. *American Scientist,* 1979, *67,* 293–299.

Chief Medical Examiner, Atlanta, Georgia. Cited in F. Harper (Ed.), *Alcohol abuse and Black America.* Alexandria, Va.: Douglass Publishers, 1976.

Child, I. L., Bacon, M. K. & Barry, H. A. A cross-cultural study of drinking. *Quarterly Journal of Studies on Alcohol,* Supplement No. 3, 1965.

Chimbos, P. D. *Marital violence: A study of interspouse homicide.* San Francisco: R & E Research Associates, 1978.

Chodorkoff, B., & Baxter, S. Psychiatric and psycho-analytic theories of violence. In D. J. Mulvihill, M. M. Tumin, & L. A. Curtis (Eds.), *Crimes of violence* (Vol. 13). Washington, D.C.: U.S. Government Printing Office, 1969.

Chotlos, J. W., & Goldstein, G. The alcoholic. *Review of Existential Psychology and Psychiatry,* 1966, *6,* 71–83.

Christian Economic and Social Research Foundation. *Alcohol and crime.* London: Author, Series C(2), 1976.

Cinquemani, D. K. *Drinking and violence among Middle American Indians.* Unpublished dissertation, Columbia University, 1975.

Clark, J. P., & Tifft, L. L. Polygraph and interview validation of self-reported deviant behavior. *American Sociological Review,* 1966, *31,* 516–523.

Clark, N. *Deliver us from evil: An interpretation of American Prohibition.* New York: Norton, 1976.

Cleveland, F. P. Problems in homicide investigation. IV: The relation of alcohol to homicide. *Cincinnati Journal of Medicine,* 1955, *36,* 28–30.

Cloward, R. A., & Ohlin, L. E. *Delinquency and opportunity.* New York: The Free Press, 1960.

Cofer, C., & Appleby, M. *Motivation.* New York: Wiley, 1964.

Cohen, A. K. *Delinquent boys: The culture of the gang.* New York: The Free Press, 1955.

Cohen, A. K. Deviance and control. In A. Inkeles (Ed.), *Foundations of modern sociology series.* Englewood Cliffs, N.J.: Prentice-Hall, 1966.

Cohen, J., Dearnaley, E. J. & Hansel, C. E. M. The risk taken in driving under the influence of alcohol. *British Medical Journal,* 1958, *1,* 1438–1444.

Cole, K. E., Fisher, G., & Cole, S. S. Women who kill: A sociopsychological study. *Archives of General Psychiatry,* 1968, *19,* 1–8.

Coleman, D. H., & Straus, M. A. *Alcohol abuse and family violence*. Paper presented at the annual meeting of the American Sociological Association, Boston, August 1979.

Coleman, K. H., & Weinman, M. L. *Conjugal violence: A comparative study in a psychiatric setting*. Houston: Texas Research Institute, no date.

Collins, J. J., Jr. *Chronic offender careers*. Paper presented at the annual meeting of the American Society of Criminology, Tucson, Ariz., November 1976.

Collins, J. J., Jr., Guess, L. L., Williams, J. R., & Hamilton, C. J. *Research designs to address the relationship between alcohol consumption and assaultive criminal behavior* (draft). Unpublished manuscript, 1980. (Available from Research Triangle Institute, Research Triangle Park, N.C.)

Connor, W. D. Criminal homicide, USSR/USA: Reflections on Soviet data in a comparative framework. *Journal of Criminal Law, Criminology, and Police Science*, 1973, *64*, 111–117.

Cook, S. A. Criminal behavior and the use of beverage alcohol. *Canadian Journal of Corrections*, 1962, *4*, 83–102.

Coopersmith, S. The effects of alcohol on reactions to affective stimuli. *Quarterly Journal of Studies on Alcohol*, 1964, *25*, 459–475.

Coopersmith, S. & Woodrow, K. Basal conductance levels of normals and alcoholics. *Quarterly Journal of Studies on Alcohol*, 1967, *28*, 27–32.

Cosper, R., & Mozersky, K. Social correlates of drinking and driving. *Quarterly Journal of Studies on Alcohol*, 1968, Suppl. No. 4.

Cox, C. T., & Longwell, B. Reliability of interview data concerning current heroin use from heroin addicts on methadone. *International Journal of the Addictions*, 1974, *9*, 161–165.

Coyne, A. C., Whitbourne, S. K., & Glenwick, D. S. Adult age differences in reflection-impulsivity. *Journal of Gerontology*, 1978, *33*(3), 402–407.

Criminal Justice Commission. *Criminal homicide in Baltimore, Maryland, 1960–1964* (An analysis prepared by the staff of the Criminal Justice Commission Inc.). Baltimore, Md.: Author, 1967.

Cuthbert, T. M. A portfolio of murders. *British Journal of Psychiatry*, 1970, *116*, 1–10.

Davis, D. I., Berenson, D., Steinglass, P., & Davis, S. The adaptive consequences of drinking. *Psychiatry*, 1974, *37*, 209–215.

Deardorff, C. M., Melges, F. T., Hout, C. N., & Savage, D. J. Situations related to drinking alcohol. *Journal of Studies on Alcohol*, 1976, *36*(9), 1184–1195.

DeVito, R. A., Flaherty, L. A., & Mozdzierz, G. Toward a psychodynamic theory of alcoholism. *Diseases of the Nervous System*, 1970, *31*(1), 43–49.

Dewsbury, A. R. Family violence seen in general practice. *Royal Society of Health Journal*, 1975, *95*, 290–294.

Distefano, M. K., Pryer, M. W., & Garrison, J. L. Internal–external control among alcoholics. *Journal of Clinical Psychology*, 1972, *28*, 36–37.

Dobash, R. E., & Dobash, R. *Violence against wives: A case against the patriarchy*. New York: The Free Press, 1979.

Dollard, J., Doob, L. W., Miller, N. E., Mowrer, O. H., & Sears, R. R. *Frustration and aggression*. New Haven, Conn.: Yale University Press, 1939.

Donovan, D. M., & O'Leary, M. R. A comparison of perceived and experienced control among alcoholics and nonalcoholics. *Journal of Abnormal Social Psychology*, 1975, *84*, 726–728.

East, W. N. The problem of alcohol and drug addiction in relation to crime. *British Journal of Inebriety*, 1939, *37*, 56–73.

Edwards, G., Hensman, C., & Peto, J. Drinking problems among recidivist prisoners. *Psychological Medicine*, 1971, *1*, 388–399.

Edwards, G., Kyle, E., & Nicholls, P. Alcoholics admitted to four hospitals in England. III: Criminal records. *Journal of Studies on Alcohol,* 1977, *38,* 1648–1664.

Einstadter, W. J. The social organization of armed robbery. *Social Problems,* 1969, *17*(1), 64–83.

Elliott, W. C. *A working paper on the relation between crime offense seriousness and informing the police of victimization.* Analytical Studies in Victimization by Crime, LEAA Grant No. 75 SS 99-0013, Technical Report No. 2, March 1977.

Emerson, C. D. Family violence: A study by the Los Angeles County Sheriff's Department. *The Police Chief,* 1979, *46*(6), 48–50.

Endicott, J., Andreasen, N., & Spitzer, R. L. *Family history—Research diagnostic criteria.* New York: Biometrics Research, New York State Psychiatric Institute, 1975.

Epstein, R. Aggression towards outgroups as a function of authoritarianism and imitation of aggressive models. *Journal of Personality and Social Psychology,* 1966, *3,* 574–580.

Epstein, S., & Taylor, S. P. Instigation to aggression as a function of degree of defeat and perceived aggressive intent of the opponent. *Journal of Personality,* 1967, *35,* 265–289.

Epstein, T. *A socio-legal examination of intoxication in the criminal law.* Berkeley, Calif.: Social Research Group, 1977.

Epstein, T., Cameron, T., & Room, R. Alcohol and family abuse. In M. Aarens, T. Cameron, J. Roizen, R. Roizen, R. Room, D. Schneberk, & D. Wingard (Eds.), *Alcohol, casualties and crime.* Berkeley, Calif.: Social Research Group, 1977.

Ervin, F. The biology of individual violence: An overview. In D. J. Mulvihill, M. M. Tumin, & L. A. Curtis (Eds.), *Crimes of violence* (Vol. 13). Washington, D.C.: U.S. Government Printing Office, 1969.

Eysenck, H. J., & Eysenck, S. B. G. *Personality structure and measurement.* London: Routledge & Kegan Paul, 1969.

Fallding, H. *Drinking, community and civilizations.* New Brunswick, N.J.: Rutgers Center for Alcohol Studies, 1974.

Fattah, E. A. *A study of the deterrent effect of capital punishment with special reference to the Canadian situation* (Department of the Solicitor General, Canada Research Centre, Report 2). Ottawa: Information Canada, 1972.

Federal Bureau of Investigation. *Crime in the United States—1977* (Uniform Crime Reports). Washington, D.C.: U.S. Government Printing Office, 1977.

Federal Bureau of Investigation. *Crime in the United States, 1978* (Uniform Crime Reports). Washington, D.C.: U.S. Government Printing Office, 1979.

Fenna, D., Mix, L., Schaefer, O., & Gilbert, J. A. L. Ethanol metabolism in various racial groups. In M. W. Everett, J. O. Waddell, & D. B. Heath (Eds.), *Cross-cultural approaches to the study of alcohol.* The Hague: Mouton Publishers, 1976.

Feldman, M. P. *Criminal behavior: A psychological analysis.* London: Wiley, 1977.

Fillmore, K. M. Relationships between specific drinking problems in early adulthood and middle age: An exploratory 20 year follow-up study. *Quarterly Journal of Studies on Alcohol,* 1975, *36,* 819–840.

Fine, E., Scoles, P., & Mulligan, M. *Incidences and type of alcohol abuse in first offenders for driving while intoxicated.* Paper presented at the Sixth Annual International Conference on Alcohol, Drugs and Traffic Safety, Toronto, September 1974.

Flynn, W. R. Frontier justice: A contribution to the theory of child battery. *American Journal of Psychiatry,* 1970, *127,* 151–155.

Fontana, V. J. Which parents abuse children? *Medical Insight,* 1971, *3,* 16–21.

Forst, B., Lucianovic, J., & Cox, S. J. *What happens after arrest?* Washington, D.C.: Institute for Law and Social Research, August 1977.

Freed, E. X. Alcohol and mood: An updated review. *International Journal of the Addictions,* 1978, *13,* 173–200.

Friedman, C. J., & Friedman, A. S. Drug abuse and delinquency among lower social class, court adjudicated adolescent boys. In National Commission on Marijuana and Drug Abuse, *Drug use in America: Problem in perspective* (Appendix, Vol. 1). Washington, D.C.: U.S. Government Printing Office, 1973.

Frum, H. S. Adult criminal offense trends following juvenile delinquency. *Journal of Criminal Law and Criminology,* May/June 1958, *49,* 29–49.

Garbarino, J. The human ecology of child maltreatment: A conceptual model for research. *Journal of Marriage and the Family,* 1977, *39,* 721–735.

Gayford, J J. Wife battering: A preliminary survey of 100 cases. *British Medical Journal,* 1975, *1,* 194–197.

Geen, R., & Berkowitz, L. Name-mediated aggressive cue properties. *Journal of Personality,* 1966, *34,* 456–465.

Geer, J. H., & Buss, A. H. Supplementary report: Generalization of nonverbal response to aggressive verbal stimuli. *Journal of Experimental Psychology,* 1962, *63*(4), 413–414.

Gelles, R. J. *The violent home: A study of physical aggression between husbands and wives.* Beverly Hills, Calif.: Sage, 1972.

Gelles, R. J. *Theoretical approaches to the issue of intrafamily violence.* Paper presented at the annual meeting of the American Society of Criminology, Philadelphia, November 1979.(a)

Gelles, R. J. Violence toward children in the United States. In R. J. Gelles (Ed.), *Family violence.* Beverly Hills, Calif.: Sage, 1979.(b)

Gelles, R. J., & Straus, M. A. Determinants of violence in the family: Toward a theoretical integration. In W. R. Burr, R. Hill, F. I. Nye, & I. L. Reiss (Eds.), *Contemporary theories about the family.* New York: The Free Press, 1979.(a)

Gelles, R. J., & Straus, M. A. Violence in the American family. *Journal of Social Issues,* 1979, *35,* 15–39. (b)

Gerber, S. R. *Coroner's statistical report.* Cleveland, Ohio: Cuyahoga County, 1974.

Gerson, L. W. Alcohol-related acts of violence: Who was drinking and where the acts occurred. *Journal of Studies on Alcohol,* 1978, *39,* 1294–1296.

Gibbens, T. C. N., & Silberman, M. Alcoholism among prisoners. *Psychological Medicine,* 1970, *1,* 73–78.

Gibbons, D. Observations on the study of crime causation. *American Journal of Sociology,* 1971, *77*(2), 262–278.

Gibbons, D. *Society, crime and criminal careers.* Englewood Cliffs, N.J.: Prentice-Hall, 1976.

Gil, D. G. *Violence against children: Physical child abuse in the United States.* Cambridge, Mass.: Harvard University Press, 1970.

Gillies, H. Murder in the west of Scotland. *British Journal of Psychiatry,* 1965, *3,* 1087–1094.

Gillis, J. S. Effects of chlorpromazine and thiothixene on acute schizophrenic patients. In K. R. Hammond & C. R. B. Joyce (Eds.), *Psychoactive drugs and social judgment.* New York: Wiley, 1975.

Giove, C. Alcoholic epilepsy. *Ospedale Psichiatric,* 1964, *32,* 195–270.

Glaser, F. B., Greenberg, S. W., & Barrett, H. *A systems approach to alcohol treatment.* Toronto, Ont.: Addiction Research Foundation, 1978.

Glatt, M. M. Crime, alcohol and alcoholism. *Howard Journal of Penology,* 1965, *11,* 274–284.

Glatt, M. M. Alcoholism disease concept and loss of control revisited. *British Journal of Addiction,* 1976, *71,* 135–144.

Gliedman, L. H. Temporal orientation and alcoholism. *Alcoholism,* 1956, *3,* 11–14.

Globetti, G., Bennett, W., & Alsikafi, M. *Alcohol and crime: Previous drinking careers of convicted offenders.* Paper presented at Midwest Sociological Society meetings, Omaha, Neb., April 3–6, 1974.

Glueck, S., & Glueck, E. *Later criminal careers.* New York: The Commonwealth Fund, 1937.

Gold, M. *Delinquent behavior in an American city.* Belmont, Calif.: Wadsworth, 1970.

Goldman, M. S. To drink or not to drink: An experimental analysis of group drinking decisions by four alcoholics. *American Journal of Psychiatry,* 1974, *131*(10), 1123–1130.

Goldstein, G. The significance of perception and cognition in understanding the alcoholic. In G. Goldstein & C. Neuringer (Eds.), *Empirical studies of alcoholism.* Cambridge, Mass.: Ballinger, 1976.

Goldstein, J. H. *Aggression and crimes of violence.* New York: Oxford University Press, 1975.

Gomberg, E. S. *Risk factors related to alcohol problems among women: Proneness and vulnerability.* Paper presented at NIAAA Workshop on Alcoholism and Alcohol Abuse among Women, Jekyll Island, Ga., April 1978.

Good, W. Violence among intimates. In D. J. Mulvihill, M. M. Tumin, & L. A. Curtis (Eds.), *Crimes of violence* (Vol. 13). Washington, D.C.: U.S. Government Printing Office, 1969.

Goode, W. J. Force and violence in the family. *Journal of Marriage and the Family,* 1971, *33,* 624–636.

Goodwin, D. W. Alcohol in suicide and homicide. *Quarterly Journal of Studies on Alcohol,* 1973, *34,* 144–156.

Goodwin, D. W. The bad-habit theory of drug abuse. In D. J. Lettieri, M. Sayers, & H. W. Pearson (Eds.), *Theories on drug abuse* (NIDA Research Monograph No. 30). Rockville, Md.: National Institute on Drug Abuse Research, March 1980.

Goodwin, D. W., Crane, B., & Guze, S. B. Felons who drink: An 8-year followup. *Quarterly Journal of Studies on Alcohol,* 1971, *32,* 136–147.

Gorwitz, K., Bahn, A., Warthern, F. J., & Cooper, M. Some epidemiological data on alcoholics in Maryland. *Quarterly Journal of Studies on Alcohol,* 1970, *31,* 423–443.

Goss, A., & Morosko, T. F. Relation between a dimension of internal–external control and the MMPI with an alcoholic population. *Journal of Consulting Clinical Psychology,* 1970, *34,* 189–192.

Gould, J. R. *Client profile: Children's Trauma Center* (Report for State Maternal and Child Health Contract No. 74-50733). Oakland, Calif.: Children's Trauma Center, 1976.

Gove, W. R. Sleep deprivation: A cause of psychotic disorganization. *American Journal of Sociology,* 1969–1970, *75,* 782–799.

Green, E. Race, social status, and criminal arrest. *American Sociological Review,* 1970, *35*(3), 476–490.

Greenberg, R., & Pearlman, C. Delirium tremens and dreaming. *American Journal of Psychiatry,* 1967, *124,* 133–142.

Greenberg, S. W. The relationship between crime and amphetamine abuse: An empirical review of the literature. *Contemporary Drug Problems,* 1976, *5,* 101–147.

Gresham, S., Webb, W., & Williams, R. Alcohol and caffeine: Effect on inferred visual dreaming. *Science,* 1963, *140,* 1226–1227.

Grigsby, S. E. The Raiford study: Alcohol and crime. *Journal of Criminal Law, Criminology and Police Science,* 1963, *54*(3), 296–306.

Grislain, J. R., Mainard, R., & DeBerranger, P. Les sévices commis sur les enfants: Problèmes sociaux et juridiques. *Annales de Pédiatrie,* 1968, *15,* 440–448.

Gross, M. M., & Goodenough, D. R. Sleep disturbances in the acute alcoholic psychoses. In J. O. Cole (Ed.), *Clinical research in alcoholism* (Psychiatric Research Report No. 24). Washington, D.C.: American Psychiatric Association, 1968.

Gusfield, J. R. *Symbolic crusade.* Urbana: University of Illinois Press, 1963.

Guze, S. B., Goodwin, D. W., & Crane, J. B. Criminality and psychiatric disorders. *Archives of General Psychiatry,* 1969, *20,* 583–591.

Guze, S. B., Tuason, V. B., Gatfield, P. D., Stewart, M. A., & Picken, B. Psychiatric illness and crime with particular reference to alcoholism: A study of 223 criminals. *Journal of Nervous and Mental Disease,* 1962, *134*(6), 512.

Haberman, P. W., & Baden, M. M. Alcoholism and violent death. *Quarterly Journal of Studies on Alcohol,* 1974, *35,* 221-231.

Hagnell, O., Nyman, E., & Tunving, K. Dangerous alcoholics: Personality varieties in aggressive and suicidally inclined subjects. *Scandinavian Journal of Social Medicine,* 1973, *1,* 125-131.

Hamparian, D. M., Schuster, R., Dinitz, S., & Conrad, J. P. *The violent few: A study of dangerous juvenile offenders.* Lexington, Mass.: Lexington Books, 1978.

Harlan, H. Five hundred homicides. *Journal of Criminal Law and Criminology,* 1950 (March-April), 736-752.

Harper, F. D. (Ed.). *Alcohol abuse and Black America.* Alexandria, Va: Douglass Publishers, 1976.

Hartford, T. C., & Mills, G. S. Aged-related trends in alcohol consumption. *Journal of Studies on Alcohol,* 1978, *39,* 207-210.

Hartocollis, P. Drunkenness and suggestion: An experiment with intravenous alcohol. *Quarterly Journal of Studies on Alcohol,* 1962, *23,* 376-389.

Hassall, C., & Foulds, G. A. Hostility among young alcoholics. *British Journal of the Addictions,* 1968, *63,* 203-208.

Heath, D. B. Anthropological perspectives on alcohol: An historical review. In M. W. Everett, J. O. Waddell, & D. B. Heath (Eds.), *Cross-cultural approaches to the study of alcohol.* The Hague: Mouton Publishers, 1976.

Herjanic, M., & Meyer, D. A. Alcohol consumption and homicide. In F. A. Seixas (Ed), *Currents in alcoholism* (Vol. 2). New York: Grune & Stratton, 1977.

Herman, V., Sekso, M., Trinajstic, M., Vidovic, V., & Cabrijan, T. Hypoglycemic conditions in the course of chronic alcoholism. *Alcoholism,* 1970, *6,* 87-90.

Hetherington, E. M., & Wrey, N. P. Aggression, need for social approval and humor preferences. *Journal of Abnormal and Social Psychology,* 1964, *68,* 685-689.

Hicks, D. J. Imitation and retention of film-mediated aggressive peer and adult models. *Journal of Personality and Social Psychology,* 1965, *2,* 97.

Higgins, R. Experimental studies of the tension-reduction hypothesis. In G. Goldstein & C. Neuringer (Eds.), *Empirical studies of alcoholism.* Cambridge, Mass.: Ballinger, 1976.

Higgins, R. L., & Marlatt, G. A. Fear of interpersonal evaluation as a determinant of the alcohol consumption in male social drinkers. *Journal of Abnormal Psychology,* 1975, *84,* 644-651.

Hilberman, E., & Munson, K. Sixty battered women. *Victimology,* 1977-1978, *2,* 460-470.

Hills, H. E., Belleville, R. E., & Wilker, A. Motivational determinants in modification of behavior by morphine and pentobarbital. *Archives of Neurology and Psychiatry,* 1957, *77,* 28-35.

Hindelang, M. J. Age, sex, and the versatility of delinquent involvements. *Social Problems,* 1971, *18,* 522-535.

Hindelang, M. J. Race and involvement in common law personal crimes. *American Sociological Review,* 1978, *43* (February), 93-109.

Hirschi, R. *Causes of delinquency.* Berkeley, Calif.: University of California Press, 1969.

Hoffman, H., & Nelson, P. C. Personality characteristics of alcoholism in relation to age and intelligence. *Psychological Reports,* 1971, *29,* 143-146.

Hollis, S. On the etiology of criminal homicides: The alcohol factor. *Journal of Police Science and Administration,* 1974, *2,* 50-53.

Homans, G. C. *The human group.* New York: Harcourt, Brace, 1950.

Hope, K. The study of hostility in the temperaments of spouses: Definitions and methods. *British Journal of Mathematical and Statistical Psychology,* 1969, *22*(1), 67–95.

Hyman, H. *Survey design and analysis: Principles, cases and procedures.* Glencoe, Ill.: The Free Press, 1955.

Hyman, M. M. Accident vulnerability and blood alcohol concentrations of drivers by demographic characteristics. *Quarterly Journal of Studies on Alcohol,* 1968, Suppl. No. 4.

Institute for Scientific Analysis. *Drinking patterns and criminal careers: A study of 310 imprisoned male felons* (Final Report). San Francisco: Scientific Analysis Corporation, 1978.

Irwin, J. *The felon.* Englewood Cliffs, N.J.: Prentice-Hall, 1970.

Janzen, C. Families in the treatment of alcoholism. *Quarterly Journal of Studies on Alcohol,* 1977, *38*(1), 114–130.

Jellinek, E. M. Phases of alcohol addiction. *Quarterly Journal of Studies on Alcohol,* 1952, *13,* 673–684.

Jellinek, E. M. *The disease concept of Alcoholism.* Highland Park, N.J.: Hillhouse Press, 1960.

Jellinek, E. M., & McFarland, R. A. Analysis of psychological experiments on the effects of alcohol. *Quarterly Journal of Studies on Alcohol,* 1940, *1,* 272–371.

Jessor, R., Graves, T., Hanson, R., & Jessor, S. *Society, personality, and deviant behavior: A study of a tri-ethnic community.* New York: Holt, Rinehart, & Winston, 1968.

Jessor, R., & Jessor, S. L. Adolescent development and the onset of drinking—A longitudinal study. *Journal of Studies on Alcohol,* 1975, *36,* 27–51.

Jessor, R., & Jessor, S. L. *Problem behavior and psychosocial development: A longitudinal study of youth.* New York: Academic Press, 1977.

Johnson, B., & Morse, H. A. Injured children and their parents. *Children,* 1968, *15,* 147–152.

Johnson, L. C., & Burdick, J. A., & Smith, J. Sleep during alcohol intake and withdrawal in the chronic alcoholic. *Archives of General Psychiatry,* 1970, *22,* 406–418.

Johnson, S. D., Gibson, L., & Linden, R. Alcohol and rape in Winnipeg, 1966–1975. *Journal of Studies on Alcohol,* 1978, *39*(11) 1877–1894.

Joyce, C. R. B. Placebo reactions. In P. Hopkins & H. H. Wolff (Eds.), *Principles of treatments of psychosomatic disorders.* London: Pergamon, 1965.

Joyce, C. R. B. Can drugs affect personality? In I. T. Ramsey & R. Porter (Eds.), *Personality and science.* London: Churchill Livingston, 1971.

Justice, B., & Justice, R. *The abusing family.* New York: Human Sciences Press, 1976.

Kalant, H. The pharmacology of alcohol intoxication. *Quarterly Journal of Studies of Alcohol,* 1961, Suppl. No. 1, 1–23.

Kalin, R. Social drinking in different settings. In D. C. McClelland, W. N. Davis, R. Kalin, & E. Wanner (Eds.), *The drinking man.* New York: The Free Press, 1972.

Kalin, R., McClelland, D. C., & Kahn, M. The effects of male social drinking on fantasy. In D. C. McClelland, W. N. Davis, R. Kalin, & E. Wanner (Eds.), *The drinking man.* New York: The Free Press, 1972.

Kaplun, D., & Reich, R. The murdered child and his killers. *American Journal of Psychiatry,* 1976, *133,* 809–813.

Kastl, A. J. Changes in ego functioning under alcohol. *Quarterly Journal of Studies on Alcohol,* 1969, *30,* 371–382.

Katkin, E. S., Hayes, W. N., Teger, A. I. & Pruitt, D. G. Effects of alcoholic beverages differing in congener content on psychomotor tasks and risk taking. *Quarterly Journal of Studies on Alcohol,* 1970, Suppl. No. 5, 101–114.

Kaufmann, H., & Marcus, A. M. Aggression as a function of similarity between aggressor and victim. *Perceptual and Motor Skills,* 1965, *20,* 1013–1020.

King, L. J., Murphy, G. E., Robins, L. N., & Darvish, H. Alcohol abuse: A critical factor in the social problems of Negro men. *American Journal of Psychiatry,* 1969, *125*(12), 1682–1691.

Kissin, B., & Hankoff, L. The acute effects of ethyl alcohol on the Funkenstein mecholyl response in male alcoholics. *Quarterly Journal of Studies on Alcohol,* 1959, *20,* 696–703.

Kitsuse, J. I., & Cicourel, A. V. A note on the uses of official statistics. *Social Problems,* 1963, *11,* 131–139.

Klausner, S. Z. Life-span environmental psychology: Methodological issues. In P. B. Baltes & K. W. Schaie (Eds.), *Life-span developmental psychology—Personality and socialization.* New York: Academic Press, 1973.

Klockars, C. B. *The professional fence.* New York: The Free Press, 1974.

Knowles, J. B., Laverty, S. G., & Kuechler, H. A. Effects of alcohol on REM sleep. *Quarterly Journal of Studies on Alcohol,* 1968, *29,* 342–349.

Knupfer, G., & Room, R.Abstainers in a metropolitan community. *Quarterly Journal of Studies on Alcohol,* 1970, *31,* 108–131.

Kogan, N. Creativity and cognitive style: A life-span perspective. In P. B. Baltes & K. W. Schaie (Eds.), *Life-span developmental psychology—Personality and socialization.* New York: Academic Press, 1973.

Kogan, N., & Wollack, M. A. Age changes in values and attitudes. *Journal of Gerontology,* 1961, *16,* 272–280.

Kohlberg, L. Continuities in childhood and adult moral development revisited. In P. B. Baltes & K. W. Schaie (Eds.), *Life-span developmental psychology—Personality and socialization.* New York: Academic Press, 1973.

Korman, M., Knopf, I. J., & Austin, R. B. Effects of alcohol on serial learning under stress conditions. *Psychological Reports,* 1960, *7,* 217–220.

Kuhn, T. S. *The structure of scientific revolutions.* Chicago: University of Chicago Press, 1970.

Lahelma, E. *Scandinavian research on alcohol's role in casualties and crime: A review essay and informative abstracts.* Berkeley, Calif.: Social Research Group, 1977.

Lang, A. R., Goeckner, D. J., Adesso, V. J., & Marlatt, G. A. Effects of alcohol on aggression in male social drinkers. *Journal of Abnormal Psychology,* 1975, *84*(5), 508–518.

Leake, C. D., & Silverman, M. *Alcohol beverages in clinical medicine.* Chicago: Year Book Medical Publishers, 1966.

Leland, J. *Firewater myths.* New Brunswick, N.J.: Rutgers Center for Alcohol Studies, 1976.

Lemert, E. M. *Human deviance, social problems, and social control.* Englewood Cliffs, N.J.: Prentice-Hall, 1967.

Lenke, L. *Valdbrott och alkohol: En studie i misshandelsbrottslighetens utveckling* [Violent crime and alcohol: A study of the developments in assaultive crime]. Stockholm: Department of Criminology, University of Stockholm, 1975.

Lenke, L. Alkohol och valdbrottslighet [Alcohol and criminal violence]. *Alkohol och Narkotika,* 1976, *70,* 8–17.

Leppa, S. *A review of robberies in Helsinki 1963–1973* (Research Institute of Legal Policy, Publication No. 2). Helsinki: The Institute, 1974.

LeRoux, L. C., & Smith, L. S. Violent deaths and alcoholic intoxification. *Journal of Forensic Medicine,* 1964, *11,* 131–147.

Leven, R., & Vandre, V. California study of relationships between drinking and crime. *Police,* 1961, *6,* 18–21.

Levine, H. *Colonial and 19th century American thought about alcohol as a cause of crime and accidents* (Paper E48). Berkeley, Calif.: Social Research Group, 1977.

Levinger, G. Source of marital dissatisfaction among applicants for divorce. *American Journal of Orthopsychiatry,* 1966, *36,* 803–807.

Levinson, D. The New York City skid row Negro: Some research findings. *Mental Hygiene,* 1970, *54,* 548–552.

Levinson, D. The etiology of skid rows in the U.S. *International Journal of Social Psychiatry,* 1974, *20*(1/2), 25–33.

Levy, J., & Kunitz, S. *Indian drinking.* New York: Wiley, 1974.

Lewis, H. *Blackways of Kent.* Chapel Hill: University of North Carolina Press, 1955.

Liebow, E. *Tally's corner.* Boston: Little, Brown, 1967.

Light, R. J. Abused and neglected children in America: A study of alternative polices. *Harvard Educational Review,* 1973, *43,* 556–598.

Lindelius, R., & Salum, I. Alcoholism and criminality. *Acta Psychiatrica Scandinavica,* 1973, *49,* 306–314.

Lindelius, R., & Salum, I. Alcoholism and crime: A comparative study of three groups of alcoholics. *Journal of Studies on Alcohol,* 1975, *36,* 1452–1447.

Locke, B. Z., & Duvall, H. J. Alcoholism among first admissions to Ohio Public Mental Health Hospital. *Quarterly Journal of Studies on Alcohol,* 1974, *25,* 521–534.

Locke, B. Z., Kramer, M., & Pasamanick, B. Alcoholic psychosis among first admissions to a public mental health hospital in Ohio. *Quarterly Journal of Studies on Alcohol,* 1960, *21,* 452–474.

Lofland, J. *Deviance and identity.* Englewood Cliffs, N.J.: Prentice-Hall, 1969.

Lombroso, C. *Crime: Its causes and remedies.* Montclair, N.J.: Patterson Smith, 1968.

MacAndrew, C., & Edgerton, R. B. *Drunken comportment: A social explanation.* Chicago: Aldine, 1969.

Macdonald, J. M. *The murderer and his victim.* Springfield, Ill.: C. C. Thomas, 1961.

MacDonnell, M. F., & Ehmer, M. Some effects of ethanol on aggressive behavior in cats. *Quarterly Journal of Studies on Alcohol,* 1969, *30,* 312–319.

Mack, J. A. The able criminal. *British Journal of Criminology,* 1972, *12,* 44–54.

Maddux, J. F., & Desmond, D. P. Reliability and validity of information from chronic heroin users. *Journal of Psychiatric Research,* 1975, *12,* 87–95.

Maden, M. F., & Wrench, D. F. Significant findings in child abuse research. *Victimology,* 1977, *2,* 196–224.

Maisto, S. A. Lauerman, R., & Adesso, V. J. A comparison of two experimental studies of the role of cognitive factors in alcoholics' drinking. *Journal of Studies on Alcohol,* 1977, *38*(1), 145–149.

Mäkelä, K. *Level of consumption and social consequences of drinking.* Unpublished report, 1976. (Available from Social Research Group, Berkeley, Calif. 94709.)

Maletzky, B. M. The diagnosis of pathological intoxication. *Journal of Studies on Alcohol,* 1976, *37*(9), 1215–1228.

Malik, M. O. A., & Sawi, O. A profile of homicide in the Sudan. *Forensic Science,* 1976, *7,* 141–150.

Malzberg, B. A study of first admissions with alcohol psychosis in New York State, 1943–1944. *Quarterly Journal of Studies on Alcohol,* 1947, *8,* 274–295.

Mandell, W., & Ginzburg, H. M. Youthful alcohol use, abuse and alcoholism. In B. Kissin & H. Begleiter (Eds.), *The biology of alcoholism. Vol. 4: Social aspects of alcoholism.* New York: Plenum, 1976.

Marek, Z., Widacki, J., & Hanausek, T. Alcohol as a victimogenic factor in robberies. *Forensic Science,* 1974, *4,* 119–223.

Marinacci, A. A. A special type of temporal lobe (psychomotor) seizures following ingestion of alcohol. *Bulletin of the Los Angeles Neurological Society,* 1963, *28,* 241–250.

Mark, V. H., & Ervin, F. R. *Violence and the brain.* New York: Harper & Row, 1970.

Marlatt, G. A., Demming, B. A., & Reid, J. B. Loss of control drinking in alcoholics: An experimental analogue. *Journal of Abnormal psychology,* 1973, *81,* 223–241.

Marlatt, G. A., Kosturn, C. F., & Lang, A. R. Provocation to anger and opportunity for retaliation as determinants of alcohol consumption in social drinkers. *Journal of Abnormal Psychology,* 1975, *84*(6), 652–659.

Marlatt, G. A., & Rohsenow, D. *Cognitive process in alcohol use: Expectancy and the balanced placebo design.* Unpublished manuscript, University of Washington, 1979.

Martin, J. B. *My life in crime: The autobiography of a professional criminal.* New York: Harper, 1952.

Matheson, J. C. M. Alcohol and female homicides. *British Journal of Inebriety,* 1939, *37,* 87–90.

Maule, H. G., & Cooper, J. Alcoholism and crime: A study of the drinking and criminal habits of 50 discharged prisoners. *British Journal of Addiction,* 1966, *61,* 201–212.

Mawson, A. R. Aggression, attachment behavior, and crimes of violence. In T. Hirschi & M. Gottfredson (Eds.), *Understanding crime.* Beverly Hills, Calif.: Sage, 1980.

Mayer, J., & Black, R. The relationship between alcoholism and child abuse and neglect. In F. A. Seixas (Ed.), *Currents in alcoholism.* New York: Grune & Stratton, 1977.

Mayfield, D. *Alcoholism, alcohol intoxication and assaultive behavior.* Paper presented at the 30th International Congress on Alcoholism and Drug Dependence, Amsterdam, 1972.

Mayfield, D. Alcoholism, alcohol intoxication, and assaultive behavior. *Diseases of the Nervous System,* 1976, *37,* 228–291.

McCaghy, C. H. Drinking and deviance disavowal: The case of child molesters. *Social Problems,* 1968, *16,* 43–49.

McClearn, G. E. Biological bases of social behavior with specific reference to violent behavior. In D. J. Mulvihill, M. M. Tumin, & L. A. Curtis (Eds.), *Crimes of violence* (Vol. 13). Washington, D.C.: U.S. Government Printing Office, 1969.

McCleary, C. P., & Mensk, I. N. Personality differences associated with age in law offenders. *Journal of Gerontology,* 1977, *32*(2), 164–167.

McClelland, D. C. *Power: The inner experience.* New York: Irvington Publishers, 1975.

McClelland, D. C., & Davis, W. N. The influence of unrestrained power concerns on drinking in working-class men. In D. C. McClelland, W. N. Davis, R. Kalin, & E. Wanner (Eds.), *The drinking man.* New York: The Free Press, 1972.

McClelland, D. C., Davis, W. N., Kalin, R., & Wanner, E. (Eds.). *The drinking man.* New York: The Free Press, 1972.

McCord, W., & McCord, J. A longitudinal study of the personality of alcoholics. In D. J. Pittman & C. R. Snyder (Eds.), *Society, culture, and drinking patterns.* New York: Wiley, 1962.

McGeorge, J. Alcohol and crime. *Medicine, Science, and the Law,* 1963, *3,* 27–48.

Megargee, E. I. A critical review of theories of violence. In D. J. Mulvihill, M. M Tumin, & L. A. Curtis (Eds.), *Crimes of violence* (Vol. 13). Washington, D.C.: U.S. Government Printing Office, 1969.

Melges, F. T., & Harris, R. F. Anger and attack: A cybernetic model of violence. In D. N. Daniels, M. F. Gilula, & F. M. Ochberg (Eds.), *Violence and the struggle for existence. Part 1: Theories of aggression and violence.* Boston: Little, Brown, 1970.

Mello, N. K., & Mendelson, J. H. A quantitative analysis of drinking patterns in alcoholics. *Archives of General Psychiatry,* 1971, *25,* 527–539.

Mello, N. K., & Mendelson, J. H. Androgens and aggression in alcohol addicts. In *Scientific proceedings in summary form: The one hundred and twenty-sixth annual meeting of the American Psychiatric Association,* Honolulu, 1973.

Mendelson, J. H., LaDou, J., & Solomon, P. Experimentally induced chronic intoxication and withdrawal in alcoholics. Part 3: Psychiatric findings. *Quarterly Journal of Studies on Alcohol,* 1964, Suppl. No. 2, 40–52.

Merton, R. K. *Social theory and social structure.* Glencoe, Ill.: The Free Press, 1957.

Merton, R. K. *Social theory and social structure.* New York: The Free Press, 1968.

Meyer, C. K., Magedanz, T., Kieselhorst, D. C., & Chapman, S. G. *A social-psychological analysis of police assailants.* Norman, Okla.: Bureau of Government Research, University of Oklahoma, April, 1978.

Milgram, S. *Obedience to authority.* London: Tavistock, 1974.

Miller, D. P. *Alcoholism and California: Criminal offenders and drinking involvement.* Sacramento: Department of Public Health, Division of Alcoholic Rehabilitation, 1964.

Miller, P. M., Hersen, M., Eisler, R. M., Epstein, L. H., & Wooten, L. S. Relationship of alcohol cues to the drinking behavior of alcoholics and social drinkers: An analogue study. *Psychological Record,* 1974, *24,* 61–66.(a)

Miller, P. M., Hersen, M., Eisler, R. M., & Hilsman, G. Effects of social stress on operant drinking of alcoholics and social drinkers. *Behaviour Research and Therapy,* 1974, *12,* 67–72.(b)

Moskowitz, H., & DePry, D. Differential effect of alcohol on auditory vigilance and divided attention tasks. *Quarterly Journal of Studies on Alcohol,* 1968, *29,* 54–62.

Moyer, K. E. *The psychobiology of aggression.* New York: Harper & Row, 1976.

Moynihan, N. H. Alcohol and blood sugar. *Alcoholism,* 1965, *1,* 180–187.

Mulvihill, D. J., & Tumin, M. M. (Eds.). *Crimes of violence* (Vol. 12). Washington, D.C.: U.S. Government Printing Office, 1969.

Mulvihill, D. J., Tumin, M. M., & Curtis, L. A. (Eds.). *Crimes of violence* (Vol. 13). Washington, D. C.: U.S. Government Printing Office, 1969.

Myers, M. *Determinants of conviction: The prosecutional roles of the victim and the defendant.* Paper presented at the International Victimology Symposium, Boston, September, 1976.

Nardi, A. H. Person-perception research and the perception of life-span development. In P. B. Baltes & D. W. Schaie (Eds.), *Life-span developmental psychology—Personality and socialization.* New York: Academic Press, 1973.

Nathan, P. E., & Lisman, S. A. Behavioral and motivational patterns. In R. E. Tarter & A. A. Sugerman (Eds.), *Alcoholism: Interdisciplinary approaches to an enduring problem.* Reading, Mass.: Addison-Wesley, 1976.

Nathan, P. E., & O'Brien, J. S. An experimental analysis of the behavior of alcoholics and nonalcoholics during prolonged experimental drinking. *Behavior Therapy,* 1971, *2,* 455–476.

Nathan, P. E., Lipson, A. G., Vettraino, A. P., & Solomon, P. The social ecology of an urban clinic for alcoholism: Racial differences in treatment entry and outcome. *International Journal of the Addictions,* 1968, *3*(1), 55–63.

Nathan, P. E., Titler, N. A., Lowenstein, L. H., Solomon, P., & Rossi, A. M. Behavioral analysis of chronic alcoholism. *Archives of General Psychiatry,* 1970, *22,* 419–430.

National Criminal Justice Information and Statistics Service. *Profile of state prison inmates: Sociodemographic findings from the 1974 survey of inmates of state correctional facilities.* Washington, D.C.: U.S. Government Printing Office, August 1979.

National Institute of Alcohol Abuse and Alcoholism. *Third special report to the Congress on alcohol and health* (E. P. Noble, Ed.). Washington, D.C.: U.S. Government Printing Office, 1978.

Nau, E. Kindemisshandlung. *Mischrift fuer Kinderheilkunde,* 1967, *115,* 192–194.

Nelson, J. D., Gelfand, D. M., & Hartmann, D. P. Children's aggression following competition and exposure to an aggressive model. *Journal of Child Development,* 1969, *40,* 1085.

Neugarten, B. L., & Datan, N. Sociological perspectives of the life cycle. In P. B. Baltes &

K. W. Schaie (Eds.), *Life-span developmental psychology—Personality and sociali-zation.* New York: Academic Press, 1973.

Nicol, A. R., Gunn, J. C., Gristwood, J., Foggitt, R. H., & Watson, J. P. The relationship of alcoholism to violent behaviour resulting in long-term imprisonment. *British Journal of Psychiatry,* 1973, *123,* 47-51.

Nisonoff, L., & Bitman, I. Spouse abuse: Incidence and relationship to selected demographic variables. *Victimology,* 1979, *4,* 131-140.

Normandeau, A. *Trends and patterns in crimes of robbery with special reference to Phila-delphia, Pennsylvania, 1960 to 1966.* Ann Arbor, Mich.: University Microfilms, 1968.

Nowlis, V., & Nowlis, H. H. The description and analysis of mood. *Annals of the New York Academy of Sciences,* 1956, *65,* 345-356.

Nurco, D. N., & DuPont, R. L. A preliminary report on crime and addiction within a com-munity-wide population of narcotic addicts. *Drug and Alcohol Dependence,* 1977, *2,* 109-121.

O'Brien, J. E. Violence in divorce-prone families. *Journal of Marriage and the Family,* 1971, *33,* 692-698.

O'Connor, J. *The young drinkers: A cross national study of social and cultural influences.* London: Tavistock, 1978.

O'Donnell, J. A., Voss, H. L., Clayton, R. R., Slatin, G. T., & Room, R. G. W. *Young men and drugs—A nationwide survey.* Washington, D.C.: National Institute for Drug Abuse, 1976.

O'Leary, M. R., Donovan, D. M., Freeman, C. W., & Chaney, E. Relationship between psychopathology, experienced control and perceived locus of control: In search of alcoholic subtypes. *Journal of Clinical Psychology,* 1976, *32*(4), 899-904.

O'Leary, M. R., Donovan, D. M., & Hague, W. H. Relationships between locus of control and MMPI scales among alcoholics. *Journal of Clinical Psychology,* 1974, *30,* 312-314.

Olson, M. R. *Predicting seriousness of official police contact careers: An exploratory analy-sis* (revised). Iowa City: Iowa Urban Community Research Center and Department of Sociology, University of Iowa, June 1978.

Parker, E. Psychological effects of alcohol on humans. Report prepared for *Alcohol and Health,* 1977.

Parker, T., & Allerton, R. *The courage of his convictions.* New York: W. W. Norton, 1962.

Pearce, J., & Garrett, H. D. A comparison of the drinking behavior of delinquent youth versus non-delinquent youth in the states of Idaho and Utah. *Journal of School Health,* 1970, *40,* 131-135.

Pernanen, K. Alcohol and crimes of violence. In B. Kissin & H. Begleiter (Eds.), *The biology of alcoholism. Vol. 4: Social aspects of alcoholism.* New York: Plenum, 1976.

Pernanen, K. *Experiences of violence and their association with alcohol use in the general population of a community.* Paper presented at the annual meeting of the American Society of Criminology, Philadelphia, November 1979.(a)

Pernanen, K. *Alcohol and aggressive behaviour: A community study with a cross-cultural perspective* (Addiction Research Foundation Substudy No. 1050). Toronto: The Foundation, 1979.(b)

Pernanen, K. *Alcohol and aggressive behaviour: Report on a community study.* In prep-aration.

Petersilia, J., Greenwood, P. W., & Lavin, M. *Criminal careers of habitual felons.* Washing-ton, D.C.: U.S. Government Printing Office, 1978.

Peterson, M. A., & Braiker, H. *Doing crime: A survey of California prison inmates* (draft, with S. M. Polich). Santa Monica, Calif.: Rand Corporation, May 1978.

Piaget, J. *The moral judgment of the child.* Glencoe, Ill.: The Free Press, 1948. (Originally published, 1932.)

Pittman, D. J., & Gordon, G. W. Criminal careers of the chronic police case inebriate. *Journal of Studies on Alcohol,* 1958, *19,* 225–268.

Pittman, D. J., & Handy, W. Patterns in criminal aggravated asault. *Journal of Criminal Law, Criminology and Police Science,* 1964, *55*(4), 462–470.

Pittman, D. J., & Handy, W. Patterns in criminal aggravated assault. In B. J. Cohen (Ed.), *Crime in America.* Stasca, Ill.: Peacock, 1970.

Plaut, T. F *Alcohol problems: A report to the nation by the Cooperative Commission on the Study of Alcoholism.* New York: Oxford University Press, 1967.

Pliner, P., & Cappell, H. Modification of affective consequences of alcohol: A comparison of social and solitary drinking. *Journal of Abnormal Psychology,* 1974, *83,* 418–425.

Pollack, D. Coping and avoidance in inebriated alcoholics and normals. *Journal of Abnormal Psychology,* 1966, *71*(6), 417–419.

Preble, E., & Miller, T. Methadone, wine and welfare. In R. S. Weppner (Ed.), *Street ethnography.* Beverly Hills, Calif.: Sage, 1977.

Prescott, J. W. Somatosensory affectional deprivation (SAD) theory of drug and alcohol use. In D. J. Lettieri, M. Sayers, & H. W. Pearson (Eds.), *Theories on drug abuse* (NIDA Research Monograph No. 30). Rockville, Md.: National Institute on Drug Abuse, March 1980.

Rachal, J. V., Williams, J. R., Brehm, M. L., Cavanaugh, B., Moore, R. P., & Eckerman, W. C. *Adolescent drinking behavior, attitudes and correlates.* Research Triangle Park, N.C.: Research Triangle Institute, 1975.

Rada, R. T. Alcoholism and forcible rape. *American Journal of Psychiatry,* 1975, *132,* 444–446.

Rappaport, J. *Personality development: The chronology of experience.* Glenview, Ill.: Scott, Foresman, 1972.

Raynes, A. E., & Ryback, R. S. Effect of alcohol and congeners on aggressive response in Betta Splendens. *Quarterly Journal of Studies on Alcohol,* 1970, Suppl. No. 5, 130–135.

Reckless, W. C. *The crime problem* (4th ed.). New York: Appleton-Century-Crofts, 1967.

Renson, G. J., Adams, J. E., & Tinklenberg, J. R. Russ–Durkee assessment and validation with violent versus nonviolent chronic alcohol abusers. *Journal of Counseling Clinical Psychology,* 1978, *46,* 360–361.

Research Triangle Institute: *Overview: Treatment outcome prospective study (TOPS).* Research Triangle Park, N.C.: Author, July 1980.

Riley, M. W., & Waring J. Age cohorts and drug use. In D. B. Kandel (Ed.), *Longitudinal research on drug abuse.* New York: Wiley, 1978.

Robin, G. O. Gang member delinquency: Its extent, sequence and typology. *Journal of Criminal Law,* 1964, *55,* 59–70.

Robins, L. *Deviant children grow up.* Baltimore: Williams & Wilkins, 1966.

Robins, L., & Guze, S. Drinking practices and problems in urban ghetto populations. In N. Mello & J. Mendelson (Eds.), *Recent advances in studies in alcoholism.* Washington, D.C.: U.S. Government Printing Office, 1970.

Robins, L. N., Bates, W. M., & O'Neal, P. Adult drinking patterns of former problem children. In D. J. Pittman & C. R. Snyder (Eds.), *Society, culture and drinking patterns.* New York: Wiley, 1962.

Robins, L. N., Murphy, G. E., & Breckenridge, M. B. Drinking behavior of young urban Negro men. *Quarterly Journal of Studies on Alcohol,* 1968, *29,* 657–684.

Robinson, D. *From drinking to alcoholism—A sociological commentary.* London: Wiley, 1976.

Roebuck, J., & Johnson, R. The Negro drinker and assaulter as a criminal type. *Crime and Delinquency,* 1962, *8*(1), 21-33.

Rohan, W. P. Drinking behavior and "alcoholism." *Journal of Studies on Alcohol,* 1975, *36*(7), 908-916.

Roizen, J. *Alcohol as an excuse for crime: A reevaluation of the deviance disavowal hypothesis* (Working Paper). Berkeley, Calif.: Social Research Group, 1977.

Roizen, J., & Schneberk, D. Alcohol and crime. In M. Aarens, T. Cameron, J. Roizen, R. Roizen, R. Room, D. Schneberk, & D. Wingard (Eds.), *Alcohol, casualties and crime.* Berkeley, Calif.: Social Research Group, 1977.(a)

Roizen, J., & Schneberk, D. *Alcohol and crime.* Special report to the National Institute on Alcohol Abuse and Alcoholism, March 1977.(b)

Roizen, R., Naming names: A note on drinker self-characterizations. *The Drinking and Drug Practices Surveyor,* 1974, *9,* 18-21.

Roizen, R., Cahalan, D., & Shanks, P. Spontaneous remission among untreated problem drinkers. In D. B. Kandel (Ed.), *Longitudinal research on drug abuse.* New York: Wiley, 1978.

Room, R. Drinking patterns in large U.S. cities: A comparison of San Francisco and national samples. *Quarterly Journal of Studies on Alcohol,* May 1972, Suppl. No. 6.

Room, R. *The measurement and distribution of drinking patterns and problems in general populations.* Geneva: World Health Organization, 1975.

Room, R. *Alcohol as an instrument of intimate domination.* Unpublished manuscript, (Available from Social Research Group, Berkeley, Calif. 94709.)

Rorabaugh, W. J. *The alcoholic republic: An American tradition.* New York: Oxford University Press, 1979.

Rosenberg, M. *The logic of survey analysis.* New York: Basic Books, 1968.

Roslund, B., & Larson, C. A. Crimes of violence and alcohol abuse in Sweden. *International Journal of the Addictions,* 1979, *14*(8), 1103-1115.

Rounsaville, B. J. Theories in marital violence: Evidence from a study of battered women. *Victimology,* 1978, *3,* 11-31.

Roy, M. A current survey of 150 cases. In M. Roy (Ed.), *Battered women: A psychosociological study of domestic violence.* New York: Van Nostrand Reinhold, 1977.

Sadoun, R., Lolli, G., & Silverman, M. *Drinking in French culture.* New Brunswick, N.J.: Rutgers Center for Alcohol Studies, 1965.

Samuels, F. G. *The Negro tavern: A microcosm of slum life.* San Francisco: R & E Research Associates, 1976.

Satir, V. *Conjoint family therapy.* Palo Alto, Calif.: Science & Behavior Publishers, 1967.

Schachter, S. The interaction of cognitive and physiological determinants of emotional state. In P. H. Leiderman & D. Shapiro (Eds.), *Psychobiological approaches to social behavior.* Stanford, Calif.: Stanford University Press, 1964.

Schachter, S., & Singer, J. E. Cognitive, social, and physiological determinants of emotional state. *Psychological Review,* 1962, *69,* 379-399.

Schachter, S., & Wheeler, L. Epinephrine, chlorpromazine and amusement. *Journal of Abnormal Psychology,* 1962, *65,* 121-128.

Scott, M. B., & Lyman, S. M. Accounts. *American Sociological Review,* 1968, *33,* 46-62.

Scott, P. D. Offenders, drunkenness, and murder. *British Journal of the Addictions,* 1968, *63,* 221-226.

Scott, P. D. Fatal battered baby cases. *Medicine, Science and the Law,* 1973, *13,* 197-206.

Scott, P. D. Battered wives. *British Journal of Psychiatry,* 1974, *125,* 433-441.

Seligman, E. R. A., & Johnson, A. (Eds.). *Encyclopedia of the social sciences* (Vol. 3). New York: Macmillan, 1959.

Sellin, T., & Wolfgang, M. E. *The measurement of delinquency.* New York: Wiley, 1974.

Selling, L. S. The role of alcoholism in the commission of sex offenses. *Medical Record,* 1940, *151,* 289–291.

Sellitz, C., Jahoda, M., Deutsch, M., & Cook, S. W. *Research methods in social relations.* New York: Holt, Rinehart, & Winston, 1951.

Shannon, L. W. *Predicting adult criminal careers from juvenile careers* (Progress Report). Iowa City: Iowa Urban Community Research Center, September 1977.(a)

Shannon, L. W. *Assessing the relationship of adult criminal careers to juvenile careers.* Iowa City: Iowa Urban Community Research Center and Department of Sociology, University of Iowa, 1977.(b)

Shannon, L. W. *Changing trends in the relationships of juvenile delinquency to adult crime.* Paper presented at the annual meeting of the Pacific Sociological Association, Anaheim, Calif.: April 4–7, 1979.

Shaw, C. *The jackroller: A delinquent boy's own story.* Chicago: University of Chicago Press, 1930.

Shaw, C. *The natural history of a delinquent career.* Philadelphia: Albert Saifer, 1931.

Shoham, S. G., Ben-David, S., & Rahav, G. Interaction in violence. *Human Relations,* 1974, *27*(5), 417.

Shuntich, R. J., & Taylor, S. P. The effects of alcohol on human physical aggression. *Journal of Experimental Research in Personality,* 1972, *6,* 34–38.

Shupe, L. M. Alcohol and crime. *Journal of Criminal Law, Criminology and Police Science,* 1954, *44,* 661–664.

Siegler, L. M., Osmond, H., & Newell, S. Models of alcoholism. *Quarterly Journal of Studies on Alcohol,* 1968, *29,* 511–591.

Sila, A. Psychopathologic traits of homicide perpetrators. *Social Psychiatry (Zagreb),* 1977, *5,* 3–87.

Silberman, C. E. *Criminal violence, criminal justice.* New York: Random House, 1978.

Simons, B., Downs, E. F., Hurster, M. M., & Archer, M. Child abuse: Epidemiologic study of medically reported cases. *New York State Journal of Medicine,* 1966, *66,* 2783–2788.

Singelmann, P. Exchange or symbolic interaction: Convergencies between two theoretical perspectives. *American Sociological Review,* 1972, *37,* 414–424.

Siu, R. G. H. *Should American pharmacologists learn how to play Chinese baseball?* Banquet talk, American Society for Pharmacology and Experimental Therapeutics, Dallas, Tex., April, 1979.

Sjoberg, L. Alcohol and gambling. *Psychopharmacologia (Berlin),* 1969, *14,* 284.

Skelton, W. D. Alcohol, violent behavior and the electroencephalogram. *Southern Medical Journal,* 1970, *63,* 465–466.

Skogan, W. G. Measurement problems in official survey crime rates. *The Journal of Criminal Justice,* 1975, *3,* 17–32.

Smelser, N. *Theory of collective behavior.* New York: The Free Press, 1963.

Smith, S. M., Hanson, R., & Noble, S. Parents of battered babies: A controlled study. *British Medical Journal,* 1973, *4,* 388–391.

Snyder, C. *Alcohol and the Jews.* New Haven, Conn.: Yale Center for Alcohol Studies, 1958.

Snyder, C. Inebriety, alcoholism and anomie. In M. Clinard (Ed.), *Anomie and deviant behavior.* New York: The Free Press, 1964.

Sobell, L. C., & Sobell, M. B. Drunkenness, a "special circumstance" in crimes of violence: Sometimes. *The International Journal of the Addictions,* 1975, *10*(5), 869–882.

Spain, D. M., Bradess, V. A., & Eggston, A. A. Alcohol and violent death: A one-year study of consecutive cases in a representative community. *Journal of the American Medical Association,* 1951, *146,* 334–335.

Spinetta, J. J., & Rigler, D. The child-abusing parent: A psychological review. *Psychological Bulletin,* 1972, *77,* 296–304.

Starkweather, J. A. Individual and situational influences on drug effects. In R. M. Feather-stone & A. Simon (Eds.), *A pharmacologic approach to the study of the mind*. Spring-field, Ill.: C. Thomas, 1959.

Steele, B. F., & Pollock, C. B. A psychiatric study of parents who abuse infants and small children. In R. E. Helfer & C. H. Kempe (Eds.), *The battered child* (2nd ed.). Chi-cago: University of Chicago Press, 1974.

Steinglass, P. Experimenting with family treatment approaches to alcoholism, 1950–1975: A review. *Family Process,* 1976, *15*(1), 97–123.

Steinmetz, S. K., & Straus, M. A. (Eds.). *Violence in the family*. New York: Dodd, Mead, 1974.

Stephens, R. The truthfulness of addict respondents in research projects. *International Journal of the Addictions,* 1972, *7,* 549–558.

Sterne, M. W., & Pittman, D. J. *Drinking practices in the ghetto,* (2 vols.). St Louis, Mo.: Social Science Institute, Washington University, 1972.

Steward, O. Questions regarding American Indian criminality. *Human Organization,* 1964, *23,* 61–66.

Stinchcombe, A. L. *Constructing social theories*. New York: Harcourt, Brace, & World, 1968.

Stivers, R. *A hair of the dog: Irish drinking and American stereotype*. University Park: Pennsylvania State University Press, 1976.

Story, R. I. Effects on thinking of relationships between conflict arousal and oral fixation. *Journal of Abnormal Psychology,* 1968, *73*(5), 440–448.

Straus, M. A. A general systems theory approach to a theory of violence between family members. *Social Science Information,* 1973, *12,* 105–125.

Straus, M. A. Sexual inequality, cultural norms, and wife-beating. *Victimology,* 1976, *1,* 54–70.

Straus, M. A. Wife-beating: How common and why? *Victimology,* 1977–1978, *2,* 443–458.

Straus, R. Alcohol and alcoholism. In R. K. Merton & R. Nisbet (Eds.), *Contemporary social problems* (3rd ed.). New York: Harcourt Brace Jovanovich, 1971.

Strayer, R. A Study of the Negro alcoholic. *Quarterly Journal of Studies on Alcohol,* 1961, *22,* 111–123.

Sutherland, E. H. *The professional thief*. Chicago: University of Chicago Press, 1937.

Sutherland, E. H., & Cressey, D. R. *Criminology* (9th ed.). Philadelphia: J. B. Lippincott, 1974.

Sutker, P. B., Archer, R. P., Brantley, P. J., & Kilpatrick, D. G. Alcoholics and opiate addicts: Comparison of personality characteristics. *Journal of Studies on Alcohol,* 1979, *40*(7), 635–644.

Sutton, W. *Where the money was* (with Edward Linn). New York: Viking, 1976.

Sykes, G. M., & Matza, D. Techniques of neutralization: A theory of delinquency. In M. E. Wolfgang, L. Savitz, & N. Johnston (Eds.), *The sociology of crime and delinquency*. New York: Wiley, 1962.

Takala, H. Alkoholstrejkens inverkan pa uppdagad brottslighet [The effect of the alcohol strike on reported crime]. *Alkoholpolitik,* 1973, *36,* 14–16.

Takala, M., Pihkanen, T. A., & Markkanen, T. *The effects of distilled and brewed beverages: A physiological, neurological and psychological study*. Helsinki: Finnish Foundation for Alcohol Studies, 1957.

Tamerin, J. S., Weiner, S., & Mendelson, J. H. Alcoholics' expectancies and recall of exper-iences during intoxication. *American Journal of Psychiatry,* 1970, *126,* 1697–1704.

Tannenbaum, P. H. Studies in film and television mediated arousal and aggression. In G. A. Comstock, E. A. Rubenstein, & J. P. Murray (Eds.), *Television and social behavior* (Vol. 5). Washington, D.C.: U.S. Government Printing Office, 1972.

Tarter, R. E., Jones, B. M., Simpson, C. D., & Vega, A. Effects of task complexity and practice on performance during acute alcohol intoxication. *Perceptual and Motor Skills,* 1971, *33,* 307–318.

Taylor, S. P. Aggressive behavior and physiological arousal as a function of provocation and the tendency to inhibit aggression. *Journal of Personality,* 1967, *35,* 297–310.

Taylor, S. P., & Gammon, C. B. Effects of type and dose of alcohol on human physical aggression. *Journal of Personality and Social Psychology,* 1975, *32*(1), 169–175.

Taylor, S. P., & Gammon, C. B. Aggressive behavior of intoxicated subjects: The effect of third-party intervention. *Quarterly Journal of Studies on Alcohol,* 1976, *37,* 917–930.

Taylor, S. P., Gammon, C. B., & Capasso, D. R. Aggression as a function of the interaction of alcohol and threat. *Journal of Personality and Social Psychology,* 1976, *34,* 938–941.

Taylor, S. P., Schmutte, G. T., & Leonard, K. E., Jr. Physical aggression as a function of alcohol and frustration. *Bulletin of Psychonomic Society,* 1977, *9,* 217–218.

Thornberry, T. P., & Figlio, R. M. *Juvenile and adult offense careers in the Philadelphia birth cohort of 1945.* Paper presented at the annual meeting of the American Society of Criminology, Dallas, Tex., November 1978.

Tinklenberg, J. R. Alcohol and violence. In P. Bourne & R. Fox (Eds.), *Alcoholism: Progress in research and treatment.* New York: Academic Press, 1973.

Tinklenberg, J. R., Roth, W. T., Kopell, B. S., & Murphy, P. Cannabis and alcohol effects on assaultiveness in adolescent delinquents. *Annals of the New York Academy of Sciences,* 1976, *282,* 85–94.

Toch, H. *Violent men.* Chicago: Aldine, 1969.

Toulmin, S. E. *The philosophy of science.* London: Hutchinson University Library, 1953.

Tripkovic, D. Problem drinkers in the penitentiary at Sremska Mitrovica. *Quarterly Journal of Studies on Alcohol,* 1967, *28,* 738–741.

Tupin, J. P., Mohry, D., & Smith, D. Two types of violent offenders with psychosocial descriptors. *Diseases of the Nervous System,* 1973, *34,* 356–363.

United States Department of Justice, LEAA. *Surveys of inmates of state corrections facilities—Advance report.* Washington, D.C.: National Criminal Justice Information and Statistics Service, 1975.

United States Department of Justice. *Crime in the United States: FBI Uniform Crime Reports.* Washington, D.C.: U.S. Government Printing Office, 1977.

Van der Spuy, H. I. J. The influence of alcohol on the mood of the alcoholic. *British Journal of the Addictions,* 1972, *67,* 255–265.

Vanicelli, M. Mood and self-perception of alcoholics when sober and intoxicated. *Quarterly Journal of Studies on Alcohol,* 1972, *33,* 341–357.

Vartia, O. K., Forsander, O. A., & Krusius, F. E. Blood sugar levels in hangover. *Quarterly Journal of Studies on Alcohol,* 1960, *21,* 597–604.

Vera Institute of Justice. *Felony arrests: Their prosecution and disposition in New York City's courts.* New York: Author, 1977.

Viamontes, G. A., & Powell, B. J. Demographic characteristics of black and white male alcoholics. *International Journal of the Addictions,* 1974, *9*(3), 489–494.

Virkkunen, M. M. D. Alcohol as a factor precipitating aggression and conflict behavior leading to homicide. *British Journal of the Addictions,* 1974, *69,* 149–154.

Vitols, M. M. Culture patterns of drinking in Negro and white alcoholics. *Diseases of the Nervous System,* 1968, *29,* 391–394.

Vogel-Sprott, M. D. Alcoholism and learning. In B. Kissin & H. Begleiter (Eds.), *The biology of alcoholism. Vol. 2: Physiology and behavior.* New York: Plenum, 1976.

Vojtechovsky, M., Safratova, V., & Havrankova, O. Effect of threshold doses of lysergic acid diethylamide (LSD) on social interaction in healthy students. *Activitas Nervosa Superior,* 1972, *14,* 115–116.

Voss, H. L., & Hepburn, J. R. Patterns in criminal homicide in Chicago. *Journal of Criminal Law, Criminology and Police Science,* 1968, *59*(4), 499–508.

Wanberg, K. W. Prevalence of symptoms found among excessive drinkers. *The International Journal of the Addictions,* 1969, *4*(2), 169–185.

Ward, D. A., Jackson, M., & Ward, R. E. *Crimes of violence by women.* Consultation paper submitted to National Commission on the Causes and Prevention of Violence, 1969.

Warren, G. H., & Raynes, A. E. Mood changes during three conditions of alcohol intake. *Quarterly Journal of Studies on Alcohol,* 1972, *33*, 979–989.

Washburne, C. Alcohol, self and the group. *Quarterly Journal of Studies on Alcohol,* 1956, *17*, 108–123.

Washburne, C. *Primitive drinking.* New York: College & University Press, 1961.

Wasikhongo, J. M. Uniformities in aggravated assaults in St. Louis (Missouri) and Mombasa (Kenya): A cross-cultural replication. *International Journal of Criminology and Penology,* 1976, *4*, 9–24.

Welch, B. L. Symposium summary. In S. Garatinni & E. B. Sigg (Eds.), *Aggressive behavior.* New York: Wiley, 1969.

West, D. J. *Who becomes delinquent: Second report of the Cambridge study in delinquent development.* London: Heinemann Educational Books, 1973.

West, D. J., & Farington, D. P. *The delinquent way of life: Third report of the Cambridge study in delinquent development.* London: Heinemann Educational Books, 1977.

Westermeyer, J., & Brantner, J. Violent death and alcohol use among the Chippewa in Minnesota. *Minnesota Medicine,* 1972, *55*, 749–752.

Wexberg, L. E. Alcoholism as a sickness. *Quarterly Journal of Studies on Alcohol,* 1951, *12*, 217–230.

Wilentz, W. C. The alcohol factor in violent deaths. *American Practitioner and Digest of Treatment,* 1953, *4*, 21–24.

Williams, A. F. The alcoholic personality. In B. Kissin & H. Begleiter (Eds.), *The biology of alcoholism. Vol. 4: Social aspects of alcoholism.* New York: Plenum, 1976.

Williams, C. B., & Vantress, F. E. Control and aggression. *Journal of Psychology,* 1969, *71*, 59–61.

Williams, T. K. *The ethanol-induced loss of control concept in alcoholism.* Unpublished dissertation, Western Michigan University, 1970.

Wilsnack, S. C. The effects of social drinking on women's fantasy. *Journal of Personality,* 1974, *42*, 43–61.

Winick, C. A theory of drug dependence based on role, access to and attitudes toward drugs. In D. J. Lettieri, M. Sayers, & H. W. Pearson (Eds.), *Theories on drug abuse* (NIDA Research Monograph No. 30). Rockville, Md.: National Institute on Drug Abuse, March 1980.

Winkler, E. G., Weissman, M., & McDermaid, G. Alcoholism and anti-social behavior. *Psychiatric Quarterly Supplement,* 1954, *28*, 242–254.

Wirt, R. D., Winokur, G., & Roff, M. (Eds.). *Life history research in psychopathology* (Vol. 4). Minneapolis: University of Minnesota Press, 1975.

Wittgenstein, L. *Tractatus Logico-Philosophicus: Annalen der Naturphilosophie.* London: Blackwell, 1961.

Wohlwill, J. F. The age variable in psychological research. *Psychological Review,* 1970, *77*, 49–64.

Wolfgang, M. E. *Patterns in criminal homicide.* Philadelphia: University of Pennsylvania, 1958.

Wolfgang, M. E., & Collins, J. J. *Offender careers and restraint: Probabilities and policy implications* (Final Report). Philadelphia: Center for Studies in Criminology and Criminal Law, University of Pennsylvania, 1978.

Wolfgang, M. E., & Ferracuti, F. *The subculture of violence.* London: Tavistock, 1967.

Wolfgang, M. E., Figlio, R. M., & Sellin, T. *Delinquency in a birth cohort.* Chicago: University of Chicago Press, 1972.

Wolfgang, M. E., & Strohm, R. B. The relationship between alcohol and criminal homicide. *Quarterly Journal of Studies on Alcohol,* 1956, *17,* 411–425.

Woodruff, D. S., & Birren, J. E. Age changes and cohort differences in personality. *Developmental Psychology,* 1972, *6*(2), 252–259.

Young, L. *Wednesday's child: A study of child neglect and abuse.* New York: McGraw-Hill, 1964.

Yules, R. B., Freedman, D. X., & Chandler, K. A. The effect of ethyl alcohol on man's electroencephalographic sleep cycle. *Electroencephalography and Clinical Neurophysiology,* 1966, *20,* 109–111.

Zachariadis, N., & Varonos, D. Effects of methylphenidate and barbiturate on normal subjects. In K. R. Hammond & C. R. B. Joyce (Eds.), *Psychoactive drugs and social judgment.* New York: Wiley, 1975.

Zacker, J., & Bard, M. Further findings on assaultiveness and alcohol use in interpersonal disputes. *American Journal of Community Psychology,* 1977, *5,* 373–383.

Zillmann, D. Excitation transfer in communication-mediated aggressive behavior. *Journal of Experimental Social Psychology,* 1971, *7,* 419.

Zucker, R. A. Sex-role identity patterns and drinking behavior of adolescents. *Quarterly Journal of Studies on Alcohol,* 1968, *29,* 868–884.

Zuckerman, M. *Sensation seeking: Beyond the optimal level of arousal.* Hillsdale, N.J.: Erlbaum, 1979.

Zylman, R. Race and social status discrimination and police action in alcohol-affected collisions. *Journal of Safety Research,* 1972, *4*(2), 75–84.

Author Index

339

Keuchler, H. A., 20, 327*n.*
Kieselhorst, D. C., 290, 330*n.*
Kilpatrick, D. G., 123, 335*n.*
King, L. J., 219, 326*n.*
Kissin, B., 130, 327*n.*
Kitsuse, J. I., 169, 327*n.*
Klausner, S. Z., 153, 205, 327*n.*
Klockars, C. B., 185, 186, 327*n.*
Knopf, I. J., 130, 327*n.*
Knowles, J. B., 20, 327*n.*
Knupfer, G., 238, 242, 327*n.*
Kogan, N., 204, 327*n.*
Kohlberg, L., 201, 204, 298, 327*n.*
Koppell, B. S., 312, 336*n.*
Korman, M., 130, 327*n.*
Kosturn, C. F., 128, 329*n.*
Kramer, M., 235, 328*n.*
Krusius, F. E., 19, 336*n.*
Kuhn, T. S., 39, 327*n.*
Kunitz, S., 148, 328*n.*
Kyle, E., 190, 322*n.*

L

LaDou, J., 131, 329*n.*
Lahelma, E., 71, 327*n.*
Lang, A. R., 128, 139, 215, 302, 308, 327*n.*, 329*n.*
Larson, C. A., 290, 333*n.*
Lauerman, R., 128, 328*n.*
Laverty, S. G., 20, 327*n.*
Lavin, M., 89, 169, 313, 331*n.*
Leake, C. D., 133, 327*n.*
Leland, J., 148, 327*n.*
Lenke, L., 3, 22, 59, 327*n.*
Leonard, K. E., Jr., 138, 336*n.*
Leppa, S., 68, 304, 327*n.*
LeRoux, L. C., 74, 78, 85, 92, 95, 327*n.*
Leven, R., 85, 87, 95, 98, 100, 101, 327*n.*
Levine, H., 148, 327*n.*
Levinger, G., 265, 266, 327*n.*
Levinson, D., 235, 328*n.*
Levy, J., 148, 328*n.*
Lewis, H., 238, 245, 250, 328*n.*
Liebow, E., 235, 328*n.*
Light, R. J., 277, 328*n.*
Lindelius, R., 77–79, 90, 101, 102, 106, 189, 328*n.*
Linden, R., 290, 326*n.*
Linton, 125
Lion, J. R., 124, 293, 317*n.*

Lipson, A. G., 236, 330*n.*
Lisman, S. A., 111, 119, 127, 130, 330*n.*
Locke, B. Z., 235, 328*n.*
Lofland, J., 145, 149, 328*n.*
Lolli, G., 133, 333*n.*
Lombroso, C., xv, xvi, 328*n.*
Longwell, B., 95, 321*n.*
Lowenstein, L. H., 120, 130, 330*n.*
Lucianovic, J., 83, 322*n.*
Lumio, M., 133, 319*n.*
Lyman, S. M., 303, 333*n.*

M

MacAndrew, C., 37, 61, 148, 197, 216, 301, 308, 328*n.*
Macdonald, J. M., 32, 35, 328*n.*
MacDonnell, M. F., 14, 328*n.*
Mack, J. A., 184, 328*n.*
Maddux, J. F., 95, 328*n.*
Maden, M. F., 257, 277, 328*n.*
Magedanz, T., 290, 330*n.*
Malnard, R., 278, 324*n.*
Maisto, S. A., 128, 328*n.*
Mäkelä, K., 133, 244, 319*n.*, 328*n.*
Maletzky, B. M., 124, 328*n.*
Malik, M. O. A., 85, 95, 328*n.*
Malzberg, B., 235, 328*n.*
Mandell, W., 161, 162, 297, 328*n.*
Marcus, A. M., 121, 326*n.*
Marek, Z., 85, 95, 97, 98, 328*n.*
Marinacci, A. A., 18, 328*n.*
Mark, V. H., 161, 293, 328*n.*
Markkanen, T., 136, 335*n.*
Marlatt, G. A., 128, 139, 215, 302, 325*n.*, 327*n.*–329*n.*
Martin, J. B., 185–187, 196, 329*n.*
Matheson, J. C. M., 85, 95, 329*n.*
Matza, D., 36, 303, 335*n.*
Maule, H. G., 87, 100, 329*n.*
Mawson, A. R., 258, 260, 329*n.*
Mayer, J., 277, 283, 285, 329*n.*
Mayfield, D., 74, 76, 82, 85, 87, 95, 96, 98, 100, 101, 104, 223, 226, 228, 290, 329*n.*
McCaghy, C. H., 94, 302, 329*n.*
McClearn, G. E., 111, 329*n.*
McCleary, C. P., 203, 329*n.*
McClelland, D. C., 25, 30, 32, 127, 137, 156, 297, 298, 326*n.*, 329*n.*
McCord, J., 33, 200, 297, 306, 329*n.*

Subject Index